FTCE

ELEMENTARY
EDUCATION K–6

By: Sharon Wynne, M.S.

XAMonline, INC.
Boston

To obtain permission(s) to use the material from this work for any purpose including workshops or seminars, please submit a written request to:

XAMonline, Inc.
21 Orient Avenue
Melrose, MA 02176
Toll Free 1-800-509-4128
Email: info@xamonline.com
Web: www.xamonline.com
Fax: 1-617-583-5552

Library of Congress Cataloging-in-Publication Data

Wynne, Sharon A.
    FTCE Elementary Education K–6 / Sharon A. Wynne.
    ISBN 978-1-60787-506-2
    1. FTCE Elementary Education K–6
    2. Study Guides
    3. FTCE
    4. Teachers' Certification & Licensure
    5. Careers

Disclaimer:

The opinions expressed in this publication are the sole works of XAMonline and were created independently from the National Education Association, Educational Testing Service, or any State Department of Education, National Evaluation Systems or other testing affiliates.

Between the time of publication and printing, state specific standards as well as testing formats and Web site information may change and therefore would not be included in part or in whole within this product. Sample test questions are developed by XAMonline and reflect content similar to that on real tests; however, they are not former test questions. XAMonline assembles content that aligns with state standards but makes no claims nor guarantees teacher candidates a passing score. Numerical scores are determined by testing companies such as NES or ETS and then are compared with individual state standards. A passing score varies from state to state.

Printed in the United States of America   œ-1

FTCE Elementary Education K–6
ISBN: 978-1-60787-506-2

Table of Contents

DOMAIN I
LANGUAGE ARTS AND READING

COMPETENCY 1
KNOWLEDGE OF THE READING PROCESS 5

Skill 1.1: Identify the content of emergent literacy *(e.g., oral language development, phonological awareness, alphabet knowledge, decoding, concepts of print, motivation, text structures, written language development)*.......................................5

Skill 1.2: Identify the processes, skills, and stages of word recognition that lead to effective decoding *(e.g., pre-alphabetic, partial-alphabetic, full alphabetic, grapho-phonemic, morphemic)*..13

Skill 1.3: Select and apply instructional methods for the development of decoding skills *(e.g., continuous blending, chunking)*....................17

Skill 1.4: Distinguish among the components of reading fluency *(e.g., accuracy, automaticity, rate, prosody)*....................................19

Skill 1.5: Choose and apply instructional methods for developing reading fluency *(e.g., practice with high-frequency words, readers theatre, repeated readings)*...25

Skill 1.6: Identify and differentiate instructional methods and strategies for vocabulary acquisition across content areas *(e.g., word analysis, author's word choice, context clues, multiple exposures)*...27

Skill 1.7: Identify and evaluate instructional methods and strategies for facilitating students' reading comprehension *(e.g., summarizing, self-monitoring, questioning, use of graphic and semantic organizers, think-alouds, recognizing story structure)*.......................32

Skill 1.8: Identify essential comprehension skills *(e.g., main idea, supporting details and facts, author's purpose, point of view, inference, conclusion)*..36

Skill 1.9: Determine appropriate uses of multiple representations of information for a variety of purposes *(e.g., charts, tables, graphs, pictures, print and non-print media)*..42

Skill 1.10: Determine and analyze strategies for developing critical-thinking skills such as analysis, synthesis, and evaluation *(e.g., making connections and predictions, questioning, summarizing, question generating)*.........................43

Skill 1.11: Evaluate and select appropriate instructional strategies for teaching a variety of informational and literary text...........................46

COMPETENCY 2
KNOWLEDGE OF LITERARY ANALYSIS AND GENRES 48

Skill 2.1: Differentiate among characteristics and elements of a variety of literary genres *(e.g., realistic fiction, fantasy, poetry, informational texts)*...48

Skill 2.2: Identify and analyze terminology and intentional use of literary devices *(e.g., simile, metaphor, personification, onomatopoeia, hyperbole)*...51

Skill 2.3: Evaluate and select appropriate multicultural texts based on purpose, relevance, cultural sensitivity, and developmental appropriateness 55

Skill 2.4: Identify and evaluate appropriate techniques for varying student response to texts *(e.g., think-pair-share, reading response journals, evidence-based discussion)*...56

COMPETENCY 3

KNOWLEDGE OF LANGUAGE AND THE WRITING PROCESS...57

Skill 3.1: Identify and evaluate the developmental stages of writing *(e.g., drawing, dictating, writing)*..................57

Skill 3.2: Differentiate stages of the writing process *(i.e., prewriting, drafting, revising, editing, publishing)*..................58

Skill 3.3: Distinguish among the modes of writing *(e.g., narrative, informative/explanatory, argument)*..................61

Skill 3.4: Select the appropriate mode of writing for a variety of occasions, purposes, and audiences..................64

Skill 3.5: Identify and apply instructional methods for teaching writing conventions *(e.g., spelling, punctuation, capitalization, syntax, word usage)*..................64

Skill 3.6: Apply instructional methods for teaching writer's craft across genres *(e.g., precise language, figurative language, linking words, temporal words, dialogue, sentence variety)*..................75

Skill 3.7: Identify and determine how text structure *(e.g., compare/contrast, cause and effect, etc.)* affects comprehension..................75

COMPETENCY 4

KNOWLEDGE OF LITERACY INSTRUCTION AND ASSESSMENTS...77

Skill 4.1: Distinguish among different types of assessments *(e.g., norm-referenced, criterion-referenced, diagnostic, curriculum-based)* and their purposes and characteristics..................77

Skill 4.2: Select and apply oral and written methods for assessing student progress *(e.g., informal reading inventories, fluency checks, rubrics, story retelling, portfolios)*..................79

Skill 4.3: Analyze assessment data *(e.g., screening, progress monitoring, diagnostic)* to guide instructional decisions and differentiate instruction..................84

Skill 4.4: Analyze and interpret students' formal and informal assessment results to inform students and stakeholders..................85

Skill 4.5: Evaluate the appropriateness of assessment instruments and practices..................88

Skill 4.6: Select appropriate classroom organizational formats *(e.g., literature circles, small groups, individuals, workshops, reading centers, multiage groups)* for specific instructional objectives..................90

Skill 4.7: Evaluate methods for the diagnosis, prevention, and intervention of common emergent literacy difficulties..................91

COMPETENCY 5

KNOWLEDGE OF COMMUNICATION AND MEDIA LITERACY...94

Skill 5.1: Identify characteristics of penmanship *(e.g., legibility, letter formation, spacing)*..................94

Skill 5.2: Distinguish among listening and speaking strategies *(e.g., questioning, paraphrasing, eye contact, voice, gestures)*..................95

Skill 5.3: Identify and apply instructional methods *(e.g., collaborative conversation, collaborative discussion, presentation)* for developing listening and speaking skills..................97

Skill 5.4: Select and evaluate a wide array of resources *(e.g., Internet, printed material, artifacts, visual media, primary sources)* for research and presentation..................100

Skill 5.5: Determine and apply the ethical process *(e.g., citation, paraphrasing)* for collecting and presenting authentic information while avoiding plagiarism..................101

Skill 5.6: Identify and evaluate current technology for use in educational settings..................102

DOMAIN II
SOCIAL SCIENCES

COMPETENCY 6
KNOWLEDGE OF EFFECTIVE INSTRUCTIONAL PRACTICES AND ASSESSMENT OF THE SOCIAL SCIENCES.............107

Skill 6.1: Select appropriate resources for instructional delivery of social science concepts, including complex informational text.............107

Skill 6.2: Identify appropriate resources for planning for instruction of social science concepts.................108

Skill 6.3: Choose appropriate methods for assessing social science concepts.................108

Skill 6.4: Determine appropriate learning environments for social science lessons.................109

COMPETENCY 7
KNOWLEDGE OF TIME, CONTINUITY, AND CHANGE (I.E., HISTORY).................110

Skill 7.1: Identify and analyze historical events that are related by cause and effect.................110

Skill 7.2: Analyze the sequential nature of historical events using timelines.................111

Skill 7.3: Analyze examples of primary and secondary source documents for historical perspective.................111

Skill 7.4: Analyze the impacts of the cultural contributions and technological developments of Africa; the Americas; Asia, including the Middle East; and Europe.................112

Skill 7.5: Identify the significant historical leaders and events that have influenced Eastern and Western civilizations.................117

Skill 7.6: Determine the causes and consequences of exploration, settlement, and growth on various cultures.................121

Skill 7.7: Interpret the ways that individuals and events have influenced economic, social, and political institutions in the world, nation, or state.................127

Skill 7.8: Analyze immigration and settlement patterns that have shaped the history of the United States.................130

Skill 7.9: Identify how various cultures contributed to the unique social, cultural, economic, and political features of Florida.................133

Skill 7.10: Identify the significant contributions of the early and classical civilizations.................140

COMPETENCY 8
KNOWLEDGE OF PEOPLE, PLACES, AND ENVIRONMENT (I.E., GEOGRAPHY).................141

Skill 8.1: Identify and apply the six essential elements of geography (i.e., the world in spatial terms, places and regions, physical systems, human systems, environment and society, uses of geography), including the specific terms for each element.................141

Skill 8.2: Analyze and interpret maps and other graphic representations of physical and human systems.................142

Skill 8.3: Identify and evaluate tools and technologies (e.g., maps, globe, GPS, satellite imagery) used to acquire, process, and report information from a spatial perspective.................147

Skill 8.4: Interpret statistics that show how places differ in their human and physical characteristics.................147

Skill 8.5: Analyze ways in which people adapt to an environment through the production and use of clothing, food, and shelter.................148

Skill 8.6: Determine the ways tools and technological advances affect the environment.................149

Skill 8.7: Identify and analyze physical, cultural, economic, and political reasons for the movement of people in the world, nation, or state.................150

Skill 8.8: Evaluate the impact of transportation and communication networks on the economic development in different regions.................152

Skill 8.9: Compare and contrast major regions of the world, nation, or state.................153

COMPETENCY 9

KNOWLEDGE OF GOVERNMENT AND THE CITIZEN (I.E., GOVERNMENT AND CIVICS) 156

Skill 9.1: Distinguish between the structure, functions, and purposes of federal, state, and local government...................................156

Skill 9.2: Compare and contrast the rights and responsibilities of a citizen in the world, nation, state, and community 159

Skill 9.3: Identify and interpret major concepts of the U.S. Constitution and other historical documents 159

Skill 9.4: Compare and contrast the ways the legislative, executive, and judicial branches share powers and responsibility.......................163

Skill 9.5: Analyze the U.S. electoral system and the election process...164

Skill 9.6: Identify and analyze the relationships between social, economic, and political rights and the historical documents that secure these rights in the United States...166

Skill 9.7: Identify and analyze the processes of the U.S. legal system 167

COMPETENCY 10

KNOWLEDGE OF PRODUCTION, DISTRIBUTION, AND CONSUMPTION (I.E., ECONOMICS) 170

Skill 10.1: Determine ways that scarcity affects the choices made by governments and individuals.................................170

Skill 10.2: Compare and contrast the characteristics and importance of currency...171

Skill 10.3: Identify and analyze the role of markets from production through distribution to consumption 171

Skill 10.4: Identify and analyze factors to consider when making consumer decisions 172

Skill 10.5: Analyze the economic interdependence between nations *(e.g., trade, finance, movement of labor)*.................................174

Skill 10.6: Identify human, natural, and capital resources and evaluate how these resources are used in the production of goods and services 176

DOMAIN III
SCIENCE

COMPETENCY 11

KNOWLEDGE OF EFFECTIVE SCIENCE INSTRUCTION...181

Skill 11.1: Analyze and apply developmentally appropriate researched-based strategies for teaching science practices 181

Skill 11.2: Select and apply safe and effective instructional strategies to utilize manipulatives, models, scientific equipment, real-world examples, and print and digital representations to support and enhance science instruction...................................181

Skill 11.3: Identify and analyze strategies for formal and informal learning experiences to provide science curriculum that promotes students' innate curiosity and active inquiry *(e.g., hands-on experiences, active engagement in the natural world, student interaction)* 183

Skill 11.4: Select and analyze collaborative strategies to help students explain concepts, to introduce and clarify formal science terms, and to identify misconceptions...185

Skill 11.5: Identify and apply appropriate reading strategies, mathematical practices, and science-content materials to enhance science instruction for learners at all levels...186

Skill 11.6: Apply differentiated strategies in science instruction and assessments based on student needs 187

Skill 11.7: Identify and apply ways to organize and manage a classroom for safe, effective science teaching that reflect state safety procedures and restrictions *(e.g., procedures, equipment, disposal of chemicals, classroom layout, use of living organisms)* 187

Skill 11.8: Select and apply appropriate technology, science tools and measurement units for students' use in data collection and the pursuit of science 191

Skill 11.9: Select and analyze developmentally appropriate diagnostic, formative and summative assessments to evaluate prior knowledge, guide instruction, and evaluate student achievement 192

Skill 11.10: Choose scientifically and professionally responsible content and activities that are socially and culturally sensitive 193

COMPETENCY 12
KNOWLEDGE OF THE NATURE OF SCIENCE

....194

Skill 12.1: Analyze the dynamic nature of science models, laws, mechanisms, and theories that explain natural phenomena *(e.g., durability, tentativeness, replication, reliance on evidence)* 194

Skill 12.2: Identify and apply science and engineering practices through integrated process skills *(e.g., observing, classifying, predicting, hypothesizing, designing and carrying out investigations, developing and using models, constructing and communicating explanations)* 195

Skill 12.3: Differentiate between the characteristics of experiments *(e.g., multiple trials, control groups, variables)* and other types of scientific investigations *(e.g., observations, surveys)* 197

Skill 12.4: Identify and analyze attitudes and dispositions underlying scientific thinking *(e.g., curiosity, openness to new ideas, appropriate skepticism, cooperation)* 198

Skill 12.5: Identify and select appropriate tools, including digital technologies, and units of measurement for various science tasks 199

Skill 12.6: Evaluate and interpret pictorial representations, charts, tables, and graphs of authentic data from scientific investigations to make predictions, construct explanations, and support conclusions 200

Skill 12.7: Identify and analyze ways in which science is an interdisciplinary process and interconnected to STEM disciplines *(i.e., science, technology, engineering, mathematics)* 201

Skill 12.8: Analyze the interactions of science and technology with society including cultural, ethical, economic, political, and global factors 202

COMPETENCY 13
KNOWLEDGE OF PHYSICAL SCIENCES

....204

Skill 13.1: Identify and differentiate among the physical properties of matter *(e.g., mass, volume, texture, hardness, freezing point)* 204

Skill 13.2: Identify and differentiate between physical and chemical changes *(e.g., tearing, burning, rusting)* 205

Skill 13.3: Compare the properties of matter during phase changes through the addition and/or removal of energy *(e.g., boiling, condensation, evaporation)* 206

Skill 13.4: Differentiate between the properties of homogeneous mixtures *(i.e., solutions)* and heterogeneous mixtures 207

Skill 13.5: Identify examples of and relationships among atoms, elements, molecules, and compounds...207

Skill 13.6: Identify and compare potential and kinetic energy 209

Skill 13.7: Differentiate among forms of energy, transformations of energy, and their real-world applications *(e.g., chemical, electrical, mechanical, heat, light, sound)* 210

Skill 13.8: Distinguish among temperature, heat, and forms of heat transfer *(e.g., conduction, convection, radiation)* 211

Skill 13.9: Analyze the functionality of an electrical circuit based on its conductors, insulators, and components.................................213

Skill 13.10: Identify and apply the characteristics of contact forces *(e.g., push, pull, friction)*, at-a-distance forces *(e.g., magnetic, gravitational, electrostatic)*, and their effects on matter *(e.g., motion, speed)* 214

COMPETENCY 14

KNOWLEDGE OF EARTH AND SPACE 216

Skill 14.1: Identify characteristics of geologic formations *(e.g., volcanoes, canyons, mountains)* and the mechanisms by which they are changed *(e.g., physical and chemical weathering, erosion, deposition)* 216

Skill 14.2: Identify and distinguish among major groups and properties of rocks and minerals and the processes of their formations........221

Skill 14.3: Identify and analyze the characteristics of soil, its components and profile, and the process of soil formation 222

Skill 14.4: Identify and analyze processes by which energy from the Sun is transferred *(e.g., radiation, conduction, convection)* through Earth's systems *(e.g., biosphere, hydrosphere, geosphere, atmosphere, cryosphere)*........................223

Skill 14.5: Identify and analyze the causes and effects of atmospheric processes and conditions *(e.g., water cycle, weather, climate)*...........225

Skill 14.6: Identify and analyze various conservation methods and their effectiveness in relation to renewable and nonrenewable natural resources 229

Skill 14.7: Analyze the Sun-Earth-Moon system in order to explain repeated patterns such as day and night, phases of the Moon, tides, and seasons 232

Skill 14.8: Compare and differentiate the composition and various relationships among the objects of our Solar System *(e.g., Sun, planets, moons, asteroids, comets)*........................235

Skill 14.9: Identify major events in the history of space exploration and their effects on society 238

COMPETENCY 15

KNOWLEDGE OF LIFE SCIENCE 240

Skill 15.1: Identify and compare the characteristics of living and nonliving things 240

Skill 15.2: Analyze the cell theory as it relates to the functional and structural hierarchy of all living things...................241

Skill 15.3: Identify and compare the structures and functions of plant and animal cells..................243

Skill 15.4: Classify living things into major groups *(i.e., Linnaean system)* and compare according to characteristics *(e.g., physical features, behaviors, development)* 245

Skill 15.5: Compare and contrast the structures, functions, and interactions of human and other animal organ systems *(e.g., respiration, reproduction, digestion)*..................246

Skill 15.6: Distinguish among infectious agents *(e.g., viruses, bacteria, fungi, parasites)*, their transmission, and their effects on the human body 254

Skill 15.7: Identify and analyze the processes of heredity and natural selection and the scientific theory of evolution...................257

Skill 15.8: Analyze the interdependence of living things with each other and with their environment *(e.g., food webs, ecosystems, pollution)*..................259

Skill 15.9: Identify and analyze plant structures and the processes of photosynthesis, transpiration, and reproduction *(i.e., sexual, asexual)*..................260

Skill 15.10: Predict the responses of plants to various stimuli *(e.g., heat, light, gravity)*..................261

Skill 15.11: Identify and compare the life cycles and predictable ways plants and animals change as they grow, develop, and age..................262

DOMAIN IV
MATHEMATICS

COMPETENCY 16
KNOWLEDGE OF STUDENT THINKING AND INSTRUCTIONAL PRACTICES 267

Skill 16.1: Analyze and apply appropriate mathematical concepts, procedures, and professional vocabulary *(e.g., subitize, transitivity, iteration, tiling)* **to evaluate student solutions.** 267

Skill 16.2: Analyze and discriminate among various problem structures with unknowns in all positions in order to develop student understanding of operations *(e.g., put-together/take-apart, arrays/area)*..............................267

Skill 16.3: Analyze and evaluate the validity of a student's mathematical model or argument *(e.g., inventive strategies, standard algorithms)* **used for problem solving**..268

Skill 16.4: Interpret individual student mathematics assessment data *(e.g., diagnostic, formative, progress monitoring)* **to guide instructional decisions and differentiate instruction.** 269

Skill 16.5: Select and analyze structured experiences for small and large groups of students according to the cognitive complexity of the task...270

Skill 16.6: Analyze learning progressions to show how students' mathematical knowledge, skills, and understanding develop over time 271

Skill 16.7: Distinguish among the components of math fluency *(i.e., accuracy, automaticity, rate, flexibility)*......................271

COMPETENCY 17
KNOWLEDGE OF OPERATIONS, ALGEBRAIC THINKING, COUNTING AND NUMBER IN BASE TEN 273

Skill 17.1: Interpret and extend multiple representations of patterns and functional relationships by using tables, graphs, equations, expressions, and verbal descriptions..273

Skill 17.2: Select the representation of an algebraic expression, equation, or inequality that models a real-world situation.........................276

Skill 17.3: Analyze and apply the properties of equality and operations in the context of interpreting solutions 278

Skill 17.4: Determine whether two algebraic expressions are equivalent by applying properties of operations or equality 281

Skill 17.5: Evaluate expressions with parentheses, brackets, and braces 282

Skill 17.6: Analyze and apply strategies *(e.g., models, estimation, reasonableness)* **to solve multistep word problems**....................282

Skill 17.7: Apply number theory concepts *(e.g., primes, composites, multiples, factors, parity, rules of divisibility)*..............................282

Skill 17.8: Identify strategies *(e.g., compensation, combining tens and ones)* **based on place value to perform multidigit arithmetic**...............287

COMPETENCY 18
KNOWLEDGE OF FRACTIONS, RATIOS, AND INTEGERS...294

Skill 18.1: Compare fractions, integers, and integers with integer exponents and place them on a number line..........................294

Skill 18.2: Convert among standard measurement units within and between measurement systems *(e.g., metric, U.S. customary)* **in the context of multistep, real-world problems** 300

Skill 18.3: Solve problems involving addition, subtraction, multiplication, and division of fractions, including mixing whole numbers and fractions, decimals and percents by using visual models and equations to represent the problems and their solutions 301

Skill 18.4: Select the representation *(e.g., linear, area, set model)* **that best represents the problem and solution, given a word problem or equation involving fractions** 302

Skill 18.5: Solve real-world problems involving ratios and proportions..303

COMPETENCY 19

KNOWLEDGE OF MEASUREMENT, DATA, AND STATISTICS 305

Skill 19.1: Calculate and interpret statistics of variability *(e.g., range, mean absolute deviation)* **and central tendency** *(e.g., mean, median)*...305

Skill 19.2: Analyze and interpret data through the use of frequency tables and graphs...306

Skill 19.3: Select appropriate measurement units to solve problems involving estimates and measurements...................309

Skill 19.4: Evaluate the choice of measures of center and variability, with respect to the shape of the data distribution and the context in which the data were gathered 310

Skill 19.5: Solve problems involving distance, time, liquid volume, mass, and money, which may include units expressed as fractions or decimals...311

COMPETENCY 20

KNOWLEDGE OF GEOMETRIC CONCEPTS...312

Skill 20.1: Apply geometric properties and relationships to solve problems involving perimeter, area, surface area, and volume.................312

Skill 20.2: Identify and locate ordered pairs in all four quadrants of a rectangular coordinate system...................................319

Skill 20.3: Identify and analyze properties of three-dimensional shapes using formal mathematical terms such as volume, faces, edges, and vertices...320

Skill 20.4: Classify two-dimensional figures in a hierarchy based on mathematical properties 322

SAMPLE TESTS

LANGUAGE ARTS AND READING...329

Language Arts and Reading Answer Key 339

Language Arts and Reading Rigor Table 339

Language Arts and Reading Answers with Rationales...340

SOCIAL SCIENCES 355

Social Sciences Answer Key 364

Social Sciences Rigor Table 364

Social Sciences Answers with Rationales...365

SCIENCE 381

Science Answer Key...390

Science Rigor Table 390

Science Answers with Rationales...391

MATHEMATICS 405

Mathematics Answer Key...414

Mathematics Rigor Table...414

Mathematics Answers with Rationales 415

FTCE
ELEMENTARY EDUCATION K–6

SECTION 1

ABOUT XAMONLINE

XAMonline—A Specialty Teacher Certification Company

Created in 1996, XAMonline was the first company to publish study guides for state-specific teacher certification examinations. Founder Sharon Wynne found it frustrating that materials were not available for teacher certification preparation and decided to create the first single, state-specific guide. XAMonline has grown into a company of over 1,800 contributors and writers and offers over 300 titles for the entire PRAXIS series and every state examination. No matter what state you plan on teaching in, XAMonline has a unique teacher certification study guide just for you.

XAMonline—Value and Innovation

We are committed to providing value and innovation. Our print-on-demand technology allows us to be the first in the market to reflect changes in test standards and user feedback as they occur. Our guides are written by experienced teachers who are experts in their fields, and our content reflects the highest standards of quality. Comprehensive practice tests with varied levels of rigor means that your study experience will closely match the actual in-test experience.

To date, XAMonline has helped nearly 600,000 teachers pass their certification or licensing exams. Our commitment to preparation exceeds simply providing the proper material for study—it extends to helping teachers **gain mastery** of the subject matter, giving them the **tools** to become the most effective classroom leaders possible, and ushering today's students toward a **successful future**.

SECTION 2

ABOUT THIS STUDY GUIDE

Purpose of This Guide

Is there a little voice inside of you saying, "Am I ready?" Our goal is to replace that little voice and remove all doubt with a new voice that says, "I AM READY. **Bring it on!**" by offering the highest quality of teacher certification study guides.

Organization of Content

You will see that while every test may start with overlapping general topics, each is very unique in the skills they wish to test. Only XAMonline presents custom content that analyzes deeper than a title, a subarea, or an objective. Only XAMonline presents content and sample test assessments along with **focus statements**, the deepest-level rationale and interpretation of the skills that are unique to the exam.

Title and field number of test

→Each exam has its own name and number. XAMonline's guides are written to give you the content you need to know for the specific exam you are taking. You can be confident when you buy our guide that it contains the information you need to study for the specific test you are taking.

Subareas

→These are the major content categories found on the exam. XAMonline's guides are written to cover all of the subareas found in the test frameworks developed for the exam.

Objectives

→These are standards that are unique to the exam and represent the main subcategories of the subareas/content categories. XAMonline's guides are written to address every specific objective required to pass the exam.

Focus statements

→These are examples and interpretations of the objectives. You find them in parenthesis directly following the objective. They provide detailed examples of the range, type, and level of content that appear on the test questions. **Only XAMonline's guides drill down to this level.**

How Do We Compare with Our Competitors?

XAMonline—drills down to the focus statement level
CliffsNotes and REA—organized at the objective level
Kaplan—provides only links to content
MoMedia—content not specific to the state test

Each subarea is divided into manageable sections that cover the specific skill areas. Explanations are easy to understand and thorough. You'll find that every test answer contains a rationale so if you need a refresher or further review after taking the test, it's easy to identify the section you need to return to for further review.

How to Use This Book

Our informal polls show that most people begin studying up to eight weeks prior to the test date, so start early. Then ask yourself some questions: How much do you really know? Are you coming to the test straight from your teacher-education program or are you having to review subjects you haven't considered in ten years? Either way, take a **diagnostic or assessment test** first. Also, spend time on sample tests so that you become accustomed to the way the actual test will appear.

This guide comes with an online diagnostic test of 30 questions found online at *www.XAMonline.com*. It is a little boot camp to get you ready for the task and reveal things about your compendium of knowledge in general. Although this guide is structured to follow the order of the test, you are not required to study in that order. By finding a time-management and study plan that fits your life, you will be more effective. The results of your diagnostic or self-assessment test can be a guide for how to manage your time and point you toward an area that needs more attention.

After taking the diagnostic exam, fill out the **Personalized Study Plan** page at the beginning of each chapter. Review the competencies and skills covered in that chapter and check the boxes that apply to your study needs. If there are sections you already know you can skip, check the "skip it" box. Taking this step will give you a study plan for each chapter.

Week	Activity
8 weeks prior to test	Take a diagnostic test found at www.XAMonline.com
7 weeks prior to test	Build your Personalized Study Plan for each chapter. Check the "skip it" box for sections you feel you are already strong in. ✘ SKIP IT ☐
6-3 weeks prior to test	For each of these four weeks, choose a content area to study. You don't have to go in the order of the book. It may be that you start with the content that needs the most review. Alternately, you may want to ease yourself into your plan by starting with the most familiar material.
2 weeks prior to test	Take the sample test, score it, and create a review plan for the final week before the test.
1 week prior to test	Following your plan (which will likely be aligned with the areas that need the most review) go back and study the sections that align with the questions you may have gotten wrong. Then go back and study the sections related to the questions you answered correctly. If need be, create flashcards and drill yourself on any area that you makes you anxious.

SECTION 3

ABOUT THE FTCE ELEMENTARY EDUCATION K–6 EXAM

The Florida Teacher Certification Examination is a computer-based exam designed to ensure that candidates possess the skills and knowledge necessary to meet the needs of Florida students. The test consists of four subtests or sections. The table below indicates the respective number of questions and time allowed for each section.

For candidates taking the test for the first time, it is necessary to register to take the **full test** (all four subtests) in one session. After the first attempt, candidates may take any combination of the subtests in one session.

Testing takes place throughout the year by appointment at testing centers throughout the state and around the country. **Unofficial** pass/no pass results are issued on completion of the test, and official results are available within four weeks.

	Number of questions	Time allowed
Subtest 1	Approximately 60 multiple choice questions	1 hour and 5 minutes
Subtest 2	Approximately 55 multiple choice questions	1 hour and 5 minutes
Subtest 3	Approximately 55 multiple choice questions	1 hour and 10 minutes
Subtest 4	Approximately 50 multiple choice questions	1 hour and 10 minutes

For candidates who take three or more subtests in one sitting, there is a 15 minute break.

To pass the test, candidates must earn a scaled score of 200 or higher per subtest and pass each subtest.

This book includes details about the skills covered by each competency for review and study.

Detailed breakdown of the test by subject area

Language Arts and Reading

Competency	Approx. percentage of total questions from this subtest
Knowledge of the reading process	29%
Knowledge of literary analysis and genres	16%
Knowledge of language and the writing process	16%
Knowledge of literacy instruction and assessments	23%
Knowledge of communication and media literacy	16%

Social Science

Competency	Approx. percentage of total questions from this subtest
Knowledge of effective instructional practices and assessment of the social sciences	19%
Knowledge of time, continuity, and change (i.e., history)	26%
Knowledge of people, places, and environment (i.e., geography)	18%
Knowledge of government, and the citizen (i.e., government and civics)	20%
Knowledge of production, distribution, and consumption (i.e., economics)	17%

Science

Competency	Approx. percentage of total questions from this subtest
Knowledge of effective science instruction	20%
Knowledge of the nature of science	18%
Knowledge of physical sciences	20%
Knowledge of Earth and space	19%
Knowledge of life science	23%

Mathematics

For this subtest, there will be an on-screen reference sheet.

Competency	Approx. percentage of total questions from this subtest
Knowledge of student thinking and instructional practices	26%
Knowledge of operations, algebraic thinking, counting and number in base ten	28%
Knowledge of fractions, ratios, and integers	18%
Knowledge of measurement, data, and statistics	16%
Knowledge of geometric concepts	12%

Question Types

You're probably thinking, *enough already, I want to study!* Indulge us a little longer while we explain that there is actually more than one type of multiple-choice question. You can thank us later after you realize how well prepared you are for your exam.

1. **Complete the Statement.** The name says it all. In this question type you'll be asked to choose the correct completion of a given statement. For example:

> The Dolch Basic Sight Words consist of a relatively short list of words that children should be able to:
>
> A. Sound out
>
> B. Know the meaning of
>
> C. Recognize on sight
>
> D. Use in a sentence

The correct answer is C. In order to check your answer, test out the statement by adding the choices to the end of it.

2. **Which of the Following.** One way to test your answer choice for this type of question is to replace the phrase "which of the following" with your selection. Use this example:

> Which of the following words is one of the twelve most frequently used in children's reading texts:
>
> A. There
>
> B. This
>
> C. The
>
> D. An

Don't look! Test your answer. _____ is one of the twelve most frequently used in children's reading texts. Did you guess C? If so, you guessed correctly!

3. **Roman Numeral Choices.** This question type is used when there is more than one possible correct answer. For example:

> **Which of the following two arguments accurately supports the use of cooperative learning as an effective method of instruction?**
>
> I. Cooperative learning groups facilitate healthy competition between individuals in the group.
> II. Cooperative learning groups allow academic achievers to carry or cover for academic underachievers.
> III. Cooperative learning groups make each student in the group accountable for the success of the group.
> IV. Cooperative learning groups make it possible for students to reward other group members for achieving.
>
> A. I and II
> B. II and III
> C. I and III
> D. III and IV

Notice that the question states there are **two** possible answers. It's best to read all the possibilities first before looking at the answer choices. In this case, the correct answer is D.

4. **Negative Questions.** This type of question contains words such as "not," "least," and "except." Each correct answer will be the statement that does **not** fit the situation described in the question. Such as:

> **Multicultural education is not**
>
> A. An idea or concept
> B. A "tack-on" to the school curriculum
> C. An educational reform movement
> D. A process

Think to yourself that the statement could be anything but the correct answer. This question form is more open to interpretation than other types, so read carefully and don't forget that you're answering a negative statement.

5. **Questions that Include Graphs, Tables, or Reading Passages.** As always, read the question carefully. It likely asks for a very specific answer and not a broad interpretation of the visual. Here is a simple (though not statistically accurate) example of a graph question:

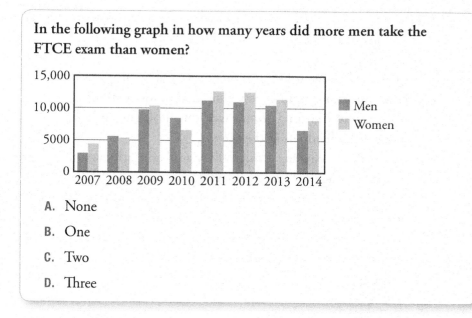

In the following graph in how many years did more men take the FTCE exam than women?

A. None

B. One

C. Two

D. Three

It may help you to simply circle the two years that answer the question. Make sure you've read the question thoroughly and once you've made your determination, double check your work. The correct answer is C.

Scenario:

A typical learning scenario, problem, or observation is given. Examine the situation carefully in order to answer the question, choose the best course of action, identify the correct teacher evaluation, or the best teacher response.

SECTION 4

HELPFUL HINTS

Study Tips

1. **You are what you eat.** Certain foods aid the learning process by releasing natural memory enhancers called CCKs (cholecystokinin) composed of tryptophan, choline, and phenylalanine. All of these chemicals enhance the neurotransmitters associated with memory and certain foods release memory enhancing chemicals. A light meal or snacks of one of the following foods fall into this category:

   - Milk
   - Rice
   - Eggs
   - Fish
   - Nuts and seeds
   - Oats
   - Turkey

   The better the connections, the more you comprehend!

2. **The pen is mightier than the sword.** Learn to take great notes. A by-product of our modern culture is that we have grown accustomed to getting our information in short doses. We've subconsciously trained ourselves to assimilate information into neat little packages. Messy notes fragment the flow of information. Your notes can be much clearer with proper formatting. *The Cornell Method* is one such format. This method was popularized in *How to Study in College*, Ninth Edition, by Walter Pauk. You can benefit from the method without purchasing an additional book by simply looking up the method online. Below is a sample of how *The Cornell Method* can be adapted for use with this guide.

← 2½" →	← 6" →
Cue Column	**Note Taking Column**
	1. Record: During your reading, use the note-taking column to record important points.
	2. Questions: As soon as you finish a section, formulate questions based on the notes in the right-hand column. Writing questions helps to clarify meanings, reveal relationships, establish community, and strengthen memory. Also, the writing of questions sets the state for exam study later.
	3. Recite: Cover the note-taking column with a sheet of paper. Then, looking at the questions or cue-words in the question and cue column only, say aloud, in your own words, the answers to the questions, facts, or ideas indicated by the cue words.
	4. Reflect: Reflect on the material by asking yourself questions.
	5. Review: Spend at least ten minutes every week reviewing all your previous notes. Doing so helps you retain ideas and topics for the exam.
↑ 2" ↓	**Summary** After reading, use this space to summarize the notes from each page.

Adapted from How to Study in College, Ninth Edition, by Walter Pauk, ©2008 Wadsworth

3. **See the forest for the trees.** In other words, get the concept before you look at the details. One way to do this is to take notes as you read, paraphrasing or summarizing in your own words. Putting the concept in terms that are comfortable and familiar to you may increase retention.

4. **Question authority.** Ask why, why, why? Pull apart written material paragraph by paragraph and don't forget the captions under the illustrations. For example, if a heading reads *Stream Erosion* put it in the form of a question (Why do streams erode? What is stream erosion?) then find the answer within the material. If you train your mind to think in this manner, you will learn more and prepare yourself for answering test questions.

5. **Play mind games.** Using your brain for reading or puzzles keeps it flexible. Even with a limited amount of time your brain can take in data (much like a computer) and store it for later use. In ten minutes you can: read two paragraphs (at least), quiz yourself with flash cards, or review notes. Even if you don't fully understand something on the first pass, your mind stores it for recall, which is why frequent reading or review increases chances of retention and comprehension.

6. **Place yourself in exile and set the mood.** Set aside a particular place and time to study that best suits your personal needs and biorhythms. If you're a night person, burn the midnight oil. If you're a morning person, set yourself up with some coffee and get to it. Make your study time and place as free from distraction as possible and surround yourself with what you need, be it silence or music. Studies have shown that music can aid in concentration, absorption, and retrieval of information. Not all music, though. Classical music is said to work best

7. **Get pointed in the right direction.** Use arrows to point to important passages or pieces of information. It's easier to read than a page full of yellow highlights. Highlighting can be used sparingly, but add an arrow to the margin to call attention to it.

8. **Check your budget.** You should at least review all the content material before your test, but allocate the most amount of time to the areas that need the most refreshing. It sounds obvious, but it's easy to forget. You can use the study rubric above to balance your study budget.

The proctor will write the start time where it can be seen and then, later, provide the time remaining, typically fifteen minutes before the end of the test.

Testing Tips

1. **Get smart, play dumb.** Sometimes a question is just a question. No one is out to trick you, so don't assume that the test writer is looking for something other than what was asked. Stick to the question as written and don't overanalyze.

2. **Do a double take.** It's common to transpose words or miss important details, so read test questions and answer choices at least twice. If you have no idea what the correct answer is, skip it and come back later if there's time. If you're still clueless, it's okay to guess. Remember, you're scored on the number of questions you answer correctly and you're not penalized for wrong answers. The worst case scenario is that you miss a point from a good guess.

3. **Turn it on its ear.** The syntax of a question can often provide a clue, so make things interesting and turn the question into a statement to see if it changes the meaning or relates better (or worse) to the answer choices.

4. **Get out your magnifying glass.** Look for hidden clues in the questions because it's difficult to write a multiple-choice question without giving away part of the answer in the options presented. In most questions you can readily eliminate one or two potential answers, increasing your chances of answering correctly to 50/50, which will help you if you've skipped a question and gone back to it (see tip #2).

5. **Call it intuition.** Often your first instinct is correct. If you've been studying the content you've likely absorbed something and have subconsciously retained the knowledge. On questions you're not sure about, trust your instincts because a first impression is usually correct.

6. **Become a clock-watcher.** You have a set amount of time to answer the questions. Don't get bogged down laboring over a question you're not sure about when there are ten others you could answer more readily. If you choose to follow the advice of tip #2, be sure you leave time near the end to go back and fill in the scan sheet.

Do the Drill

No matter how prepared you feel, it's sometimes a good idea to apply Murphy's Law. So the following tips might seem silly, mundane, or obvious, but we're including them anyway.

1. **Remember, you are what you eat, so bring a snack.** Choose from the list of energizing foods that appear earlier in the introduction.

2. **You're not too sexy for your test.** Wear comfortable clothes. You'll be distracted if your belt is too tight or if you're too cold or too hot.

3. **Lie to yourself.** Even if you think you're a prompt person, pretend you're not and leave plenty of time to get to the testing center. Map it out ahead of time and do a dry run if you have to. There's no need to add road rage to your list of anxieties.

4. **No ticket, no test.** Bring your admission ticket as well as **two** forms of identification, including one with a picture and signature. You will not be admitted to the test without these things.

5. **You can't take it with you.** Leave any study aids, dictionaries, notebooks, computers, and the like at home. Certain tests **do** allow a scientific or four-function calculator, so check ahead of time to see if your test does.

6. **Prepare for the desert.** Any time spent on a bathroom break **cannot** be made up later, so use your judgment on the amount you eat or drink.

7. **Quiet, Please!** Keeping your own time is a good idea, but not with a timepiece that has a loud ticker. If you use a watch, take it off and place it nearby but not so that it distracts you. Also, **silence your cell phone**.

To the best of our ability, we have compiled the content you need to know in this book and in the accompanying online resources. The rest is up to you. You can use the study and testing tips or you can follow your own methods. Either way, you can be confident that there aren't any missing pieces of information and there shouldn't be any surprises in the content on the test.

If you have questions about test fees, registration, electronic testing, or other content verification issues please visit *www.fl.nesinc.com*.

Good luck!

Sharon Wynne
Founder, XAMonline

DOMAIN I
LANGUAGE ARTS AND READING

PERSONALIZED STUDY PLAN

PAGE	COMPETENCY AND SKILL	KNOWN MATERIAL/ SKIP IT
5	**1: Knowledge of the reading process**	☐
	1.1: Identify the content of emergent literacy	☐
	1.2: Identify the processes, skills, and stages of word recognition that lead to effective decoding	☐
	1.3: Select and apply instructional methods for the development of decoding skills	☐
	1.4: Distinguish among the components of reading fluency	☐
	1.5: Choose and apply instructional methods for developing reading fluency	☐
	1.6: Identify and evaluate instructional methods and strategies for facilitating students' reading comprehension	☐
	1.7: Identify essential comprehension skills	☐
	1.8: Determine appropriate uses of multiple representations of information for a variety of purposes	☐
	1.9: Determine and analyze strategies for developing critical-thinking skills such as analysis, synthesis, and evaluation	☐
	1.10: Evaluate and select appropriate instructional strategies for teaching a variety of informational and literary text	☐
	1.11: Evaluate and select appropriate instructional strategies for teaching a variety of informational and literary text	☐
47	**2: Knowledge of literary analysis and genres**	☐
	2.1: Differentiate among characteristics and elements of a variety of literary genres	☐
	2.2: Identify and analyze terminology and intentional use of literary devices	☐
	2.3: Evaluate and select appropriate multicultural texts based on purpose, relevance, cultural sensitivity, and developmental appropriateness	☐
	2.4: Identify and evaluate appropriate techniques for varying student response to texts	☐
	2.5: Identify and evaluate the developmental stages of writing	☐
56	**3: Knowledge of language and the writing process**	☐
	3.1: Distinguish among the modes of writing	☐
	3.2: Select the appropriate mode of writing for a variety of occasions, purposes, and audiences	☐
	3.3: Identify and apply instructional methods for teaching writing conventions	☐
	3.4: Apply instructional methods for teaching writer's craft across genres	☐
	3.5: Distinguish among different types of assessments and their purposes and characteristics	☐

PERSONALIZED STUDY PLAN

KNOWN MATERIAL/ SKIP IT

PAGE	COMPETENCY AND SKILL	
75	**4: Knowledge of literacy instruction and assessments**	☐
	4.1: Select and apply oral and written methods for assessing student progress	☐
	4.2: Analyze assessment data to guide instructional decisions and differentiate instruction	☐
	4.3: Analyze and interpret students' formal and informal assessment results to inform students and stakeholders	☐
	4.4: Evaluate the appropriateness of assessment instruments and practices	☐
	4.5: Select appropriate classroom organizational formats for specific instructional objectives	☐
	4.6: Evaluate methods for the diagnosis, prevention, and intervention of common emergent literacy difficulties	☐
	4.7: Identify characteristics of penmanship	☐
92	**5: Knowledge of communication and media literacy**	☐
	5.1: Distinguish among listening and speaking strategies	☐
	5.2: Identify and apply instructional methods for developing listening and speaking skills	☐
	5.3: Select and evaluate a wide array of resources for research and presentation	☐
	5.4: Determine and apply the ethical process for collecting and presenting authentic information while avoiding plagiarism	☐
	5.5: Identify and evaluate current technology for use in educational settings	☐

COMPETENCY 1
KNOWLEDGE OF THE READING PROCESS

> **SKILL 1.1** **Identify the content of emergent literacy** *(e.g., oral language development, phonological awareness, alphabet knowledge, decoding, concepts of print, motivation, text structures, written language development).*

EMERGENT LITERACY refers to a child's speech and language development. It begins at birth and continues into the preschool years, during which time the child learns how to use and understand language in order to communicate. In the school-age years, emergent literacy refers to the way the spoken language relates to reading and writing for the child.

> **EMERGENT LITERACY:**
> a child's speech and language development

In 2000, the National Reading Panel released its now well-known report on teaching children to read. In a small way, this report put to rest the debate over phonics and whole language. It argued, essentially, that while word-letter recognition is important, understanding what the text means is equally important. The report's "big 5" critical areas of reading instruction are as follows:

1. Phonemic awareness
2. Phonics
3. Fluency
4. Comprehension
5. Vocabulary

Areas of Emerging Evidence

- Experiences with print (through reading and writing) help preschool children develop an understanding of the conventions, purposes, and functions of print. Children learn about print from a variety of sources and in the process come to realize that print carries the story. They also learn how text is structured visually (i.e., text begins at the top of the page, moves from left to right, and carries over to the next page when the page is turned). While knowledge of the conventions of print enables children to understand the physical structure of language, the conceptual knowledge that printed words convey a message also helps children bridge the gap between oral and written language.

- Phonological awareness and letter recognition contribute to initial reading acquisition by helping children develop efficient word recognition strategies (e.g., detecting pronunciations and storing associations in memory). Phonological awareness and knowledge of print-speech relations play an important role in facilitating reading acquisition. Therefore, phonological awareness instruction should be an integral component of early reading programs. Within the emergent literacy research, viewpoints diverge on whether acquisition of phonological awareness and letter recognition are preconditions of literacy acquisition or whether they develop interdependently with literacy activities such as storybook reading and writing.

- Storybook reading affects children's knowledge about, strategies for, and attitudes toward reading. Of all the strategies intended to promote growth in literacy acquisition, none is as commonly practiced, nor as strongly supported across the emergent literacy literature, as storybook reading. Children in different social and cultural groups have differing degrees of access to storybook reading. For example, it is not unusual for a teacher to have students who have experienced thousands of hours of story-reading time along with others who have had little or no such exposure.

Knowledge of Text Structure

In nonfiction, particularly in textbooks, and sometimes in fiction, text structure gives readers important clues about what to look for.

In nonfiction, particularly in textbooks, and sometimes in fiction, text structure gives readers important clues about what to look for. Students often do not know how to make sense of all the headings in a textbook and do not realize that, for example, the sidebar story about a character in history is not the main text on a particular page in the history textbook. Teaching students how to interpret text structures gives them the tools they need for tackling other similar texts.

The concepts of print

Understanding that print carries meaning is demonstrated every day in the elementary classroom as the teacher holds up a selected book to read aloud to the class. The teachers explicitly and deliberately think aloud about how to hold the book, how to focus the class on looking at its cover, where to start reading, and in what direction to begin.

Even in writing the morning message on the board, the teacher targets the children on the placement of the message and its proper place at the top of the board to be followed by additional activities and a schedule for the rest of the day.

When a teacher challenges children to make letter posters of a single letter and the items in the classroom, their home, or their knowledge base that start with that letter, the children are making concrete the understanding that print carries meaning.

Teachers should look for five basic behaviors in students:

1. Do students know how to hold the book?

2. Can students match speech to print?

3. Do students know the difference between letters and words?

4. Do students know that print conveys meaning?

5. Can students track print from left to right?

In order for students to understand concepts of print, they must be able to recognize text and understand the various mechanics that text contains. These include:

- All text contains a message

- The English language has a specific structure

- In order to decode words and read text, students must be able to understand that structure

The structure of the English language consists of rules of grammar, capitalization, and punctuation. For younger children, this means being able to recognize letters and form words. For older children, it means being able to recognize different types of text, such as lists, stories, and signs, and knowing the purpose of each one.

> The structure of the English language consists of rules of grammar, capitalization, and punctuation.

When reading to children, teachers point to words as they read them. Illustrations and pictures also contribute to being able to understand the meaning of the text. Therefore, teachers should also discuss illustrations related to the text. Teachers also discuss the common characteristics of books, such as the author, title page, and table of contents. Asking students to predict what the story might be about is a good strategy to help teach students about the cover and its importance to the story. Pocket charts, big books, and song charts provide ample opportunity for teachers to point to words as they read.

Instructional Strategies

Using Big Books in the Classroom	Gather the children around you in a group with the big book placed on a stand. This allows all children to see the words and pictures. As you read, point to each word. It is best to use a pointer so that you are not covering any other words or part of the page. When students read from the big book on their own, have them also use the pointer for each word. When students begin reading from smaller books, have them transfer what they have learned about pointing to the words by using their finger to track the reading. Observation is a key point in assessing students' ability to track words and speech.
A Classroom Rich in Print	Having words from a familiar rhyme or poem in a pocket chart lends itself to an activity where the students arrange the words in the correct order and then read the rhyme. This is an instructional strategy that reinforces directionality of print. It also reinforces punctuation, capitalization, and matching print to speech. Using highlighters or sticky tabs to locate upper and lower case letters or specific words can help students isolate words and learn about the structure of language they need to have for reading. There should be plenty of books in the classroom for children to read on their own or in small groups. As you observe each of these groups, take note of how the child holds the book in addition to how he or she tracks and reads the words.
Word Wall	A word wall is a great teaching tool for words in isolation and for writing. Each of the letters of the alphabet is displayed with words that begin with that letter under each one. Students are able to find the letter on the wall and read the words under each one.
Sounds of the Letters	In addition to teaching the letter names, students should learn the corresponding sound of each letter. This is a key feature of decoding when beginning to read. The use of rhyming words is an effective way to teach letter sounds so that children have a solid background.

Sites with information on using word walls:

http://www.teachingfirst.net/wordwallact.htm

http://www.theschoolbell.com/Links/word_walls/words.html

Students should be exposed to daily opportunities for viewing and reading texts. Teachers can do this by engaging the students in discussions about books during shared, guided, and independent reading times. The teacher should draw the students' attention to the conventions of print and discuss with them the reasons for choosing different books. For example, teachers should let the students know that it is perfectly acceptable to return a book and select another if they think it is too hard for them.

Predictable books help engage the students in reading. Once the students realize what words are repeated in the text, they will eagerly chime in to repeat the words at the appropriate time during the reading. Rereading helps students learn individual words and develop fluency as they recognize and repeat whole lines of text.

Development of Oral Language

Oral language begins to develop during the earliest vocal interactions infants experience with their caregivers, and it is an ongoing process. Throughout their youngest years, children observe oral communication in their home, their schools, and their interactions with others. During the preschool years, children acquire cognitive skills in oral language that they later apply to reading comprehension. Reading aloud to young children is one of the most important things that an adult can do because adults are teaching them how to monitor, question, predict, and confirm what they hear in the stories.

Reading aloud to young children is one of the most important things that an adult can do.

Oral language is said to develop in three stages: protolinguistic, transition, and language. Around the time a child learns to crawl, the child is often also in the protolinguistic phase of oral development, which includes baby noises, physical movements, and interactions with others. In the transition phase (around the time the child begins to walk), the child begins to move beyond baby language in order to mimic words and sounds in the child's native tongue. In the final stage, language, the child is able to communicate about shared experiences with others. At this point children are aware that there is more in the world than just what they experience, and they can begin to use language to learn about and share the experiences of others.

Reid (1988) described four metalinguistic abilities that young children acquire through early involvement in reading activities:

Once children reach the language phase, they can begin to see how language, in all of its forms, plays a role in the world around them.

1. **Word consciousness:** Children who have access to books can tell the story through the pictures before they can read. Gradually, they begin to realize the connection between the spoken words and the printed words. The beginning of letter and word discrimination begins in the early years.

2. **Language and conventions of print:** During this stage children learn how to hold a book, where to begin to read, the left-to-right motion, and how to continue from one line to another.

3. **Functions of print:** Children discover that print can be used for a variety of purposes and functions, including entertainment and information.

4. **Fluency:** Through listening to adult models, children learn to read in phrases and use intonation.

Motivation

Readiness for subject-area learning is dependent not only on prior knowledge but also on affective factors such as interest, motivation, and attitude. These factors are often more influential on student learning than the preexisting cognitive base.

Self-motivation is the best tool for learning. Children need to challenge themselves through constant exploration and experimentation. Activities should suit the developmental age of the child so that she can perform them with minimal outside assistance. An adult should act as an assistant who provides help only when it is required.

> *Self-motivation is the best tool for learning. Children need to challenge themselves through constant exploration and experimentation.*

Strategies for promoting awareness of the relationship between spoken and written language

- Write down what the children are saying on a chart.

- Highlight and celebrate the meanings and uses of print products found in the classroom. These products include: posters, labels, yellow sticky-pad notes, labels on shelves and lockers, calendars, rule signs, and directions.

- Read big-print and oversized books to children to teach print conventions such as directionality.

- Use practice exercises in reading to others (for K-1/2), where young children practice how to handle a book, how to turn pages, how to find tops and bottoms of pages, and how to tell the difference between the front and back covers of a book.

- Create search-and-discuss adventures in word awareness and close observation where children are challenged to identify and talk about the length, appearance, and boundaries of specific words and the letters that make them up.

- Have children match oral words to printed words by forming an echo chorus. As the teacher reads the story aloud, children echo the reading. This often works best with poetry or rhymes.

- Have the children combine, manipulate, switch, and move letters around to change words and spelling patterns.

- Work with letter cards to create messages and respond to the messages that the children create.

Methods used to teach these skills are often featured in a "balanced literacy" curriculum that focuses on the use of skills in various instructional contexts. For example, with independent reading, students independently choose books that are at their reading levels; with guided reading, teachers work with small groups of students to help them with their particular reading problems; with whole-group reading, the entire class reads the same text, and the teacher incorporates activities to help students learn phonics, comprehension, fluency, and vocabulary. In addition to these components of balanced literacy, teachers incorporate writing so students can learn the structures of communicating through text.

Design Principles and Instructional Strategies for Emergent Literacy

Conspicuous strategies

As an instructional priority, conspicuous strategies are sequences of teaching events and teacher actions used to help students learn new literacy skills and relate them to their existing knowledge. Conspicuous strategies can be incorporated in beginning reading instruction to ensure that all learners have basic literacy concepts. For example, during storybook reading, teachers can show students how to recognize the fronts and backs of books, locate titles, or look at pictures and predict the story, rather than assume children will learn this through incidental exposure. Similarly, teachers can give students a strategy for holding a pencil appropriately or checking the form of their letters against an alphabet sheet on their desks or the classroom wall.

Mediated scaffolding

Mediated scaffolding can be accomplished in a number of ways to meet the needs of students with diverse literacy experiences. To link oral and written language, for example, teachers may use texts that simulate speech by incorporating oral language patterns or children's writing. Teachers can also use daily storybook reading to discuss book-handling skills and directionality—concepts that are particularly important for children who are unfamiliar with printed texts. Repeated readings will provide students with multiple exposures to unfamiliar words or extended opportunities to look at books with predictable patterns, as well as provide support by modeling the behaviors associated with reading. Teachers can act as scaffolds during these storybook reading activities by adjusting their demands (e.g., asking increasingly complex questions or encouraging children to take on portions of the reading) or by reading more complex texts as students gain knowledge of beginning literacy components.

Strategic integration

Many children have difficulty making connections between old and new information.

In the classroom, strategic integration of old and new learning can be accomplished by providing access to literacy materials in classroom writing centers and libraries. Students should also have opportunities to integrate and extend their literacy skills by reading aloud, listening to other students read aloud, and listening to recordings in reading corners.

Primed background knowledge

All children bring some level of background knowledge (e.g., how to hold a book, awareness of directionality of print) to beginning reading. Teachers can utilize children's background knowledge to help them link their personal literacy experiences to beginning reading instruction, while also closing the gap between students with rich literacy experiences and those with impoverished literacy experiences. Activities that draw upon background knowledge include incorporating oral language activities (which discriminate between printed letters and words) into daily read-alouds, as well as frequent opportunities to retell stories, looking at books with predictable patterns, writing messages with invented spelling, and responding to literature through drawing.

Emergent literacy

Emergent literacy research examines early literacy knowledge and the contexts and conditions that foster that knowledge. Despite differing viewpoints on the relationship between emerging literacy skills and reading acquisition, strong support exists in the literature for the important contribution that early childhood exposure to oral and written language makes to the facility with which children learn to read.

Reading for comprehension of factual material—content area textbooks, reference books, and newspapers—is closely related to study strategies in middle or junior high school. Organized study models, such as the SQ3R (Survey, Question, Read, Recite, and Review) method, a technique that makes it possible and feasible to learn the content of even large amounts of text, teach students to locate main ideas and supporting details, to recognize sequential order, to distinguish fact from opinion, and to determine cause and effect relationships.

SKILL 1.2 **Identify the processes, skills, and stages of word recognition that lead to effective decoding** (e.g., pre-alphabetic, partial-alphabetic, full alphabetic, grapho-phonemic, morphemic).

Word analysis (also called phonics or decoding) is the process readers use to figure out unfamiliar words based on written patterns. Word recognition is the process of automatically determining the pronunciation and, to some degree, the meaning of an unknown word. Fluent readers recognize most written words easily and correctly without consciously decoding or breaking them down. The elements of literacy described below are skills all readers need for word recognition.

Phonological Awareness

PHONOLOGICAL AWARENESS is the ability of the reader to recognize the sound of spoken language. This recognition includes how sounds can be blended together, segmented (divided up), and manipulated (switched around). This awareness then leads to phonics, a method for teaching children to read. It helps them "sound out" words.

> **PHONOLOGICAL AWARENESS:** the ability of the reader to recognize the sound of spoken language

Development of phonological skills may begin during the pre-K years. Indeed, by the age of five, a child who has been exposed to rhyme can recognize a rhyme. Such a child can demonstrate phonological awareness by filling in the missing rhyming word in a familiar rhyme or rhymed picture book.

Children learn phonological awareness when they learn the sounds made by particular letters and various combinations of letters, and how to recognize individual sounds in words.

Phonological awareness skills include:

- Rhyming and syllabification
- Blending sounds into words (such as pic-tur-bo-k)
- Identifying the beginning or starting sounds of words and the ending or closing sounds of words
- Breaking words down into sounds, also called "segmenting" words
- Recognizing other smaller words in a larger word by removing starting sounds, such as *hear* to *ear*

Instructional methods to teach phonological awareness may include auditory games and drills. These games allow students to recognize and manipulate the sounds of words, separate or segment the sounds of words, take out sounds, blend sounds, add in new sounds, or take apart sounds and recombine them in new ways.

Phonemic Awareness

PHONEMIC AWARENESS is the idea that words are composed of sounds. To be phonemically aware means that the reader and listener can recognize and manipulate specific sounds in spoken words. Phonemic awareness is concerned with sounds in spoken words. The majority of phonemic awareness tasks, activities, and exercises are oral.

Theorist Marilyn Jager Adams, who researches early reading, has outlined five basic types of phonemic awareness tasks:

PHONEMIC AWARENESS TASKS	
The ability to hear rhymes and alliteration	The children listen to a poem, rhyming picture book, or song and identify the rhyming words they hear, which the teacher might then record or list on an experiential chart
The ability to do oddity tasks (recognize the member of a set that is different, or odd, among the group)	The children look at pictures of a blade of grass, a garden, and a rose and identify which starts with a different sound
The ability to orally blend words and split syllables	The children say the first sound of a word and then the rest of the word and put it together as a single word
The ability to orally segment words	This is the ability to count sounds; the children are asked as a group to count the sounds in the word hamburger
The ability to do phonics manipulation tasks	Children replace the *r* sound in the word *rose* with a *p* sound

Since the ability to distinguish between individual sounds, or phonemes, within words is a prerequisite to the association of sounds with letters and manipulating sounds to blend words—a fancy way of saying "reading"—the teaching of phonemic awareness is crucial to emergent literacy (early childhood K-2 reading instruction). Children need a strong background in phonemic awareness in order for phonics instruction (sound–spelling relationship in printed materials) to be effective.

Instructional methods that may be effective for teaching phonemic awareness include:

- Clapping syllables in words

- Distinguishing between a word and a sound

- Using visual cues and movements to help children understand when the speaker goes from one sound to another

- Incorporating oral segmentation activities that focus on easily distinguished syllables rather than sounds

- Singing familiar songs (e.g., "Happy Birthday," "Knick-Knack, Paddy-Whack") and replacing key words in them with words that have a different ending or middle sound (oral segmentation)

- Dealing children a deck of picture cards and having them sound out the words for the pictures on their cards, or calling for a picture by asking for its first and second sound

Alphabetic Principle

The alphabetic principle is sometimes called graphophonemic awareness. This multisyllabic technical reading foundation term describes the understanding that written words are composed of patterns of letters that represent the sounds of spoken words.

The alphabetic principle has two parts:

1. An understanding that words are made up of letters and that each letter has a specific sound.

2. The correspondence between sounds and letters leads to phonological reading. This consists of reading regular and irregular words and doing advanced analysis of words.

Since the English language depends on the alphabet, being able to recognize and sound out letters is the first step for beginning readers. Relying simply on memorization for recognition of words is not a feasible way for children to learn to recognize words. Therefore, decoding is essential. The most important goal for beginning reading teachers is to teach students to decode text so they can read fluently and with understanding.

There are four basic features of the alphabetic principle:

1. Students need to be able to take spoken words apart and blend different sounds together to make new words

2. Students need to apply letter sounds to all of their reading

3. Teachers need to use a systematic, effective program to teach children to read

4. The teaching of the alphabetic principle usually begins in kindergarten

Some children already know the letters and sounds before they come to school. Others may catch on to this quickly and still others need one-on-one instruction in order to learn to read.

The alphabetic principle is sometimes called grapho-phonemic awareness. It describes the understanding that written words are composed of patterns of letters that represent the sounds of spoken words.

Critical skills that students need to learn are:

- Letter–sound correspondence

- How to sound out words

- How to decode text to make meaning

When a child decodes a word, the child makes a connection between it and a word she knows. This is very difficult for the child learning English at the same time she is learning to read because that word may not be in her vocabulary. This makes it hard for the child to make a connection between text and speech, which is a vital step in learning to read.

Morphology

MORPHOLOGY: the study of word structure

MORPHOLOGY is the study of word structure. When readers develop morphemic skills, they are developing an understanding of patterns they see in words. For example, English speakers realize that cat, cats, and caterpillar share some similarities in structure. This understanding helps readers recognize words more quickly and easily since each word doesn't need individual decoding.

Syntax

SYNTAX: refers to the rules or patterned relationships that correctly create phrases and sentences from words

SYNTAX refers to the rules or patterned relationships that correctly create phrases and sentences from words. When readers develop an understanding of syntax, they begin to understand the structure of how sentences are built, and eventually the beginning of grammar.

> *"I am going to the movies."*

This statement is syntactically and grammatically correct.

> *"They am going to the movies."*

This statement is syntactically correct since all the words are in their correct place, but the use of the word *They* rather than *I* makes it grammatically incorrect.

Semantics

SEMANTICS: refers to the meaning expressed when words are arranged in a specific way

SEMANTICS refers to the meaning expressed when words are arranged in a specific way. This is where connotation and denotation of words play a role in reading.

All of these skill sets are important for developing effective word recognition skills, which help emerging readers develop fluency.

Prompts that teachers can use to alert children to semantic cues include:

- You said _____ (the child's statement and incorrect attempt). Does that make sense to you?

- If someone said _____ (repeat the child's attempt), would you know what he or she meant?

- You said _____ (child's incorrect attempt). Would you write that?

Children need to use meaning to predict what the text says so the relevant information can prompt the correct words to surface as they identify the words.

If children come to a word they can't immediately recognize, they need to try to figure it out using their past reading experiences, background knowledge, and what they can deduce from the text itself.

Pragmatics

PRAGMATICS concerns the difference between the writer's meaning and the literal meaning of the sentence based on social context. When someone is competent in pragmatics, he or she is able to understand what the writer is trying to convey.

For example, a child sitting beside her mother at a fancy restaurant after her great-grandmother's funeral looks over to the table next to them. She sees a very elderly woman eating her dessert. "Mom?" she asks, patiently waiting for a response. When her mother addresses her, she states loudly, "That woman is old like Grandma. Is she going to die soon too?" Embarrassed, the mother hushes her child. However, this is a simple example of immature pragmatics. The child has the vocabulary, the patience to wait her turn, and some knowledge of conversational rules. She is not aware, however, that certain topics are socially inappropriate and therefore does not adapt her language to the situation.

> **PRAGMATICS:** the difference between the writer's meaning and the literal meaning of the sentence based on social context

---

SKILL 1.3 **Select and apply instructional methods for the development of decoding skills** *(e.g., continuous blending, chunking).*

In the late 1960s and the 1970s, many reading specialists, most prominently Fries (1962), believed that successful decoding resulted in reading comprehension. This meant that if children could sound out the words, they would then automatically be able to comprehend the words. Many teachers of reading and many reading texts still subscribe to this theory after more than thirty years.

DECODE: to change communication signals into messages

ENCODE: to change a message into symbols

Reading comprehension requires that the reader learn the code in which a message is written and be able to decode it to get the message.

To **DECODE** means to change communication signals into messages. Reading comprehension requires that the reader learn the code in which a message is written and be able to decode it to understand the message.

To **ENCODE** means to change a message into symbols. Some examples of encoding include changing oral language into writing (spelling), putting an idea into words, or representing a mathematical idea using appropriate mathematical symbols.

Although effective reading comprehension requires identifying words automatically (Adams, 1990; Perfetti, 1985), children do not have to be able to identify every single word or know the exact meaning of every word in a text to understand the text. Indeed, Nagy (1988) says that children can read a work with a high level of comprehension even if they do not fully know as many as 15 percent of the words in a given text.

Children develop the ability to decode and recognize words automatically. They can then extend their ability to decode to multisyllabic words.

Procedure for letter–sound investigations

The following procedure for letter-sound investigations helps to support beginning decoding.

1. Focus on a particular letter or letters that you want the child to investigate. It is good to choose one from a shared text with which the children are familiar. Make certain that the teacher's directions to the children are clear and either ask them to look for a specific letter or listen for sounds.

2. Begin a list of words that meet the task given to the children. Use chart paper to list the words the children identify. This list can be continued into the next week as long as the children's focus stays on the list. This can be easily done by challenging the children to identify a specific number of letters or sounds and "daring" them as a class team to go beyond those words or sounds.

3. Continue to add to the list. At the beginning of the day, have the children focus on the goal of adding their own words to the list. Give each child an adhesive note (sticky-pad sheet) on which they can write down the words they find. They can then attach their newly found words with their names on them to the chart. This provides the children with a sense of ownership and pride in their letter-sounding abilities. During shared reading, discuss the children's proposed additions and have the group decide if they meet the criteria. If all the children agree that they do meet the criteria, include the words on the chart.

4. Do a word sort from all the words generated and have the children put the words into categories that demonstrate similarities and differences. They can be prompted to see if the letter appeared at the beginning of the word or in the middle of the word. They might also be prompted to see that one sound could have two different letter representations. The children can then "box" the word differences and similarities by using colors established in a chart key.

5. Finally, before the children go off to read, ask them to look for new words in the texts, which they can now recognize because of the letter-sound relationships on their chart. During shared reading, make certain that they have time to share the words that they were able to decode.

SKILL 1.4 **Distinguish among the components of reading fluency** *(e.g., accuracy, automaticity, rate, prosody).*

When students practice fluency, they practice reading connected pieces of text. In other words, instead of looking at a word as just a word, they might read a sentence straight through. Students who are not fluent in reading would sound each letter or word out slowly and pay more attention to the phonics of each word. A fluent reader, on the other hand, might read a sentence out loud using appropriate intonation. The best way to test for fluency is to have a student read something out loud, preferably a few sentences in a row. Fluency is considered to be a good predictor of comprehension. A child who is focusing too much on sounding out each word will not be paying attention to the essential meaning of the text.

A child who is focusing too much on sounding out each word will not be paying attention to the meaning.

Accuracy

One way to evaluate reading fluency is to look at student accuracy, and one way to do this is to keep running records of students during oral reading. Calculating the reading level lets you know if a book is at a level the child can read independently or comfortably with guidance or if the book is at too high a level, which will frustrate the child.

As part of the informal assessment of primary grade reading, it is important to record the child's word insertions, omissions, requests for help, and attempts to get the word. In informal assessment, the rate of accuracy can be estimated from the ratio of errors to total words read.

Results of running record informal assessments can be used for teaching based on accuracy. If a child reads from 95–100 percent correctly, the child is ready for independent reading. If a child reads from 92–97 percent correctly, the child is ready for guided reading. If a child reads below 92 percent correctly, the child needs a read-aloud or shared reading activity.

Automaticity

Fluency in reading depends on automatic word identification, which assists the student in achieving comprehension of the material. Even slight difficulties in word identification can significantly increase the time it takes a student to read material, may require rereading parts or passages of the material, and reduces the level of comprehension. A student who experiences reading as a constant struggle will avoid reading whenever possible and consider it a negative experience. The ability to read for comprehension, and learning in general, will suffer if all aspects of reading fluency are not presented to the student as skills that can be acquired with the appropriate effort.

Fluency in reading depends on automatic word identification.

Automatic reading involves developing strong orthographic representations, which allows for fast, accurate identification of whole words made up of specific letter patterns. Most young students move easily from using alphabetic strategies to using orthographic representations, which can be accessed automatically. Initially, word identification is based on the application of phonic word-accessibility strategies (letter-sound associations). These strategies are in turn based on the development of phonemic awareness, which is necessary to learn how to relate speech to print.

Six syllable types

One of the most useful devices for developing automaticity in young students is through the visual pattern provided in the six syllable types.

EXAMPLES OF THE SIX SYLLABLE TYPES	
Not (Closed)	<u>Closed</u> in by a consonant—vowel makes its **short** sound
No (Open)	<u>Ends</u> in a vowel—vowel makes its **long** sound
Note (Silent "E")	<u>Ends</u> in vowel consonant "e"—vowel makes its **long** sound
Nail (Vowel Combination)	<u>Two vowels together</u> make the sound
Bird ("R" Controlled)	<u>Contains</u> a vowel plus 4—vowel sound is changed
Table (Consonant "L"-"E")	<u>Applied</u> at the end of a word

These **orthographic** (letter) patterns signal vowel pronunciation to the reader. Students must become able to apply their knowledge of these patterns to recognize the syllable types and to see these patterns automatically and ultimately in order to read words as wholes. The move from decoding letter symbols to identify recognizable terms to automatic word recognition is a substantial move toward fluency.

A significant tool for helping students move through this phase was developed by Anna Gillingham, who incorporated an activity using phonetic word cards into the Orton-Gillingham lesson plan (Gillingham and Stillman, 1997). This activity involves having students practice reading words (and some nonwords) on cards as wholes, beginning with simple syllables and moving systematically through the syllable types to complex syllables and two-syllable words. The words are divided into groups that correspond to the specific sequence of skills being taught.

The student's development of the elements necessary for automaticity continually moves through stages. Another important stage involves the automatic recognition of single graphemes as a critical first step to the development of the letter patterns that make up words or word parts.

English orthography is made up of four basic word types:

1. Regular, for reading and spelling (e.g., *cat, print*)

2. Regular, for reading but not for spelling (e.g., *float, brain*—could be spelled *flote* or *brane*, respectively)

3. Rule based (e.g., *canning*—doubling rule, *faking*—drop *e* rule)

4. Irregular (e.g., *beauty*)

Students must be taught to recognize all four types of words automatically in order to be effective readers. Repeated practice in pattern recognition is often necessary. Practice techniques can include speed drills in which students read lists of isolated words with contrasting vowel sounds that are signaled by the syllable type. One way to do this is to randomly arrange several closed syllable and vowel-consonant e words containing the vowel *a* on pages containing about twelve lines and have the child read for one minute. Individual goals are established and charts are kept of the number of words read correctly in successive sessions. The same word lists are repeated in sessions until the goal has been achieved for several succeeding sessions. When selecting words for these lists, the use of high-frequency words in a syllable category increases the likelihood of generalization to text reading.

Rate

A student whose reading rate is slow, or halting and inconsistent, exhibits a lack of reading fluency. According to an article by Mastropieri, Leinart, and Scruggs (1999), some students have developed accurate word pronunciation skills but read at a slow rate. They have not moved to the phase where decoding is automatic, and their limited fluency may affect performance in the following ways:

- They read less text than their peers and have less time to remember, review, or comprehend the text

- They expend more cognitive energy than their peers trying to identify individual words

- They may be less able to retain text in their memories and less likely to integrate those segments with other parts of the text

The simplest means of determining a student's reading rate is to have the student read aloud from a prescribed passage that is at the appropriate reading level for age and grade and contains a specified number of words. The passage should not be too familiar for the student (some will try to memorize or "work out" difficult bits ahead of time) and should not contain more words than can be read comfortably and accurately by a normal reader in one or two minutes.

Count only the words *correctly* pronounced on first reading, and divide this word count by the elapsed time to determine the student's reading rate. To determine the student's standing and progress, compare this rate with the norm for the class and the average for all students who read fluently at that specific age/grade level.

The following general guidelines can be applied for reading lists of words with a speed drill and a one-minute timing:

- 30 wpm for first- and second-grade children

- 40 wpm for third-grade children;

- 60 wpm for mid-third-grade

- 80 wpm for students in fourth grade and higher

Various techniques are useful with students who have acquired some proficiency in decoding but whose skill levels are lower than their oral language abilities. Such techniques have certain common features:

- Students listen to text as they follow along with the book

- Students follow the print using their fingers as guides

- Use of reading materials that students would be unable to read independently

Experts recommend that a beginning reading program incorporate partner reading, practice reading difficult words prior to reading the text, timings for accuracy and rate, opportunities to hear books read, and opportunities to read to others.

Experts recommend that a beginning reading program incorporate partner reading, practice reading difficult words prior to reading the text, timings for accuracy and rate, opportunities to hear books read, and opportunities to read to others.

Prosody

PROSODY is versification of text and involves such matters as which syllable of a word is accented. With regard to fluency, it is that aspect which translates reading into the same experience as listening in the reader's mind. It involves intonation and rhythm through such devices as syllable accent and punctuation.

In their article for *Perspectives* (Winter 2002), Pamela Hook and Sandra Jones proposed that teachers can begin to develop awareness of the prosodic features of language by introducing a short three-word sentence with each of the three different words underlined for stress (e.g., *He is sick. He is sick. He is sick.*). The teacher can then model the three sentences while discussing the possible meaning for each variation. The students can practice reading them with different stress until they are fluent. These simple three-word sentences can be modified and expanded to include various verbs, pronouns, and tenses (e.g., *You are sick. I am sick. They are sick.*). This strategy can also be used while increasing the length of phrases and emphasizing the different meanings (e.g., *Get out of bed. Get out of bed. Get out of bed now.*) Teachers can also practice fluency with common phrases that frequently occur in texts.

Using prepositional phrases

Prepositional phrases are good syntactic structures for this type of work (e.g., *on the _____, in the _____, over the _____*). Teachers can pair these printed phrases with oral intonation patterns that include variations of rate, intensity, and pitch. Students can infer the intended meaning as the teacher presents different prosodic variations of a sentence. For example, when speakers want to stress a concept, they often slow their rate of speech and may speak in a louder voice (e.g., *Joshua, get-out-of-bed-**NOW!***). Often, the only text marker for this sentence will be the exclamation point (!), but the speaker's intent will affect the manner in which it is delivered.

Using the alphabet

Practicing oral variations and then mapping the prosodic features onto the text will assist students in making the connection when reading. This strategy can also be used to alert students to the prosodic features present in punctuation marks. In the early stages, using the alphabet helps to focus a student on the punctuation marks without having to deal with meaning. The teacher models for the students and

> **PROSODY:** versification of text and involves such matters as which syllable of a word is accented

> *Practicing oral variations and then mapping the prosodic features onto the text will assist students in making the connection when reading.*

then has them practice the combinations using the correct intonation patterns to fit the punctuation mark (e.g., ABC. DE? FGH! IJKL? or ABCD! EFGHI? KL.).

Using two- or three-word sentences

Teachers can then move to simple two-word or three-word sentences. The sentences are punctuated with a period, question mark and exclamation point and the differences in meaning that occur with each different punctuation mark (e.g., *Chris hops. Chris hops? Chris hops!*) are discussed. It may help students to point out that the printed words convey the fact that someone named Chris is engaged in the physical activity of hopping, but the intonation patterns get their cue from the punctuation mark. The meaning extracted from an encounter with a punctuation mark is dependent upon a reader's prior experiences or background knowledge in order to project an appropriate intonation pattern onto the printed text. Keeping the text static while changing the punctuation marks helps students to attend to prosodic patterns.

Using chunking

Students who read word-for-word may benefit initially from practicing phrasing with the alphabet rather than words because letters do not tax the meaning system. The letters are grouped, an arc is drawn underneath, and students recite the alphabet in chunks (e.g., ABC DE FGH IJK LM NOP QRS TU VW XYZ). Once students understand the concept of phrasing, it is recommended that teachers help students chunk text into syntactic (noun phrases, verb phrases, prepositional phrases) or meaning units until they are proficient. There are no hard and fast rules for chunking, but syntactic units are most commonly used.

Using slashes

For better readers, teachers can mark the phrasal boundaries with slashes for short passages. Eventually, the slashes are used only at the beginning of long passages and then students are asked to continue "phrase reading" even after the marks end. Marking phrases can be done together with students, or those on an independent level may divide passages into phrases themselves. Comparisons can be made to clarify reasons for differences in phrasing. Another way to encourage students to focus on phrase meaning and prosody, in addition to word identification, is to provide tasks that require them to identify or supply a paraphrase of an original statement.

> **SKILL 1.5** **Choose and apply instructional methods for developing reading fluency** *(e.g., practice with high-frequency words, readers theatre, repeated readings).*

At some point it is crucial that the early reader integrate graphophonic cues with semantic and structural cues and move toward fluency. Before this happens, early readers sound stilted when they read aloud, which, does not promote the enjoyment of reading.

Expressive Reading

When modeling reading, the teacher should be theatrical so that children can hear the beauty and nuances that are contained in the texts whose print they are tracking so anxiously. Children love to mimic their teachers and will do so if the teacher takes time each day to recite a poem with them. The poem might be posted on chart paper and stay up on the board for a week.

First, the teacher can model the fluent and expressive reading of the poem. Then, with the use of a pointer, the class can recite it with the teacher. As the week progresses, students can recite it on their own.

Illustrations

Illustrations can be key supports for emergent and early readers. Teachers should not only use wordless stories (books that tell their stories through pictures alone), but can also make targeted use of Big Books for read-alouds, so that young children become habituated to illustrations as an important tool for constructing meaning. The teacher should teach children how to reference an illustration for help in identifying a word the child does not recognize in the text.

> *Illustrations can be key supports for emergent and early readers.*

Of course, children can also go on a picture walk with the teacher as part of a mini-lesson or guided reading and anticipate the story (narrative) using the pictures alone to construct meaning.

Decodability

Use literature that contains examples of letter-sound correspondences you wish to teach. First, read the literature with the children or read it aloud to them. Take a specific example from the text and have the children reread it as you point out the letter-sound correspondence. Then ask the children to go through the now-familiar literature to find other letter-sound correspondences. Once the children have correctly made the text-sound correspondence, have them share other similar correspondences they find in other works of literature.

Cooper (2004) suggests that children can be taught to become word detectives so they can independently and fluently decode on their own. The child should learn the following word detective routines in order to function as an independent, fluent reader who can decode words on his own:

- First, the child should read to the end of the sentence

- Next, the child should search for known word parts and also try to decode the word from the letter sounds

- As a last resort, the child should ask someone for help or look up the word in the dictionary

Independent, Instructional, and Frustration Reading Levels

Instructional reading is generally judged to be at the 95 percent accuracy level, although Taberski places it between 92 and 97 percent. Taberski tries to enhance the independent reading levels by making sure that readers on the instructional reading levels read a variety of genres and have a range of available and interesting books of a particular genre to read.

Taberski's availability for reading conferences helps her to both assess first-hand her children's frustration levels and to model ongoing teacher/reader book conversations by scheduling child-initiated reading conferences where she personally replenishes their book bags.

In order to allay children's frustration levels in their reading and to foster their independent reading, it is important to some children that the teacher personally take time to hear them read aloud and to check for fluency and expression. After hearing them read aloud, teachers can help reduce student's frustration by encouraging them to read without pointing and to try chunking words into phrases that mimic natural speech.

> In order to allay children's frustration levels in their reading and to foster their independent reading, it is important to some children that the teacher personally take time out to hear them read aloud and to check for fluency and expression.

Assessment of the reading development of individual students

Using pictures and illustrations

For young readers who are from ELL backgrounds, even if they were born in the United States, the use of pictures validates their story-authoring and story-telling skills and provides them with access and equity to the literary discussion and book talk of their native English-speaking peers. These children can also demonstrate their story-telling abilities by drawing sequels or prequels to the story detailed in the illustrations alone. They might even be given the opportunity to share the story aloud in their native language or to comment on the illustrations in their native language.

Since many stories today are recorded in two or even three languages discussing story events or analyzing pictures in a different native language is a beneficial practice.

Use of pictures and illustrations can also help the K–3 educator assess the capabilities of children who are struggling readers because they are children whose learning strengths are spatial. Through targeted questions about how the pictures would change if different plot twists occurred, or how the child might transform the story through changing the illustrations, the teacher can begin to assess struggling reader deficits and strengths.

Use of pictures and illustrations can also help the K–3 educator assess the capabilities of children who are struggling readers because they are children whose learning strength is spatial.

Using recorded readings

Children from ELL backgrounds can benefit from listening to a recorded version of a particular story with which they can read along. This gives them another opportunity to "hear" the story correctly pronounced and presented and to begin to internalize its language structures. In the absence of recorded versions of some key stories or texts, the teacher may want to make sound recordings.

Highly proficient readers can also be involved in creating these literature recordings for use with ELL peers or younger peers. This, of course, develops oral language proficiency but also introduces these skilled readers to the intricacies of supporting ELL English language reading instruction. When they actually see their tapes being used by children, they will be tremendously gratified.

SKILL 1.6 **Identify and differentiate instructional methods and strategies for vocabulary acquisition across content areas** *(e.g., word analysis, author's word choice, context clues, multiple exposures).*

Vocabulary knowledge plays a crucial role in academic success. Students with limited vocabulary often face challenges in building content area knowledge in all subject areas, not just in English Language Arts. A variety of factors contribute to each student's existing vocabulary, including language background, reading habits, previous experiences, learning difficulties, etc. As a result, it is important that each teacher be able to implement a range of instructional methods for vocabulary acquisition in order to differentiate for students with different needs.

Word Analysis: Identification of Common Morphemes, Prefixes, and Suffixes

Working with students to identify common morphemes, prefixes, and suffixes provides them with essential tools for determining the meaning of unfamiliar words. Especially as vocabulary becomes more complex and varied, being able to employ the tools of word analysis can help students to become more confident, independent readers as they look for structural elements in words that they can use to help them determine meaning. As an example, understanding of the root of solitary can help students to unlock the meanings of a number of other words including 'sole', 'solitude', 'isolate', 'solitaire', and 'soliloquy'.

KEY COMPONENTS OF WORD ANALYSIS	
Root Words	A word from which another word is developed; the second word has its "root" in the first. This component lends itself to a tree-with-roots illustration. Students may also want to literally construct root words using cardboard trees and roots to create word-family models.
Base Words	A stand-alone linguistic unit, which cannot be deconstructed or broken down into smaller words. For example, in the word *retell*, the base word is *tell*.
Contractions	Shortened forms of two words in which a letter or letters have been deleted. The deleted letters are replaced by an apostrophe.
Prefixes	Units of meaning that can be added (the word for this type of structural addition is *affixed*) to the beginning of a base word or root word. They are also sometimes known as "bound morphemes," meaning that they cannot stand alone as a base word. An example is *retell*. The prefix in this word is *re*.
Suffixes	Units of meaning that can be "affixed," or added on, to the ends of root or base words. Suffixes transform the original meanings of base and root words. Like prefixes, they are also known as "bound morphemes," because they cannot stand alone as words. In the word *comfortable*, the suffix is *able*.
Compound Words	These occur when two or more base words are connected to form a new word. The meaning of the new word is in some way connected with that of the base words. For example, the word *bedroom* is a compound word made of the two base words *bed* and *room*.
Inflectional Endings	Types of suffixes that impart a new meaning to the base or root word. These endings, in particular, change the gender, number, tense, or form of the base or root words. Like other suffixes, these are also called "bound morphemes." In the word *telling*, the inflectional ending *-ing* determines the tense of the verb *tell*.

Context Clues

When children encounter unknown words in a sentence, they rely on their background knowledge to choose a word that makes sense. Errors of younger children therefore are often substitutions of words in the same syntactic class. Poor readers often fail to make use of context clues to help them identify words or activate the background knowledge that would help them with comprehension. Instead of "chunking" phrases and clauses, poor readers also tend to process sentences word by word, resulting in a slow pace that focuses on the decoding rather than comprehension. Poor readers also have problems answering *wh-* questions (who, what, where, when, why?) as a result of these problems with syntax.

One strategy, contextual redefinition, helps children use context more effectively by presenting them with sufficient context *before* they begin reading. It models the use of contextual clues to make informed guesses about word meanings.

To apply this strategy, the teacher should first select two or three unfamiliar words for teaching. The teacher should then write a sentence in which sufficient clues are supplied for the child to successfully figure out the meaning. The types of context clues the teacher can use include compare/contrast, synonyms, and direct definition.

The teacher should then present the words only on the experiential chart or as letter cards and have the children pronounce the words. As they pronounce them, challenge them to come up with a definition for each word. After several definitions have been offered, encourage the children to decide as a group what the definition is. Write down their agreed-upon definition without commenting on it. Then share the contexts (sentences the teacher wrote with the words and explicit context clues). Ask the children to read the sentences aloud and have them come up with a definition for each word. Make sure not to comment as they present their definitions. Ask them to justify their definitions by making specific references to the context clues in the sentences. As the discussion continues, direct the children's attention to their previously agreed-upon definition of the word. Facilitate a discussion of the differences between their guesses about the word when they saw only the word and their guesses about the word when they read it in context. Finally, have the children check their use of context skills to correctly define the word by looking it up.

This type of direct teaching of word definitions is useful when children have dictionary skills or another way of looking up the words and the teacher is aware that there are insufficient context clues to help the students define it. In addition, struggling readers and students from ELL backgrounds may benefit tremendously from being walked through this process that successful readers apply automatically.

Choice of Words

Teachers can allow students to develop a personalized vocabulary word journal based on their own interests. Teachers can then encourage them to create their own vocabulary word lists and research their words' various meanings. Teachers can ask students to write down a personal interest, ask the rest of the class for vocabulary words that pertain to the student's answer. The teacher can then write the vocabulary words on the board. For example, if a student says, "I like to play basketball," ask the class to suggest vocabulary words in that subject area (e.g., basketball, net, slam dunk, hoop). Have students locate definitions in the dictionary, in the thesaurus, or on the computer. Students can then write a story describing their interest using the new words they have learned. Have students meet in groups to share their journals, while encouraging them to discuss one another's words.

Pre-teaching vocabulary

The pre-teaching of vocabulary involves identifying words that students are likely to be unfamiliar with in upcoming activities or readings. By introducing students to these words before the activities either through explicit instruction or activities involving word analysis, prediction, inference, and context, students are able to reinforce their understanding when they encounter the words in the authentic context of the learning activities, while at the same time being better able to understand and interpret the text they have to work with.

Repeated exposure

For most students, repeated exposure will be a key to truly mastering new vocabulary. Through varied texts, games, oral language activities, and cooperative learning situations, students will have multiple opportunities to encounter target vocabulary and actually use it. Seeing words in different contexts builds a deeper understanding and increases the likelihood that students are able to use words independently.

Word maps and graphic organizers

The purpose of this method is to build students' understanding of target vocabulary by helping them to relate new words to prior knowledge, familiar vocabulary and important concepts. Students make connect related words either on their own word maps or the class can maintain an ongoing one on the wall for all students to see.

Annotation of texts

In some cases, teachers may want to annotate class texts, adding vocabulary clues or even definitions to help students reinforce target vocabulary. This may be particularly well suited to very challenging texts with quite a bit of challenging vocabulary.

Word awareness

Creating a learning environment in which words and language are highly valued can be a powerful motivator for building vocabulary. Drawing attention to the ways in which words are used for vivid description, for humor, or to make a powerful point can be a way to engage students with language.

The National Reading Panel (2000) has published the following conclusions about vocabulary instruction.

1. There is a need for direct instruction of vocabulary items required for a specific text.

2. Repetition and multiple exposures to vocabulary items are important. Students should be given items that are likely to appear in many contexts.

3. Learning in rich contexts is valuable for vocabulary learning. Vocabulary words should be those that the learner will find useful in many contexts. When vocabulary items are derived from content learning materials, the learner will be better equipped to deal with specific reading matter in content areas.

4. Vocabulary tasks should be restructured as necessary. It is important to be certain that students fully understand what is asked of them in the context of reading rather than focusing only on the words to be learned.

5. Vocabulary learning is effective when it entails active engagement in learning tasks.

6. Computer technology can be used effectively to help teach vocabulary.

7. Vocabulary can be acquired through incidental learning. Much of a student's vocabulary will have to be learned in the course of doing things other than explicit vocabulary learning. Repetition, richness of context, and motivation may also add to the efficacy of incidental learning of vocabulary.

8. Dependence on a single vocabulary instruction method will not result in optimal learning. A variety of methods can be used effectively with emphasis on multimedia aspects of learning, richness of context in which words are to be learned, and the number of exposures to words that learners receive.

The panel found that a critical feature of effective classrooms is the teaching of specific words including lessons and activities in which students apply their vocabulary knowledge and strategies to reading and writing. Included in the activities were discussions in which teachers and students talked about words, their features, and strategies for understanding unfamiliar words.

There are many methods for directly and explicitly teaching words. Through its research, the panel found twenty-one methods teachers could use in the classroom to teach vocabulary. Many emphasize the underlying concept of a word and its connections to other words, such as semantic mapping and diagrams that use graphics. The keyword method uses words and illustrations that highlight salient features of meaning. Another effective method is visualizing or drawing a picture.

Effective classrooms provide multiple ways for students to learn and interact with words.

Many words cannot be learned in this way, of course, so it should be used as only one method among others. Effective classrooms provide multiple ways for students to learn and interact with words. The panel also found that computer-assisted activities could have a positive role in vocabulary development.

SKILL 1.7 **Identify and evaluate instructional methods and strategies for facilitating students' reading comprehension** *(e.g., summarizing, self-monitoring, questioning, use of graphic and semantic organizers, think-alouds, recognizing story structure).*

The point of comprehension instruction is not to focus simply on the text(s) students are using at the moment of instruction, but rather to help them learn strategies they can use independently with other texts.

COMMON METHODS OF TEACHING COMPREHENSION	
Summarization	When summarizing, either in writing or verbally, students review the main point of the text, along with strategically chosen details that highlight the main point. This is not the same as paraphrasing, which is saying the same thing in different words. Teaching students how to summarize is very important, as it will help them look for the most critical areas in a text. In nonfiction, for example, it helps them distinguish between main arguments and examples. In fiction, it helps them learn how to focus on the main characters and events and distinguish them from the lesser characters and events.
Question Answering	While this method tends to be overused in many classrooms, it is a valid method of teaching comprehension. As the name implies, students answer questions regarding a text, either out loud, in small groups, or individually on paper. The best questions are those that require students to think about the text (rather than just find an answer in the text).
Question Generating	This is the opposite of question answering, although students can then be asked to answer their own questions or the questions of other students. In general, students should be taught to constantly question texts as they read. This is important because it makes them more critical readers. Teaching students to generate questions helps them to learn the types of questions they can ask, and it gets them thinking about how to be critical of texts.

Continued on next page

Graphic Organizers	Graphic organizers are visual representations of content within a text. For example, Venn diagrams can be used to highlight the differences between two characters in a novel or two similar political concepts in a social studies textbook. A teacher can use flowcharts with students to talk about the steps in a process (for example, the steps of setting up a science experiment or the chronological events of a story).
Semantic Organizers	These are similar to graphic organizers in that they visually display information. The difference, usually, is that semantic organizers focus on words or concepts. For example, a word web can help students make sense of a word by mapping from the central word all the similar and related concepts to that word.
Text Structures	In nonfiction, particularly in textbooks, and sometimes in fiction, text structures give readers important clues about what to look for. Often students do not know how to make sense of all the types of headings in a textbook and do not realize that, for example, the sidebar story about a character in history is not the main text on a particular page in the history textbook. Teaching students how to interpret text structures gives them tools they can use to tackle other similar texts.
Monitoring Comprehension	Students need to be aware of their comprehension, or lack of it, in particular texts. It is important to teach students what to do when the text suddenly stops making sense. For example, students can go back and reread the description of a character. They can go back to the table of contents or the first paragraph of a chapter to see where they are headed.
Discussion	Small-group or whole-class discussion stimulates thoughts about texts and gives students a larger picture of their impact. For example, teachers can strategically encourage students to discuss concepts related to the text. This helps students learn to consider texts within larger societal and social contexts. Teachers can also encourage students to provide personal opinions in discussion. Listening to other students' opinions helps all students in a class to see the wide range of interpretations of and thoughts about one text.
Textual Marking	This is when students interact with the text as they read. For example, armed with sticky notes, students can insert questions or comments regarding specific sentences or paragraphs within the text. This helps them focus on the importance of the small things, particularly when they are reading larger works (such as novels in high school). It also gives students a reference point to go back into the text when they need to review something.

Knowledge of Story Structure

Most works of fiction contain a common set of elements that make them come alive to readers. Even though writers do not consciously think about each of these story elements when they sit down to write, all stories essentially contain these "markers" that make them the stories that they are. Even though all stories have these elements, they are a lot like fingerprints: Each story's story elements are just a bit different.

Plot

The most commonly discussed story element in fiction is plot. PLOT is the series of events in a story. Typically, but not always, plot moves in a predictable fashion:

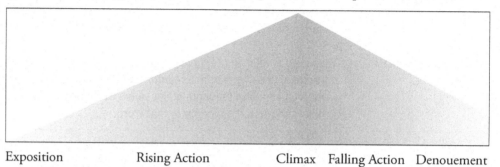

Exposition   Rising Action   Climax   Falling Action   Denouement

Exposition is where characters and their situations are introduced. **Rising action** is the point at which conflict starts to occur. **Climax** is the highest point of conflict, often a turning point. **Falling action** is the result of the climax. **Dénouement** is the final resolution of the plot.

Character

Character is another commonly studied story element. Stories contain heroes, villains, comedic characters, dark characters, etc. When we examine the characters of a story, we look to see who they are and how their traits contribute to the story. Often, plot elements become more interesting because of the characters' particular traits. For example, authors may pair unlikely characters together who, in turn, create specific conflict.

Setting

The SETTING of a story is the place, or location, where it occurs. Often, the specific place is not as important as some of the specifics about the setting. For example, the setting of F. Scott Fitzgerald's novel *The Great Gatsby* is New York, which is not as significant as the fact that it takes place among extreme wealth. Conversely, John Steinbeck's novel *The Grapes of Wrath*, although it takes place in Oklahoma and California, has a more significant setting of poverty. In fact, as the story takes place *around* other migrant workers, the setting is even more significant. In a way, the setting serves as a reason for various conflicts to occur.

Theme

The THEME of a story is the underlying message that a writer wants to convey. Common themes in literature are jealousy, money, love, man or woman against corporation or government, etc. These themes are never explicitly stated; rather, they are the result of the portrayal of characters, settings, and plots.

Mood

Finally, the **MOOD** of a story is the atmosphere or attitude the writer conveys through descriptive language. Often, mood fits in nicely with theme and setting. For example, in Edgar Allan Poe's stories, we often find a mood of horror and darkness that comes from the descriptions of characters and the setting, as well as from specific plot elements. Mood helps us better understand the writer's theme and intentions through descriptive, stylistic language.

> **MOOD:** the atmosphere or attitude the writer conveys through descriptive language

Multiple-Strategy Instruction

Students' attitudes and perceptions about learning are the most powerful factors influencing academic focus and success. When instructional objectives center on students' interests and are relevant to their lives, effective learning occurs. Students must believe that the tasks they are asked to perform have value and that they have the ability and resources to perform them. If a student thinks a task is unimportant, he will not put much effort into it. If a student thinks he lacks the ability or resources to successfully complete a task, even attempting the task becomes too great a risk. The teacher must not only understand the student's abilities and interests but also help the student develop positive attitudes and perceptions about tasks and learning.

Good readers do not rely on a single strategy to comprehend what they read. They apply different strategies at different points in a text, switching tactics as the text or reading activity demands. *Reciprocal teaching, concept-oriented reading instruction*, and *transactional strategy instruction* are three examples of multiple-strategy instructional techniques that have demonstrated classroom success.

Reciprocal teaching

This technique begins with the teacher and a group of students discussing a text. The discussion is structured by four strategies: summarizing, questioning, clarifying, and predicting—with the teacher modeling each strategy. After the modeling, students take turns leading the discussion about specific parts of the text.

> *Reciprocal teaching, concept-oriented reading instruction, and transactional strategy instruction are three examples of multiple-strategy instructional techniques that have demonstrated classroom success.*

Teachers should also change instructional strategies based on students' questions and comments. If students express confusion about the content of the lesson, the teacher should immediately take another approach to presenting the lesson. Sometimes this can be accomplished by simply rephrasing an explanation.

Concept-Oriented Reading Instruction (CORI)

CORI integrates comprehension strategies for which the National Reading Panel found firm scientific bases for effectiveness (e.g., cooperative learning, comprehension monitoring, summarizing) with inquiry science. Inquiry science includes hands-on activities such as observation of real-world phenomena and experimentation, designed to support student understanding of scientific concepts. Students use texts to confirm and extend the knowledge they gain through the hands-on activities. The effective teacher uses advanced communication skills such as clarification, reflection, perception, and summarization as a means to facilitate communication. The ability to communicate with students, listen effectively, identify relevant and irrelevant information, and summarize students' messages facilitates the establishment and ongoing development of an optimum classroom learning environment.

Transactional Strategy Instruction (TSI)

TSI takes place in small groups and concerns the transaction among the reader, the text, and the context. Specifically, TSI helps students link their prior knowledge to a text through discussion and involves constructing meaning through group collaboration rather than individual interpretation. The dynamics of the group determine the responses of all group members, including the teacher.

The following are instructional strategy guidelines that teachers may implement:

- Select appropriate text
- Select the strategy
- Give a clear explanation

- Model the strategy
- Support student practice
- Have students apply the strategy

After the teacher has presented a skill or concept lesson, students must be given time to practice the skill or concept. During this time teachers can circulate among students to check for understanding. If the teacher observes that any of the students did not clearly understand the skill or concept, she can immediately readdress the issue using another technique or approach.

SKILL 1.8 **Identify essential comprehension skills** (e.g., main idea, supporting details and facts, author's purpose, point of view, inference, conclusion).

Main Idea

TOPIC: what a paragraph or story is about

MAIN IDEA: the important idea(s) that the author wants the reader to know about a topic

The TOPIC of a paragraph or story is what the paragraph or story is about. The MAIN IDEA of a paragraph or story is the important idea(s) that the author wants the reader to know about a topic. The topic and main idea of a paragraph or story are sometimes directly stated. There are times, however, when the topic and main idea are not directly stated, but simply implied.

Look at this paragraph:

> *Henry Ford was an inventor who developed the first affordable automobile. The cars that were being built before Mr. Ford created his Model-T were very expensive. Only rich people could afford to have cars.*

The topic of this paragraph is Henry Ford. The main idea is that Henry Ford built the first affordable automobile.

The **TOPIC SENTENCE** indicates what a passage is about. It is the subject of that portion of the narrative. The ability to identify the topic sentence in a passage will enable the student to focus on the concept being discussed and better comprehend the information provided.

You can find the main ideas by examining how paragraphs are written. A **PARAGRAPH** is a group of sentences about one main idea. Paragraphs usually have two types of sentences: a topic sentence, which contains the main idea, and two or more detail sentences that support, prove, provide more information, explain, or give examples. You can only tell if you have a detail or topic sentence by comparing the sentences with each other.

Look at this sample paragraph:

> *Fall is the best of the four seasons. The leaves change colors to create a beautiful display of golds, reds, and oranges. The air turns crisp and windy. The scent of pumpkin muffins and apple pies fills the air. Finally, Halloween marks the start of the holiday season. Fall is my favorite time of year!*

Breakdown of sentences:

> *Fall is the best of the four seasons. (TOPIC SENTENCE)*
>
> *The leaves change colors to create a beautiful display of golds, reds, and oranges. (DETAIL)*
>
> *The air turns crisp and windy. (DETAIL)*
>
> *The scent of pumpkin muffins and apple pies fill the air. (DETAIL)*
>
> *Finally, Halloween marks the start of the holiday season. (DETAIL)*
>
> *Fall is my favorite time of year! (CLOSING SENTENCE—Often a restatement of the topic sentence)*

The first sentence introduces the main idea and the other sentences support and provide more details and information.

TOPIC SENTENCE: indicates what a passage is about

PARAGRAPH: a group of sentences about one main idea

Tips for Finding the Topic Sentence

How can you be sure that you have a topic sentence? Try this trick: Switch the sentence you think is the topic sentence into a question. If the other sentences seem to "answer" the question, then you've got it.

- The topic sentence is usually first, but could be in any position in the paragraph.

- A topic sentence is usually more general than the other sentences; that is, it talks about many things and looks at the big picture. Sometimes it refers to more than one thing. Plurals and the words *many*, *numerous*, or *several* often signal a topic sentence.

- Detail sentences are usually more specific than the topic; that is, they usually talk about one single or small part of an idea. The words *for example, i.e., that is, first, second, third, etc.,* and *finally* often signal a detail.

- Most of the detail sentences support, give examples, prove, talk about, or point toward the topic sentence in some way.

For example, reword the topic sentence "Fall is the best of the four seasons" in one of the following ways:

> *"Why is fall the best of the four season?"*
>
> *"Which season is the best season?"*
>
> *"Is fall the best season of the year?"*

Then, as you read the remaining sentences (the ones you didn't pick), you will find that they answer (support) your question. If you attempt this with a sentence other than the topic sentence, it won't work.

For example, in the sample paragraph about fall, suppose you select "Halloween marks the start of the holiday season," and you reword it in the following way:

> *"Which holiday is the start of the holiday season?"*

You will find that the other sentences fail to help you answer (support) your question.

Summary Statements

The introductory statement should be at the beginning of the passage. An introductory statement provides a bridge between any previous, relevant text and the content to follow. It provides information about, and sets the tone and parameters for, the text to follow. The old axiom regarding presenting a body of information suggests that you should always "tell them what you are going to tell them; tell it to them; tell them what you just told them." The introductory statement is where the writer tells the readers what he or she is going to tell them.

The summary statement should be at or near the end of the passage, and is a concise presentation of the essential data from the passage. In terms of the old axiom, the content portion (the main body of the narrative) is where the writer "tells it to them." The summary statement is where the writer tells the readers what he or she has just told them.

Restating the main idea

An accurate restatement of the main idea from a passage usually summarizes the concept in a concise manner, and it often presents the same idea from a different perspective. A restatement should always demonstrate complete comprehension of the main idea.

To select an accurate restatement, identifying the main idea of the passage is essential. Once you comprehend the main idea of a passage, evaluate your choices to see which statement restates the main idea while eliminating statements that restate a supporting detail. Walk through the steps below the sample paragraph to see how to select the accurate restatement.

> *Fall is the best of the four seasons. The leaves change colors to create a beautiful display of golds, reds, and oranges. The air turns crisp and windy. The scent of pumpkin muffins and apple pies fill the air. Finally, Halloween marks the start of the holiday season. Fall is my favorite time of year!*

Steps

1. Identify the main idea. ("Fall is the best of the four seasons.")

2. Decide which statement below restates the topic sentence:

   A. The changing leaves turn gold, red, and orange.

   B. The holidays start with Halloween.

   C. Of the four seasons, fall is the greatest of them all.

   D. Crisp wind is a fun aspect of fall.

The answer is C because it rephrases the main idea of the first sentence, the topic sentence.

Supporting Details

SUPPORTING DETAILS are sentences that provide more information about the topic and the main idea.

The supporting details in the paragraph about Henry Ford would be that he was an inventor and that before he created his Model T only rich people could afford cars because they were too expensive.

> *An accurate restatement of the main idea from a passage usually summarizes the concept in a concise manner, and it often presents the same idea from a different perspective.*

> **SUPPORTING DETAILS:** sentences that provide more information about the topic and the main idea

Fact and Opinion

A fact is something that is true and can be proved.

An opinion is something that a person believes, thinks, or feels.

Consider the following examples:

> Joe DiMaggio, a Yankees center fielder, was replaced by Mickey Mantle in 1952.

This is a fact. If necessary, evidence can be produced to support this statement.

> First-year players are more ambitious than seasoned players.

This is an opinion. There is no proof to support this statement.

Author's Purpose

An author's purpose may be to entertain, to persuade, to inform, to describe, or to narrate.

There are no tricks or rules to follow in attempting to determine an author's purpose. It is up to the reader to use his or her judgment. Read the following paragraph.

> Charles Lindbergh had no intention of becoming a pilot. He was enrolled in the University of Wisconsin until a flying lesson changed the entire course of his life. He began his career as a pilot by performing daredevil stunts at fairs.

The author wrote this paragraph primarily to:

A. Describe

B. Inform

C. Entertain

D. Narrate

Since the author is simply telling us or informing us about the life of Charles Lindbergh, the correct answer here is B.

An author may have more than one purpose in writing, such as to entertain, persuade, inform, describe, or narrate.

Author's Tone and Point of View

The AUTHOR'S TONE is attitude reflected in the statement or passage. The author's choice of words helps the reader determine the overall tone of a statement or passage.

AUTHOR'S TONE: attitude reflected in the statement or passage

Read the following paragraph.

> *I was shocked by your article, which said that sitting down to breakfast was a thing of the past. Many families consider breakfast time to be family time. Children need to realize the importance of having a good breakfast. It is imperative that they be taught this at a young age. I cannot believe that a writer with your reputation has difficulty comprehending this.*

The author's tone in this passage is one of:

- A. Concern
- B. Anger
- C. Excitement
- D. Disbelief

Since the author directly states that he "cannot believe" that the writer feels this way, the answer is D, disbelief.

Inferences and Conclusions

In order to draw inferences and make conclusions, a reader must use prior knowledge and apply it to the current situation. A conclusion or inference is never stated. You must rely on your common sense.

Read the following passage.

> *The Smith family waited patiently around carousel number 7 for their luggage to arrive. They were exhausted after their five-hour trip and were eager to get to their hotel. After about an hour, they realized that they no longer recognized any of the other passengers' faces. Mrs. Smith asked the person who appeared to be in charge if they were at the right carousel. The man replied, "Yes, this is it, but we finished unloading that baggage almost half an hour ago."*

From the man's response we can infer that:

- A. The Smiths were ready to go to their hotel
- B. The Smiths' luggage was lost
- C. The man had their luggage
- D. They were at the wrong carousel

Since the Smiths were still waiting for their luggage, we know that they were not yet ready to go to their hotel. From the man's response, we know that they were not at the wrong carousel and that he did not have their luggage. Therefore, though not directly stated, it appears that their luggage was lost. Choice B is the correct answer.

> **SKILL 1.9** Determine appropriate uses of multiple representations of information for a variety of purposes *(e.g., charts, tables, graphs, pictures, print and non-print media)*.

While the teaching of writing undoubtedly involves an enormous amount of work on the composition of text, it also involves teaching students to convey ideas in the best possible manner. Although a teacher could explain the results of a survey in words, they might be easier to understand in a graph, table, or chart. If that is the case, why present them in words? The important point is for the information to be conveyed.

As students write reports and respond to ideas in writing, they can learn how to incorporate various graphic representations into written text. While this is fairly easy to do, given the word processing technology available today, students struggle with this. They can learn to do this in three ways: explanation, observation/modeling, and practice.

First, students need to have clear explanations from teachers on appropriate forms of graphical representations in text, as well as the methods by which to include those representations. They need to see plenty of examples of how it is done. Second, they need to be able to see teacher-modeled examples where text has been replaced or enhanced by graphical representations. The more examples they see, the clearer the concepts will be to them.

Deciding which type of representation to use and how to use it is challenging. Generally, graphical representations should be used only if they can convey information better than written text can. This is an important principle that students will need to learn through constant practice.

Finally, students need a chance to practice incorporating graphical representations in their writing. This, of course, requires technology and plenty of feedback.

Emergent readers often need as many comprehension strategies as possible in order to determine meaning. Often they will look at the pictures in a story and sound out the words but fail to make the connection between the two. Therefore, the use of picture clues should be stressed as an applicable and effective strategy by which emergent readers can efficiently gain comprehension of the text they are reading.

Most early readers are attracted to pictures and illustrations, and as beginning readers they should be encouraged to use them as they try to make sense of print. Children can use pictures and prior knowledge to construct a story, with little attention to the print, gradually using the pictures to help them predict and identify individual words in the text. As they become more knowledgeable they will develop other comprehension strategies and become more fluent readers, relying less and less on the pictures. However, even fluent readers should be encouraged to create mental images as they read texts with fewer illustrations.

Teachers can demonstrate the value of visual clues in reading comprehension by reading a story that depends on pictorial representations for meaning (e.g., a picture book). Young readers can then accurately decipher meaning by using the picture clues provided. Teachers can also use picture clues to teach reading comprehension in a variety of children's literature by using materials such as maps, graphs, charts, posters, and Venn diagrams.

Strategies to Encourage Reading Comprehension

- Have students predict what the book will be about from the picture on the front cover

- Take "picture walks" through books before reading

- Encourage students to glance through a wordless picture book, guessing the storyline from the pictures. Next, allow the students to dictate or write a story corresponding to the pictures

- Have students "write" a story. Then ask them to illustrate their stories using their picture clues

- Have students illustrate their own wordless picture books and ask someone to predict the storyline

SKILL 1.10 Determine and analyze strategies for developing critical-thinking skills such as analysis, synthesis, and evaluation (e.g., making connections and predictions, questioning, summarizing, question generating).

Teachers should have a toolkit of instructional strategies, materials, and technologies to encourage and teach students how to problem solve and think critically about subject content. There is an established level of academic performance and proficiency in public schools that students are required to master. Research of national and state standards indicates that there are benchmarks and learning objectives in the subject areas of science, foreign language, English language arts, history, art, health, civics, economics, geography, physical education, mathematics, and social studies that students are required to master in state assessments (Marzano & Kendall, 1996).

A critical thinking skill is a skill target that teachers help students develop to sustain learning in specific subject areas that they can apply in other subject areas. For example, when learning algebraic concepts to solve a math word problem on how much fencing material is needed to build a fence around an 8' x 12' backyard area, a math student must understand the order of numerical expression to simplify algebraic expressions. Teachers can provide instructional strategies that show students how to group the fencing measurements into an algebraic word problem that, with minor addition, subtraction, and multiplication, can produce a simple number equal to the amount of fencing materials needed to build the fence.

Higher-Order Thinking Skills

> *Developing critical thinking skills in students is not as simple as developing other, simpler, skills.*

Developing critical thinking skills in students is not as simple as developing other, simpler, skills. Critical thinking skills must be taught within the context of specific subject matter. For example, language arts teachers can teach critical thinking skills through novels; social studies teachers can teach critical thinking skills through primary source documents or current events; and science teachers can teach critical thinking skills by having students develop hypotheses prior to conducting experiments.

The three main types of critical thinking skills are: analysis, synthesis, and evaluation.

Analysis

> **ANALYSIS:** the systematic exploration of a concept, event, term, piece of writing, element of media, or any other complex item

ANALYSIS is the systematic exploration of a concept, event, term, piece of writing, element of media, or any other complex item. Usually, people think of analysis as the exploration of the parts that make up a whole. For example, when someone analyzes a piece of literature, that person might focus on small pieces of the novel; yet, as they focus on the small pieces, they also call attention to the big picture and show how the small pieces create significance for the whole novel.

To carry this example further, if one were to analyze a novel, she might investigate a particular character to determine how that character adds significance to the novel. In something more concrete, like biology, one could analyze the findings of an experiment to see if the results might be of significance for something even larger than the experiment itself. It can be easier to analyze political events. For example, a social studies teacher might ask students to analyze the events leading up to World War II; doing so would require that students look at the small pieces (e.g., smaller world events prior to World War II) and determine how those small pieces, when added together, caused the war.

Synthesis

> **SYNTHESIS:** examining different concepts and drawing a global conclusion

SYNTHESIS is usually thought of as the opposite of analysis. In analysis, one takes a whole, breaks it up into pieces, and looks at the pieces. With synthesis, one takes different things and makes them one whole thing. A language arts teacher could ask students to synthesize two works of literature. For example, *The Scarlet Letter* and *The Crucible* are two works featuring Puritan life in America, written nearly a century apart. A student could synthesize the two works and come to conclusions about Puritan life. An art teacher could ask students to synthesize two paintings from the Impressionist era and come to conclusions about the features that distinguish that style of art.

Evaluation

Finally, **EVALUATION** involves making judgments. Whereas analysis and synthesis seek answers and hypotheses based on investigations, evaluation is based on opinions. A social studies teacher could ask students to evaluate the quality of Richard Nixon's resignation speech. To do so, they would judge whether or not they felt it was good. In contrast, analysis would keep judgment out of the assignment. Rather, it might have students focus on the structure of the speech (i.e., does the argument move from emotional to logical?).

> **EVALUATION:** drawing conclusions based on judgments

When evaluating a speech, a novel, a movie, or a painting, one must determine whether it is good or not. However, teaching evaluation skills requires not just that students learn how to determine whether something is good. It requires that students learn how to support their evaluations. If a student claims that Nixon's speech was effective in what the president intended the speech to do, the student would need to explain how this is so. Notice that evaluation often utilizes the skills of analysis and/or synthesis, but that the purpose is ultimately different.

Encouraging Independent Critical Thinking

Questioning is an effective tool to build students up to these higher-level thinking skills. Low-order questions are useful to begin the process. If the objective is for students to be able to read and understand the story "Goldilocks and the Three Bears," the teacher may wish to start with low-order questions, for example, "What are some things Goldilocks did while in the bears' home?" (knowledge) or "Why didn't Goldilocks like the Papa Bear's chair?" (analysis).

> *Because most teachers want their students to use higher-level thinking skills, they need to direct students to these higher levels on the taxonomy.*

Through a series of questions, the teacher can move students up the taxonomy: For example, "If Goldilocks had come to your house, what are some things she might have used?" (application); "How might the story have differed if Goldilocks had visited the three fishes?" (synthesis); or "Do you think Goldilocks was good or bad? Why?" (evaluation). The teacher can guide the thinking process of the class through questioning. As students become more involved in the discussion, they are systematically led to higher-level thinking.

To develop a critical-thinking approach to the world, children need to know enough about valid and invalid reasoning to ask questions. Bringing speeches or essays that demonstrate examples of both valid and invalid reasoning into the classroom can be useful in helping students develop the ability to question the reasoning of others. These examples should be by published writers or televised speakers so students can see that they are able to question even ideas that are accepted by some adults and talk about what is wrong in the thinking of those apparently successful communicators.

If the teacher stays on the cutting edge of children's experience, children will become more and more curious about things they don't know. A good way to introduce the outside world could be a lesson on a foreign country that the children may not know exists. This kind of lesson would reveal what life is like in other countries for children their own age. The lesson could use different types of media for variety and greater impact. In such lessons, positive aspects of the lives of those "other" children should always be included. Perhaps correspondence with children in a foreign country could be established.

> Political speeches are a good example of texts to use in the classroom.

Political speeches are a good example of texts to use in the classroom. Students will become better analyzers, synthesizers, and evaluators if they understand some of the basics of political speeches. Therefore, a teacher might introduce concepts such as rhetoric, style, persona, audience, diction, imagery, and tone. The best way to introduce these concepts would be to provide students with good examples of these things. Once they are familiar with these critical tools, students will be better able to apply them individually to political speeches—and then be able to analyze, synthesize, and evaluate political speeches on their own.

SKILL 1.11 Evaluate and select appropriate instructional strategies for teaching a variety of informational and literary text.

> **TEXT STRUCTURE:** the patterns of textual organization in a piece of writing

TEXT STRUCTURE refers to the patterns of textual organization in a piece of writing. Authors arrange their writing in various structures to make their content more comprehensible. When explaining a historical event, an author, for example, may arrange the text in a cause-effect structure; in other words, the text presents causes of an event followed by a description of the potential or actual effects. Or, if an author is telling a story, such as in a literary narrative, he may decide to present the text in a basic, chronological sequence. The author could also provide flashbacks or other disruptions in a sequence, and that would change the text structure.

> Particularly in informational texts, text structure helps readers make sense of the content.

Particularly in informational texts, text structure helps readers make sense of the content. When readers can identify a text structure, they usually have an easier time comprehending the text. In an essay that contains one paragraph explaining an opinion about a political issue and nine or ten paragraphs recounting stories about people, one might believe that the essay is merely a collection of stories about people. However, it is entirely possible that the text structure works like this:

Opinion
Example
Example
Example
Example
Example
…and so on

How do teachers help students understand the concept of text structure and use it in their own reading? Modeling and then giving students the opportunity to practice text-structure analysis is effective. Graphic organizers also provide a visual tool to help students make sense of text structure. In general, giving students the chance to practice identifying the structures in texts will help them do it on their own with the books and shorter texts they read outside of school.

COMPETENCY 2
KNOWLEDGE OF LITERARY ANALYSIS AND GENRES

> SKILL 2.1 Differentiate among characteristics and elements of a variety of literary genres (e.g., realistic fiction, fantasy, poetry, informational texts).

The major literary genres include allegory, ballad, drama, epic, epistle, essay, fable, novel, poem, romance, and the short story.

MAJOR LITERARY GENRES	
Allegory	A story in verse or prose with characters representing virtues and vices. There are two meanings, symbolic and literal. John Bunyan's *The Pilgrim's Progress* is the most well-known text of this genre.
Ballad	An *in medias res* story, told or sung, usually in verse and accompanied by music. Literary devices found in ballads include the refrain, or repeated section, and incremental repetition, or anaphora, for effect. Earliest forms were anonymous folk ballads. Later forms include Coleridge's Romantic masterpiece, "The Rime of the Ancient Mariner."
Drama	Plays—comedy, modern, or tragedy—typically in five acts. Traditionalists and neoclassicists adhere to Aristotle's unities of time, place, and action. Plot development is advanced via dialogue. Literary devices include asides, soliloquies, and the chorus representing public opinion. Greatest of all dramatists/playwrights is William Shakespeare. Other well-known playwrights include Ibsen, Williams, Miller, Shaw, Stoppard, Racine, Moliére, Sophocles, Aeschylus, Euripides, and Aristophanes.
Epic	Long poem usually of book length reflecting values inherent in the generative society. Epic devices include an invocation to a Muse for inspiration, purpose for writing, universal setting, protagonist and antagonist who possess supernatural strength and acumen, and interventions of a god or gods. Understandably, there are very few epics: Homer's *Iliad* and *Odyssey*, Virgil's *Aeneid*, Milton's *Paradise Lost*, Spenser's *The Fairie Queene*, Barrett Browning's *Aurora Leigh*, and Pope's mock-epic, *The Rape of the Lock*.
Epistle	A letter that is not always originally intended for public distribution, but due to the fame of the sender and/or recipient, becomes public. Paul wrote epistles that were later placed in the Bible.
Essay	Typically a limited length prose work focusing on a topic and propounding a definite point of view and authoritative tone. Great essayists include Carlyle, Lamb, DeQuincy, Emerson, and Montaigne, who is credited with defining this genre.

Continued on next page

Fable	Terse tale offering up a moral or exemplum. Chaucer's "The Nun's Priest's Tale" is a fine example of a *bête fabliau* or beast fable in which animals speak and act characteristically human, illustrating human foibles.
Legend	A traditional narrative or collection of related narratives, popularly regarded as historically factual but actually a mixture of fact and fiction.
Myth	Stories that are more or less universally shared within a culture to explain its history and traditions.
Novel	The longest form of fictional prose containing a variety of characterizations, settings, and regionalism. Most have complex plots, expanded description, and attention to detail. Some of the great novelists include Austin, the Brontes, Twain, Tolstoy, Hugo, Hardy, Dickens, Hawthorne, Forster, and Flaubert.
Poem	The only requirement is rhythm. Subgenres include fixed types of literature such as the sonnet, elegy, ode, pastoral, and villanelle. Unfixed types of literature include blank verse and dramatic monologue.
Romance	A highly imaginative tale set in a fantastical realm dealing with the conflicts between heroes, villains and/or monsters. "The Knight's Tale" from Chaucer's *Canterbury Tales*, *Sir Gawain and the Green Knight* and Keats' "The Eve of St. Agnes" are prime representatives.
Short Story	Typically a terse narrative, with less developmental background about characters than a novel. Short stories may include description, author's point of view, and tone. Poe emphasized that a successful short story should create one focused impact. Hemingway, Faulkner, Twain, Joyce, Shirley Jackson, Flannery O'Connor, de Maupassant, Saki, Edgar Allan Poe, and Pushkin are considered to be great short story writers.
Children's Literature	A genre of its own that emerged as a distinct and independent form in the second half of the eighteenth century. *The Visible World in Pictures* by John Amos Comenius, a Czech educator, was one of the first printed works and the first picture book. For the first time, educators acknowledged that children are different from adults in many respects. Modern educators acknowledge that introducing elementary students to a wide range of reading experiences plays an important role in their mental/ social/psychological development.

LITERATURE SPECIFICALLY FOR CHILDREN	
Traditional Literature	Traditional literature opens up a world where right wins out over wrong, where hard work and perseverance are rewarded, and where helpless victims find vindication—all worthwhile values that children identify with even as early as kindergarten. In traditional literature, children will be introduced to fanciful beings, humans with exaggerated powers, talking animals, and heroes that will inspire them. For younger elementary children, these stories in Big Book format are ideal for providing predictable and repetitive elements that can be grasped by these children.
Folktales/ Fairy Tales	Adventures of animals or humans and the supernatural characterize these stories. The hero is usually on a quest and is aided by other-worldly helpers. More often than not, the story focuses on good and evil and reward and punishment. Some examples: *The Three Bears*, *Little Red Riding Hood*, *Snow White*, *Sleeping Beauty*, *Puss-in-Boots*, *Rapunzel*, and *Rumpelstiltskin*.
Fables	Animals that act like humans are featured in these stories, which usually reveal human foibles or sometimes teach a lesson. Example: Aesop's *Fables*.
Myths	These stories about events from the earliest times, such as the origin of the world, are considered true in their own societies.
Legends	These are similar to myths except that they tend to deal with events that happened more recently. Example: Arthurian legends.
Tall Tales	These are purposely exaggerated accounts of individuals with superhuman strength. Examples: Paul Bunyan, John Henry, and Pecos Bill.
Modern Fantasy	Many of the themes found in these stories are similar to those in traditional literature. The stories start out based in reality, which makes it easier for the reader to suspend disbelief and enter worlds of unreality. Little people live in the walls in *The Borrowers* and time travel is possible in *The Trolley to Yesterday*. Including some fantasy tales in the curriculum helps elementary-grade children develop their senses of imagination. These often appeal to ideals of justice and issues having to do with good and evil; and because children tend to identify with the characters, the message is more likely to be retained.
Science Fiction	Robots, spacecraft, mystery, and civilizations from other ages often appear in these stories. Most presume advances in science on other planets or in a future time. Most children like these stories because of their interest in space and the "what if" aspect of the stories. Examples: *Outer Space and All That Junk* and *A Wrinkle in Time*.
Modern Realistic Fiction	These stories are about real problems that real children face. By finding that their hopes and fears are shared by others, young children can find insight into their own problems. Young readers also tend to experience a broadening of interests as the result of this kind of reading. It's good for them to know that a child can be brave and intelligent and can solve difficult problems.

Continued on next page

Historical Fiction	The stories are presented in a historically accurate setting. One example of this kind of story is *Rifles for Watie*. This story is about a young boy who serves in the Union army. He experiences great hardship but discovers that his enemy is an admirable human being. It provides a good opportunity to introduce younger children to history.
Biography	Reading about inventors, explorers, scientists, political and religious leaders, social reformers, artists, sports figures, doctors, teachers, writers, and war heroes helps children to see that one person can make a difference. They also open new vistas for children to think about when they choose an occupation to fantasize about.
Informational Books	These are ways to learn more about something you are interested in or something that you know nothing about. Encyclopedias are good resources, of course, but a book like *Polar Wildlife* by Kamini Khanduri shows pictures and facts that will capture the imaginations of young children.

SKILL 2.2 Identify and analyze terminology and intentional use of literary devices (e.g., simile, metaphor, personification, onomatopoeia, hyperbole).

Imagery

IMAGERY can be described as a word or sequence of words that refers to any sensory experience—that is, anything that can be seen, tasted, smelled, heard, or felt on the skin or with the fingers. While writers of prose also use imagery, it is most common in poetry. The poet intends to make an experience available to the reader. In order to do that, the poet must choose words that appeal to one of the senses. The poet will deliberately paint a scene in such a way that the reader can see it. However, the purpose is not simply to stir the visceral feeling, but also to stir the emotions.

> **IMAGERY:** a word or sequence of words that refers to any sensory experience; anything that can be seen, tasted, smelled, heard, or felt on the skin or with the fingers

A good example is "The Piercing Chill" by Taniguchi Buson (1715–1783):

> The piercing chill I feel:
> My dead wife's comb, in our bedroom,
> Under my heel . . .

In only a few short words, the reader can feel many things: the shock that might come from touching the corpse, a literal sense of death, and the contrast between the death of the wife and the memories the husband has of her when she was alive. Imagery might be defined as speaking of the abstract in concrete terms, a powerful device in the hands of a skilful poet.

Symbols

A **SYMBOL** is an object or action that can be observed with the senses and that suggests other things. The lion is a symbol of courage; the color green, a symbol of envy. Symbols used in literature are usually of a different sort. They tend to be private and personal; their significance is only evident in the context of the work in which they are used. A good example is the huge pair of spectacles on a billboard in *The Great Gatsby* by F. Scott Fitzgerald. They are interesting as a part of the landscape, but they can also be a symbol for divine myopia. A symbol can certainly have more than one meaning, and the meaning may be as personal as the memories and experiences of the particular reader. In analyzing a poem or a story, it is important to identify symbols and their possible meanings.

Looking for symbols is often challenging, especially for novice poetry readers. However, these suggestions may be useful: First, pick out all references to concrete objects, such as a newspaper or a black cat. Note any that the poet emphasizes by describing them in detail, repeating, or by placing them at the very beginning or end of a poem. Ask yourself, "What is the poem about? What does it mean?" Paraphrase the poem and determine whether the meaning depends on certain concrete objects. Then, one by one, think about what each concrete object potentially symbolizes in this particular poem. A symbol may be a part of a person's body, such as the eye of the murder victim in Edgar Allan Poe's short story "The Tell-Tale Heart," or a look, a voice, or a mannerism.

The following are some things a symbol is *not*: an abstraction such as truth, death, or love; in narrative, a well developed character who is not at all mysterious; or the second term in a metaphor. In Emily Dickinson's "The Lightning Is a Yellow Fork," the symbol is the lightning, not the fork.

An **ALLUSION** is very much like a symbol. In *Merriam-Webster's Encyclopedia of Literature*, an allusion is defined as "an implied reference to a person, event, thing, or a part of another text." Allusions are based on the assumption that there is a common body of knowledge shared by the poet and the reader and that a reference to that body of knowledge will be immediately understood. Allusions to the Bible and classical mythology are common in Western literature on the assumption that they will be immediately understood. This is not always the case, of course. T. S. Eliot's *The Waste Land* requires research and annotation for understanding. The author assumed more background on the part of the average reader than actually exists. However, when Michael Moore headlines an article on the war in Iraq: "Déjà Fallouja: Ramadi surrounded, thousands of families trapped, no electricity or water, onslaught impending," we understand immediately that this refers to a repeat of the human disaster in New Orleans, although the "onslaught" is not a storm but an invasion by American and Iraqi troops.

The use of allusion is a sort of shortcut for poets. They can use fewer words and count on meaning to come from the reader's own experience.

Figures of Speech

Figurative language is also referred to as figures of speech. If all figures of speech that have ever been identified were listed, it would be a very long list. However, for purposes of analyzing poetry, a few are sufficient:

1. **Simile:** Direct comparison between two things. "My love is like a red-red rose."

2. **Metaphor:** Indirect comparison between two things; the use of a word or phrase denoting one kind of object or action in place of another to suggest a comparison between them. While poets use them extensively, they are also integral to everyday speech. For example, it is said that chairs have "legs" and "arms," although everyone knows that inanimate objects do not have limbs.

3. **Parallelism:** The arrangement of ideas in phrases, sentences, and paragraphs that balance one element with another of equal importance and similar wording. An example from Francis Bacon's "Of Studies:" "Reading maketh a full man, conference a ready man, and writing an exact man."

4. **Personification:** Attributing human characteristics to an inanimate object, an abstract quality, or an animal. John Bunyan exemplified this by writing about characters named Death, Knowledge, Giant Despair, Sloth, and Piety in his Pilgrim's Progress. The metaphor of "an arm of a chair" is a form of personification.

5. **Euphemism:** The substitution of an agreeable or inoffensive term for one that might offend or suggest something unpleasant. Many euphemisms, such as "passed away," "crossed over," or "passed," are used to refer to death to avoid using the real word.

6. **Hyperbole:** Deliberate exaggeration for effect or comic effect. Seen here is an example from Shakespeare's *The Merchant of Venice*:

> *Why, if two gods should play some heavenly match*
> *And on the wager lay two earthly women,*
> *And Portia one, there must be something else*
> *Pawned with the other, for the poor rude world*
> *Hath not her fellow.*

7. **Climax:** A number of phrases or sentences are arranged in ascending order of rhetorical forcefulness. Here is an example from Melville's Moby Dick:

> *All that most maddens and torments; all that stirs up the lees of things; all truth with malice in it; all that cracks the sinews and cakes the brain; all the subtle demonisms of life and thought; all evil, to crazy Ahab, were visibly personified and made practically assailable in Moby Dick.*

8. **Bathos:** A ludicrous attempt to portray pathos; that is, to evoke pity, sympathy, or sorrow. It may result from inappropriately dignifying the commonplace, elevated language to describe something trivial, or greatly exaggerated pathos.

9. **Oxymoron:** A contradiction in terms deliberately employed for effect. It is usually seen in a qualifying adjective whose meaning is contrary to that of the noun it modifies, such as "wise folly."

10. **Irony:** Expressing something other than and particularly opposite the literal meaning, such as words of praise when the author or speaker intends blame. In poetry, it is often used as a sophisticated or resigned awareness of contrast between what is and what ought to be and expresses a controlled pathos without sentimentality. This form of indirection avoids overt praise or censure. An early example is the Greek comic character Eiron, a clever underdog who by his wit repeatedly triumphs over the boastful character Alazon.

11. **Alliteration:** The repetition of consonant sounds in two or more neighboring words or syllables. In its simplest form, it reinforces one or two consonant sounds, for example, Shakespeare's "Sonnet #12:" "When I do count the clock that tells the time."

> *Some poets have used more complex patterns of alliteration by creating consonants both at the beginning of words and at the beginning of stressed syllables within words; for example, Shelley's "Stanzas Written in Dejection Near Naples": "The **C**ity's voi**c**e it**s**elf is **s**oft like **S**olitude's."*

12. **Onomatopoeia:** The naming of a thing or action by a vocal imitation of the sound associated with it, such as *buzz* or *hiss* or the use of words whose sound suggests the sense. The following is a good example from "The Brook" by Tennyson:

> *I chatter over stony ways,*
> *In little sharps and trebles,*
> *I bubble into eddying bays,*
> *I babble on the pebbles.*

13. **Malapropism:** A verbal blunder in which one word is replaced by another that is similar in sound but different in meaning. Thinking of the geography of contiguous countries, Mrs. Malaprop in Richard Brinsley Sheridan's *The Rivals* (1775) spoke of the "geometry" of "contagious countries."

Poets use figures of speech to sharpen the effect and meaning of their poems and to help readers see things in ways they have never seen them before. In her poem "A Grave," Marianne Moore observes that a fir tree has "an emerald turkey-foot at the top." This poem makes the reader aware of something not previously noticed. The sudden recognition of the likeness yields pleasure in the reading.

Figurative language allows for the statement of truths that more literal language cannot. Skillfully used, figures of speech will help the reader see more clearly and focus upon particulars. They add dimensions of richness to our reading and understanding of a poem; they also provide many opportunities for analysis. In analyzing a poem on the basis of its figures of speech, one should ask the questions: What do they do for the poem? Do they underscore meaning? Do they intensify understanding? Do they increase the intensity of our response?

> *Figurative language allows for the statement of truths that more literal language cannot.*

SKILL 2.3 **Evaluate and select appropriate multicultural texts based on purpose, relevance, cultural sensitivity, and developmental appropriateness.**

Living in a multicultural society, it is important that teachers think beyond the classics of literature (or even simply the works of literature they personally enjoy and are familiar with) and consider literature that is representative of the various cultures in this country and their particular classrooms, and instructive to students about how to interact with people who are not like themselves.

When selecting multicultural literature, a few things need to be considered:

- Is the literature, in general, appropriate?
- Does the literature accurately portray a particular culture?
- Will students be able to utilize the literature for a greater social purpose?

When selecting a piece of literature for classroom use, teachers need to ensure that it is appropriate. Has the board of education in the teacher's district approved the text for classroom use? If it is up to the teacher to decide whether the text is appropriate, the teacher must determine whether the text contains violence, vulgar language, sexual explicitness, negative values, or racism. If so, the text is probably not appropriate. In addition, is the text at the appropriate reading level for the class? These considerations are necessary for all texts, whether or not they are multicultural selections.

The next issue to consider is the extent to which the text accurately portrays other cultures. Often, in general literature, there are gross misrepresentations of some cultures, which can give students incorrect perceptions of those cultures. In addition, teachers should consider whether students who are members of the cultures portrayed feel that the portrayals are accurate. If not, it could be damaging to those students, as well as to their relationships with other students.

Finally, the literature should help students learn how to live in a multicultural society. The literature students read in school may provide one of the few opportunities they have to learn how to interact with people in different cultures. By selecting literature that offers good role models, teachers can assist students in developing positive habits of mind. While not all literature must serve this purpose, it is important that, at various times throughout the school year, students get some "life instruction" through their classroom reading materials.

> ### SKILL 2.4 Identify and evaluate appropriate techniques for varying student response to texts *(e.g., think-pair-share, reading response journals, evidence-based discussion).*

Simply presenting good literature to students is not enough. They need active involvement with the literature. They also need opportunities to respond to it in a variety of ways. Response helps students personalize the literature. It helps them understand that the literature comes from human instincts and issues, it helps them as they make sense of meaning, and it helps them to appreciate the literature more.

Appropriate response to literature comes in many forms. Many students learn by responding with additional works of art—whether it is through further literature (poetry, fiction, etc.), visual art, or music. For example:

- Students can write a poem expressing the mood of a character

- They can draw a picture that portrays a scene in a novel

- They can rewrite the end of a story

Giving students the opportunity to be creative in this way helps them to "enter" into the literature more fully. It gives them a real opportunity to interact with the ideas, characters, setting, and author.

Analytic writing is also a good way to respond to literature. Of course, students may not enjoy this as much, but analytic writing allows them to see that there is more than one way to view literature. They learn more when they understand that even unconventional ways of understanding literature must be defended with clear examples from the text.

The list of appropriate responses to literature could go on and on. Not every type of response works well for all students and for all types of literature, so careful selection is important.

Drama is an effective tool for responding to literature. When students act out scenes from a novel, for example, they begin to understand character motives more clearly.

COMPETENCY 3
KNOWLEDGE OF LANGUAGE AND THE WRITING PROCESS

> **SKILL 3.1** **Identify and evaluate the developmental stages of writing** *(e.g., drawing, dictating, writing).*

Young learners go through several stages before becoming fluent in writing.

Beginning Sounds Emerge

At this stage, students begin to see the differences between a letter and a word, but they may not use spacing between words. Their message makes sense and matches the picture, especially when they choose the topic.

Consonants Represent Words

Students begin to leave spaces between their words and may often mix upper- and lowercase letters in their writing. They begin using punctuation and usually write sentences that tell ideas.

Initial, Middle, and Final Sounds

Students in this phase may spell correctly some sight words, siblings' names, and environmental print, but other words are spelled the way they sound. Children easily hear sounds in words, and their writing is very readable.

Transitional Phases

Writing is readable and approaches conventional spelling. The students' writing is interspersed with words that are in standard form and have standard letter patterns.

Standard Spelling

Students in this phase can spell most words correctly and are developing an understanding of root words, compound words, and contractions. This understanding helps students spell similar words.

Writing is a process that flows gradually. Since writing is a process and stages are connected, learners may show evidence of more than one stage in a single piece of writing. Providing a literacy-rich environment with plenty of opportunities to engage in writing is the best way to ensure fluency in writing skills.

SKILL 3.2 **Differentiate stages of the writing process** *(i.e., prewriting, drafting, revising, editing, publishing).*

Writing is an iterative process. As students engage in the various stages of writing, they develop and improve not only their writing skills, but their thinking skills as well. Students must understand that writing is a process and typically involves many steps: prewriting, drafting, revision and editing, proofreading, and publishing.

Prewriting

Students gather ideas before writing. Prewriting may include clustering, listing, brainstorming, mapping, free writing, and charting. Providing many ways for students to develop ideas on a topic will increase their chances of success.

Remind students that, as they prewrite, they need to consider their audience. Prewriting strategies assist students in a variety of ways. Listed below are the most common prewriting strategies students can use to explore, plan, and write on a topic. It is important to remember when teaching these strategies that not all prewriting must eventually produce a finished piece of writing. In fact, in the initial lesson about prewriting strategies, it might be more effective to have students practice prewriting strategies without the pressure of having to produce a finished product.

- Keep an idea book for jotting down ideas that come to mind.

- Write in a daily journal.

- Write down whatever comes to mind; this is called free writing. Students do not stop to make corrections or interrupt the flow of ideas.

  A variation of this technique is focused free writing—writing on a specific topic—to prepare for an essay.

- Make a list of all ideas connected with their topic (brainstorming).

- Ask the questions Who? What? When? Where? How? Help the writer approach a topic from several perspectives.

- Create a visual map on paper to gather ideas. Cluster circles and lines to show connections between ideas.

- Observe details of sight, hearing, taste, and touch.

- Visualize by making mental images of something and writing down the details in a list.

After they have practiced each of these prewriting strategies, ask them to pick out the ones they prefer and have them discuss how they might use the techniques to help them with future writing assignments. It is important to remember that they can use more than one prewriting strategy at a time. They may also find that different writing situations may suggest certain techniques.

Make sure students know that keeping lists works best when they let their minds work freely. After completing the list, students should analyze it to find a pattern or way to group the ideas.

Students should try to identify the relationships that exist between their ideas. If they cannot see the relationships, have them pair up, exchange papers, and have their partners look for some related ideas.

Drafting

Students compose the first draft. They should follow their notes or writing plan from the prewriting stage.

Revising and Editing

The word **revise** comes from the Latin word **revidere**, meaning "to see again." Revision is probably the most important step in the writing process. In this step, students examine their work and make changes in wording, details, and ideas. Often, students write a draft and feel that they're done. On the contrary, they must be encouraged to develop, change, and enhance their writing as they go, as well as after they've completed a draft.

Effective teachers realize that revision and editing go hand in hand, and that students often move back and forth between these stages during the course of one written work. Also, these stages must be practiced in small groups, pairs, and/or individually. Students must learn to analyze and improve their own work as well as the work of their peers. Some methods to use include:

- Students, working in pairs, analyze sentences for variety

- Students work in pairs or groups to ask questions about unclear areas in the writing or to help students add details, more information, etc.

- Students perform final edit

Many teachers introduce a Writer's Workshop to their students to maximize learning about the writing process. Writer's Workshops vary across classrooms, but the main idea is for students to become comfortable with the writing process and to produce written work. A basic Writer's Workshop includes a block of classroom time committed to writing various projects (e.g., narratives, memoirs, book summaries, fiction, book reports). Students use this time to write, meet with others to review and edit writing, make comments on writing, revise their own work, proofread, meet with the teacher, and publish their work.

Teachers who facilitate effective Writer's Workshops are able to meet with students one at a time and guide them in their individual writing needs. This approach allows the teacher to differentiate instruction for each student's writing level.

Students need to be trained to become effective at proofreading, revising, and editing strategies. Desk-side and scheduled conferences are excellent opportunities to help students develop their editing skills. Listed below are some strategies for guiding students through the final stages of the writing process (these can easily be incorporated into a Writer's Workshop).

> *Students need to be trained to become effective at proofreading, revising, and editing strategies.*

- Provide some guide sheets or forms for students to use during peer responses

- Allow students to work in pairs and limit the agenda

- Model the use of the guide sheet or form for the entire class

- Give students a time limit or a particular number of written pieces to be completed in a specific amount of time

- Have students read their partner's papers and ask at least three who, what, when, why, or how questions to start their discussion

- At this point in the writing process, a mini-lesson that focuses on some of the problems that students are having would be appropriate

Provide students with a series of questions and instructions to assist them in revising their writing such as:

1. Do the details give a clear picture? Add details that appeal to more than just the sense of sight.

2. How effectively are the details organized? Reorder the details if necessary.

3. Are the thoughts and feelings of the writer included? Add personal thoughts and feelings about the subject.

As you discuss revision, begin with discussing the definition of *revise* and the fact that all writing must be revised to make it better.

Proofreading

Students proofread the draft for punctuation and mechanical errors. There are a few key points to remember when helping students learn to edit and proofread their work:

- It is crucial that students are not taught grammar in isolation, but in the context of the writing process

- Ask students to check for specific errors in their work, such as using a subordinate clause as a sentence

- Provide students with a proofreading checklist to guide them as they edit their work

Publishing

Students may have their work displayed on a bulletin board, read aloud in class, or printed in a literary magazine or school anthology.

It is important to realize that these steps are iterative; as a student engages in the writing process, he or she may begin with prewriting and then write, revise, write, revise, edit, and publish. Students do not engage in this process in a lockstep manner; it is more circular.

SKILL **Distinguish among the modes of writing** *(e.g., narrative, informative/*
3.3 *explanatory, argument).*

Discourse, whether spoken or written, falls naturally into four different forms: narrative, descriptive, expository, and persuasive. The first question to ask when *reading* a written piece, *listening* to a presentation, or *writing* is: "What is the point?" The "point" is usually called the **THESIS**. If you are reading an essay, when you've finished, you want to be able to say, "The point of this piece is that the foster-care system in America is a disaster." If you are reading a play, you should be able to say, "The point of this play is that good overcomes evil." The same is true of any written document or performance. If it doesn't make a point, the reader/listener/viewer is confused or feels that it's not worth the effort. It is helpful to keep this in mind when one sits down to write something, be it essay, poem, or speech. What point do you want to make? We make our points in the forms that have structured western thinking since the Greek rhetoricians.

THESIS: the main point of discourse

Narration

NARRATION: discourse that is arranged chronologically

NARRATION is discourse that is arranged chronologically: Something happened, and then something else happened, and then something else happened. News reports are often narrative in nature, as are records of trips, etc.

Description

DESCRIPTION: discourse that makes an experience available through one of the five senses: seeing, smelling, hearing, feeling, or tasting

DESCRIPTION is discourse that makes an experience available through one of the five senses: seeing, smelling, hearing, feeling, or tasting. Descriptive words make it possible for the reader to see with the mind's eye, hear through the mind's ear, smell through the mind's nose, taste with the mind's tongue, and feel with the mind's fingers. This is how language moves people. Only by experiencing an event can the reader's emotions become involved. Poets are experts in descriptive language.

Exposition

EXPOSITION: discourse that is informative in nature

EXPOSITION is discourse that is informative in nature. Expository writing is not intended to change anyone's mind or get anyone to take a certain action. Its purpose is to give information. Examples of expository writing include driving directions to a particular location or the instructions for putting together a toy that arrives unassembled. The writer doesn't care whether the reader follows the directions or not. The only purpose is to provide the information in case the reader does decide to use it.

Research reports are a special kind of expository writing. A topic is researched—explored by searching literature, interviewing experts, or conducting experiments—and the findings are written up in such a way that a particular audience may know what was discovered. They can be very simple, such as delving into the history of an event or very complex, such as a report on a scientific phenomenon that requires complicated testing and reasoning to explain. A research report often includes multiple possible conclusions, but puts forth one as the best answer to the question that inspired the research in the first place. This conclusion becomes the thesis of the report.

Letters are often expository in nature; their purpose is to give information. However, letters are also often persuasive; the writer wants to persuade the recipient to do something. They are also sometimes descriptive or narrative; the writer will share an experience or tell about an event.

Persuasion

PERSUASION is a piece of writing—a poem, a play, or a speech—whose purpose is to change the minds of readers or audience members or to get them to do something. This can be achieved in many ways:

- The credibility of the writer or speaker might lead listeners or readers to a change of mind or a recommended action.

- Reasoning is important in persuasive discourse. No one wants to accept a new viewpoint or go out and take action just because he likes or trusts the person who recommends it. Logic comes into play in reasoning that is persuasive.

- The most powerful force that leads to acceptance or action is emotional appeal. Even if people have been persuaded logically and reasonably that they should believe something, they are unlikely to act on it unless they are moved emotionally. A man with financial resources might be convinced that people suffered in New Orleans after Hurricane Katrina, but may not feel the need to donate to a relief agency unless moved emotionally, for example, by the sight of elderly people stranded in houses. Sermons are an example of persuasive discourse.

Persuasive writing often uses all forms of discourse. The introduction may be a history or background of the idea being presented (exposition). Details supporting some of the points may be stories (narrations). Descriptive writing will be used to make sure the point is established emotionally.

> **PERSUASION:** a piece of writing—a poem, a play, or a speech—whose purpose is to change the minds of readers or audience members or to get them to do something

Paraphrase and Summary

PARAPHRASE is the rewording of a piece of writing. The result will not necessarily be shorter than the original. It will use different vocabulary and possibly a different arrangement of details. Paraphrases are sometimes written to clarify a complex piece of writing. Sometimes, material is paraphrased because copyright prohibits use of the original material.

SUMMARY is a distillation of the elements of a piece of writing or speech. A summary is much shorter than the original. To write a good summary, the writer must determine what the "bones" of the original piece are. What is its structure? What is the thesis, and what are the sub-points? A summary does not make judgments about the original; it simply reports the original in condensed form.

> **PARAPHRASE:** rewording a piece of writing

> **SUMMARY:** a distillation of the elements of a piece of writing or speech

> **SKILL 3.4** Select the appropriate mode of writing for a variety of occasions, purposes, and audiences.

See Skill 3.3

> **SKILL 3.5** Identify and apply instructional methods for teaching writing conventions *(e.g., spelling, punctuation, capitalization, syntax, word usage).*

Candidates should be cognizant of proper rules and conventions of punctuation, capitalization, and spelling. Competency exams generally test the ability to apply the more advanced skills; thus, a limited number of more frustrating rules are presented here. Rules should be applied according to the American style of English, i.e., spelling *theater* instead of *theatre* and placing terminal marks of punctuation almost exclusively within other marks of punctuation.

Subject-Verb Agreement

A verb should always agree in number with its subject. Making them agree relies on the ability to properly identify the subject.

> <u>One</u> of the boys <u>was playing</u> too rough.
>
> <u>No one</u> in the class, not the teacher nor any student, <u>was listening</u> to the message from the intercom.
>
> The <u>candidates</u>, including a grandmother and a teenager, <u>are debating</u> some controversial issues.

If two singular subjects are connected by *and*, the verb must be plural.

> A man and his dog <u>were jogging</u> on the beach.

If two singular subjects are connected by *or* or *nor*, a singular verb is required.

> Neither Dot nor Joyce <u>has missed</u> a day of school this year. Either Fran or Paul <u>is</u> missing.

If one singular subject and one plural subject are connected by *or* or *nor*, the verb agrees with the subject nearest to the verb.

> Neither the coach nor the players <u>were able</u> to sleep on the bus.

If the subject is a collective noun, its sense of number in the sentence determines the verb: It is singular if the noun represents a group or unit and plural if the noun represents individuals.

> The House of Representatives <u>has adjourned</u> for the holidays.

Pronoun-Antecedent Agreement

A noun is any word that names a person, place, thing, idea, quality, or activity. A pronoun is a word that is used in place of a noun or other pronoun. The word or word group that a pronoun stands for (or refers to) is called its ANTECEDENT.

We use pronouns in many of the sentences that we write. Pronouns enable us to avoid monotonous repetition of nouns. They also help us maintain coherence within and among sentences. Pronouns must agree with their antecedents in number and person. Therefore, if the antecedent is plural, use a plural pronoun; if the antecedent is feminine, use a feminine pronoun.

Specific types of pronouns include: personal, possessive, indefinite, reflexive, reciprocal, intensive, interrogative, relative, and demonstrative.

To help students revise their work to correct errors, have them complete the following steps:

- Read focusing only on pronouns
- Circle each pronoun, and draw an arrow to its antecedent
- Replace the pronoun with a noun to eliminate a vague pronoun reference
- Supply missing antecedents where needed
- Place the pronoun so that the nearest noun is its antecedent

After students have focused on pronoun-antecedent agreement a few times, they will progress from correcting errors to avoiding errors. The only way to develop their skill with pronoun references, however, is focused and adequate practice.

> **ANTECEDENT:** the word or word group that a pronoun stands for (or refers to)

Verbs (Tense)

PRESENT TENSE is used to express that which is currently happening or is always true.

> Randy is playing the piano.
> Randy plays the piano like a pro.

> **PRESENT TENSE:** expresses that which is currently happening or is always true

PAST TENSE: expresses action that occurred in a past time

FUTURE TENSE: expresses action or a condition of future time

PRESENT PERFECT TENSE: expresses action or a condition that started in the past and is continued or completed in the present

PAST PERFECT TENSE: expresses action or a condition that occurred as a precedent to some other past action or condition

FUTURE PERFECT TENSE: expresses action that started in the past or the present and will conclude at some time in the future

PAST TENSE is used to express action that occurred in a past time.

> *Randy learned to play the piano when he was six years old.*

FUTURE TENSE is used to express action or a condition of future time.

> *Randy will probably earn a music scholarship.*

PRESENT PERFECT TENSE is used to express action or a condition that started in the past and is continued or completed in the present.

> *Randy has practiced the piano every day for the last ten years.*
> *Randy has never been bored with practice.*

PAST PERFECT TENSE expresses action or a condition that occurred as a precedent to some other past action or condition.

> *Randy had considered playing clarinet before he discovered the piano.*

FUTURE PERFECT TENSE expresses action that started in the past or the present and will conclude at some time in the future.

> *By the time he goes to college, Randy will have been an accomplished pianist for more than half of his life.*

Use of verbs: mood

Indicative mood is used to make unconditional statements; **subjunctive mood** is used for conditional clauses or wish statements that pose conditions that are untrue. Verbs in subjunctive mood are plural with both singular and plural subjects.

> *If I were a bird, I would fly.*
> *I wish I were as rich as Donald Trump.*

Conjugation of verbs

The conjugation of verbs follows the patterns used in the discussion of tense above. However, the most common errors in verb use stem from the improper formation of the past and past participial forms.

> Regular verb: *believe, believed, (have) believed*
> Irregular verbs: *run, ran, run; sit, sat, sat; teach, taught, taught*

Other errors stem from the use of verbs that are the same in some tenses but have different forms and different meanings in other tenses.

> I lie on the ground. I lay on the ground yesterday. I have lain down. I lay the blanket on the bed. I laid the blanket there yesterday. I have laid the blanket down every night.
>
> The sun rises. The sun rose. The sun has risen.
>
> He raises the flag. He raised the flag. He had raised the flag.
>
> I sit on the porch. I sat on the porch. I have sat in the porch swing.
>
> I set the plate on the table. I set the plate there yesterday. I had set the table before dinner.

Two other common verb problems stem from misusing the preposition *of* for the verb auxiliary *have* and misusing the verb *ought* (now rare).

Incorrect: *I should of gone to bed.*

Correct: *I should have gone to bed.*

Incorrect: *He hadn't ought to get so angry.*

Correct: *He ought not to get so angry.*

Adjectives

An adjective should agree in number with the word it modifies.

> Those apples are rotten. This one is ripe. These peaches are hard.

With some exceptions, comparative adjectives end in *-er* and superlatives in *-est*, like *worse* and *worst*. Some adjectives that cannot easily make comparative inflections are preceded by *more* and *most*.

> Mrs. Carmichael is the better of the two basketball coaches. That is the hastiest excuse you have ever contrived.

Avoid double comparatives and superlatives.

Incorrect: *This is the worstest headache I ever had.*

Correct: *This is the worst headache I ever had.*

When comparing one thing to others in a group, exclude the thing under comparison from the rest of the group.

Incorrect: *Joey is larger than any baby I have ever seen. (Since you have seen him, he cannot be larger than himself.)*

Correct: *Joey is larger than any other baby I have ever seen. (Include all necessary words to make a comparison clear in meaning.)*

> I am as tall as my mother. I am as tall as she (is).
> My cats are better behaved than those of my neighbor.

Plurals

The multiplicity and complexity of spelling rules based on phonics, letter doubling, and exceptions to rules that are not mastered by adulthood should be replaced by a good dictionary. As spelling mastery is also difficult for adolescents, the recommendation is the same: Learning the uses of a dictionary and a thesaurus are strategic solutions to this common problem.

Most plurals of nouns that end in hard consonants or in hard consonant sounds followed by a silent *e* are made by adding -*s*. Plurals of some words ending in vowels are formed by adding only -*s*.

> fingers, numerals, banks, bugs, riots, homes, gates, radios, bananas

For nouns that end in soft consonant sounds—*s, j, x, z, ch,* and *sh*—the plurals are formed by adding -*es*. Plurals of some nouns ending in *o* are formed by adding -*es*.

> dresses, waxes, churches, brushes, tomatoes

For nouns ending in *y* preceded by a vowel, just add -*s*.

> boys, alleys

For nouns ending in *y* preceded by a consonant, change the *y* to *i* and add -*es*.

> babies, corollaries, frugalities, poppies

Some nouns' plurals are formed irregularly or remain the same.

> sheep, deer, children, leaves, oxen

Some nouns derived from foreign words, especially Latin words, are made plural in two different ways. Sometimes the meanings are the same; other times the two plural forms are used in slightly different contexts. It is always wise to consult the dictionary.

> appendices, appendixes   criterion, criteria
>
> indexes, indices   crisis, crises

Make the plurals of closed (solid) compound words in the usual way.

> timelines, hairpins
>
> cupfuls, handfuls

Make the plurals of open or hyphenated compounds by adding the change in inflection to the word that changes in number.

> fathers-in-law, courts-martial, masters of art, doctors of medicine

Make the plurals of letters, numbers, and abbreviations by adding -s.

> fives and tens, IBMs, 1990s, ps and qs (Note that letters are italicized.)

Possessives

Make the possessives of singular nouns by adding an apostrophe followed by the letter *s* (*'s*).

> baby's bottle, mother's job, elephant's eye, teacher's desk,
>
> sympathizer's protests, week's postponement

Make the possessives of singular nouns ending in *s* by adding either an apostrophe or an apostrophe followed by the letter *s*, depending upon common usage or sound. When the possessive sounds awkward, use a prepositional phrase instead. Even with the sibilant ending, with a few exceptions, it is advisable to use the *'s* construction.

> dress's color, species' characteristics (or characteristics of the species),
>
> James' hat (or James's hat), Dolores's shirt

Make the possessives of plural nouns ending in *s* by adding an apostrophe after the *s*.

> horses' coats, jockeys' times, four days' time

Make the possessives of plural nouns that do not end in s by adding 's, just as with singular nouns.

> children's shoes, deer's antlers, cattle's horns

Make the possessives of compound nouns by adding the inflection at the end of the word or phrase.

> the mayor of Los Angeles' campaign, the mailman's new truck, the mailmen's new trucks, my father-in-law's first wife, the keepsakes' values, several daughters-in-law's husbands

Note: *Because a gerund functions as a noun, any noun preceding it and operating as a possessive adjective must reflect the necessary inflection. However, if the gerundive following the noun is a participle, no inflection is added.*

The general was perturbed by the private's sleeping on duty. (The word **sleeping** *is a gerund, the object of the preposition* **by***.)*
—BUT—
The general was perturbed to see the private sleeping on duty. (The word **sleeping** *is a participle modifying* **private***.)*

Pronouns

A pronoun used as a direct object, indirect object, or object of a preposition requires the objective case form.

> The teacher praised him. She gave him an A on the test. Her praise of him was appreciated. The students whom she did not praise will work harder next time.

Common pronoun errors occur from misuse of reflexive pronouns:

Singular: *myself, yourself, herself, himself, itself*
Plural: *ourselves, yourselves, themselves.*

Incorrect: *Jack cut hisself shaving.*

Correct: *Jack cut himself shaving.*

Incorrect: *They backed theirselves into a corner.*

Correct: *They backed themselves into a corner.*

Capitalization

Capitalize all proper names of persons (including specific organizations or agencies of government), places (countries, states, cities, parks, and specific geographical areas), things (political parties, structures, historical and cultural terms, and calendar and time designations), and religious terms (deities, revered persons or groups, and sacred writings).

> Percy Bysshe Shelley, Argentina, Mount Rainier National Park, Grand Canyon, League of Nations, the Sears Tower, Birmingham, Lyric Theater, Americans, Midwesterners, Democrats, Renaissance, Boy Scouts of America, Easter, Bible, Dead Sea Scrolls, Koran

Capitalize proper adjectives and titles used with proper names.

> *California gold rush, President John Adams, French fries, Homeric epic, Romanesque architecture, Senator John Glenn*

Note: Some words that represent titles and offices are not capitalized unless used with a proper name.

Capitalized	Not Capitalized
Congressman McKay	*the congressman from Hawaii*
Commander Alger	*the commander of the Pacific Fleet*
Queen Elizabeth	*the queen of England*

Capitalize all main words in titles of works of literature, art, and music.

Punctuation

Quotation marks

In a quoted statement that is either declarative or imperative, place the period inside the closing quotation marks.

> *"The airplane crashed on the runway during takeoff."*

If other words in the sentence follow the quotation, place a comma inside the closing quotations marks and a period at the end of the sentence.

> *"The airplane crashed on the runway during takeoff," said the announcer.*

Usually, when a quoted title or expression occurs at the end of a sentence, the period is placed before the single or double quotation marks.

> *"The middle school readers were unprepared to understand Bryant's poem 'Thanatopsis.'"*
>
> *Early book-length adventure stories such as* **Don Quixote** *and* **The Three Musketeers** *were known as "picaresque novels."*

The final quotation mark precedes the period if the content of the sentence is about a speech or quote.

> *The first thing out of his mouth was "Hi, I'm home."*
>
> *–BUT–*
>
> *The first line of his speech began: "I arrived home to an empty house".*

In interrogatory or exclamatory sentences, the question mark or exclamation point should be positioned outside the closing quotation marks if the quote itself is a statement, command, or cited title.

> Who decided to lead us in the recitation of the "Pledge of Allegiance"?
>
> Why was Tillie shaking as she began her recitation, "Once upon a midnight dreary..."?
>
> I was embarrassed when Mrs. White said, "Your slip is showing"!

In declarative sentences, where the quotation is a question or an exclamation, place the question mark or exclamation point inside the quotation marks.

> The hall monitor yelled, "Fire! Fire!"
>
> "Fire! Fire!" yelled the hall monitor.
>
> Cory shrieked, "Is there a mouse in the room?" (In this instance, the question supersedes the exclamation.)

Quotations—whether words, phrases, or clauses—should be punctuated according to the rules of the grammatical function they serve in the sentence.

> The works of Shakespeare, "the Bard of Avon," have been contested as originating with other authors.
>
> "You'll get my money," the old man warned, "when 'hell freezes over'."
>
> Sheila cited the passage that began "Four score and seven years ago . . . ." (Note the ellipsis followed by an enclosed period.)
>
> "Old Ironsides" inspired the preservation of the U.S.S. Constitution.

Use quotation marks to enclose the titles of shorter works: songs, short poems, short stories, essays, and chapters of books. (See "Dashes and Italics" for rules on punctuating longer titles.)

> "The Tell-Tale Heart" "Casey at the Bat" "America the Beautiful"

Using Periods with Parentheses

Place the period inside the parentheses or brackets if they enclose a complete sentence that is independent of the other sentences around it.

> Stephen Crane was a confirmed alcohol and drug addict. (He admitted as much to other journalists in Cuba.)

If the parenthetical expression is a statement inserted within another statement, the period in the enclosure is omitted.

> *Mark Twain used the character Indian Joe (he also appeared in* **The Adventures of Tom Sawyer***) as a foil for Jim in* **The Adventures of Huckleberry Finn.**

Commas

Separate two or more coordinate adjectives that modify the same word and three or more nouns, phrases, or clauses in a list.

> *It was a dank, dark day.*
>
> *Maggie's hair was dull, dirty, and lice-ridden.*
>
> *Dickens portrayed the Artful Dodger as a skillful pickpocket, loyal follower of Fagin, and defender of Oliver Twist.*
>
> *Ellen daydreamed about getting out of the rain, taking a shower, and eating a hot dinner.*
>
> *In Elizabethan England, Ben Johnson wrote comedy, Christopher Marlowe wrote tragedies, and William Shakespeare composed both.*

Use commas to separate antithetical or complementary expressions from the rest of the sentence.

> *The veterinarian, not his assistant, would perform the delicate surgery.*
>
> *The more he knew about her, the less he wished he had known.*
>
> *Randy hopes to, and probably will, get an appointment to the Naval Academy.*
>
> *His thorough, though esoteric, scientific research could not easily be understood by high school students.*

Semicolons

Use semicolons to separate independent clauses when the second clause is introduced by a transitional adverb. (These clauses may also be written as separate sentences, preferably by placing the adverb within the second sentence.)

> *The Elizabethans modified the rhyme scheme of the sonnet; thus, it was called the English sonnet.*
>
> **or**
>
> *The Elizabethans modified the rhyme scheme of the sonnet. Thus, it was called the English sonnet.*

Use semicolons to separate items in a series that are long and complex or have internal punctuation.

> *The Italian Renaissance produced masters in the fine arts: Dante Alighieri, author of the* **Divine Comedy**; *Leonardo da Vinci, painter of* **The Last Supper**; *and Donatello, sculptor of the* **Quattro Coronati**, *the four saints.*

> *The leading scorers in the WNBA were Zheng Haixia, averaging 23.9 points per game; Lisa Leslie, 22; and Cynthia Cooper, 19.5.*

Colons

Place a colon at the beginning of a list of items. (Note its use in the sentence about Renaissance Italians in the previous section.)

> *The teacher directed us to compare Faulkner's three symbolic novels:* **Absalom, Absalom**; **As I Lay Dying**; *and* **Light in August**.

Do not use a colon if the list is preceded by a verb.

> *Three of Faulkner's symbolic novels are* **Absalom, Absalom**; **As I Lay Dying**; *and* **Light in August**.

Dashes and Italics

Place **EM DASHES** to denote sudden breaks in thought.

> *Some periods in literature—the Romantic Age, for example—spanned different periods in different countries.*

EM DASHES: used to denote sudden breaks in thought or if commas are already used in the sentence for amplification or explanation

Use dashes instead of commas if commas are already used elsewhere in the sentence for amplification or explanation.

> *The Fireside Poets included three Brahmans—James Russell Lowell, Henry David Wadsworth, and Oliver Wendell Holmes.*

Use **ITALICS** to punctuate the titles of long works of literature, names of periodical publications, musical scores, works of art, and motion picture, television, and radio programs. (If italic type is unavailable, students should be instructed to use underlining where italics would be appropriate.)

ITALICS: used to punctuate the titles of long works of literature, names of periodical publications, musical scores, works of art, and motion picture, television, and radio programs

The Idylls of the King	*Hiawatha*	*The Sound and the Fury*
Mary Poppins	*Newsweek*	*The Nutcracker Suite*

SKILL 3.6 Apply instructional methods for teaching writer's craft across genres (e.g., precise language, figurative language, linking words, temporal words, dialogue, sentence variety).

To get students started with writing, it is necessary to get them thinking about possible topics to write about. This can be done through:

- Brainstorming about people, places, and events
- Talking and listening to others
- Looking at pictures
- Listening to music
- Looking through books
- Making a list of ideas
- Looking through newspaper articles

After students have generated ideas for topics, teachers can discuss the possible audience who would read the writing. Teachers should help students consider the point of view they want to take, the purpose of the writing, and the format the writing will take. Ask students to consider whom they are writing for and whether they want to entertain, inform, describe, persuade, or inquire in their writing.

Outlines, webs, charts, and maps can help students organize the information they want to present. Examples of various types of writing should be available so that students are aware of the different stylistic options for the assignment. Some of these examples might include reports, journal entries, advertisements, book reviews, speeches, comic strips, directions, songs, and stories.

See also Skill 3.2

Ask students to consider who they are writing for and whether they want to entertain, inform, describe, persuade, or inquire in their writing.

Students need numerous opportunities to write for various purposes. Writing should be a daily activity in all classrooms.

SKILL 3.7 Identify and determine how text structure (e.g., compare/contrast, cause and effect, etc.) affects comprehension

The structure of different texts types can affect comprehension, especially when students are unfamiliar with them. Working with students to recognize the features of different texts can facilitate understanding and allow deeper analysis. It can also help students improve their writing, as they will be familiar with the way in which different text types make meaning. They can also incorporate stylistic choices and structural features into their own work.

For example, a typical compare and contrast essay follows one of two formats. It will often introduce a topic, compare similarities, contrast differences, and then draw a conclusion about the subject. Another common format goes step by step through the arguments for one of the items being compared and then methodically does the same with the other. When students are aware of the general structure of compare and contrast writing, they can more easily recognize arguments, locate evidence, and come to an opinion of their own.

Pursuing this analysis of different types of texts will support comprehension as texts become more complex. As students progress through different grade levels they will encounter increasingly difficult readings that are context-reduced. Knowing how texts are structured can help compensate.

Similarly, teaching students to recognize the language common to different text types will help them to more quickly understand what they are reading. Certain words can 'signal' the writer's intent. For example, words like 'however' or 'instead' indicate the writer's intent to show disagreement or a differing viewpoint. Words like 'therefore' or 'consequently' can indicate a cause-effect relationship.

KNOWLEDGE OF LITERACY INSTRUCTION AND ASSESSMENTS

COMPETENCY 4

KNOWLEDGE OF LITERACY INSTRUCTION AND ASSESSMENTS

SKILL 4.1	**Distinguish among different types of assessments** (e.g., norm-referenced, criterion-referenced, diagnostic, curriculum-based) **and their purposes and characteristics.**

Types of Assessment

The process of collecting, quantifying, and qualifying student performance data is called **ASSESSMENT**. A comprehensive assessment system must include a variety of assessment tools, such as norm-referenced, criterion-referenced, performance-based, or any student-generated alternative assessments that can measure learning outcomes and goals for student achievement and success in school communities.

> **ASSESSMENT:** the process of collecting, quantifying, and qualifying student performance data

There are four main types of assessment:

1. **Observation:** Noticing a student and judging his/her work habits, behavior, and work.

2. **Nonstructured informal continuous assessment:** Less structured assessment that occurs periodically, on a daily or weekly basis.

3. **Structured informal continuous assessment:** More structured assessment, which involves setting up assessment situations periodically. An assessment situation is an activity you organize so that the learners can be assessed. It could be a quiz. It could also be a group activity in which the participants are assessed.

4. **Formal assessment:** A structured, infrequent measure of learner achievement. It involves the use of tests and exams to measure the learners' progress.

The purpose of informal assessment is to help students learn more effectively. This form of assessment helps the teacher monitor student learning and progress. Informal assessment can be applied to homework assignments, field journals, and daily class work, which are good indicators of student progress and comprehension. The purpose of the assessment is to determine where the students need help or challenges and to set the tone for the instruction.

TEACHER CERTIFICATION STUDY GUIDE

Formal assessment, on the other hand, is highly structured, keeping the learner in mind. It must be done at regular intervals, and if the progress is not satisfactory, parent involvement is essential. A test or exam is a good example of formal assessment. A science project is also a formal assessment.

Formal assessments

Norm-referenced assessments

NORM-REFERENCED TESTS (NRTs) are used to classify student learners into a ranking category for homogenous groupings based on ability levels or basic skills. In many school communities, NRTs are used to classify students into Advanced Placement (AP), honors, regular, or remedial classes that can have a significant impact on their future educational opportunities or success. NRTs are also used by national testing companies such as the Iowa Test of Basic Skills (Riverside), the Florida Achievement Test (McGraw-Hill), and other major test publishers to test a national sample of students to use as a norm against standard test-takers. Stiggins (1994) states clearly that "Norm-referenced tests are designed to highlight achievement differences between and among students to produce a dependable rank order of students across a continuum of achievement from high achievers to low achievers."

Educators may select NRTs to focus on student learners with lower basic skills, which could limit the development of curriculum content that needs to provide students with the essential academic learning to accelerate student skills from basic to higher skill application in order to address the state assessments and core subject expectations. NRT ranking ranges from 1 to 99 with 25 percent of students scoring in the lower ranking of 1 to 25 and 25 percent of students scoring in the higher ranking of 76 to 99. Florida uses a variety of NRTs for student assessments that range from Iowa Basic Skills Testing to California Battery Achievement testing to measure student learning in reading and math.

Criterion-referenced assessments

CRITERION-REFERENCED ASSESSMENTS look at specific student learning goals and performance compared to a norm group of student learners. According to Bond (1996), "Educators or policy makers may choose to use a criterion-referenced test (CRT) when they wish to see how well students have learned the knowledge and skills which they are expected to have mastered." Many school districts and states use CRTs to ascertain whether schools are meeting national and state learning standards. The latest national educational mandate of "No Child Left Behind" (NCLB) and Adequate Yearly Progress (AYP) use CRTs to measure student learning, school performance, and school improvement goals as structured accountability expectations in school communities. CRTs are generally used in learning environments to reflect the effectiveness of curriculum implementation and learning outcomes.

Performance-based assessments

PERFORMANCE-BASED ASSESSMENTS are currently being used in a number of state testing programs to measure the learning outcomes of individual students in subject content areas. For example, Washington State uses performance-based assessments for the Washington Assessment of Student Learning (WASL) in reading, writing, math, and science to measure student-learning performance. Attaching a graduation requirement to passing the required state assessment for the class of 2008 has created high-stakes testing and educational accountability for both students and teachers in meeting the expected skill-based requirements for tenth-grade students taking the test.

In today's classrooms, performance-based assessments in core subject areas must have established specific performance criteria that start with pretesting in a subject area and maintain daily or weekly testing to gauge student learning goals and objectives. To understand a student's learning is to understand how a student processes information. Effective performance assessments show the gaps or holes in student learning, allowing the teacher to identify student needs and to focus on addressing nonsequential learning gaps.

Typical performance assessments include oral and written student work in the form of research papers, oral presentations, class projects, journals, student portfolio collections of work, and community service projects.

> **PERFORMANCE-BASED ASSESSMENTS:** tests that measure the learning outcomes of individual students in subject content areas

---

> **SKILL 4.2** Select and apply oral and written methods for assessing student progress *(e.g., informal reading inventories, fluency checks, rubrics, story retelling, portfolios).*

Evaluation of student progress has two primary purposes: *summative*, to measure student progress or achievement, and *formative*, to provide feedback to students to help them learn. The types of assessment discussed below represent many of the more common types, but the list is not comprehensive.

Anecdotal Records

These are notes recorded by the teacher concerning an area of interest in or concern about a particular student. These records should focus on observable behaviors and should be descriptive in nature. They should not include assumptions or speculations regarding effective areas such as motivation or interest. These records are usually compiled over a period of several days to several weeks.

Rating Scales and Checklists

These assessments are generally self-appraisal instruments completed by the students or observation-based instruments completed by the teacher. The focus of these is frequently on behavior or effective areas such as interest and motivation.

Informal Reading Inventories

The setting in which you administer the informal reading inventory (IRI) should be as quiet and isolated as possible. Speak in a relaxed tone and reassure the student that this is not for a "grade." An informal reading inventory can be used to estimate a student's reading level and also to assess a student's ability to use word identification strategies. Specifically, the IRI will help you assess a student's strengths and needs in these areas:

- Word recognition

- Word meaning

- Reading strategies

- Comprehension

The IRI can assist a teacher in determining reading fluency as well as strengths and weaknesses in the progress of reading comprehension. It may suggest directions for instruction or complete a profile of a student's reading ability. The inventory provides graded word lists and graded passages that assess oral reading, silent reading, and listening comprehension. Some IRIs provide narrative and expository passages with longer-passage options. After reading a passage, the student answers questions or retells the passage.

The IRI can assist a teacher in determining reading fluency as well as strengths and weaknesses in the progress of reading comprehension.

Fluency Checks

Fluency is a student's ability to read a text accurately and quickly. Students can make connections among the ideas in the text and their background knowledge. In other words, fluent readers are able to recognize words and comprehend at the same time. Fluent readers read aloud effortlessly and with expression. Readers who have not yet developed fluency read slowly, word by word. Their oral reading is choppy and plodding.

To complete a fluency check, teachers should have a student read independently during a teacher-student conference. The teacher will select a passage (100 words) from the student's independent reading book. The student will then read the passage while the teacher times her and takes a running record of the student's oral reading. The student will be assessed using the fluency standard expectations for that grade level. The number of words read correctly per minute is an indicator of a student's progress in all aspects of reading: decoding, fluency, and comprehension.

Minimum fluency rates

An expected quantitative level of 60 words per minute (wpm) for first grade and 90 wpm for second grade is to be met by the end of the year. The expected quantitative level of 110 wpm is required for the third grade and 118 wpm for the fourth grade. To put these rates into perspective, fluent adults read about 200 wpm during oral passage reading.

Think-Alouds

Poor readers are often delayed at the basic level of comprehension as they concentrate on decoding words and sentences. They often don't see how various parts of a whole text relate to each other and work together to create a larger meaning. Struggling readers often cannot draw on background knowledge or make predictions as they read. They frequently cannot visualize the events of a text as they are reading. These students often have trouble thinking about the text while they are reading it.

Think-alouds can be used to improve reading comprehension by getting students to reflect on the process of thinking aloud as they read. Teachers can encourage students to recognize the difference between reading the words and comprehending the text by implementing coached practice.

Have students read a short passage to you. Tell them to continually pause and ask themselves, "Does this make sense to me?" Remind them that you will be stopping occasionally to ask them what they are thinking about as they are reading. When students share their thoughts, and the connection to the text is not clear, encourage the students to explain themselves. If students are having trouble with this task, focus on a single strategy such as prediction.

Running Records

Running records permit teachers to determine students' reading strengths, weaknesses, readability levels, and fluency. A teacher can do a running record by asking a student to read a book he has never seen before or one that has been read only once or twice. This will often give a more accurate measure of a child's ability to handle text at the assessed level. The running record, for example, requires that each child read 100 words of text out loud to the teacher. The teacher notes the time it takes the child to read the passage and the accuracy with which the child reads the passage.

The teacher tallies the errors during the reading whenever a child does any of the following:

- Substitutes a word

- Omits a word

- Inserts an erroneous word

- Has to be told a word by the person administering the running record

Teachers can administer this type of assessment multiple times during the year to note progress in fluency as well as accuracy in reading.

Running records should be administered with greater frequency at the earlier stages of reading.

Story retelling

After the student has read the target book and the teacher has done a running record, have the child do an oral retelling of the story. Ask the student to close the book and then tell you about the story in as much detail as he can remember. If the child has difficulty retelling parts of the story or remembering certain details, the teacher can use prompts such as, "Tell me more about Character X" or "What happened after…?"

Retelling checklist

- Can the child tell you what happened in the story or what the factual book was about in his or her own words?

- Does the child include details about the characters in the retelling? Can she explain the relationships between the characters?

- Can the child describe the setting? How detailed is the description?

- Can the child recall the events of the story, and can she place them in the correct sequence?

Portfolio Assessment

The use of student portfolios for some aspects of assessment has become quite common. The purpose, nature, and policies of portfolio assessment vary greatly from one setting to another. In general, a student's portfolio contains samples of work collected over an extended period of time. The nature of the subject, age of the student, and scope of the portfolio all contribute to the specific mechanics of analyzing, synthesizing, and otherwise evaluating the portfolio's contents.

In most cases, the student and teacher make joint decisions regarding which work samples go into the student's portfolio. A collection of work compiled over an extended time period allows teacher, student, and parents to view the student's progress from a unique perspective. Qualitative changes over time can be readily apparent from work samples. Such changes are difficult to establish with strictly quantitative records like the scores recorded in the teacher's grade book.

Questioning

One of the most frequently used forms of assessment in the classroom is oral questioning by the teacher. As the teacher questions students, he can collect a considerable amount of information about how much students have learned and potential sources of confusion for students. While questioning is often viewed as a component of instructional methodology, it is also a powerful assessment tool.

Tests

Tests and similar direct-assessment methods are the most easily identified types of assessment. Thorndike (1997) identifies three types of assessment instruments:

1. Standardized achievement tests

2. Assessment material packaged with curricular materials

3. Teacher-made assessment instruments:
   - Pencil-and-paper tests
   - Oral tests
   - Product evaluations
   - Performance tests
   - Effective measures (p. 199)

Kellough and Roberts (1991) take a slightly different perspective. They describe "three avenues for assessing student achievement: a) what the learner says, b) what the learner does, and c) what the learner writes…" (p. 343).

Types of tests

Formal tests are tests that have been standardized on a large sample population. The process of standardization provides various comparative norms and scales for the assessment instrument. The term **informal test** includes all other tests. Most publisher-provided tests and teacher-made tests are informal tests by this definition. Note clearly that an "informal" test is not necessarily unimportant. A teacher-made final exam, for example, is informal by definition because it has not been standardized, but is a very important assessment tool.

> *Formal tests are tests that have been standardized on a large sample population. The process of standardization provides various comparative norms and scales for the assessment instrument.*

> **SKILL 4.3** Analyze assessment data *(e.g., screening, progress monitoring, diagnostic)* to guide instructional decisions and differentiate instruction.

Purposes of Assessment

There are a number of different classification systems used to identify the various purposes of assessment. A compilation of several lists identifies some common purposes:

1. Diagnostic assessments are used to determine individual weaknesses and strengths in specific areas

2. Readiness assessments measure prerequisite knowledge and skills

3. Interest and attitude assessments attempt to identify topics of high interest or areas in which students may need extra motivational activities

4. Evaluation assessments are generally program- or teacher-focused

5. Placement assessments are used for purposes of grouping students or determining appropriate beginning levels in leveled materials

6. Formative assessments provide ongoing feedback on student progress and the success of instructional methods and materials

7. Summative assessments define student accomplishments to determine the degree of student mastery or learning that has taken place

Key terms used in assessment

- **Formative:** Sets targets for student learning and creates an avenue to provide data on whether students are meeting the targets

- **Diagnostic:** Testing used to determine students' skill levels and current knowledge

- **Normative:** Establishes rankings and comparative levels of student performance against an established norm of achievement

- **Alternative:** Nontraditional method of helping students construct responses to problem solving

- **Authentic:** Real-life assessments that are relevant and meaningful in a student's life. (For example, calculating a 20 percent discount on an iPod, for a student learning math percentages, creates a more personalized approach to learning.)

- **Performance-based:** Judged according to preestablished standards

- **Traditional:** Diverse teacher assessments that either come with the textbooks or are directly created from the textbooks

Assessment skills should be an integral part of teacher training, so teachers are able to monitor student learning using pre- and post-assessments of content areas, to analyze assessment data in terms of individualized support for students and instructional practice for teachers, and to design lesson plans that have measurable outcomes and definitive learning standards.

For example, in an Algebra I class, teachers can use assessment to see whether students have learned the prior knowledge to engage in the subject area. If the teacher provides students with a pre-assessment on algebraic expression and ascertains that the lesson plan should be modified to include a pre-algebraic expression lesson unit to refresh student understanding of the content area, then the teacher can produce quantifiable data to support the need of additional resources to support student learning. Once the teacher has taught the unit on algebraic expression, a post-assessment test can be used to test student learning, and a mastery exam can be used to test how well students understand and can apply the knowledge to the next math unit.

Teachers can use assessment data to inform instructional practices by making inferences about teaching methods and gathering clues on student performance. By analyzing the various types of assessments, teachers can gather more definitive information on projected student academic performance. Instructional strategies for teachers would provide learning targets for student behavior, cognitive thinking skills, and processing skills that can be employed to diversify student learning opportunities.

> *Assessment information should be used to provide performance-based criteria and academic expectations for all students in evaluating whether students have learned the expected skills and content of the subject area.*

SKILL 4.4 Analyze and interpret students' formal and informal assessment results to inform students and stakeholders.

There are a number of reliable reading tests that can be administered to provide empirical data to let the teacher know where the students' reading skills lie. The school or the district can probably recommend some. Some of these can be given at the beginning of the school year and again at the end to help teachers assess the effectiveness of their instructional methods.

Assessment and evaluation should be ongoing in the reading classroom. When a teacher asks a student to retell a story, it is a form of assessment. After the child retells the story, the teacher can judge how accurate it is and give it a grade or score and make anecdotal comments in the course of listening to the child's retelling of the story.

> *Assessment and evaluation should be ongoing in the reading classroom.*

Informal assessment utilizes observations and other nonstandardized procedures to compile anecdotal and observational evidence of student progress and may include checklists, observations, and performance assessments and tasks. Formal assessment involves standardized tests and procedures that are carried out under prescribed conditions and includes state tests, standardized achievement tests, NAEP tests, etc.

Characteristics of Effective Assessment

Effective assessment should have the following characteristics:

- It should be an ongoing process with the teacher making some kind of informal or formal assessment almost every time the student speaks, listens, reads, writes, or views something in the classroom.

- The most effective assessment is integrated into the ongoing instruction and is not intrusive.

- Assessment should reflect the actual reading and writing experiences for which that classroom learning has prepared the student.

- Assessment needs to be a collaborative and reflective process. Teachers can learn from what the students reveal about their own individual assessments. Teachers should encourage students to continually and routinely ask themselves questions, thus assessing their own reading progress.

- High-quality valid assessment is multidimensional and may include samples of writing, student retellings, running records, anecdotal teacher observations, and self-evaluations. This not only enables the teacher to derive a consistent level of performance but also to design additional instruction that will enhance that level of performance.

- Assessment must take into account the student's age and cultural patterns of learning.

- The purpose of assessment is to teach students from their strengths, not their weaknesses. Teachers should determine which reading behaviors students demonstrate well and then design instruction to support those behaviors.

- Assessment should be part of children's learning process; it should not be done *on* them, but rather done *with* them.

Communicating with Students

How can a teacher provide good feedback so that students will learn from their assessments? First, language should be helpful and constructive. Critical language does not usually help students learn. Language that is constructive and helpful will guide students to specific actions and recommendations that will help them improve in the future.

Critical language does not usually help students learn.

When teachers provide timely feedback, they increase the chance that students will reflect on the thought processes they went through when they originally produced the work. When feedback comes weeks after the production of an assignment, the student may not remember what it is that caused him or her to respond in a particular way.

Specific feedback is particularly important. Comments like, "This should be clearer," and "Your grammar needs work" provide information that students may already know. Students can benefit from commentary that includes specific actions they can take to make something clearer or to improve their grammar.

When teachers provide feedback on a set of assignments, for example, they enhance their students' learning by teaching students how to use the feedback. Teachers can ask students to do additional things to work with their original products, or they can even ask students to take small sections and rewrite them based on the feedback. While written feedback will enhance student learning, having students do something with the feedback encourages even deeper learning and reflection.

Teachers can also show students how to use scoring guides and rubrics to evaluate their own work, particularly before they turn it in. One particularly effective way of doing this is to have students examine models and samples of proficient work. Teachers should collect samples of good work, remove names and other identifying factors, and show these to students so that they understand what is expected of them. Often, when teachers do this, they're surprised to see how much students gain in terms of their ability to assess their own performance.

> *Teachers should collect samples of good work, remove names and other identifying factors, and show these to students so that they understand what is expected of them.*

Finally, teachers can help students develop plans for revising and improving their work, even if the teacher does not evaluate it in the preliminary stages. For example, teachers can have students keep track of words they commonly misspell, or they can have students make personal lists of areas they feel they need to focus on.

Communicating with Parents

The major questions for parents in understanding student performance criterion-referenced data assessment are, "Are students learning?" and "How well are students learning?" Providing parents with data related to student achievement and performance is a quantifiable response to these questions. The National Study of School Evaluation (NSSE) 1997 research study, "School Improvement: Focusing on Student Performance," adds the following additional questions for parent focus on student learning outcomes:

- What are the types of assessments of student learning that are used in the school?

- What do the results of the data assessments indicate about the current levels of student learning performance? About future predictions? What were the learning objectives and goals?

- What are the strengths and limitations of student learning and achievement?

- How prepared are students for further education or promotion to the next level of education?

- What are the trends seen in student learning in various subject areas or overall academic learning?

Providing parents with opportunities to attend in-service workshops on data discussions with teachers and administrators allows parents to ask questions and become actively involved in monitoring their student's educational progress. With state assessments, parents should look for the words *passed* or *met/exceeded standards* in interpreting the numerical data on student reports. Parents who maintain an active involvement in their student's education will take advantage of opportunities provided by the school to promote their understanding of academic and educational achievement.

> **SKILL 4.5** Evaluate the appropriateness of assessment instruments and practices.

Curriculum Alignment

> **CURRICULUM ALIGNMENT:** the combination of curriculum, instruction, standards, and assessment practices

CURRICULUM ALIGNMENT is the combination of curriculum, instruction, standards, and assessment practices. The identification of assessments that are included in the curriculum alignment document should measure how the students' learning of the standards and the development of a plan measures the effectiveness of the curricular alignment system as it relates to the curricular area being studied. However, these separate components are prepared at the state, district, and school levels with various degrees of complexity. Because of these factors, gaps exist between what is outlined in the written curriculum, what gets taught, and what gets tested. States, districts, and schools have varied and distinct responsibilities.

The state department of education ensures that state tests are aligned with state standards and state curriculum frameworks. The district writes or adopts a curriculum that is aligned with state documents and supports teachers in delivering and monitoring implementation and results. The school provides teachers with opportunities for periodic review of curriculum documents, alignment of instructional strategies and classroom assessments in order to meet state standards and to plan relevant professional development.

Research has shown that improved student performance on standardized tests can result when teachers carefully align instruction with learning goals and assessments. For most teachers, assessment purposes vary according to the situation. It may be helpful to consult several sources to help formulate an overall assessment plan.

Purposes of Assessment

Kellough and Roberts (1991) identify six purposes of assessment:

1. To evaluate and improve student learning

2. To identify student strengths and weaknesses

3. To assess the effectiveness of a particular instructional strategy

4. To evaluate and improve program effectiveness

5. To evaluate and improve teacher effectiveness

6. To communicate to parents their children's progress

Bias

Bias exists in assessment when it is obvious that demographic variables account for score variation. For example, in a test question intended to assess a student's understanding of a science concept that has been taught in class, if the teacher uses an example that assumes all students have the same cultural background, this question would be assumed to be biased.

There are a few ways to systematically notice potential bias. First, when test questions are developed, they should focus on assessing discrete skills or areas of knowledge that have been taught. Test questions should be written simply, contain basic vocabulary, and should not include elements that pertain to any one culture or religion.

How can teachers eliminate bias in the assessments they create themselves? They can work to ensure that everything tested has been taught. Teachers should carefully examine their tests for material that students would have no way of knowing. They should also be sensitive to the things they take for granted. Something as simple as forgetting that different religions celebrate different holidays can lead to bias.

Teachers may notice that an entire demographic group has performed worse than other demographic groups on a particular question. This might be a clue to possible bias.

> SKILL 4.6 **Select appropriate classroom organizational formats** (e.g., literature circles, small groups, individuals, workshops, reading centers, multiage groups) **for specific instructional objectives.**

It used to be that when teachers would think about varying instruction, they would be thinking mainly about content. Methods of instruction were fairly constant. In older grade levels, lecture—and possibly some discussion—was the primary method of instructional delivery. In younger grades, independent work, as well as some group work, was standard fare for most instructional topics. Today, however, teachers know that for the enormous variety of content to be taught, there are multiple varieties of instructional methods they can use. A good way to think about the variety of instructional methods is to classify them into organizational formats. While there are literally hundreds of instructional ideas for just about any K-12 curricular topic, teachers can make the job easier by thinking of how organizational formats essentially organize their instructional ideas.

As the standard states, widely used organizational formats include literature circles, small groups, individual work, workshops, reading centers, and multiage groups. These formats are described in the table below. It is important to remember, however, that other ideas are possible; for example, whole-class drama. In whole-class drama, after reading a book or story, the entire class acts out various portions of the text.

CLASSROOM ORGANIZATIONAL FORMATS	
Literature Circles	Group activities in which each individual in the group has a particular "job." Jobs may include discussion leader, artist (for representing the discussion through art, perhaps), word leader (someone who looks up definitions and informs the group about specific vocabulary words), and many others. The point of these jobs is to keep a student-centered conversation of literature alive. These jobs assist the group in maintaining a conversation without teacher assistance.
Small-Group Activities	Activities that allow a few students to work together. While teachers circulate around the room and assist where necessary, small-group activities give students a chance to help each other and work together on a common problem. Often, small groups are beneficial because they can be prearranged by the teacher to serve various purposes. Sometimes teachers want to have homogeneous groups (groups of the same ability); other times, it is preferable to mix groups up so that highly skilled students can assist less-skilled students.
Individual Work	This format should not be ruled out, although there is a movement to get away from it. Individual work is beneficial when the teacher wants to ensure that all students get the practice they need to become proficient on their own in a certain area.

Continued on next page

CLASSROOM ORGANIZATIONAL FORMATS	
Workshops	Structures that allow students to work on different products simultaneously. Writing workshops are common in language arts classrooms. While there may be times when, for example, teachers want all students to work on the same writing assignment (which would be considered individual work), at other times teachers want students to have choices about what they write. In workshops, one student might be writing a short story while another student is writing an essay. Students can get feedback from one another in a workshop, and they can also get assistance from the teacher.
Reading Centers	Structured places in the room where, while the teacher is working with an individual or a small group, students can complete certain reading activities without teacher assistance. Usually, students spend a little time at each center and then rotate to the next center. Common centers include computer terminals (so students can use reading instruction software), student desks (so students can read silently), and reading activity tables (where students, in groups, can do a reading activity together).
Multiage Groups	These groups are coordinated among teachers. Sometimes it is preferable to have homogeneous groups on certain topics. Thus, a third-grade teacher might have some of his students go to the fourth-grade class if they read at a fourth-grade level, and the fourth-grade teacher would send his third-grade readers to the third-grade room. This allows teachers to work with students on their specific reading difficulties.

When classroom organizational concepts are considered, teachers are then free to expand their repertoires of classroom activities for the variety of content they teach.

SKILL 4.7 **Evaluate methods for the diagnosis, prevention, and intervention of common emergent literacy difficulties.**

Assessment of Oral Language Skills

Assessment information should be used to provide performance-based criteria and academic expectations for all students in evaluating whether students have learned the expected skills and content of the subject area. By analyzing the various types of assessments, teachers can gather more definitive information on projected student academic performance. Instructional strategies for teachers would provide learning targets for student behavior, cognitive thinking skills, and processing skills that can be employed to diversify student learning opportunities.

Assessment drives the instruction. Some of the methods teachers can employ to assess for learning involve both formative and summative evaluation. Formative assessment consists of testing; however, teachers can make summative assessment part of their daily routine by using such measures as:

- Anecdotal records
- Portfolios
- Checklists
- Running records

- Listening to children read
- Oral presentations
- Samples of work
- Self-evaluation

Informal assessment

For informal assessment, teachers can observe students during their everyday classroom activities. Teachers should make a point to evaluate a student multiple times at different times of the day and during different types of tasks. They can keep records, notes, or checklists of the child's oral skills. This type of assessment can include other students, for example, in cooperative learning environments. This type of assessment is often particularly authentic because the student will display typical oral skills while at ease. Students in higher grades can learn how to assess themselves using checklists, journals, portfolios, and other types of self-evaluation.

Formal assessment

Formal assessments take more planning. The teacher typically targets certain oral skills utilizing specific tasks and assessment methods. A formal assessment can be an oral interview that is recorded in some manner; picture-cued description/stories; oral prompts; text retelling; or role-playing. There are also formal assessment tests teachers can obtain to formally record a student's oral skill development.

Speech or Language Delays

Speech or language delays in children can be cause for concern or intervention Understanding the development of language in young children can provide information on delays or differences. Parents and teachers must understand the difference between developmental speech, word development, and language delays/differences that may prevent oral language acquisition. The ability to differentiate between the natural development of children's language patterns and the delayed development of those patterns should be the focus of the adult caregivers who provide the environmental stimulis and language experiences for children.

Age/language acquisition guidelines

- Children at the age of 2 should have speech patterns that are about 70 percent intelligible.

- Children at the age of 3 should have a speech pattern that is about 80 percent intelligible.

- Children at the age of 4 should have a speech pattern that is about 90 percent intelligible.

- Children at the age of 5 should have a speech pattern that is 100 percent intelligible.

- Children over the age of 5 will develop speech patterns that continue at 100 percent intelligibility with increased vocabulary.

Teachers and parents who have concerns about a child's language development should be proactive in addressing them. Early intervention is critical. Effective steps in addressing language delays or differences include: contacting a speech pathologist to evaluate a child's speech, allowing an auditory specialist to test for hearing disorders, consulting a pediatrician to test for motor-function delays, and allowing a pediatrician to test for motor-function delays, and utilizing other assessment resources for evaluation.

Stimulating Development of Children's Oral Language Skills

In order to stimulate the development of their oral language skills, children should be exposed to a challenging environment that is rich in opportunities. Teachers should remain focused on oral language skills throughout the day, even while teaching other subjects.

Activities that encourage development of oral language skills

- Encourage meaningful conversation
- Allow dramatic playtime
- Let children share personal stories
- Sing the alphabet song

- Teach the art of questioning
- Read rhyming books
- Play listening games
- Encourage sharing of information

If an educational program is child-centered, it will surely address the developmental abilities and needs of the students because it will take its cues from students' interests, concerns, and questions.

COMPETENCY 5
KNOWLEDGE OF COMMUNICATION AND MEDIA LITERACY

> **SKILL 5.1** **Identify characteristics of penmanship** *(e.g., legibility, letter formation, spacing).*

Penmanship refers to handwriting, which is printing the letters in the early grades. Students learn how to make letters individually, both upper- and lowercase letters, and gradually start putting them together to form words. This takes a lot of practice. Lined paper is essential and, for students in K–2, the paper should be double-lined so that students can make the lowercase letters between the middle and lower line and use the upper line for the uppercase letters.

As students progress with making the printed forms of the letters, they start cursive writing. The same process is used with practicing writing each letter and then learning how to join letters together. It is a slow process that often takes several years to master.

The important part of learning penmanship is to ensure that the writing is legible. As students start writing, they often make the letters very large and gradually learn how to decrease the size.

Posture is important in legible writing, as is the manner in which one holds the pencil or pen.

There are many different workbooks and worksheets that teachers can use to teach penmanship, with the proper format of each letter written on the top line. Students begin by tracing letters and, eventually, learn how to write letters and words on their own.

In perfect penmanship, the letters are slanted slightly to the right. However, many students write the letters straight up and down.

Posture is important in legible writing, as is the manner in which the student holds the pencil or pen. The body should be relaxed and the grip on the writing instrument should not be rigid. Sometimes writing that contains letters, such as *b* and *d*, that are not properly closed is hard to decipher. Students may need extra practice to learn how to make these letters properly.

The spacing between the handwritten words has an effect on legibility. One technique to use when teaching handwriting is to have students place a finger on the page after each word to show them that they must have a space between the words. After practicing this technique, students will start to use it automatically without having to use their finger as a guide for spacing.

Analyzing the speech of others is an excellent technique for helping students improve their public speaking abilities. In most circumstances, students cannot view themselves as they give speeches and presentations. When they get the opportunity to critique, question, and analyze others' speeches, they begin to learn what works and what doesn't work in effective public speaking. However, an important word of warning: Do not have students critique each other's public speaking skills. It could be very damaging to students to have their peers point out what did not work in a speech. Instead, use recorded examples. Any appropriate example of public speaking can be used in the classroom for students to analyze and critique.

Some of the things students should pay attention to include:

- **Volume:** Speakers should use an appropriate volume—not so loud as to be annoying, but not so soft as to be inaudible.

- **Pace:** The rate at which words are spoken should be appropriate—not so fast as to make the speech difficult to understand, and not so slow as to allow listeners' minds to wander.

- **Pronunciation:** A speaker should make sure words are spoken clearly. Listeners are not able to go back and reread things they didn't catch.

- **Body language:** While animated body language can help a speech, too much of it can be distracting. Body language should help convey the message, not detract from it.

- **Word choice:** The words speakers choose should be consistent with their intended purpose and the audience.

- **Visual aids:** Like body language, visual aids should enhance a message. Many visual aids can be distracting, and that detracts from the message.

Overall, instead of telling students to keep these factors in mind when presenting information orally, having them view speakers who do these things well and poorly will help them remember what to do the next time they give a speech.

PUBLIC SPEAKING STRATEGIES	
Voice	Many people fall into one of two traps when giving a speech: talking with a monotone voice or talking too quickly. These are both caused by anxiety. Monotone speech restricts natural inflection, but can be remedied by releasing tension in upper- and lower-body muscles. Talking too fast, on the other hand, is not necessarily a bad thing if the speaker is exceptionally articulate. If not, though, or if the speaker is talking about very technical things, it becomes easy for the audience to become lost. When you talk too fast and begin tripping over your words, consciously pause after every sentence you say. Don't be afraid of brief silences. The audience needs time to absorb what you are saying.
Volume	Problems with volume, whether too soft or too loud, can usually be overcome with practice. If you tend to speak too softly, have someone stand in the back of the room and give you a signal when the volume is strong enough. If possible, have someone in the front of the room as well to make sure you're not overcompensating with excessive volume. Conversely, if you have a problem with speaking too loudly, have the person in the front of the room signal to you when your voice is soft enough, and check with the person in the back to make sure it is still loud enough to be heard. In both cases, note your volume level for future reference. Don't be shy about asking your audience, "Can you hear me in the back?" Appropriate volume is beneficial for both you and the audience.
Pitch	Pitch refers to high or low tones. In oral performance, pitch reflects one's emotional arousal level. More variation in pitch typically corresponds to more emotional arousal, but can also be used to convey sarcasm or highlight specific words.
Posture	Maintain a straight, but not stiff, posture. Instead of shifting weight from hip to hip, point your feet directly at the audience, and distribute your weight evenly. Keep shoulders oriented toward the audience. If you have to turn your body to use a visual aid, turn 45 degrees, and continue speaking in the direction of the audience.
Movement	Instead of staying glued to one spot or pacing back and forth, stay within four to eight feet of the front row of your audience, and take a step or half-step to the side every once in a while. If you are using a lectern, feel free to move to the front or side of it to engage your audience more. Avoid distancing yourself from the audience; you want them to feel involved and connected.
Gestures	Gestures are a great way to keep a natural atmosphere when speaking publicly. Use them just as you would when speaking to a friend. They shouldn't be exaggerated, but they should be utilized for added emphasis. Avoid keeping your hands in your pockets or locked behind your back, wringing your hands, fidgeting nervously, or keeping your arms crossed.
Eye Contact	Many people are intimidated by eye contact when speaking to large groups. Interestingly, eye contact usually *helps* speakers overcome speech anxiety by connecting them with their attentive audience and easing feelings of isolation. Instead of looking at a spot on the back wall or at your notes, scan the room and make eye contact with various audience members for one to three seconds per person.

Organizing a Presentation

Class presentations are an opportunity for students to demonstrate their understanding of a topic and to explain it to an audience. Teachers can emphasize these main points for organizing a presentation:

- State your main point clearly

- Explain your main point

- Support your main point with evidence from credible sources

- Conclude and restate your main point

Audience Feedback

After a presentation, audience members are often allowed to give feedback to the presenter. Teachers should emphasize that while students are listening to feedback about their presentation, they should not be overly sensitive to their classmates' comments because other students may feel uncomfortable about giving feedback and may not phrase their comments properly.

Teacher Feedback

Teachers should instruct students about the distinction between criticism and feedback. Feedback describes what took place and what did not take place in terms of goals. Teachers should not offer feedback as critical examination, but should include a variety of comments. Feedback can be in the form of suggestions, questions, or in response to a student-generated form.

> Feedback describes what took place and what did not take place in terms of goals.

SKILL 5.3 **Identify and apply instructional methods** *(e.g., collaborative conversation, collaborative discussion, presentation)* **for developing listening and speaking skills.**

When complex or new information is provided to us orally, we must analyze and interpret that information. What is the author's most important point? How do figures of speech affect meaning? How are conclusions determined? Often, making sense of information can be difficult when it is presented orally—first, because we have no way to go back and review material already stated; second, because oral language is so much less predictable than written language. However, when we focus on extracting the meaning, message, and speaker's purpose, rather than just "listening" and waiting for things to make sense to us, then we have greater success in interpreting speech.

> When we are more active in our listening, then we have greater success in interpreting speech.

In the classrooms of exceptional teachers, students are captivated by the reading aloud of good literature. It is refreshing and enjoyable to just sit and soak in language, stories, and poetry being read aloud. Therefore, we must teach students how to listen and enjoy such work. We do this by making reading fun and providing many opportunities and alternatives to appeal to the wide array of interests in each classroom.

Large- and small-group conversation requires more than just listening; it involves feedback and active involvement. This can be particularly challenging because, in our culture, we are trained to move conversations along and to avoid silences in a conversation. This poses significant problems for the art of listening. In a discussion, for example, when we are preparing our next response instead of listening to what others are saying, we do a large disservice to the entire discussion. Students need to learn how listening carefully to others in discussions actually promotes better responses on the part of subsequent speakers. One way teachers can encourage this in both large- and small-group discussions is to expect students to respond directly to previous comments before moving ahead with their new comments. This will encourage them to add their new comments in light of the comments that came before their turn.

Listening to Messages

Speech can be difficult to follow. First, we have no written record by which to "reread" things we didn't hear or understand. Second, it can be much less structured and have far more variation in volume, tone, and rate than written language.

Speech can be difficult to follow. First, we have no written record by which to "reread" things we didn't hear or understand. Second, it can be much less structured and have far more variation in volume, tone, and rate than written language. Yet, aside from rereading, many of the skills and strategies that help us in reading comprehension can help us in listening comprehension. For example, as soon as we start listening to something new, we can tap into our prior knowledge in order to attach new information to what we already know. This not only helps us understand the new information more quickly, it also helps us remember the material.

We can also look for transitions between ideas. Sometimes, we can notice voice tone or body language changes. Of course, we don't have the luxury of looking at paragraphs in oral language, but we do have the animation that comes along with live speech. Human beings have to try very hard to be completely nonexpressive in their speech. Listeners should pay attention to the way speakers change character and voice in order to signal a transition of ideas.

Often, in speech, elements like irony are not indicated at all by the actual words, but rather through tone and nonverbal cues.

Listeners can also better comprehend the underlying intent of a speaker when they attend to the nonverbal cues of the speaker. The expression on a speaker's face can do more to communicate irony, for example, than the actual words.

One good way to follow speech is to take notes and outline major points. Because speech can be less linear than written text, notes and outlines can be of great assistance in keeping track of a speaker's message. Students can practice this strategy in the classroom by taking notes of their teachers' oral messages and of other students' presentations and speeches.

Other classroom methods can help students learn good listening skills. For example, teachers can have students practice following complex directions. They can also have students retell stories or retell oral presentations of stories or other materials. These activities give students direct practice with important listening skills.

Oral language (listening and speaking) involves receiving and understanding messages sent by other people and also expressing our own feelings and ideas. Students must learn that listening is a communication process and that they must be active participants in the process.

> *In active listening, students must determine and evaluate the meaning of a message before they can respond appropriately.*

Responding to Messages

The way students respond to messages is more than communication going from a student's mouth to a teacher's ear. In addition to the words, messages are transmitted by eye contact, physical closeness, tone of voice, visual cues, and overall body language. Speech employs gestures, visual clues, and vocal dynamics to convey information between teachers and students. Children first learn to respond to messages by listening to and understanding what they hear (supported by overall body language); next, they experiment with expressing themselves through speaking.

As children become proficient in language, they expect straight messages from teachers. A straight message is one in which words, vocal expression, and body movements are all congruent. Students need to feel secure and safe. If the message is not straight—if the words say one thing but the tone and facial expression say another—children get confused. When they are confused, they often feel threatened.

Remembering Message Content

Reading is more than pronouncing words correctly; readers have to gain meaning from the words. A competent reader can pronounce the words on a page, remember what the words mean, and learn from them.

Processes that enhance students' ability to remember include:

- **Association:** When you associate, you remember things by relating them to each other in some way.

- **Visualization:** Visualization helps you create a strong, vivid memory. Try to picture in your mind what you wish to remember.

- **Concentration:** Concentration can be defined as focusing attention on one thing only. When you read for a particular purpose, you will concentrate on what you read.

- **Repetition:** When you have difficulty remembering textbook information, you should repeat the procedures for association, visualization, and concentration. The repetition helps store the information in your memory.

SKILL 5.4 **Select and evaluate a wide array of resources** (e.g., Internet, printed material, artifacts, visual media, primary sources) **for research and presentation.**

Technology in the classroom is multifaceted. While one teacher might have students utilizing computers to do research and write reports, another, perhaps just next door, might use a computer for record keeping only. Technology offers schools and classrooms a wide range of uses. Some examples are:

- **Instructional support:** A variety of programs actually assist students in learning important skills. Some programs assist students with reading problems; others give students practice on math problems. Additionally, the Internet and various databases help students with research.

- **Word processing:** There are a number of programs that help students type, format, organize, and present written text.

- **Assessment:** Quizzes and progress-monitoring assessments can be done on the computer. For example, many reading programs include weekly tests that keep track of each student's progress.

- **Record keeping:** Teachers can use various programs to keep track of grades, student achievement, and other important student information. Record-keeping programs should be protected with passwords, as they often contain sensitive data.

Technology is increasingly important in schools today. Some of the most important tools include:

- **Computers:** Personal computing, word processing, research, and multimedia devices that utilize memory in order to save, transform, and process information. Unfortunately, many economically disadvantaged children throughout the country still do not have basic computing skills. Indeed, many teachers must be taught to utilize some of the more advanced computing skills that could help them with their daily work.

- **Internet:** Platform for the sharing and organization of information throughout the world. It began with simple telephone connectors between dozens of computers in the 1970s and 80s. In the 90s, it became a standard feature on virtually every computer. Essentially, the Internet allows people to view, post, and find any information that has been made available for public viewing. This is helpful when it comes to classroom research; however, there is a considerable amount of material that is both inappropriate for children and irrelevant to school. Care should be taken to filter out what is important for students and what is not.

- **Video projection:** Video in the classroom is a common tool to enhance student learning. Indeed, video has become a "text" in itself, much like literature. While the Internet has been a good source of information, video continues to be an excellent source of refined, carefully structured information for teachers and students. It can also be a creative way for students to express themselves through original productions.

> **SKILL 5.5** **Determine and apply the ethical process** *(e.g., citation, paraphrasing)* **for collecting and presenting authentic information while avoiding plagiarism.**

Collecting Information

Before teachers assign reports, they should spend time teaching students how to locate the information they need and assess whether or not it answers the questions they want to cover in their assignment.

Teachers should spend several periods teaching students how to take notes on the information they gather so they can separate relevant information from the irrelevant. This activity can start with note-taking from content-area textbooks. The students should take notes in their own words to make the material their own.

Students should be made aware at an early age that plagiarism is illegal.

Students must also learn how to determine whether or not the material they find is credible. This involves teaching the difference between primary and secondary sources.

For young students, collecting information can take the form of a simple worksheet in which they have to find answers to questions by using a specific text or web site. As they become used to this process in the early grades, they will be able to find the information on their own in the elementary years.

It is important to teach students how to determine whether the source of information they use is reliable. They need to know how to access the site in order to determine whether the information they find is the opinion of the writer or if it is based on fact.

Using a checklist

One of the ways to help students is to provide them with a checklist to use when gathering their information. This helps them identify specific questions they need to answer in their research and keywords they can use to help them find the information they need in their search.

Other aspects of this checklist can include:

- Identifying potential sources of information
- Planning how they will present the final product
- Determining the audience of the final product (this will affect the type of information and the method of presentation)
- Use of rubrics to understand how the final product will be assessed (students should have the rubric in advance to help them plan the presentation format and the type of information they will need)
- Analyzing the information with respect to its relevance to the topic
- Preparation of the report

Citing Sources

Citing the sources of information is an essential part of presenting credible and reliable information. Students should be taught how to prepare a bibliography and footnotes for their presentations.

SKILL 5.6 Identify and evaluate current technology for use in educational settings.

See Skill 5.4

DOMAIN II
SOCIAL SCIENCES

PERSONALIZED STUDY PLAN

PAGE	COMPETENCY AND SKILL	KNOWN MATERIAL/ SKIP IT
105	**6: Knowledge of effective instructional practices and assessment of the social sciences**	☐
	6.1: Select appropriate resources for instructional delivery of social science concepts, including complex informational text	☐
	6.2: Identify appropriate resources for planning for instruction of social science concepts	☐
	6.3: Choose appropriate methods for assessing social science concepts	☐
	6.4: Determine appropriate learning environments for social science lessons	☐
108	**7: Knowledge of time, continuity, and change (i.e., history)**	☐
	7.1: Identify and analyze historical events that are related by cause and effect	☐
	7.2: Analyze the sequential nature of historical events using timelines	☐
	7.3: Analyze examples of primary and secondary source documents for historical perspective	☐
	7.4: Analyze the impacts of the cultural contributions and technological developments of Africa; the Americas; Asia, including the Middle East; and Europe	☐
	7.5: Identify the significant historical leaders and events that have influenced Eastern and Western civilizations	☐
	7.6: Determine the causes and consequences of exploration, settlement, and growth on various cultures	☐
	7.7: Interpret the ways that individuals and events have influenced economic, social, and political institutions in the world, nation, or state	☐
	7.8: Analyze immigration and settlement patterns that have shaped the history of the United States	☐
	7.9: Identify how various cultures contributed to the unique social, cultural, economic, and political features of Florida	☐
	7.10: Identify the significant contributions of the early and classical civilizations	☐
139	**8: Knowledge of people, places, and environment (i.e., geography)**	☐
	8.1: Identify and apply the six essential elements of geography, including the specific terms for each element	☐
	8.2: Analyze and interpret maps and other graphic representations of physical and human systems	☐
	8.3: Identify and evaluate tools and technologies used to acquire, process, and report information from a spatial perspective	☐
	8.4: Interpret statistics that show how places differ in their human and physical characteristics	☐
	8.5: Analyze ways in which people adapt to an environment through the production and use of clothing, food, and shelter	☐
	8.6: Determine the ways tools and technological advances affect the environment	☐

PERSONALIZED STUDY PLAN

PAGE		COMPETENCY AND SKILL	KNOWN MATERIAL/ SKIP IT
	8.7:	Identify and analyze physical, cultural, economic, and political reasons for the movement of people in the world, nation, or state	☐
	8.8:	Evaluate the impact of transportation and communication networks on the economic development in different regions	☐
	8.9:	Compare and contrast major regions of the world, nation, or state	☐
154	9:	**Knowledge of government and the citizen (i.e., government and civics)**	☐
	9.1:	Distinguish between the structure, functions, and purposes of federal, state, and local government	☐
	9.2:	Compare and contrast the rights and responsibilities of a citizen in the world, nation, state, and community	☐
	9.3:	Identify and interpret major concepts of the U.S. Constitution and other historical documents	☐
	9.4:	Compare and contrast the ways the legislative, executive, and judicial branches share powers and responsibility	☐
	9.5:	Analyze the U.S. electoral system and the election process	☐
	9.6:	Identify and analyze the relationships between social, economic, and political rights and the historical documents that secure these rights in the United States	☐
	9.7:	Identify and analyze the processes of the U.S. legal system	☐
168	10:	**Knowledge of production, distribution, and consumption (i.e., economics)**	☐
	10.1:	Determine ways that scarcity affects the choices made by governments and individuals	
	10.2:	Compare and contrast the characteristics and importance of currency	☐
	10.3:	Identify and analyze the role of markets from production through distribution to consumption	☐
	10.4:	Identify and analyze factors to consider when making consumer decisions	☐
	10.5:	Analyze the economic interdependence between nations	☐
	10.6:	Identify human, natural, and capital resources and evaluate how these resources are used in the production of goods and services	☐

COMPETENCY 6

KNOWLEDGE OF EFFECTIVE INSTRUCTIONAL PRACTICES AND ASSESSMENT OF THE SOCIAL SCIENCES

> **SKILL 6.1** Select appropriate resources for instructional delivery of social science concepts, including complex informational text.

Teaching strategies useful for studying social structures in various industries and sectors include presenting an overview of the industry, explaining what that industry is about, and what its different components are, and examining the different groups that are involved in the industry or sector and how those groups interact.

For example, teachers can have students:

- Examine the labor movement as it occurred in these industries and look at the conflicts between labor and management

- Explore the reasons why these conflicts occurred and why union organization was required to solve the problems

- Explain how and why these groups interact differently in the presence of a union

- Examine the process and functions of the union, as well as the different parts of the collective bargaining agreement

- Evaluate the negotiation process and the different tactics that each side can employ

- Role-play the different steps in the process

- Study the effects industries and sectors have had on the population and on the economy

The teacher can have students analyze the role of communications and transportation (communications enhanced commerce, just as transportation did).

SKILL 6.2 Identify appropriate resources for planning for instruction of social science concepts.

Appropriate Resources

There are many resources available for teaching social science concepts. Materials should be developmentally appropriate, and you should use a variety of resources to meet the needs of all learners when teaching social science concepts.

A good textbook is helpful, and audiovisual aides are also beneficial in the classroom environment. Many people are visual learners and retain information more easily when it is in visual form. Audiovisual presentations, like short clips or movies, can give students concepts in pictures and motion that they will retain easily. The media center has an abundance of resources, including books and magazines, with which students should become familiar at an early age. Younger children, particularly, like to look at pictures.

Computers are invaluable as teaching tools and resources. The Internet and online applications and programs provide a wealth of information on all topics suitable for any age group. Presenting material in a game-like format also can be a good teaching tool. Making puzzles for vocabulary or letting students present information in the form of a story or a play helps them learn and retain concepts. Field trips, if possible, are a good way to expose children to various aspects of social science. Trips to museums, stock market exchanges, or the Federal Reserve are things students enjoy and remember.

SKILL 6.3 Choose appropriate methods for assessing social science concepts.

Assessment

Assessment is always important in teaching. Assessment basically means asking a question and receiving a response from the student, whether written or verbal. The test is the usual method in which students answer questions on the material they have studied. Tests can be written or oral. Tests for younger children can be game-like.

Students can be asked to draw lines connecting various associated symbols or to pick pictures that represent things like landmarks in various countries. Another assessment method is writing essays. Essays don't have to be long—just long enough for the students to demonstrate that they have adequate knowledge of a subject. Oral reports can accomplish the same goal. Younger children studying culture or geography, or even history, can role-play or act out various parts. They can even put on a play about events or aspects of culture or dress in ethnic costumes. This, along with facts about the culture of a country, is a more tangible experience than reading a textbook or taking a test and will help students remember material better. The experiences will be associated with the facts, and students will be better able to answer questions. They can be assessed based on their participation and knowledge of the subject. Assigning projects in which students obtain information about a subject and organize it into a written or oral report is another good way of reinforcing learning.

SKILL 6.4 Determine appropriate learning environments for social science lessons.

Appropriate Learning Environments

When instructing students in the area of social sciences, many lessons can be taught in the classroom setting. Depending on the objectives and overall goals, teachers may want to utilize other learning environments, including the media center, technology lab, or an outdoor setting.

For instance, when learning about Native Americans or other populations, the teacher may have the students create realistic models of homes using materials from the outdoors like twigs, rocks, and grass. Depending on the teaching strategies chosen, different environments will be more applicable for different lessons.

When teaching about the labor movement, for example, teachers can have students do the following, depending on available resources:

* Using online resources, examine the labor movement as it occurred in industries and look at the conflicts between labor and management

* Using an online learning application, explore the reasons why these conflicts occurred and why union organization was required to solve these problems

* Researching in the school media center to explain how and why these groups interact differently in the presence of a union

* Role-playing the steps in the unionization and collective bargaining process in the classroom, in the multipurpose room, or on stage

* Using tablets or laptops, study the effects unions in different industries and sectors have had on the population and on the economy

COMPETENCY 7
KNOWLEDGE OF TIME, CONTINUITY, AND CHANGE (I.E., HISTORY)

> **SKILL** Identify and analyze historical events that are related by cause and
> **7.1** effect.

HISTORIC CAUSATION:
the concept that events in history are linked to one another by an endless chain of cause and effect

HISTORIC CAUSATION is the concept that events in history are linked to one another by an endless chain of cause and effect. The root causes of major historical events cannot always be seen immediately and are only apparent when looking back from many years later.

When Columbus landed in the New World in 1492, the full effect of this event could not have been measured. By opening the Western Hemisphere to economic and political development by Europeans, he changed the face of the world. The native populations that existed before Columbus arrived were quickly decimated by disease and warfare. Over the following century, the Spanish conquered most of South and Central America, and English and French settlers arrived in North America, eventually displacing the native people. This gradual displacement took place over many years and could not have been foreseen by those early explorers. Looking back, it can be said that Columbus caused a series of events that had a great impact on world history.

In some cases, individual events can have an immediate, clear effect. In 1941, Europe was embroiled in war. On the Pacific Rim, Japan was engaged in military occupation of Korea and other Asian countries. The United States took a position of isolation, choosing not to become directly involved in the conflicts. This position changed rapidly, however, on the morning of December 7, 1941, when Japanese forces launched a surprise attack on the U.S. naval base at Pearl Harbor in Hawaii. The United States immediately declared war on Japan and became involved in Europe shortly afterwards. The entry of the United States into the Second World War undoubtedly contributed to the eventual victory of the Allied forces in Europe and the defeat of Japan after the U.S. dropped two atomic bombs there. The surprise attack on Pearl Harbor affected the outcome of the war and the shape of the modern world.

The surprise attack on Pearl Harbor affected the outcome of the war and the shape of the modern world.

Interactions between cultures, either by exploration, migration, or war, often contribute directly to major historical events, but other forces can influence the course of history as well. For example, the rise of Catholicism in the Middle Ages created social changes throughout Europe and culminated in the Crusades and the

110

expulsion of Muslims from Spain. Technological developments can lead to major historical events, as in the case of the Industrial Revolution, which was driven by the replacement of water power with steam power.

Social movements can also cause major historical shifts. Between the Civil War and the early 1960s, in the United States, racial segregation was practiced legally in many parts of the country through "Jim Crow" laws. Civil rights protests and demonstrations against segregation began to escalate during the late 1950s and early 1960s eventually leading to the passage in Congress of the Civil Rights Act of 1964, which ended legal segregation in the United States.

SKILL 7.2 Analyze the sequential nature of historical events using timelines.

Timelines

Timelines are a useful graphic tool that present information and dates in sequential order. Timelines can be vertical or horizontal and can span a small or large amount of time. Utilizing timelines while teaching historical events and developments can help students make sense of chronological happenings and outcomes.

SKILL 7.3 Analyze examples of primary and secondary source documents for historical perspective.

The resources used in the study of history can be divided into two major groups: primary sources and secondary sources.

Primary Sources

PRIMARY SOURCES are works, records, etc. that were created during the period being studied or immediately after it. SECONDARY SOURCES are works written significantly after the period being studied and are based on primary sources.

Primary sources include the following kinds of materials:

- Documents that reflect the immediate, everyday concerns of people: memoranda, bills, deeds, charters, newspaper reports, pamphlets, graffiti, popular writings, journals or diaries, records of decision-making bodies, letters, receipts, and snapshots.

PRIMARY SOURCES: works, records, etc. that were created during the period being studied or immediately after it

SECONDARY SOURCES: works written significantly after the period being studied and based on primary sources

- Theoretical writings, which reflect care and consideration in composition and an attempt to convince or persuade. The topic is generally deeper and more concerned with pervasive values than is the case with "immediate" documents. These may include newspaper or magazine editorials, sermons, political speeches, or philosophical writings.

- Narrative accounts of events, ideas, or trends, written with intentionality by someone contemporary with the events described.

- Statistical data, although statistics can be misleading.

- Literature—novels, stories, poetry, and essays from the period—as well as coins, archaeological artifacts, and art produced during the period.

Guidelines for use of primary sources

1. Be certain that you understand how language was used at the time of writing and that you understand the context in which it was produced.

2. Do not read history blindly; be certain that you understand both explicit and implicit references in the material.

3. Read the entire text you are reviewing; do not simply extract a few sentences to read.

4. Although anthologies of materials may help you identify primary source materials, the full original text should be consulted.

SKILL 7.4 Analyze the impacts of the cultural contributions and technological developments of Africa; the Americas; Asia, including the Middle East; and Europe.

Africa

African civilizations during the early centuries CE were few and far between. Muslim armies had conquered most of northern coastal Africa. The preponderance of deserts and other inhospitable lands restricted African settlements to a few select areas. The city of Zimbabwe became a trading center in south-central Africa in the fifth century, but didn't last long. More successful was Ghana, a Muslim-influenced kingdom that arose in the ninth century and lasted for nearly 300 years. Ghanaians had large farming areas and also raised cattle and elephants. They traded with people from Europe and the Middle East. Eventually overrunning Ghana was Mali, whose trade center, Timbuktu, survived its own empire's demise and blossomed into one of the world's greatest caravan destinations. Iron, tin, and leather came out of Mali. The succeeding civilization of the Songhai had relative success in maintaining the success of its predecessors. Religion in all of these settlements was Muslim; and even after extended contact with other cultures, there were few technological advancements.

Mesopotamia

The civilizations of the Sumerians, Amorites, Hittites, Assyrians, Chaldeans, and Persians controlled various areas of the land we call Mesopotamia. With few exceptions, monarchs and military leaders controlled most aspects of society, including trade, religions, and the laws. Each Sumerian city-state had its own patron deity. Subsequent cultures had multiple gods as well, although they had more of a national worship structure, with high priests centered in the capital city as advisers to the ruling class.

Trade was extremely important to these early civilizations. Some trading agreements led to occupation, as was the case with the Sumerians. Egypt and Phoenicia were powerful and regular trading partners of the various Mesopotamian cultures.

Legacies handed down to us from these civilizations include:

- The first use of writing, the wheel, and banking (Sumerian)

- The first written set of laws (Code of Hammurabi)

- The first epic story (Gilgamesh)

- The first library dedicated to preserving knowledge (instituted by the Assyrian ring Ashurbanipal)

The ancient civilization of the Sumerians invented the wheel; developed irrigation through use of canals, dikes, and devices for raising water; devised the system of cuneiform writing; learned to divide time; and built large boats for trade. The Babylonians devised the famous Code of Hammurabi, a code of laws.

The ancient Assyrians were warlike and aggressive due to a highly organized military and that horse-drawn chariots.

Egypt

Egypt made numerous significant contributions, including construction of the great pyramids, development of hieroglyphic writing, preservation of bodies after death, creation of paper from papyrus, developments in arithmetic and geometry, invention of the method of counting in groups of 1-10 (the decimal system), completion of a solar calendar, and laying the foundation for science and astronomy.

The earliest historical record of the **Kush** civilization is in Egyptian sources, which describe a region upstream from the first cataract of the Nile as "wretched." This civilization was characterized by a settled way of life in fortified mud-brick villages. They subsisted on hunting and fishing, herding cattle, and gathering grain. Skeletal remains suggest that the people were a blend of Negroid and Mediterranean peoples. This civilization appears to be the second oldest in Africa (after Egypt).

> **MONOTHEISM:** the worship of one God

The **ancient Israelites** instituted MONOTHEISM, which is the worship of one God—in this case Yahweh—and wrote and compiled the books of the Hebrew Bible, or Old Testament.

The **Minoans** had a system of writing using symbols to represent syllables in words. They built palaces with multiple levels containing many rooms, water, and sewage systems with flush toilets, bathtubs, hot and cold running water, and bright paintings on the walls.

The **Mycenaeans** changed the Minoan writing system to aid their own language and used symbols to represent syllables.

The **Phoenicians** were sea traders, well known for their manufacturing skills in glass and metals and the development of their famous purple dye. They became so proficient in the skill of navigation that they were able to sail by the stars at night. Further, they devised an alphabet using symbols to represent single sounds, which was an improvement over earlier symbolic and syllabic writing systems.

India

In **India**, the caste system was developed, the principle of zero in mathematics was discovered, and the major religion of Hinduism was begun. Hinduism was a continuing influence along with the rise of Buddhism. Industry and commerce developed along with extensive trading with the Near East. Outstanding advances in the fields of science and medicine were made, and India was one of the first civilizations to be active in navigation and maritime enterprises during this time.

China

China is considered by some historians to be the oldest uninterrupted civilization in the world and was in existence around the same time as the ancient civilizations founded in Egypt, Mesopotamia, and the Indus Valley. The Chinese studied nature and weather; stressed the importance of education, family, and a strong central government; followed the religions of Buddhism, Confucianism, and

Taoism; and invented such things as gunpowder, paper, printing, and the magnetic compass. China began building the Great Wall; practiced crop rotation and terrace farming; increased the importance of the silk industry; and developed caravan routes across Central Asia for extensive trade. The Chinese also increased proficiency in rice cultivation and developed a written language based on drawings or pictographs.

Persia

The ancient Persians developed an alphabet; contributed the religions/philosophies of Zoroastrianism, Mithraism, and gnosticism; and allowed conquered peoples to retain their own customs, laws, and religions.

Greece

The classical civilization of Greece reached the highest levels in man's achievements based on the foundations already laid by such ancient groups as the Egyptians, Phoenicians, Minoans, and Mycenaeans.

Among the more important contributions of Greece were the Greek alphabet, derived from the Phoenician letters, which formed the basis for the Roman alphabet and our present-day alphabet. Extensive trading and colonization resulted in the spread of the Greek civilization. The love of sports, with emphasis on a sound body, led to the tradition of the Olympic Games. Greece was responsible for the rise of independent, strong city-states. Other important contributions of classical Greece include drama, epic and lyric poetry, fables, myths, science, astronomy, medicine, mathematics, philosophy, art, architecture, and recording historical events. The conquests of Alexander the Great spread Greek ideas to the areas he conquered and brought many ideas from Asia to Greece, including the value of ideas, curiosity, and the desire to learn as much about the world as possible.

Rome

The ancient civilization of Rome lasted approximately a thousand years, including the periods of republic and empire, although its influence on Europe and its history was felt for much longer. The Romans spread and preserved the ideas of ancient Greece and other cultures. The contributions and accomplishments of the Romans are numerous, but the greatest included language, engineering, building, law, government, roads, trade, and the Pax Romana. Pax Romana was a long period of peace, which enabled free travel and trade and spread people, cultures, goods, and ideas over a vast area of the known world.

The ancient civilization of Rome lasted approximately a thousand years

Japan

The civilization in Japan appeared during the same time as that of Rome, having borrowed much of its culture from China. It was the last of these classical civilizations to develop. Although they used, accepted, and copied Chinese art, law, architecture, dress, and writing, the Japanese refined these into their own unique way of life, incorporating the religion of Buddhism into their culture. Early Japanese society focused on the emperor and the farm, in that order. The Sea of Japan protected the country from invasion, including the famous Mongol invasion that was blown back by the "divine wind." The power of the emperor declined as it was usurped during the era of the Daimyo and his loyal soldiers, the Samurai. Japan flourished economically and culturally during many of these years, although the policy of isolation the country developed kept the rest of the world from knowing it. It wasn't until the mid-nineteenth century that Japan joined the world community.

The Americas

The people who lived in the Americas before Columbus arrived had a thriving, connected society. The civilizations in North America were spread out and were in occasional conflict but maintained their sovereignty for the most part. The South American civilizations, however, tended to shape themselves into empires, with the strongest city or tribe assuming control of the lives and resources of the rest of the nearby peoples. One of the best known North American tribes was the Pueblo, who lived in what is now the American Southwest. The Pueblo are perhaps best known for the challenging vista-based villages that they constructed on the sheer faces of cliffs and rocks and for their adobe, or mud-brick, buildings that served as their living and meeting quarters.

Known for their organized government, the Iroquois lived in the American Northeast. The famous five nations of the Iroquois made treaties among themselves and shared leadership of their peoples.

South and Central America

Much is known about the empires of South and Central America: the Aztec, the Inca, and the Maya. The Aztecs dominated Mexico and Central America. They weren't the only people living in these areas, just the most powerful ones. The Aztecs had many enemies, some of whom helped Hernan Cortes precipitate the downfall of the Aztec society. The Aztecs had access to great quantities of metals and jewels, and they used the metals to make weapons and the jewels to trade for items they didn't possess. The Aztecs also conquered neighboring tribes and demanded tribute from them; this was the source of much of the Aztec riches.

The Inca Empire stretched across a vast territory down the western coast of South America. The Inca Empire, like the Aztec Empire, was a centralized state, with all income going to the state coffers and all trade going through the emperor. The Incas worshiped the dead, their ancestors, and nature, and often took part in elaborate rituals.

The most advanced Native American civilization was the Maya, who lived primarily in Central America. They were the only Native American civilization to develop writing, which consisted of a series of symbols that has only been partially deciphered. The Maya also built huge pyramids and other stone figures and sculptures, most of which were in honor of the gods they worshiped. The Maya are most famous, however, for their calendars and their mathematics (they were the first to come up with the idea of zero. The Mayan calendars were the most accurate available until the sixteenth century.

See also Skill 7.5

> The Incas are known for inventing the quipu, a string-based device that provided them with a method of keeping records.

SKILL 7.5 Identify the significant historical leaders and events that have influenced Eastern and Western civilizations.

India

India suffered from the invasion of Alexander the Great and had to spend time recovering. One strong man who met the great Alexander was Chandragupta Maurya, who began one of his country's most successful dynasties. Chandragupta conquered most of what we now call India. His grandson, Asoka, was a more peaceful ruler but powerful nonetheless. He was also a great believer in the practices and power of Buddhism, sending missionaries throughout Asia. Succeeding the Mauryas were the Guptas, who ruled India for a longer period of time and brought prosperity and international recognition to their people.

The Guptas were great believers in science and mathematics, especially their uses in the production of goods. They invented the decimal system and had a concept of zero, two things that distinguished them from other civilizations of the time. They were the first to make cotton and calico, and their medical practices were much more advanced than those in Europe and elsewhere in Asia at the time. These inventions and innovations created a high demand for Indian goods throughout Asia and Europe.

> The Guptas were great believers in science and mathematics, especially their uses in the production of goods.

The idea of a united India continued after the Gupta dynasty ended. It was especially favorable to the invading Muslims, who took over in the eleventh century, ruling the country for hundreds of years through a series of sultanates. Timur (often known as **Tamerlane** in English) founded an empire that extended from the edges of Europe through Central Asia. In 1398 he led the capture of Delhi, bringing Muslim rule to what is now India. Two of Timur's most famous descendants included Babur, who founded the Mughal Empire, and Akbar the Great (1542-1605). **Akbar** was the third ruler of the Mughal Empire and helped to consolidate Muslim control over the Indian subcontinent. Akbar believed in freedom of religion and is perhaps most well known for the series of buildings that he had built, including mosques, palaces, forts, and tombs, some of which are still standing today. During the years that Muslims ruled India, Hinduism continued to be respected, although it was a minority religion; Buddhism, however, died out almost entirely from the country that begot its founder.

China

The story of China during this time is one of dynasties controlling various parts of what is now China and Tibet. The Tang dynasty was one of the most long-lasting and proficient dynasties, inventing the idea of civil service and the practice of block printing. The Sung dynasty came next, producing some of the world's greatest paintings and porcelain pottery, but failing to unify China in a meaningful way. This would prove instrumental in the takeover of China by the Mongols, led by Genghis Khan and his most famous grandson, Kublai.

Genghis Khan was known as a conqueror and **Kublai Khan** was known as a uniter. They both extended the borders of their empire, however, and, at its height, the Mongol Empire was the largest the world has ever seen, encompassing all of China, Russia, Persia, and central Asia. Following the Mongols were the Ming and Manchu dynasties, both of which focused on isolation. As a result, China at the end of the eighteenth century knew very little of the outside world, and vice versa. Ming artists created beautiful porcelain pottery, but not much of it saw its way into the outside world until much later. The **Manchus** were known for their focus on farming and road building, which were initiated to keep up with the country's expanding population. Confucianism, Taoism, and ancestor worship—the staples of Chinese society for hundreds of years—continued to flourish during this time.

The Scientific Revolution

A Polish astronomer, **Nicolaus Copernicus**, began the Scientific Revolution. He crystallized a lifetime of observations into a book that was published about the time of his death. Copernicus argued that the Sun, not the Earth, was the center of a solar system and that other planets revolved around the Sun. This flew in the face of established Church-mandated doctrine. The Church still wielded tremendous power at this time, including the power to banish people or sentence them to prison or even death.

The Danish astronomer **Tycho Brahe** was the first to catalog his observations of the night sky. Building on Brahe's data, German scientist Johannes Kepler developed his theory of planetary movement, embodied in his famous laws of planetary motion. Using Brahe's data, Kepler also confirmed Copernicus's observations and argument that the Earth revolved around the Sun.

The most famous defender of this idea was **Galileo Galilei**, an Italian scientist who conducted many famous experiments in the pursuit of science. He is most well known, however, for his defense of the heliocentric (Sun-centered) idea. He wrote a book comparing the two theories, but most readers could tell easily that he favored the new one. He was convinced of this mainly because of what he had seen with his own eyes. He had used the relatively new invention of the telescope to see four moons of Jupiter. They certainly did not revolve around the Earth, so why should everything else? His ideas were not favored by the Church, which was still powerful enough at this time, especially in Italy, to order Galileo to be placed under house arrest.

Galileo died under house arrest, but his ideas didn't die with him. Picking up the baton was an English scientist named **Isaac Newton**, who became perhaps the most famous scientist of all. He is known as the discoverer of gravity and a pioneering voice in the study of optics (light), calculus, and physics. More than any other scientist, Newton argued for, and proved, the idea of a mechanistic view of the world: You can see and prove how the world works through observation. Until this time, people held on to traditional beliefs that were endorsed by the Church. Newton, following in the footsteps of Copernicus and Galileo, changed this.

The Enlightenment

This change led to the **Enlightenment**, a period of intense self-study that focused on ethics and logic. More so than at any time before, scientists and philosophers questioned cherished truths and widely held beliefs in an attempt to discover why the world worked—from within. "I think, therefore I am" was one of the famous sayings of the day. René Descartes, who uttered this statement, was a French scientist-philosopher whose dedication to logic and the rigid rules of observation was a blueprint for the thinkers who came after him.

One of the giants of the era was England's **David Hume**, a pioneer of the doctrine of empiricism (believing things only when you've seen the proof for yourself). Perhaps the most famous Enlightenment thinker is **Immanuel Kant** of Germany. Both a philosopher and a scientist, he took a decidedly scientific view of the world. He wrote the movement's most famous essay, "Answering the Question: What Is Enlightenment?" and answered his famous question with the motto "Dare to know." For Kant, the human being was a rational being capable of extremely creative thought and intense self-evaluation. He encouraged people to examine themselves and the world around them. He believed that the source of morality lay not in nature or in the grace of God, but in the human soul itself. He believed that men and women believed in God for practical, not religious or mystical, reasons.

Also prevalent during the Enlightenment was the idea of the "social contract," the belief that people had an agreement with the government and would submit to it as long as it protected them and didn't encroach on their basic human rights. This idea was first made famous by the Frenchman **Jean-Jacques Rousseau**, but was also adopted by England's **John Locke** and by **Thomas Jefferson** in the United States. John Locke was one of the most influential political writers of the seventeenth century. He put great emphasis on human rights and espoused the belief that when governments violate those rights people should rebel. He wrote the book *Two Treatises of Government* in 1690, which had tremendous influence on political thought in the American colonies and helped to shape the U.S. Constitution and Declaration of Independence.

Louis XIV in France

Louis XIV created a centralized government that he
ruled with absolute power.
He is often considered "the
archetype of an absolute
monarch."

Known as the Sun King, Louis XIV acceded to the throne in France shortly before his fifth birthday in 1661. During his reign, France attained cultural dominance as well as military and political superiority. Louis XIV created a centralized government that he ruled with absolute power. He is often considered "the archetype of an absolute monarch." He is quoted as claiming, "I am the State." However, many scholars believe political opponents falsely attributed this statement to him. It does, however, summarize the absolute power he held.

Louis XIV and his advisors moved France to economic strength and political power and influence in Europe. But the claim of absolute power by divine right, combined with his distrust of others, led to unique actions to maintain power and to control any who might instigate rebellion against him. One of his tactics to control the nobility was to require them to remain at the Palace of Versailles, where he could watch them and prevent them from plotting unrest in their communities. He spent lavishly on parties and distractions to keep the nobility occupied and to strengthen his control over them. He was determined to under-cut the power and influence of the nobility.

Louis also tried to control the Church. He called an assembly of the clergy in 1681. By the time the assembly ended, he had won acceptance of the "Declaration of the Clergy of France," by which the pope's power was greatly reduced and his power was greatly enhanced. The pope never accepted this declaration.

Perhaps the greatest mistake of Louis's reign was his attitude toward Protestantism and his handling of the Huguenots. In 1685, he revoked the Edict of Nantes, which resulted in the departure from the country of these French Protestants, who were among the wealthiest and most industrious people in the nation. He also alienated the Protestant countries of Europe, particularly England.

Catherine the Great in Russia

Catherine the Great (Catherine II) has often been called the "enlightened despot." She came to power in Russia through a coup that removed her husband (Peter III) from the throne and had herself proclaimed empress with the help of the military and other politically powerful individuals with whom she had cultivated relationships.

Catherine revised Russian law in an effort to make it more logical and more humane. She built many hospitals and orphanages, encouraged the people to be inoculated against smallpox, and wanted to establish schools throughout the nation to teach the people the responsibilities of citizenship. Despite her sympathy for the peasants, she did nothing to free them from serfdom. She never forgot that she ruled an empire of "barbarous peoples." In fact, to maintain control of the nobility, she made large land grants, which increased serfdom. She divided Russia into fifty provinces. She claimed to want each district to control its own local affairs, yet she empowered the governors she appointed. The end result was broader despotism rather than enlightenment.

> **SKILL 7.6** Determine the causes and consequences of exploration, settlement, and growth on various cultures.

Early Exploration and Settlement

Columbus's first trans-atlantic voyage was undertaken to try to prove his theory that Asia could be reached by sailing west. Long after Spain dispatched explorers and famed conquistadors to gather the wealth for the Spanish monarchs and their coffers, the British were searching valiantly for the Northwest Passage, a land-sea route across North America and the eventual open sea to the wealth of Asia. It was the Lewis and Clark expedition that proved conclusively that a Northwest Passage did not exist.

Spain, France, and England, with some participation by the Dutch, led the way in expanding Western European civilization in the New World. These three nations had strong monarchial governments and were struggling for dominance and power in Europe. With the defeat of Spain's mighty armada in 1588, England became the undisputed mistress of the seas. France and England carried on the rivalry, leading to eventual British control in Asia as well.

Spain's influence in the New World was in Florida, the Gulf Coast, from Texas to California, and south to the tip of South America, and included some of the islands of the West Indies. French control centered in New Orleans and reached north to what is now northern Canada. England settled the eastern seaboard of North America, including parts of Canada and the territory from Maine to Georgia.

Spanish settlement began in the Caribbean, with the establishment of colonies on Hispaniola, Puerto Rico, and Cuba. There were a number of reasons for Spanish involvement in the Americas, which included: the spirit of adventure; the desire for land; expansion of Spanish power, influence, and empire; the desire for great wealth; the expansion of Roman Catholic influence; and the conversion of native peoples.

The Native Americans who came in contact with the Spaniards were introduced to animals, plants, and seeds from the Old World that they had never seen before.

The first permanent settlement in what is now the United States was in 1565 at St. Augustine, Florida. At the peak of Spanish power, the area in the United States claimed, settled, and controlled by Spain included Florida and all land west of the Mississippi River. France and England also laid claim to the same areas. Ranches and missions were built.

Spain's control over New World colonies lasted more than three hundred years, longer than that of England or France. The Spanish settlements in North America were not commercial enterprises, but were for protection and defense of the trading and wealth from their colonies in Mexico and South America. Russians hunting seals came down the Pacific coast, English settlers moved into Florida and west into and beyond the Appalachians, and French traders and trappers made their way from Louisiana and other parts of New France into the Spanish territory. The Spanish never realized or understood that self-sustaining economic development and colonial trade were so important. Consequently, the Spanish settlements in the United States never really prospered.

The Dutch West India Company founded a colony in what was then called New Amsterdam. It was eventually captured by English settlers and renamed New York, but many of the Dutch families that had been granted large segments of land by the Dutch government were allowed to keep their estates. As hostility built between England and the colonies over the taxation of tea, colonists turned to the Dutch to supply them with this important import.

The part of North America claimed by France was called New France and consisted of the land west of the Appalachian Mountains. This area of claims and settlement included the St. Lawrence valley, the Great Lakes, the Mississippi valley and all of the land westward to the Rocky Mountains. The French established the permanent settlements of Montreal and New Orleans, thus giving them control over these two major gateways into the heart of North America.

The English colonies, with only a few exceptions, were considered commercial ventures to make a profit for the crown, the company, or whoever financed their beginnings. Settlers in these unique colonies came for various reasons, including religious freedom, political freedom, economic prosperity, and land ownership.

Colonists from England, France, Holland, Sweden and Spain all settled in North America on lands once frequented by Native Americans. Spanish colonies were mainly in the south; French colonies were mainly in the extreme north and in the middle of the continent; and the rest of the European colonies were in the northeast and along the Atlantic coast. These colonists got along with the Native Americans with varying degrees of success.

New England colonies

The **New England colonies** consisted of Massachusetts, Rhode Island, Connecticut, and New Hampshire. Life in these colonies was centered on the towns. What farming was done was completed by each family on their own plot of land, but a short summer growing season and a limited amount of good soil gave rise to other economic activities such as manufacturing, fishing, shipbuilding, and trade.

The vast majority of the settlers shared similar origins, coming from England and Scotland. Towns were carefully planned and laid out the same way. The form of government used by these settlers was the town meeting, in which all adult males participated in making laws. The legislative body and the general court consisted of an upper and lower house.

Middle Atlantic colonies

The **Middle or Middle Atlantic colonies** included New York, New Jersey, Pennsylvania, Delaware, and Maryland. These five colonies from their beginnings were considered "melting pots," with settlers from many different nations and backgrounds. The main economic activity was farming, with the settlers scattered over the countryside cultivating rather large farms. Native Americans were not as much of a threat here as they were in New England, so the colonists did not have to settle in small farming villages. The soil was very fertile, the land was gently rolling, and a milder climate provided a longer growing season. These farms produced a large surplus of food, not only for the colonists themselves but also for sale. The New York and Philadelphia seaports were constantly filled with ships being loaded with meat, flour, and other foodstuffs for export to the West Indies and England.

There were other economic activities such as shipbuilding, iron mines, and factories producing paper, glass, and textiles. The legislative body in Pennsylvania was unicameral, or consisted of one house. In the other four colonies, the legislative body had two houses.

Southern colonies

The **Southern colonies** were Virginia, North and South Carolina, and Georgia. Virginia was the first permanent successful English colony and Georgia was the last. The year 1619 was a very important year in the history of Virginia and the United States, featuring three very significant events. First, sixty women were sent to Virginia to marry and establish families. Second, twenty Africans, the first of thousands, arrived. Third, and most important, the Virginia colonists were granted the right to self-govern and began electing their own representatives to the House of Burgesses, which was their own legislative body.

Seven Years' War

The conflict that decided once and for all which nation was the most powerful in Europe began in North America in 1754 in the Ohio River valley. It was known in America as the French and Indian War. In Europe it was known as the **Seven Years' War** because it began there in 1756. The British colonies were well established and consolidated in a smaller area. British colonists outnumbered French colonists 23 to 1. Except for a small area in Canada, French settlements were scattered over a much larger area (roughly half of the continent) and were smaller. However, the French settlements were united under one government and were quick to act and cooperate when necessary. Additionally, the French had many more Native American allies than the British. Each of the British colonies had its own government; these governments seldom cooperated even when it was in their mutual interest to do so. In Europe, at that time, France was the more powerful of the two nations.

In Paris in 1763, Spain, France, and Britain met to draw up the **Treaty of Paris.** Under this treaty, Great Britain received most of India and all of North America east of the Mississippi River. Britain also gained control of Florida from Spain and returned Cuba and the islands of the Philippines, taken during the war, to Spain. France lost nearly all of its possessions in America, except for the islands of St. Pierre and Miquelon off the east coast of what is now Canada. France was allowed to keep four islands: Guadeloupe, Martinique, and Haiti on Hispaniola. France gave New Orleans and the vast territory of Louisiana, west of the Mississippi River, to Spain. Britain was now the most powerful nation without question.

Where did all of this leave the British colonies? Their colonial militias had fought with the British, and they, too, benefited. The militias and their officers gained much experience in fighting, experience which would later prove to be invaluable. The thirteen colonies began to realize that cooperating with each other was the only way to defend themselves. At the start of the war in 1754, Benjamin Franklin proposed that the thirteen colonies unite permanently to better defend themselves. This was after the French and their Native American allies had defeated Major George Washington and his militia at Fort Necessity.

Delegates from seven of the thirteen colonies met in Albany, New York, along with the representatives from the Iroquois Confederation and British officials. Franklin's proposal, known as the **Albany Plan of Union**, was totally rejected by the colonists, along with a similar proposal from the British. The delegates did not want each of the colonies to lose the right to act independently.

The War of Independence occurred due to a number of economic and political changes. By the end of the French and Indian War in 1763, Britain's American colonies were thirteen out of a total of thirty-three scattered around the globe. Like all other countries, Britain strove to have a strong economy and a favorable balance of trade. To have that delicate balance a nation needs wealth, self-sufficiency, and a powerful army and navy. This is why the overseas colonies developed. The colonies provided raw materials for the industries in the mother country and were a market for the finished products. In the case of Great Britain, a strong merchant fleet would be a school for training, providing bases of operation for the royal navy.

Trade Issues

The **Navigation Acts** of 1651 put restrictions on shipping and trade within the British Empire by requiring that only British ships be involved. This increased the strength of the British merchant fleet and greatly benefited the American colonists. Since they were British citizens, they could build and operate their own vessels. By the end of the war in 1763, the shipyards in the colonies were building one third of the merchant ships under the British flag.

The Navigation Acts of 1651 put restrictions on shipping and trade within the British Empire by requiring that only British ships be involved.

The Navigation Act of 1660 restricted the shipment and sale of colonial products to England only. In 1663, another Navigation Act stipulated that the colonies had to buy manufactured products only from England and that any European goods going to the colonies had to go to England first. These acts were a protection from enemy ships, pirates, and competition with European rivals.

The New England and Middle Atlantic colonies had started producing many of the products already being produced in Britain, but they soon found new markets for their goods and began what was known as **triangular trade**. Colonial vessels started the first part of the triangle by sailing for Africa loaded with kegs of rum from colonial distilleries. On Africa's West Coast, the rum was traded for either gold or slaves. The second part of the triangle was from Africa to the West Indies, where slaves were traded for molasses, sugar, or money. The third part of the triangle was home, bringing sugar or molasses (to make more rum), gold, and silver.

The British had been extremely lax and inconsistent in enforcement of the mercantile or trade laws passed in the years before 1754. The government itself was not particularly stable, so actions against the colonies occurred in anger, and the attitude of the British government was that they knew how to manage the colonies better than the colonists did themselves. This pointed to a lack of sufficient knowledge of conditions and opinions in the colonies. The colonists had been left on their own for nearly 150 years and, by the time the Revolutionary War began, they were quite adept at self-government and adequately handling the affairs of their daily lives. The colonists equated ownership of land or property with the right to vote. Property was considered the foundation of life and liberty, and in the colonial mind and tradition these went together.

As strains with the mother country began to increase, the issues became increasingly focused in print throughout the colonies. No doubt the published discussions and debates carried their sentiments over to the homes, taverns, and other places where the people met to discuss events of the day. An important result of this was a growing "Americanism" in the sentiments of those writers published, and a sense of connection among American people that transcended colonial boundaries.

The initial Stamp Act in 1765, the Boston Massacre in 1770, the Tea Act in 1773 (which resulted in the Boston Tea Party), and beyond kept colonial presses rife with discussion and debate about what they considered to be an unacceptable situation. Parliament intended to assert its right to tax and legislatively control the colonies of Great Britain. Most American colonists, believing themselves to be full British subjects, would deny Parliament's assertions as long as they were not provided with full and equal representation in Parliament.

Declaration of Independence

By 1776, the colonists and their representatives in the Second Continental Congress realized that things were past the point of no return. The Declaration of Independence was drafted and declared on July 4, 1776. George Washington labored against tremendous odds to wage a victorious war. The turning point in the Americans' favor occurred in 1777 with the American victory at Saratoga. After this victory, the French decided to align themselves with the Americans. With the aid of Admiral de Grasse and French warships blocking the entrance to Chesapeake Bay, British General Cornwallis, trapped at Yorktown, Virginia, surrendered in 1781 and the war was over. The Treaty of Paris officially ending the war was signed in 1783.

Manifest Destiny

The nineteenth century was the age of **MANIFEST DESTINY,** the belief in the divinely given right of the United States to expand westward and incorporate more of the continent into the nation. This belief had been expressed at the end of the Revolutionary War in the demand that Britain cede all lands east of the Mississippi River to the United States. The goal of expanding westward was further confirmed with the Northwest Ordinance (1787) and the Louisiana Purchase (1803).

The Red River basin was the next acquisition of land and came about as part of a treaty with Great Britain in 1818. It included parts of North and South Dakota and Minnesota. In 1819, Florida, both east and west, was ceded to the United States by Spain along with parts of Alabama, Mississippi, and Louisiana. Texas was annexed in 1845 and after the war with Mexico in 1848. The government paid $15 million for what would eventually become the states of California, Utah, Nevada, and parts of four other states. In 1846, the Oregon Country, which extended the nation's western border to the Pacific Ocean, was ceded to the United States. The northern U.S. boundary was established at the forty-ninth parallel. The states of Idaho, Oregon, and Washington were formed from this territory. In 1853, the **Gadsden Purchase** rounded out the present boundary of the forty-eight coterminous states with payment to Mexico of $10 million for land that makes up the present states of New Mexico and Arizona.

> **MANIFEST DESTINY:** the belief in the divinely given right of the United States to expand westward and incorporate more of the continent into the nation

SKILL 7.7 Interpret the ways that individuals and events have influenced economic, social, and political institutions in the world, nation, or state.

Founding Fathers

George Washington (1789–1797) faced a number of challenges during his two terms as president. There were boundary disputes with Spain in the Southeast and wars with the Native Americans on the western frontier.

The **French Revolution** and the ensuing war between France and England created great turmoil within the newly established United States. Thomas Jefferson, secretary of state, was pro-French and believed the United States should enter the conflict. Alexander Hamilton, secretary of the treasury, was pro-British and wanted to support England. Washington took a neutral course, believing the country was not strong enough to be engaged in a war. Washington did not interfere with the powers of Congress in establishing foreign policy. Two political parties were beginning to form by the end of his first term. In Washington's farewell address, he encouraged Americans to put an end to regional differences. He also warned the nation against long-term alliances with foreign nations.

John Adams, of the Federalist Party, was elected president in 1796. When he assumed office, the war between England and France was underway. The British seized American ships engaging in trade with France, and France refused to receive the American envoy and suspended economic relationships. The people were divided in their loyalties to France or England.

Adams focused on France and the diplomatic crisis known as the XYZ Affair. During his administration, Congress appropriated money to build three new frigates and additional ships, authorized the creation of a provisional army, and passed the Alien and Sedition Acts, which were intended to drive foreign agents from the country and to maintain the Federalist Party's dominance over the Republican Party. When the war ended, Adams sent a peace mission to France, which angered the Republicans. The election of 1800 pitted a unified and effective Republican Party against a divided and ineffective Federalist Party.

Thomas Jefferson won the election of 1800. Jefferson, a champion of states' rights, opposed a strong centralized government. He supported a strict interpretation of the Constitution. He reduced military expenditures, made budget cuts, and eliminated a tax on whiskey. At the same time, he reduced the national debt by one-third. The **Louisiana Purchase** doubled the size of the nation. During Jefferson's second term, the administration focused on keeping the country out of the Napoleonic wars. Both France and England were seizing U.S. ships and trying to deny the other access to trade. Jefferson's solution was to impose an embargo on all foreign commerce. The cost to the northeastern United States was great, and the embargo was both ineffective and unpopular.

James Madison won the election of 1808 and inherited the foreign policy issues with England. During the first year of his administration, trade was prohibited with both Britain and France. In 1810, Congress authorized trade with both England and France. Congress directed the president that if either nation would accept America's view of neutrality, he was to forbid trade with the other nation.

Napoleon pretended to comply. Madison thus banned trade with Great Britain. The British continued to harass American ships, capture sailors, and force them to become members of the British Navy (impressments). In June 1812, Madison asked Congress to declare war on Great Britain. The United States was not prepared to fight a war, especially against the strong British army.

Other Important Americans

Following is a list of well-known Americans who contributed their leadership and talents in various fields and reforms:

- Lucretia Mott and Elizabeth Cady Stanton for women's rights

- Emma Hart Willard, Catharine Esther Beecher, and Mary Lyon for education for women

- Dr. Elizabeth Blackwell, the first woman doctor

- Antoinette Louisa Blackwell, the first female minister

- Dorothea Lynde Dix for reforms in prisons and asylums

- Elihu Burritt and William Ladd for peace movements

- Robert Owen for a utopian society

- Horace Mann, Henry Barmard, Calvin E. Stowe, Caleb Mills, and John Swett for public education

- Benjamin Lundy, David Walker, William Lloyd Garrison, Isaac Hooper, Arthur and Lewis Tappan, Theodore Weld, Frederick Douglass, Harriet Tubman, James G. Birney, Henry Highland Garnet, James Forten, Robert Purvis, Harriet Beecher Stowe, Wendell Phillips, and John Brown for abolition of slavery and the Underground Railroad

- Louisa Mae Alcott, James Fenimore Cooper, Washington Irving, Walt Whitman, Henry David Thoreau, Ralph Waldo Emerson, Herman Melville, Richard Henry Dana, Nathaniel Hawthorne, Henry Wadsworth Longfellow, John Greenleaf Whittier, Edgar Allan Poe, and Oliver Wendell Holmes, famous writers

- John C. Fremont, Zebulon Pike, and Kit Carson, explorers

- Henry Clay, Daniel Webster, Stephen Douglas, and John C. Calhoun, American statespeople

- Robert Fulton, Cyrus McCormick, and Eli Whitney, inventors

- Noah Webster, American dictionary and spellers

The list could go on. The contributions of these, and many other, individuals shaped the history and culture of the United States.

See also Skill 7.4

SKILL
7.8 **Analyze immigration and settlement patterns that have shaped the history of the United States.**

Immigration from 1870 to 1916

Between 1870 and 1916, more than 25 million immigrants came into the United States, adding to the phenomenal population growth that was taking place. This tremendous growth aided business and industry in two ways:

- The number of consumers increased, creating a greater demand for products

- With increased production and expanding business, more workers were available for newly created jobs

The completion of the nation's transcontinental railroad in 1869 contributed greatly to the nation's economic and industrial growth. Many wealthy industrialists and railroad owners saw profits steadily increase due to this improved method of transportation. Another impact of interstate railroad expansion was the standardization of time zones, in order to maintain the reliability and accuracy of train schedules across long east-west routes.

Innovations in industrial processes and technology grew at a pace unmatched at any other time in American history. Thomas Edison was the most prolific inventor of the time. The abundance of resources, together with the growth of industry and the pace of capital investments, led to the growth of cities. Populations shifted from rural agricultural areas to urban industrial areas, and, by the early 1900s, a third of the nation's population lived in cities. Industry needed workers in its factories, mills, and plants, and the advances in and increasing use of farm machinery and other forms of automation displaced many rural workers.

Increased urban populations, often packed into dense tenements without adequate sanitation or clean water, led to public health challenges that required cities to establish sanitation, water, and public health departments in order to cope with and prevent epidemics. Political organizations also saw advantages through mobilizing the new industrial working class and creating vast patronage programs. These programs sometimes became notorious for corruption and big-city machine politics, such as Tammany Hall in New York.

As one of the first colonized areas in the nation, New York was a major point of entry for immigrants. The melding of the Dutch, French, and British settlers into a unified colony was the first step along the way to becoming the melting pot that New York has been to this day. The large harbor and the state's reputation for business, industry, and commerce made New York a place of special opportunity for immigrants who were seeking freedom and opportunity.

Between 1870 and 1916, more than 25 million immigrants came into the United States, adding to the phenomenal population growth that was taking place

The Dutch settlers of the early colonial period introduced many goods to North America that profoundly affected the nature of the development of both the state and the nation. The trade of the Dutch West India Company provided the foundation for an economy based on trade and commerce.

African American Migration from South to North

As African Americans left the rural South and migrated to the North in search of opportunity, many settled in Harlem in New York City. By the 1920s, Harlem had become a center of life and activity for African Americans. The music, art, and literature of this community gave birth to a cultural movement known as the Harlem Renaissance. The artistic expression that emerged from this community in the 1920s and 1930s celebrated the black experience, black traditions, and the voices of black America.

Some of the major writers and works of this movement include:

• Langston Hughes, *The Weary Blues*

• Nella Larsen, *Passing*

• Zora Neale Hurston, *Their Eyes Were Watching God*

Irish Immigration

The **Irish Famine** of 1845–1849 is alternately referred to as the Irish Potato Famine, the Great Famine, or the Great Hunger. The immediate cause of the famine was the destruction of the potato crops due to a fungus. The potato was the primary food source for much of the population of Ireland at the time. Although estimates vary, the number of people who emigrated from Ireland as a result of the famine is in the neighborhood of two million.

The Irish who emigrated to the United States for the most part became residents of cities. With no money, they were forced to remain in the port cities where they arrived. By 1850, the Irish accounted for one quarter of the population of Boston, New York City, Philadelphia, and Baltimore.

Immigration on the West Coast

On the West Coast, there was a steady increase in the number of Japanese immigrants in the early part of the twentieth century. As the number of Japanese in California grew, anti-Japanese sentiment also grew. A series of actions were taken against the Japanese immigrants:

• Labor leaders in San Francisco formed an Asiatic Exclusion League in 1905 and demanded public policies against the Japanese. They pressured the city into requiring that Japanese children attend only segregated schools with other Asian children. Protests from Japan led to intervention by President Theodore Roosevelt. The city agreed to suspend the Segregation Act in exchange for a law limiting Japanese immigration. Japan agreed in 1907 to prohibit its workers from coming to the United States.

- The Japanese immigrants were capable farmers. In an attempt to eliminate the competition, in 1913, the state legislature passed a law prohibiting anyone who was not eligible for citizenship from owning land in the state. Under federal law, Asians were ineligible for naturalization.

- In 1924, the U.S. Congress passed the National Origins Quota Act, prohibiting all further immigration from Japan.

This period of rapid economic growth and industrial expansion in California came to an abrupt end with the **stock market crash of 1929**. The worst depression in the history of California and the country ensued. With 20–25 percent of the population unemployed, nativism and a fear of foreigners rose quickly. The first to be subjected to the hostility of the natives were the Filipinos. White workers complained that the recent immigrants posed an economic threat to native-born workers. Numerous riots broke out, and Congress passed the Filipino Repatriation Act in 1935. The government offered to pay transportation expenses for any Filipinos who wished to return home.

Later, Mexican immigrants became the targets. The federal government created a program of repatriation. Some left voluntarily; others were forced to leave. Up to 100,000 deportees left California and returned to Mexico.

In the 1930s, **Dust Bowl refugees** came by the hundreds of thousands in search of a better life in California. They were called Okies because many came from Oklahoma. The situation in California was not what they expected, and they were unwelcome to many Californians. However, these refugees held on to the culture of the Southwest and created their own subculture in California.

Puerto Rican Immigration

The transition from Spanish colony to U.S. possession was not easy for the people of Puerto Rico. Residents have been U.S. citizens since 1917, but they have no representation in Congress.

Although **Puerto Rico** became a U.S. territory at the end of the Spanish-American War, there was little immigration during the first half of the century. Technically, moving from the island to the U.S. mainland is considered internal migration rather than immigration. This does not, however, recognize that leaving an island with a distinct culture and identity involves the same cultural conflicts and intellectual, language, and other adjustments as those faced by most immigrants.

In the early part of the twentieth century, a severe economic depression created widespread poverty. Few Puerto Ricans were able to afford the fare to travel by boat to the mainland. In 1910, there were only about 2,000 Puerto Ricans living on the mainland, most in small enclaves in New York City. By 1945, there were 13,000 Puerto Ricans in New York City, and, by 1946, there were more than 50,000. By the mid-1960s, there were more than a million Puerto Ricans on the mainland.

Many of the immigrant Puerto Ricans established communities in major East Coast cities and mid-Atlantic farming regions as well as in the mill towns of New England. A large number of these immigrants settled in the northeastern part of Manhattan that came to be known as Spanish Harlem. They quickly became an important factor in the city's political and cultural life. Although the first generation of immigrants faced prejudice, unemployment, discrimination, and poverty, most remained and learned to thrive.

> **SKILL 7.9** Identify how various cultures contributed to the unique social, cultural, economic, and political features of Florida.

Florida's first human inhabitants were Native Americans, as evidenced by the burial mounds found in varying locations around the state. When Europeans arrived, there were about 10,000 Native Americans belonging to as many as five major tribes. In the south were the Calusa and the Tequesta. The Ais were found on the Atlantic coast in the central part of the peninsula. The Timucans were in the central and northeast area of the state, and the Apalachee lived in the northwest part of the state.

When Europeans arrived in Florida, there were about 10,000 Native Americans belonging to as many as five major tribes

Early Spanish Explorers

Written records of life in Florida began with the arrival of the first European in 1513, the Spanish explorer and adventurer Juan Ponce de León, who was searching for the fabled fountain of youth. Sometime between April 2 and April 8 of that year, Ponce de León waded ashore on the northeast coast of Florida, possibly near present-day St. Augustine. He called the area la Florida, in honor of Pascua Florida, or "feast of the flowers," Spain's Easter-time celebration. Other Europeans may have reached Florida earlier, but no firm evidence of such achievement has been found.

The Spanish flag flew over Florida for the next 250 years. Other Spanish explorers who spent time in Florida included Panfilo de Narvaez; Hernando de Soto, who became the first European to reach the Mississippi River; and Pedro Menendez de Aviles, who put an end to French attempts to settle in eastern Florida and founded the first permanent European settlement in the present-day United States, St. Augustine.

On another voyage in 1521, Ponce de León landed on the southwestern coast of the peninsula, accompanied by two hundred people, fifty horses, and numerous beasts of burden. His colonization attempt quickly failed because of attacks by native people. However, his activities served to identify Florida as a desirable place for explorers, missionaries, and treasure seekers.

In 1539, Hernando de Soto began another expedition in search of gold and silver, which took him on a long trek through Florida and what is now the southeastern United States. For four years, de Soto's expedition wandered in hopes of finding the fabled wealth of the Native American people. De Soto and his soldiers camped for five months in the area now known as Tallahassee. De Soto died near the Mississippi River in 1542, but survivors of his expedition eventually reached Mexico.

No great treasure troves awaited the Spanish conquistadores who explored Florida. However, their stories helped inform Europeans about Florida and its relationship to Cuba, Mexico, and Central and South America, from which Spain regularly shipped gold, silver, and other products.

No great treasure troves awaited the Spanish conquistadores who explored Florida. However, their stories helped inform Europeans about Florida and its relationship to Cuba, Mexico, and Central and South America, from which Spain regularly shipped gold, silver, and other products. Groups of heavily laden Spanish vessels, called plate fleets, usually sailed up the Gulf Stream through the straits that parallel the Florida Keys. Aware of this route, pirates preyed on the fleets. Hurricanes created additional hazards, sometimes wrecking ships on the reefs and shoals along Florida's eastern coast.

The French and the British

Spain was not the only European nation that found Florida attractive. In 1562, the French Protestant Jean Ribault explored the area. Two years later, fellow Frenchman René Goulaine de Laudonnière established Fort Caroline at the mouth of the St. Johns River, near present-day Jacksonville.

These French adventurers prompted Spain to accelerate her plans for colonization. Pedro Menéndez de Avilés hastened across the Atlantic, his sights set on removing the French and creating a Spanish settlement. Menéndez arrived in 1565, at a place he called San Augustín (St. Augustine) and established the first permanent European settlement in what is now the United States. He accomplished his goal of expelling the French, attacking and killing all settlers except for noncombatants and Frenchmen who professed belief in the Roman Catholic faith. Menéndez captured Fort Caroline and renamed it San Mateo.

The French response came two years later, when Dominique de Gourgues recaptured San Mateo, killing the Spanish soldiers stationed there. This incident did not halt the Spanish advance. Their pattern of constructing forts and Roman Catholic missions continued. Spanish missions established among native people soon extended across north Florida and north along the Atlantic coast to what we now call South Carolina.

The English, also eager to exploit the wealth of the Americas, increasingly came into conflict with Spain's expanding empire. In 1586, the English captain Sir Francis Drake looted and burned the tiny village of St. Augustine, but the Spanish control of Florida was not diminished. In fact, as late as 1600, Spain's power over what is now the southeastern United States was unquestioned.

The English colonists in the Carolina colonies were particularly hostile toward Spain. Led by Colonel James Moore, the Carolinians and their Creek Native American allies attacked Spanish Florida in 1702. They destroyed the town of St. Augustine, but could not capture the fort, named Castillo de San Marcos. Two years later, they destroyed the Spanish missions between Tallahassee and St. Augustine, killing many native people and enslaving many others. The French continued to harass Spanish Florida's western border and captured Pensacola in 1719, twenty-one years after the town had been established.

Spain's adversaries moved even closer in 1733, when England founded Georgia, its southernmost continental colony. Georgians attacked Florida in 1740, assaulting the Castillo de San Marcos at St. Augustine for almost a month. While the attack was not successful, it did point out the growing weakness of Spanish Florida.

British control of Florida

Britain gained control of Florida in 1763 in exchange for Havana, Cuba, which the British had captured from Spain during the Seven Years' War (1756–1763). Spain evacuated Florida after the exchange, leaving the province virtually empty. At that time, St. Augustine was still a garrison community with fewer than five hundred houses, and Pensacola also was a small military town.

The British had ambitious plans for Florida. First, it was split into two parts: East Florida, with its capital at St. Augustine; and West Florida, with its seat at Pensacola. British surveyors mapped much of the landscape and coastline and tried to develop relations with a group of Native Americans who were moving into the area from the North. The British called these people of Creek descent Seminolies or Seminoles. Britain also attempted to attract white settlers by offering land to settle on and help for those who produced products for export. Given enough time, this plan might have converted Florida into a flourishing colony, but British rule lasted only twenty years.

The two Floridas remained loyal to Great Britain throughout the American War of Independence (1776–1783). However, Spain—participating indirectly in the war as an ally of France—captured Pensacola from the British in 1781. In 1784, it regained control of the rest of Florida as part of the peace treaty that ended the war. The second period of Spanish control lasted until 1821.

Andrew Jackson in Florida

In 1818, General Andrew Jackson made a foray into Florida. Jackson's battles with Florida's Native Americans would later be called the First Seminole War.

When the British evacuated Florida, Spanish colonists, as well as settlers from the newly formed United States, came pouring in. Many of the new residents were lured by favorable Spanish terms for acquiring property, called **land grants**. Others who came were escaped slaves, trying to reach a place where their masters had no authority and could not reach them. Instead of becoming more Spanish, the two Floridas increasingly became more "American." Finally, after several official and unofficial U.S. military expeditions into the territory, Spain formally ceded Florida to the United States in 1821, according to terms of the Adams-Onís Treaty.

Spain formally ceded Florida to the United States in 1821.

Andrew Jackson returned to Florida in 1821 to establish a new territorial government on behalf of the United States. What the United States inherited was a wilderness sparsely dotted with settlements of Native American people, African Americans, and Spaniards.

As a territory of the United States, Florida was particularly attractive to people from the older Southern plantation areas of Virginia, the Carolinas, and Georgia, who arrived in considerable numbers. After being granted territorial status, the two Floridas merged into one entity with a new capital city in Tallahassee. Established in 1824, Tallahassee was chosen because it was halfway between the existing governmental centers of St. Augustine and Pensacola.

Removal of Native Americans from their lands

As Florida's population increased through immigration, so did pressure on the federal government to remove the Native Americans from their lands. The Native American population was made up of several groups—primarily the Creek and the Miccosukee people. Many African American refugees lived among the Native American population. The removal of Native Americans was popular with white settlers because the native people occupied lands that white people wanted and because their communities often provided a sanctuary for runaway slaves from northern states.

Osceola was a Seminole war leader who refused to leave his homeland in Florida.

Among Florida's native population, the name of Osceola has remained familiar after more than a century and a half. Osceola was a Seminole war leader who refused to leave his homeland in Florida. Seminoles, already noted for their fighting abilities, won the respect of U.S. soldiers for their bravery, fortitude, and ability to adapt to changing circumstances during the Second Seminole War (1835–1842). This war, the most significant of the three conflicts between Native Americans and U.S. troops in Florida, began over the question of whether Seminoles should be moved westward across the Mississippi River into what is now Oklahoma.

Under President Andrew Jackson, the U.S. government spent $20 million to force the removal of the Seminoles. In the end, after the death of many U.S.

soldiers, Native Americans, and U.S. citizens, the outcome was not as the federal government had planned. Some Native Americans migrated "voluntarily"; some were captured and sent west under military guard; and others escaped into the Everglades, where they made a life for themselves away from contact with whites. Today, reservations occupied by Florida's Native American people exist at Immokalee, Hollywood, Brighton (near the city of Okeechobee), and along the Big Cypress Swamp. In addition to the Seminole people, Florida also has a separate Miccosukee tribe.

Statehood

By 1840, Florida was divided informally into three areas: East Florida, from the Atlantic Ocean to the Suwannee River; Middle Florida, between the Suwannee and the Apalachicola rivers; and West Florida, from the Apalachicola to the Perdido River. The southern area of the territory (south of present-day Gainesville) was sparsely settled by whites. The territory's economy was based on agriculture. Plantations were concentrated in Middle Florida, and the plantation owners established the political tone for all of Florida until after the Civil War. Florida became the twenty-seventh state in the United States on March 3, 1845. William D. Moseley was elected the new state's first governor, and David Levy Yulee, one of Florida's leading proponents for statehood, became a U.S. Senator. By 1850, the population had grown to 87,445, which included about 39,000 African American slaves and 1,000 free blacks.

Florida became the twenty-seventh state in the United States on March 3, 1845.

The slavery issue began to dominate the affairs of the new state. Most Florida voters—who were white males, age twenty-one or older—did not oppose slavery. They were, however, concerned about the growing feeling against it in the North, and during the 1850s they viewed the new antislavery Republican Party with suspicion. In the 1860 presidential election, no Floridians voted for Abraham Lincoln. Shortly after his election, a special convention drew up an ordinance that allowed Florida to secede from the Union on January 10, 1861. Within several weeks, Florida joined other southern states to form the Confederate States of America.

Civil War

During the Civil War, Florida was not ravaged as several other southern states were. Indeed, no decisive battles were fought on Florida soil. While Union forces occupied many coastal towns and forts, the interior of the state remained in Confederate hands.

Florida provided an estimated 15,000 troops and a significant number of supplies— including salt, beef, pork, and cotton—to the Confederacy, but more than two thousand Floridians, both African American and white, joined the Union army. Confederate and foreign merchant ships slipped through the Union navy blockade along the coast, bringing in needed supplies from overseas ports. Tallahassee was the only southern capital east of the Mississippi River to avoid capture during the war, spared by southern victories at Olustee (1864) and Natural Bridge (1865).

Before the Civil War, Florida had been well on its way to becoming another southern cotton state. After the war, the lives of many residents changed. The ports of Jacksonville and Pensacola again flourished due to the demand for lumber and forest products to rebuild the nation's cities. Those who had been slaves were declared free. Plantation owners tried to regain prewar levels of production by hiring former slaves to raise and pick cotton, but such programs did not work well and much of the land came under cultivation by tenant farmers and sharecroppers, both African American and white.

Beginning in 1868, the federal government instituted a congressional program of reconstruction in Florida and the other southern states. During this period, Republican officeholders tried to enact sweeping changes, many aimed at improving conditions for African Americans.

> Tallahassee was the only southern capital east of the Mississippi River to avoid capture during the war.

Development in Late Nineteenth Century

During the final quarter of the nineteenth century, large-scale commercial agriculture in Florida, especially cattle raising, grew in importance. Industries such as cigar manufacturing took root in the immigrant communities of the state. Large phosphate deposits were discovered; citrus groves were planted and cultivated; swamplands were drained; and Henry Plant and Henry Flagler built railroad lines opening the state for further growth and development.

The Florida citrus industry grew rapidly, despite occasional freezes and economic setbacks. The development of industries throughout the state prompted the large-scale construction of roads and railroads. Jobs created by the state helped develop the natural resources. Private industries' construction of paper mills resulted in conservation programs for the state's forests, and, to help preserve perishable fruits and vegetables, cooling plants were built. To aid farmers, cooperative markets and cooperative farm groups were established.

The growth of Florida's transportation industry had its origins in 1855, when the state legislature passed the Internal Improvement Act. This act offered cheap or free public land to investors, particularly those interested in transportation. It had its greatest effect in the years between the end of the Civil War and the beginning of World War I. During this period, many companies constructed railroads throughout the state and built lavish hotels near their railroad lines.

These development projects had far-reaching effects on the agricultural, manufacturing, and extractive industries of late-nineteenth-century Florida. The citrus industry especially benefited since it was now possible to pick oranges in south Florida, put them on a train heading north, and eat them in Baltimore, Philadelphia, or New York in less than a week.

In 1898, national attention focused on Florida as the Spanish-American War began. The port city of Tampa served as the primary staging area for U.S. troops bound for the war in Cuba. Many Floridians supported the Cuban people's desire to be free of Spanish colonial rule.

Florida in the Twentieth Century

By the turn of the century, Florida's population and per capita wealth were increasing rapidly, and the potential of the "Sunshine State" appeared endless. By the end of World War I, land developers had descended on this virtual gold mine. With more Americans owning automobiles, Florida became a popular vacation destination. Many visitors stayed on, and exotic projects sprang up in southern Florida. Some people moved on to land made from drained swamps. Others bought canal-crossed tracts through what had been dry land. The real estate developments quickly attracted buyers, and land in Florida was sold and resold. Profits and prices for many developers reached inflated levels. The early 1900s saw the settlement and economic development of south Florida, especially along the East Coast. A severe depression in 1926, the hurricanes of 1926 and 1928, and the Great Depression of the 1930s burst the economic bubble.

By the turn of the century, Florida's population and per capita wealth were increasing rapidly, and the potential of the "Sunshine State" appeared endless.

During World War II, many military bases were constructed as part of the vital defense interests of the state and nation. After the war, prosperity and population grew, resulting in tourism becoming the most important industry. It remains so today. Continued agricultural development and industrial expansion also played an important role in the state's economy. Such industries as paper and paper products, chemicals, electronics, and ocean and space exploration gave a tremendous boost to the labor force. From the 1950s to the present day, the Kennedy Space Center at Cape Canaveral has been a space and rocket center for launching of orbiting satellites, manned space flights, and space shuttles.

Florida Today

While Florida is often thought of as a vacation and retirement destination, the state has made headlines in recent years due to the housing boom and subsequent foreclosure crisis beginning in 2007. On the heels of the housing and banking problems was the rising unemployment rate during the nation's 2009 recession. In the middle of 2010 another economic concern arrived—BP's oil spill in the

Gulf of Mexico. Given the state's large tourism market, which brought in over $65 billion in 2008 according to VISIT FLORIDA research, the aftermath of the spill on the state's coastline could impact the tourism sector for years to come. Regardless of the recent economic concerns, Florida continues to attract residents and visitors. According to data from the U.S. Census Bureau, Florida's population increased 16 percent from 2000 to 2009. In addition to its attractions, the state provides the majority of the United State's citrus and continues to grow in the high tech, health technology, and financial sectors.

SKILL 7.10 Identify the significant contributions of the early and classical civilizations.

See Skills 7.4 and 7.5

COMPETENCY 8
KNOWLEDGE OF PEOPLE, PLACES, AND ENVIRONMENT (I.E., GEOGRAPHY)

> **SKILL** **Identify and apply the six essential elements of geography** *(i.e.,*
> **8.1** *the world in spatial terms, places and regions, physical systems, human systems, environment and society, uses of geography)*, **including the specific terms for each element.**

Geography covers eighteen learning standards that educators have grouped into six essential elements. Each of the elements has specific standards:

1. The World in Spatial Terms

    A. The proper methods of using maps and other geographic tools and representations in order to collect, process, and present information from a spatial perspective

    B. The use of mental maps as a way of processing information about people, places, and environments within a spatial context

    C. The analysis of the spatial organization of people, places, and environments on the surface of the Earth

2. Places and Regions

    A. The physical and human characteristics of locations on the Earth

    B. The reasons people create regions in order to help them interpret the complex qualities of the Earth

    C. People's perceptions of places and regions are affected by the different cultures and experiences they have

3. Physical Systems

    A. Knowledge of the physical systems that shape the patterns of the surface of the Earth

    B. Understanding of the characteristics and spatial distributions of the various ecosystems that exist on the Earth

4. Human Systems

   A. Characteristics, distribution, and migrations of human populations on the Earth

   B. Characteristics, distribution, and complexities of the Earth's cultural mosaics

   C. Patterns and networks of economic interdependence on the Earth

   D. Processes, patterns, and functions of human settlement

   E. The influence of cooperation and conflict among people in determining the division and control over areas of the Earth's surface

5. Environment and Society

   A. The way human actions can modify the physical environment

   B. The effect that physical systems have on human systems

   C. The types of changes that can occur in the importance of resources and in their meaning, use, and distribution

6. Uses of Geography

   A. Can be used to interpret the past

   B. Can be applied to what is happening in the present and used to formulate a plan for the future

---

SKILL **Analyze and interpret maps and other graphic representations of**
8.2 **physical and human systems.**

Illustrations often make it easier to demonstrate an idea visually rather than through text or speech. Among the more common illustrations used in social science are various types of **maps, graphs, and charts.**

Although maps have advantages over globes and photographs, they do have a major disadvantage: most maps are flat and the Earth is a sphere. It is impossible to reproduce an object shaped like a sphere accurately on a flat surface. In order to put the Earth's features on a map they must be stretched in some way. This stretching is called **distortion.** Distortion does not mean that maps are wrong; it simply means that they are not perfect representations of the Earth or its parts. **Cartographers,** or mapmakers, understand the problems of distortion. They try to design maps so there is as little distortion as possible.

The process of putting the features of the Earth onto a flat surface is called **projection**. All maps are really projections of the three-dimensional surface of the Earth onto a two-dimensional surface. Each one deals in a different way with the problem of distortion. Map projections are made in a number of ways. Some are done using complicated mathematics. However, the basic ideas behind map projections can be understood by looking at the three most common types.

Cylindrical Projections	These are done by taking a cylinder of paper and wrapping it around a globe. A light is used to project the globe's features onto the paper. Distortion is least where the paper touches the globe. For example, if the paper was wrapped so that it touched the globe at the equator, the map from this projection would have just a little distortion near the equator. However, the distortion would increase as you moved further away from the equator. The best known and most widely used cylindrical projection is the Mercator Projection. It was first developed in 1569 by Gerardus Mercator, a Flemish mapmaker.
Conical Projections	The name for these maps come from the fact that the projection is made onto a paper cone that touches a globe at the base of the cone only. It can also be made so that it cuts through part of the globe in two different places. The distortion is least where the paper touches the globe. If the cone touches at two different points, there is some distortion at both of them. Conical projections are most often used to map areas in the middle latitudes. Maps of the United States are most often conical projections. This is because most of the country lies within these latitudes.
Flat-Plane Projections	These are made with a flat piece of paper. It touches the globe at one point only. Areas near this point show little distortion. Flat-plane projections are often used to show the areas of the north and south poles. One such flat projection is called a Gnomonic Projection. On this kind of map all meridians appear as straight lines. Gnomonic projections are useful because any straight line drawn between points on it forms a Great-Circle Route.

Great-Circle Routes can best be described by thinking of a globe and, when using the globe, the shortest route between two points on it can be found by simply stretching a string from one point to the other. However, if the string was extended in reality, so that it took into effect the globe's curvature, it would then make a great-circle. A **GREAT-CIRCLE** is any circle that cuts a sphere, such as the globe, into two equal parts. Because of distortion, most maps do not show great-circle routes as straight lines. Gnomonic projections, however, do show the shortest distance between the two places as a straight line, which is why they are valuable for navigation. They are called Great-Circle Sailing Maps.

> **GREAT-CIRCLE:** any circle that cuts a sphere, such as the globe, into two equal parts

To properly analyze a given map one must be familiar with the various parts and symbols that most modern maps use. For the most part, these are standardized, with different maps using similar parts and symbols. These can include:

The Title	All maps should have a title, just like all books should. The title tells you what information is found on the map.
The Legend	Most maps have a legend. A legend tells the reader about the various symbols that are used on that particular map and what the symbols represent (also called a map key).
The Grid	A grid is a series of lines that are used to find exact places and locations on the map. There are several different kinds of grid systems in use; however, most maps use the longitude and latitude system, known as the Geographic Grid System.
Directions	Most maps have some directional system to show which way the map is being presented. Often on a map, a small compass will be present, with arrows showing the four basic directions: north, south, east, and west.
The Scale	This is used to show the relationship between a unit of measurement on the map versus the real world measure on the Earth. Maps are drawn to many different scales. Some maps show a lot of detail for a small area. Others show a greater span of distance. One should always be aware of what scale is being used. For instance, the scale might be something like 1 inch = 10 miles for a map of a small area. A map showing the whole world might have a scale in which 1 inch = 1,000 miles. One must look at the map key in order to see what units of measurements the map is using.

Maps have four main properties. They are:

1. The size of the areas shown on the map

2. The shapes of the areas

3. Consistent scales

4. Straight line directions

A map can be drawn so that it is correct in one or more of these properties. No map can be correct in all of them.

Equal Areas	One property that maps can have is that of equal areas. In an equal area map, the meridians and parallels are drawn so that the areas shown have the same proportions as they do on the Earth. For example, Greenland is about 118th the size of South America, thus it will be shown as 118th the size on an equal area map. The Mercator projection is an example of a map that does not have equal areas. In it, Greenland appears to be about the same size of South America. This is because the distortion is very bad at the poles and Greenland lies near the North Pole.
Conformal Map	A second map property is conformal, or correct shapes. There are no maps that can show very large areas of the Earth in their exact shapes. Only globes can do that; however, conformal maps are as close as possible to true shapes. The United States is often shown by a Lambert Conformal Conic Projection Map.
Consistent Scales	Many maps attempt to use the same scale on all parts of the map. Generally, this is easier when a map shows a relatively small part of the Earth's surface. For example, a map of Florida might be a consistent scale map. Generally maps showing large areas are not consistent scale maps. This is so because of distortion. Often such maps will have two scales noted in the key. One scale, for example, might be accurate to measure distances between points along the Equator. Another might be accurate to measure distances between the North Pole and the South Pole. Maps showing physical features often try to show information about the elevation or relief of the land. Elevation is the distance above or below the sea level. The elevation is usually shown with colors, for instance, all areas on a map which are at a certain level will be shown in the same color.
Relief Maps	These show the shape of the land's surface: flat, rugged, or steep. Relief maps usually give more detail than simply showing the overall elevation of the land's surface. Relief is sometimes shown with colors, but another way to show relief is by using contour lines. These lines connect all points of a land surface that are the same height surrounding the particular area of land.
Thematic Maps	These are used to show specific information, often on a single theme, or topic. Thematic maps show the distribution or amount of something over a certain given area—things such as population density, climate, economic information, cultural, political information, etc.

Graphs

There are two major reasons that graphs are used:

1. To visually present a model or theory, in order to show how two or more variables interrelate

2. To present real-world data visually in order to show how two or more variables interrelate

The most-often used graphs are known as bar graphs and line graphs. Graphs themselves are most useful when one wishes to demonstrate the sequential increase or decrease of a variable or to show specific correlations between two or more variables in a given circumstance.

Bar graphs are commonly used because they visually show the difference in a given set of variables, which is easy to see and understand. However, a bar graph is limited in that it cannot show the actual proportional increase, or decrease, of each given variable. In order to show a decrease, a bar graph must show the "bar" under the starting line, which is impossible in this format.

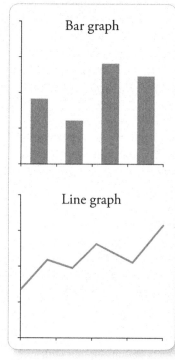

Bar graph

Line graph

Thus, in order to accomplish this, one must use a **line graph**. Line graphs can be of two types:

1. **Linear graph:** Uses a series of straight lines

2. **Nonlinear graph:** Uses a curved line

Though the lines can be either straight or curved, all of the lines are called curves.

A line graph uses a number line or **axis**. The numbers on the axis are generally placed in order, equal distances from one another. The number line is used to represent a number, degree, or some such other variable at an appropriate point on the line. Two lines are used, intersecting at a specific point. They are referred to as the X-axis and the Y-axis. The Y-axis is a vertical line the X-axis is a horizontal line. Together they form a **coordinate system**. The difference between two points on the line of the X-axis and the Y-axis is called the **slope** of the line, or the change in the value on the vertical axis divided by the change in the value on the horizontal axis. The Y-axis number is called the rise and the X-axis number is called the run; thus, the equation for slope is:

$$\text{SLOPE} = \frac{\text{RISE (change in value on the vertical axis)}}{\text{RUN (change in value on the horizontal axis)}}$$

The slope tells the amount of increase or decrease of a given variable.

To use charts correctly, one should remember the reasons one uses graphs. It is usually a question as to which, a graph or chart, is more capable of accurately portraying the information one wants to illustrate. One of the most common types of chart, because it is easiest to read and understand, is the **piechart**.

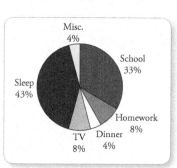

Piecharts are used often, especially when illustrating the differences in percentages among various items, or demonstrating the divisions of a whole.

Spatial organization is a description of how things are grouped in a given space. In geographical terms, this can describe people, places, and environments anywhere on Earth.

The most basic form of spatial organization for people is where they live. The vast majority of people live near other people—in villages, towns, cities, and settlements. People live near others in order to take advantage of the goods and services that naturally arise from cooperation. Villages, towns, cities, and settlements are, to varying degrees, near bodies of water. Water is a staple of survival for every person on the planet and is also a good source of energy for factories and other industries, as well as a form of transportation for people and goods.

> **SKILL Identify and evaluate tools and technologies** *(e.g., maps, globe, GPS,*
> **8.3** *satellite imagery)* **used to acquire, process, and report information from a spatial perspective.**

Satellites capture satellite images at regular intervals (usually hourly). Meteorologists use these images to forecast the weather. These images also can be used to develop maps and track data. GPS (GLOBAL POSITIONING SYSTEM) is a navigation system made up of many satellites. It originally was used for military purposes and later was made available for use by civilians.

See also Skill 8.2

> **GPS (GLOBAL POSITIONING SYSTEM):** a navigation system made up of many satellites

> **SKILL Interpret statistics that show how places differ in their human and**
> **8.4** **physical characteristics.**

DEMOGRAPHY is the branch of the science of statistics most concerned with the social well-being of people. Demographic tables may include:

> **DEMOGRAPHY:** the branch of the science of statistics most concerned with the social well-being of people

- Analysis of a population on the basis of age, parentage, physical condition, race, occupation, or civil position, giving the actual size and density of each separate area

- Changes in a population as a result of birth, marriage, and death

- Statistics on population movements and their effects, and their relation to given economic, social, and political conditions

- Statistics on crime, illegitimacy, and suicide

- Levels of education, economic status, and social statistics

Such information is similar to the area of science known as vital statistics and is indispensable in studying social trends and making important legislative, economic, and social decisions. Such demographic information is gathered from the census, registrar reports, and by state laws. In the United States, demographic

> *In the United States, demographic information is compiled and published by the Public Health Service of the U.S. Department of Health and Human Services.*

information is compiled and published by the Public Health Service of the U.S. Department of Health and Human Services.

The most important element of this information is the so-called rate, which customarily represents the average number of births and deaths for a unit of 1,000 population over a given calendar year. These general rates are called crude rates. The crude rates are then subdivided by sex, race, age, occupation, locality, and other criteria. The results are then known as refined rates.

In examining statistics and sources of statistical data, one must be aware of the methods of statistical information gathering. For instance, there are many good sources of raw statistical data. Books such as *The Statistical Abstract of the United States*, published by the U.S. Department of Commerce, *The World Factbook*, published by the Central Intelligence Agency, or the *Monthly Labor Review*, published by the Bureau of Labor Statistics, are excellent examples of good sources containing raw data. Many such yearbooks on various topics are readily available from any library or from the government itself.

However, knowing how the data was gathered is equally as important as the figures themselves. It is only through knowledge of statistical language and methodology that one can gauge the usefulness of any given data. Statistics usually deal with a specific model, hypothesis, or theory that one is attempting to prove. One should be aware that a theory can never actually be proved correct; it can only be corroborated (corroboration means that the data presented is more consistent with one theory than with any other theory, so it makes sense to use this theory.) One should be aware of what is known as CORRELATION, the joint movement of various data points, and that it does not infer CAUSATION, that a change in one data points causes the other data points to change.

Once collected, data must be arranged, tabulated, and presented for meaningful analysis and interpretation. Tests of reliability are used, bearing in mind the manner in which the data has been collected and the inherent biases of any artificially created model used to explain real-world events.

> **CORRELATION:** the joint movement of various data points

> **CAUSATION:** a change in one data points causes the other data points to change

---

SKILL 8.5 Analyze ways in which people adapt to an environment through the production and use of clothing, food, and shelter.

> *As people migrated to areas where game and fertile soil were abundant, communities began to develop.*

Humans in the earliest communities subsisted initially as gatherers. With the invention of tools, it became possible to dig for roots, hunt small animals, and catch fish from rivers and oceans. Humans observed their environments and soon learned to plant seeds and harvest crops. As people migrated to areas where game and fertile soil were abundant, communities began to develop. When people had the knowledge to grow crops and the skills to hunt game, they began to understand the division of labor. Some of the people in the community tended to agricultural needs while others hunted game.

As habitats attracted larger numbers of people, environments became crowded and competition developed. The concept of division of labor appeared and the sharing of food began. Groups of people focused on growing crops while others concentrated on hunting. Farmers began to develop new plant species, and hunters began to protect certain animal species from other predators for their own use. This ability to manage the environment led people to settle down, guard their resources, and manage them.

Camps soon became villages; villages became year-round settlements. Animals were domesticated and gathered into herds that met the needs of the village. With the settled life, it was no longer necessary to "travel light." Pottery was developed for storing and cooking food. As farming and animal husbandry skills increased, the dependence on wild game and food gathering declined.

By 8000 BCE, culture was beginning to evolve in these villages. Agriculture was developed for the production of grain crops, which led to a decreased reliance on wild plants. The domestication of animals decreased the need to hunt wild game. Life became more settled. It was then possible for people to turn their attention to such matters as managing water supplies, producing tools, and making cloth.

SKILL 8.6 Determine the ways tools and technological advances affect the environment.

Human civilization, population growth, and efforts to control the environment can have many negative effects on various habitats. Humans change their environments to suit their particular needs and interests; sometimes these changes result in the extinction of species or changes to the habitat itself. For example, **deforestation** damages the stability of mountain surfaces. One particularly devastating example of deforestation is the removal of the grasses of the Great Plains for agriculture. Tilling the ground and planting crops left the soil unprotected. Sustained drought turned the soil into dust. When windstorms occurred, the topsoil was stripped away and blown all the way to the Atlantic Ocean.

> One particularly devastating example of deforestation is the removal of the grasses of the Great Plains for agriculture.

In extreme cases, erosion can leave a plot of agricultural land unsuitable for use. Technological advances have led to a modern method of farming that relies less on plowing the soil before planting, but more on chemical fertilizers, pesticides, and herbicides. These chemicals can find their way into groundwater, and can have a major negative impact on the environment.

Cities are good examples of how technological change has allowed humans to modify their environment to suit their needs. At the end of the eighteenth century, advances made in England in the construction of canals were brought to New York, and an ambitious project to connect Lake Erie with the Hudson River by canal was planned. The Erie Canal was built through miles of virgin wilderness, opening natural areas to settlement and commerce. Towns along the canal grew and thrived, including Buffalo, Rochester, and Albany. The canal opened westward expansion beyond the borders of New York by opening a route between the Midwest and the East Coast.

Further advances in transportation and building methods allow for larger and denser communities, which affect the environment in many ways. Concentrated consumption of fuels by automobiles and home heating systems affects the quality of the air in and around cities. The lack of exposed ground means that rainwater runs off roads and rooftops into sewer systems instead of seeping into the ground, and often makes its way into nearby streams or rivers, carrying urban debris with it.

New York City, the nation's largest city, has had a considerable impact on its island environment and is making extensive use of new technology to reduce its energy use. New York City has the world's largest mass transit system, including hybrid buses that reduce emissions. New "clean" methods of energy production are being explored, such as wind power and underwater turbines that are run by tidal forces.

> **SKILL 8.7** Identify and analyze physical, cultural, economic, and political reasons for the movement of people in the world, nation, or state.

CULTURE: the way of life of a group of people

GEOGRAPHY: the study of Earth's features and living things with regard to their location, relationship with each other, how they came to be there, and why they are so important

Social scientists use the term **CULTURE** to describe the way of life of a group of people. Culture not only includes art, music, and literature but also beliefs, customs, languages, traditions, and inventions. The term **GEOGRAPHY** is defined as the study of Earth's features and living things with regard to their location, relationship with each other, how they came to be there, and why they are so important.

PHYSICAL GEOGRAPHY is concerned with the locations of such features as climate, water, and land; how these relate to and affect each other and human activities; and what forces shaped and changed them. All three of these features affect the lives of all humans and have a direct influence on what is made and produced, where it occurs, how it occurs, and what makes it possible. The combination of the different climate conditions and types of landforms as well as other surface features work together all around the Earth to give the many varied cultures unique characteristics and distinctions.

CULTURAL GEOGRAPHY studies the location, characteristics, and influence of the physical environment on different cultures around the world. Also included in these studies are the comparisons among and influences of the many varied cultures. Ease of travel and state-of-the-art communication techniques ease the difficulties of understanding cultural differences.

A **POPULATION** is a group of people living within a certain geographic area. Populations are usually measured on a regular basis by census, which also measures age, economic status, ethnicity, and other data.

When a population grows, it must either expand its geographic boundaries to make room for new people or increase its density. Population density is simply the number of people in a population divided by the geographic area in which they live. Cultures with a high population density are likely to have different ways of interacting with one another than those with low density, as people live in closer proximity to one another.

As a population grows, its economic needs change. There are more people with more basic needs, and more workers are needed to produce the goods to meet those needs. If a population's production or purchasing power does not keep pace with its growth, its economy can be adversely affected. The age distribution of a population can affect the economy as well, if the number of young and old people who are not working is disproportionate to those who are.

Growth in some areas may spur **migration** to other parts of a population's geographic region that are less densely populated. This redistribution of population also places demands on the economy, as infrastructure is needed to connect new areas to older population centers, and land is put to new use.

Populations can grow naturally when the rate of birth is higher than the rate of death, or by adding new people from other populations through **immigration**. Immigration is often a source of societal change as people from other cultures bring their institutions and language to a new area. Immigration has an impact on a population's educational and economic institutions as immigrants enter the workforce and enroll their children in schools.

Populations can decline in number, when the death rate exceeds the birth rate, or when people migrate to another area. War, famine, disease, and natural disasters can dramatically reduce a population. The economic problems caused by population decline can be similar to those from overpopulation. In extreme cases, a population may decline to the point where it can no longer perpetuate itself and its members and their culture either disappear or are absorbed into another

PHYSICAL GEOGRAPHY: concerned with the locations of such features as climate, water, and land; how these relate to and affect each other and human activities; and what forces shaped and changed them

CULTURAL GEOGRAPHY: studies the location, characteristics, and influence of the physical environment on different cultures around the world

POPULATION: a group of people living within a certain geographic area

population. When changes in human and other populations and migration, climate change, or natural disasters disrupt the delicate balance of a habitat or an ecosystem, species either adapt or become extinct.

> SKILL 8.8 **Evaluate the impact of transportation and communication networks on the economic development in different regions.**

The global economy had its origins in the early twentieth century, with the advent of the airplane, which made travel and trade easier and less time-consuming than ever. With the advent of the Internet, the world can be considered a global neighborhood. Air travel has made possible global commerce and exchange of goods on a level never before seen. Foods from all around the world can be flown across the world and, with the aid of refrigeration techniques, kept fresh long enough to sell in markets nearly everywhere. The same is true of medicine.

Trucks, trains, and ships carry cargo all over the world. Trains travel faster than ever, as do ships. There are more roads and they are usually in better repair than they have ever been.

With all of this capability has come increasing demand. Increased demand for limited natural resources can be problematic. A good example is wood, paper, and other goods that are made from trees. The demand for paper these days is staggering. In order to fulfill that demand, companies are cutting down more and more trees. Nonrenewable resources such as coal and oil are in worldwide demand and the supplies won't last forever.

Globalization has brought about welcome and unwelcome developments in the field of epidemiology. Vaccines and other important medicines can be shipped relatively quickly all around the world.

Globalization has brought about welcome and unwelcome developments in the field of epidemiology. Vaccines and other important medicines can be shipped relatively quickly all around the world. Unfortunately, the preponderance of global travel has also meant that there is now a very real threat of an infected person traveling on an international flight spreading a disease around the world.

The most recent example of technology contributing to globalization is the development of the Internet. The Internet is an extension of the telephone and cellular phone revolutions. A huge number of businesses now use cell phones and the Internet to do business, and are also using computers to track goods and receipts quickly and efficiently.

Globalization has brought financial and cultural exchange on a worldwide scale. A large number of businesses have investments in countries around the world. Financial transactions are conducted using a variety of currencies.

Along with the growing exchange of money, goods and culture has come an increase in immigration. Many people who live in less-developed nations see what is available in other places and want to move there, in order to fully take advantage of all that those more-developed nations have to offer. This can conceivably create an increase in immigration. Depending on the numbers of people who want to immigrate and the resources available, this could become a problem. The technological advances in transportation and communications have made such immigration easier than ever.

The U.S. economy is so big that there can be unemployment in one part of the country while there are labor shortages in other parts of the country. In many cases there are institutional rigidities, such as the lack of information that prevents workers from migrating in response to employment opportunities. State job services exist to provide information about available job opportunities, even though many workers are reluctant to migrate due to family situations.

Tremendous progress in communication and transportation has drawn all parts of the world closer.

SKILL 8.9 Compare and contrast major regions of the world, nation, or state.

PHYSICAL CHARACTERISTICS OF THE EARTH	
Mountains	Mountains are landforms with rather steep slopes at least 2,000 feet or more above sea level. Mountains are found in groups called mountain chains or mountain ranges. At least one range can be found on six of the Earth's seven continents. North America has the Appalachian and Rocky Mountains; South America the Andes; Asia the Himalayas; Australia the Great Dividing Range; Europe the Alps; and Africa the Atlas, Ahaggar, and Drakensburg Mountains. Mountains are commonly formed when land is thrust upward where two tectonic plates collide, or by volcanic activity.
Hills	Hills are landforms rising to an elevation of about 500 to 2,000 feet. They are found everywhere on Earth, including Antarctica, where they are covered by ice.
Plateaus	Plateaus are elevated landforms usually level on top. Depending on location, they range from being an area that is very cold to one that is cool and healthful. Some plateaus are dry because they are surrounded by mountains that keep out any moisture. One example is the Kenya Plateau in East Africa, which is very cool. The plateau extending north from the Himalayas is extremely dry, while those in Antarctica and Greenland are covered with ice and snow. Plateaus can be formed by underground volcanic activity, erosion, or colliding tectonic plates.

Continued on next page

Plains	Plains are described as areas of flat or slightly rolling land, usually lower than the landforms next to them. Sometimes called lowlands (and sometimes located along seacoasts), they support the majority of the world's people. Some are found inland and many have been formed by large rivers. This resulted in extremely fertile soil for successful cultivation of crops and numerous large settlements of people. In North America, the vast plains areas extend from the Gulf of Mexico north to the Arctic Ocean and between the Appalachian and Rocky Mountains. In Europe, rich plains extend east from Great Britain into central Europe on into the Siberian region of Russia. Plains in river valleys are found in China (the Yangtze River valley), India (the Ganges River valley), and Southeast Asia (the Mekong River valley).
Valleys	Valleys are land areas that are found between hills and mountains. Some have gentle slopes containing trees and plants; others have very steep walls and are referred to as canyons. One famous example is Arizona's Grand Canyon of the Colorado River, which was formed by erosion.
Deltas	Deltas are areas of lowlands formed by soil and sediment deposited at the mouths of rivers. The soil is generally very fertile and most fertile river deltas are important crop-growing areas. One well-known example is the delta of Egypt's Nile River, known for its production of cotton.
Deserts	Deserts are large dry areas of land receiving ten inches or less of rainfall each year. Among the better known deserts are Africa's large Sahara Desert, the Arabian Desert on the Arabian Peninsula, and the desert Outback covering roughly one third of Australia. Deserts are found mainly in the tropical latitudes and are formed when surrounding features, such as mountain ranges, extract most of the moisture from the prevailing winds.
Mesas	Mesas are the flat tops of hills or mountains usually with steep sides. Mesas are similar to plateaus, but smaller.
Basins	Basins are considered to be low areas drained by rivers or low spots in mountains.
Foothills	Foothills are generally considered a low series of hills found between a plain and a mountain range.
Marshes and Swamps	Marshes and swamps are wet lowlands providing an ecosystem for such plants as rushes and reeds.
Oceans	Oceans are the largest bodies of water on the planet. The four oceans of the Earth are the Atlantic Ocean, one-half the size of the Pacific and separating North and South America from Africa and Europe; the Pacific Ocean, covering almost one-third of the entire surface of the Earth and separating North and South America from Asia and Australia; the Indian Ocean, touching Africa, Asia, and Australia; and the ice-filled Arctic Ocean, extending from North America and Europe to the North Pole. The waters of the Atlantic, Pacific, and Indian Oceans also touch the shores of Antarctica.
Seas	Seas are smaller than oceans and are surrounded by land. Some examples include the Mediterranean Sea found between Europe, Asia, and Africa; and the Caribbean Sea, touching the West Indies, South and Central America.

Continued on next page

Lakes	A lake is a body of water surrounded by land. The Great Lakes in North America are a good example.
Rivers	Rivers, considered a nation's lifeblood, usually begin as very small streams, formed by melting snow and rainfall, flowing from higher to lower land, and emptying into a larger body of water, usually a sea or an ocean. Examples of important rivers for the people and countries affected by and/or dependent on them include the Nile, Niger, and Zaire Rivers of Africa; the Rhine, Danube, and Thames Rivers of Europe; the Yangtze, Ganges, Mekong, Hwang He, and Irrawaddy Rivers of Asia; the Murray-Darling in Australia; and the Orinoco in South America. River systems are made up of large rivers and numerous smaller rivers or tributaries flowing into them. Examples include the vast Amazon River system in South America and the Mississippi River system in the United States.
Canals	Canals are manmade water passages constructed to connect two larger bodies of water. Famous examples include the Panama Canal across Panama's isthmus connecting the Atlantic and Pacific Oceans and the Suez Canal in the Middle East between Africa and the Arabian peninsulas connecting the Red and Mediterranean Seas.

COMPETENCY 9

KNOWLEDGE OF GOVERNMENT AND THE CITIZEN (I.E., GOVERNMENT AND CIVICS)

> **SKILL 9.1** Distinguish between the structure, functions, and purposes of federal, state, and local government.

Powers of the Federal Government

1. To tax

2. To borrow and coin money

3. To establish postal service

4. To grant patents and copyrights

5. To regulate interstate and foreign commerce

6. To establish courts

7. To declare war

8. To raise and support the armed forces

9. To govern territories

10. To define and punish felonies and piracy on the high seas

11. To fix standards of weights and measures

12. To conduct foreign affairs

Powers of the States

1. To regulate intrastate trade

2. To establish local governments

3. To protect general welfare

4. To protect life and property

5. To ratify amendments

6. To conduct elections

7. To make state and local laws

Concurrent Powers of the Federal Government and States

1. Both Congress and the states may tax

2. Both may borrow money

3. Both may charter banks and corporations

4. Both may establish courts

5. Both may make and enforce laws

6. Both may take property for public purposes

7. Both may spend money to provide for the public welfare

Implied Powers of the Federal Government

1. To establish banks or other corporations implied from delegated powers to tax, borrow, and to regulate commerce

2. To spend money for roads, schools, health, insurance, etc., implied from powers to establish post roads, to tax to provide for general welfare and defense, and to regulate commerce

3. To create military academies, implied from powers to raise and support an armed force

4. To locate and generate sources of power and sell surplus implied from powers to dispose of government property, commerce, and war powers

5. To assist and regulate agriculture implied from power to tax and spend for general welfare and regulate commerce

Political parties in the United States have five major functions: (1) choose candidates who will run for public office; (2) assist in organizing the government; (3) formulate political platforms and policies; (4) obtain the funds needed to conduct election campaigns; and (5) make sure voters are aware of issues, problems to be solved, and any other information about public affairs. The two-party system in the United States operates at the national, state, and local levels.

Powers delegated to the federal government:

1. To tax

2. To borrow and coin money

3. To establish a postal service

4. To grant patents and copyrights

5. To regulate interstate and foreign commerce

6. To conduct elections

7. To make state and local laws

8. To raise and support the armed forces

9. To govern territories

10. To define and punish felonies and piracy on the high seas

11. To fix standards of weights and measures

12. To conduct foreign affairs

Powers reserved for the states:

1. To regulate intrastate trade

2. To establish local governments

3. To protect general welfare

4. To protect life and property

5. To ratify amendments

6. To establish courts

7. To declare war

Powers delegated to the local government

Florida has three levels of local government: counties, municipalities, and special districts. Planning for land development and roads within the county is the responsibility of county government. Each county keeps records for its citizens and has its own school district. An elected school board makes most decisions regarding the county's schools. Municipal governments are set up within each county. Cities and towns also set up governing bodies. A mayor is elected as the top official. A city council is elected to make policies and decisions that impact the city or town. The city charter and related laws guide the city council. Public safety is a major responsibility of municipal government. Special districts are spread throughout the state and serve special purposes. District boards make the policies and decisions regarding their purposes.

Compare and contrast the rights and responsibilities of a citizen in the world, nation, state, and community.

CITIZENSHIP is membership in a political state, such as a country or state. With citizenship comes the right to participate politically in a society. Citizenship and nationality are closely related, but they are not always the same. A person can hold citizenship in one country, for instance, but live and work in another country.

> **CITIZENSHIP:** membership in a political state, such as a country or state

Anyone born in the United States is a citizen of the United States, regardless of the nationality or citizenship of his or her parents. Other countries have different rules about obtaining citizenship that may be based on parental heritage or ethnicity. Some countries, such as Switzerland, hold local elections to determine whether a person may become a citizen.

In the past, many countries required an oath of allegiance to become a citizen, and some still do. Some countries, such as Israel, require all citizens to serve at least one term in the military.

At times, countries that grant individual citizenship may unite and create a combined political group that has citizenship rights and responsibilities of its own. The British Commonwealth and the European Union are examples of this kind of group. Citizens of the member states hold additional rights and share additional responsibilities of the larger group. They also may have the right to move freely within the member states.

In all cases, citizenship implies a responsibility to participate in the general improvement of one's society.

**SKILL
9.3** **Identify and interpret major concepts of the U.S. Constitution and other historical documents.**

Declaration of Independence

The Declaration of Independence was the founding document of the United States of America. Conceived and written in large part by Thomas Jefferson, the Declaration is not only important for what it says but also for how it is written. It is in many respects a poetic document. Instead of a simple recitation of the colonists' grievances, it set out clearly the reasons the colonists were seeking their freedom from Great Britain. They had tried all means to resolve the dispute peacefully. It was the right of a people, when all other methods of addressing their grievances have been tried and have failed, to separate themselves from that power that was keeping them from fully expressing their rights to "**life, liberty and the pursuit of happiness.**"

The Declaration's text can be divided into three main parts:

1. Statements of the general state of humanity and the natural rights inherent in all civil societies. Jefferson talks about "self-evident" truths and the unalienable rights of people to "Life, Liberty and the pursuit of Happiness," which show considerable influence from primarily French thinkers of the Enlightenment during the seventeenth and eighteenth centuries. He clearly states that a government that no longer respects these inherent rights loses its legitimacy and becomes despotic. Jefferson also states that the governed have the right to throw off such a government and impose a call for insurrection against the sovereign.

2. An enumeration of specific and detailed grievances, which point out why the current sovereign has lost the right to govern, and that lists how the king even subverted English Common Law and legal traditions dating back to antiquity.

3. The last part of the text states that the colonists had exhausted all civil and legal means of having their grievances addressed by British government and now had the right, and duty, to break with the crown and be a free and independent nation.

The final section of the Declaration contains the signatures of the representatives of the colonies to the Continental Congress in Philadelphia. Realizing that they had committed an act of treason punishable by death by hanging, Benjamin Franklin counseled unity, lest they all hang separately. It should also be noted that when the Declaration was signed, open hostilities between the British and the Colonists had already been underway for over a year. George Washington had taken command of the Continental Army, organized on June 14, 1775 at Harvard Yard, and, in the same year, the Continental Navy and the Marine Corps had been organized.

Articles of Confederation

On November 15, 1777, the Articles of Confederation were adopted, creating a league of free and independent states.

During the war, and after independence was declared, the former colonies found themselves independent states. The Second Continental Congress was conducting a war with representation by delegates from thirteen separate states. The Congress had no power to act for the states or to require them to accept and follow its wishes. A permanent united government was desperately needed. On November 15, 1777, the **Articles of Confederation** were adopted, creating a league of free and independent states.

The central government of the new United States of America consisted of a **Congress** of two to seven delegates from each state, with each state having just one vote. Some of its powers included: borrowing and coining money, directing foreign affairs, declaring war and making peace, building and equipping a navy, regulating weights and measures, and asking the states to supply men and money for an army. The delegates to Congress had no real authority, beacause each state carefully and jealously guarded its own interests and limited powers under the Articles. Also, the delegates to Congress were paid by their states and had to vote as directed by their state legislatures.

Under the Articles, the government had serious weaknesses, including lack of power over the regulation of finances, interstate trade, foreign trade, enforcing treaties, and the military. Within a few months of the adoption of the Articles of Confederation, it became apparent that there were serious defects in the system of government established for the new republic.

U.S. Constitution

The Constitutional Convention met under the presidency of George Washington, with fifty-five of the sixty-five appointed members present. A constitution was written in four months. The **Constitution of the United States** is the fundamental law of the republic. The founders of the Union established it as the highest governmental authority. The foundations were so broadly laid as to provide for the expansion of national life and to make it an instrument that would last for all time.

To maintain its stability, the framers created a difficult process for making any changes to it. No amendment can become valid until it is ratified by three-fourths of all of the states. The British system of government was part of the basis of the final document, but significant changes were necessary to meet the needs of a partnership of states that were tied together as a single federation—yet sovereign in their own local affairs. This constitution established a system of government that was unique and advanced far beyond other systems of its day.

There were, to be sure, differences of opinion. The compromises that resolved these conflicts are reflected in the final document. The first point of disagreement and compromise was related to the presidency. Some wanted a strong, centralized, individual authority. Others feared autocracy or the growth of monarchy. The compromise was to give the president broad powers but to limit the amount of time, through term of office, that any individual could exercise that power. The power to make appointments and to conclude treaties required the consent of the Senate.

The second conflict was between large and small states. The large states wanted power proportionate to their voting strength, but the small states opposed this plan. The compromise was that all states should have equal voting power in the Senate, but membership in the House of Representatives would be determined in proportion to population.

The third conflict was about slavery. The compromise was that 1) fugitive slaves should be returned by states to which they might flee for refuge, and 2) no law would be passed for twenty years prohibiting the importation of slaves.

The fourth major area of conflict was how the president would be chosen. One side argued for election by direct vote of the people. The other side thought Congress should choose the president. One group feared the ignorance of the people, while the other feared the power of a small group of people. The compromise was the **Electoral College**.

The Constitution binds the states in everything that affects the welfare of all. At the same time, it recognizes the right of the people of each state to act independently in matters that relate only to them. Since the federal Constitution is the law of the land, all other laws must conform to it.

The debates conducted during the Constitutional Convention represent the issues and arguments that led to the compromises in the final document. The debates reflect the concerns of the Founding Fathers that the rights of the people be protected from abrogation by the government itself and the determination that no branch of government should have enough power to override the others. There is, therefore, a system of **checks and balances**.

Federalist Papers

The Federalist Papers were written to win popular support for the new proposed Constitution. In these publications, the debates of the Congress and the concerns of the Founding Fathers were made available to the people of the nation. In addition to providing an explanation of the underlying philosophies and concerns of the Constitution and the compromises that were made, the Federalist Papers conducted what has frequently been called the most effective marketing and public relations campaign in human history.

Bill of Rights

The Bill of Rights consists of the first ten amendments to the U.S. Constitution. These amendments were passed almost immediately upon ratification of the Constitution by the states. They reflect the concerns raised throughout the country and by the Founding Fathers during the ratification process.

See also Skill 9.2

SKILL 9.4 **Compare and contrast the ways the legislative, executive, and judicial branches share powers and responsibility.**

In the United States, the three branches of the federal government are the executive, the legislative, and the judicial. They divide their powers in the following manner:

Legislative Branch

Article I of the Constitution established the legislative, or law-making branch of the government, called the Congress. It is made up of two houses: the House of Representatives and the Senate. Voters in all states elect the members who serve in each respective house of Congress. The legislative branch is responsible for making laws, raising and printing money, regulating trade, establishing the postal service and federal courts, approving the president's appointments, and declaring war and supporting the armed forces. The Congress has the power to change the Constitution and to impeach, or bring charges against, the president. Charges for impeachment are brought by the House of Representatives and tried in the Senate.

Executive Branch

Article II of the Constitution created the executive branch of the government, headed by the President, who leads the country, recommends new laws, and can veto bills passed by the legislative branch. As the chief of state, the President is responsible for carrying out the laws of the country and the treaties and declarations of war passed by the legislative branch. The President appoints federal judges and is commander-in-chief of the military. Other members of the executive branch include the Vice-President, who is also elected, and the cabinet members, presidential advisers, ambassadors, agencies, departments, and bureaus of the federal government.

Judicial Branch

Article III of the Constitution established the judicial branch of government headed by the Supreme Court. The Supreme Court has the power to rule that a law passed by Congress or an act of the executive branch is illegal and unconstitutional. In an appeal capacity, citizens, businesses, and government officials can also ask the Supreme Court to review a decision made in a lower court if they believe that the ruling by a judge is unconstitutional. The judicial branch includes lower federal courts known as federal district courts that have been established by Congress.

Checks and balances is a system established by the Constitution in which each branch of the federal government has the power to check or limit the actions of other branches.

Separation of powers is a system of U.S. government in which each branch of government has its own specifically designated powers and cannot interfere with the powers of another.

SKILL 9.5 **Analyze the U.S. electoral system and the election process.**

U.S. citizens have to register in order to vote and, at that time, they can declare their membership in a political party. The Democratic and Republican parties are the two with the most money and power, but other political parties abound.

Candidates affiliate themselves with political parties. Candidates then go about the business of campaigning, which includes publicizing their candidacy, what they believe in, and what they will do if elected. Candidates sometimes get together for debates, to showcase their views on important issues of the day and how those views differ from those of their opponents. Candidates give public speeches, attend public functions, and express their views to reporters, for coverage in newspapers and magazines and on radio and television. On Election Day, candidates hope that what they've done is enough.

Elections take place regularly, so voters know just how long it will be before the next election. Presidential elections are held every four years. Voters technically have the option to **recall** elected candidates. Such a measure, however, is drastic and requires a large number of signatures to get the motion on the ballot and then a large number of votes to have the measure approved. As such, recalls of elected candidates are relatively rare.

Another method of removing public officials from office is **impeachment**. This, too, is rare, but does happen. Both houses of the state or federal government have to approve the impeachment measure by a large margin. In the case of the federal government, the House of Representatives votes to impeach a federal official and the Senate votes to convict or acquit.

Electoral College

The College of Electors—or the Electoral College, as it is more commonly known—has a long and distinguished history of mirroring the political will of the American voters. On some occasions, however, Electoral College results have not been entirely in sync with that political will.

Article II of the Constitution lists the specifics of the Electoral College. The Founding Fathers included the Electoral College as one of the famous "checks and balances" for two reasons:

1. They wanted states with small populations to have more of an equal weight in the presidential election

2. They didn't trust the common people to be able to make an informed decision about which candidate would make the best president

Each state elects two members to the Senate for similar reasons as those that led to the creation of the Electoral College. The large-population states had their populations reflected in the House of Representatives. New York and Pennsylvania, two of the states with the largest populations, had the greatest number of members in the House of Representatives. But these two states still had only two senators—the same number that small-population states like Rhode Island and Delaware had. The same principle applied in the Electoral College. Each state had just one vote, regardless of how many members of the House represented that state.

Technically, the electors do not have to vote for a particular candidate. The Constitution does not require them to do so. However, tradition holds that the electors vote for the candidate chosen by their state and so the vast majority of electors do just that. The Electoral College meets a few weeks after the presidential election. This meeting is generally a formality. When all the electoral votes are counted, the candidate with the most votes wins. In most cases, the candidate who wins the popular vote also wins in the Electoral College, but this has not always been the case.

Election of 2000

In 2000 in Florida, the Supreme Court decided the election. The Democratic Party's candidate was Vice President Al Gore. The Republican Party's candidate was George W. Bush, governor of Texas and son of former president George Bush. The election was hotly contested, and many states went down to the wire, decided by only a handful of votes. The one state that seemed to be flip-flopping as election day turned into election night was Florida. In the end, Gore won the popular vote by nearly 540,000 votes. But he didn't win the electoral vote. The vote was so close in Florida that a recount was necessary under federal law. Eventually, the Supreme

Court weighed in and stopped all the recounts. The last count had Bush winning by less than a thousand votes. That gave him Florida and the White House.

SKILL 9.6 Identify and analyze the relationships between social, economic, and political rights and the historical documents that secure these rights in the United States

Citizenship in a democracy bestows on an individual certain rights, foremost being the right to participate in one's own government. Along with these rights come responsibilities, including the responsibility of a citizen to participate.

The most basic form of participation is the vote. Those who have reached the age of 18 in the United States are eligible to vote in public elections. With this right comes the responsibility to be informed before voting and not to sell or otherwise give away one's vote. Citizens also are eligible to run for public office. Along with the right to run for office comes the responsibility to represent the electors as fairly as possible and to perform the duties expected of a government representative.

In the United States, citizens are guaranteed the right to free speech, which includes the right to express an opinion on public issues. In turn, citizens have the responsibility to allow others to speak freely. At the community level, this might mean speaking at a city council hearing while allowing others with different or opposing viewpoints to have their say without interruption or comment.

The U.S. Constitution also guarantees freedom of religion. This means that the government may not impose an official religion on its citizens and that people are free to practice their religion. Citizens are also responsible for allowing those of other religions to practice freely without obstruction. Occasionally, religious issues will be put before the public at the state level in the form of ballot measures or initiatives. The extent to which religious beliefs may be expressed in a public setting, such as a public school, is a constant source of debate.

In making decisions on matters like these, the citizen is expected to become informed of the issues involved and to vote based on his or her own opinion. Being informed of how one's government works and what the effects of new legislation will be is an essential part of being a good citizen.

The U.S. Constitution also guarantees that all citizens be treated equally by the law. In addition, federal and state laws make it a crime to discriminate against citizens based on their sex, race, religion, and other factors. To ensure that all people are treated equally, citizens have the responsibility to follow these laws.

These rights and responsibilities are essentially the same whether one is voting in a local school board race, for the passage of a new state law, or for the president of the United States. Being a good citizen means exercising one's own rights while allowing others to do the same.

Almost all representative democracies in the world guarantee similar rights to their citizens and expect them to take similar responsibilities to respect the rights of others. As a citizen of the world, one is expected to respect the rights of other nations, and the people of those nations, in the same way.

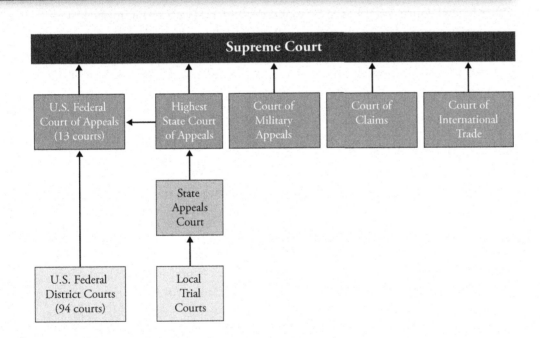

Federal Court System

The federal court system is provided for in the Constitution of the United States on the theory that the judicial power of the federal government could not be entrusted to the individual states, many of which had opposed the idea of a strong federal government. Congress passed the **Judiciary Act** in 1789, organizing the Supreme Court of the United States and establishing a system of federal courts of inferior jurisdiction. The states were left to establish their own judicial systems subject to the exclusive overall jurisdiction of the federal courts and to Article VI of the Constitution, declaring the judges of the state courts to be bound to the

Constitution and to the laws and treaties of the United States. This created a dual system of judicial power and authority.

The courts established under the powers granted by Article III, Sections 1 and 2 of the Constitution are known as constitutional courts. The president, with approval of the Senate, appoints judges of the constitutional courts for life. These courts are the **district courts, lower courts of original jurisdiction**, the **courts of appeals** (before 1948, known as the circuit courts of appeals), exercising appellate jurisdiction over the district courts, and the **Supreme Court**. A district court functions in each of the more than ninety federal judicial districts and in the District of Columbia.

The Supreme Court is the highest appellate court in the country and is a court of original jurisdiction. By virtue of its power to declare legislation unconstitutional, the Supreme Court is the final arbitrator of all Constitutional questions.

Other federal courts, established by Congress under powers to be implied in other articles of the Constitution, are called legislative courts. These courts are the **Court of Claims, the Court of Customs and Patent Appeals, the Customs Court**, and the territorial courts established in the federally administered territories of the United States.

The State Courts

In cases involving the U.S. Constitution or federal laws or treaties, the state courts are governed by the decisions of the U.S. Supreme Court and their decisions are subject to review by it.

Each state has an independent system of courts operating under the laws and constitution of that particular state. Broadly speaking, the state courts are based on the English judicial system as it existed in colonial times, but as modified by succeeding statutes. The character and names of the various courts differ from state to state, but the state courts as a whole have general jurisdiction, except in cases in which exclusive jurisdiction has by law been vested in the federal courts. In cases involving the U.S. Constitution or federal laws or treaties, the state courts are governed by the decisions of the U.S. Supreme Court and their decisions are subject to review by it.

Cases involving the federal Constitution or federal laws or treaties may be brought to either the state courts or the federal courts. Ordinary **civil suits** can be brought only to the state courts, except in cases of different state citizenship between the parties, in which case the suit may be brought to a federal court.

County courts of general original jurisdiction exercise both criminal and civil jurisdictions in most states. In a number of states, there are intermediate appellate courts between the lower courts and the supreme appellate courts. Like the federal courts of appeals, appellate courts handle a large number of cases that would otherwise be added to the overcrowded calendars of the higher courts. Courts of last resort, the highest appellate courts for the states in criminal and civil cases are usually called **state Supreme Courts**.

The state court system includes a number of minor local courts with limited jurisdictions. These courts dispose of minor offenses and relatively small civil actions. Included in this classification are police and municipal courts in various cities and towns and the courts presided over by justices of the peace in rural areas.

COMPETENCY 10

KNOWLEDGE OF PRODUCTION, DISTRIBUTION, AND CONSUMPTION (I.E., ECONOMICS)

> **SKILL 10.1** Determine ways that scarcity affects the choices made by governments and individuals.

Economics is the study of how a society allocates its scarce resources to satisfy what are basically unlimited and competing wants. Economics can also be defined as a study of the production, consumption, and distribution of goods and services. A fundamental fact of economics is that resources are scarce and that wants are infinite. The fact that scarce resources have to satisfy unlimited wants means that choices have to be made. If society uses its resources to produce good A, then it doesn't have those resources to produce good B. This tradeoff is referred to as the **opportunity cost**, or the value of the sacrificed alternative.

> *Economics is the study of how a society allocates its scarce resources to satisfy what are basically unlimited and competing wants.*

On the consumption side of the market, consumers buy the goods and services that give them satisfaction, or utility. They want to obtain the most utility they can for their dollar. The quantity of goods and services that consumers are willing and able to purchase at different prices during a given period of time is referred to as **demand**. Since consumers buy the goods and services that give them satisfaction, this means that, for the most part, they don't buy the goods and services that don't give them satisfaction. Consumers are, in effect, voting for the goods and services that they want with their dollars. This concept is referred to as **dollar voting**. A good that society wants acquires enough dollar votes for the producer to make a profit.

This process in which consumers vote with their dollars is called **consumer sovereignty**. Consumers are basically directing the allocation of scarce resources in the economy with their dollar spending. Firms, which are in business to earn profits, hire resources or inputs in accordance with consumer preferences. This is the way resources are allocated in a **market economy**.

> *The supply of a good or service is defined as the quantity of a good or service that a producer is willing and able to sell at different prices during a given period of time.*

Price plays an important role in a market economy. Demand was defined above. Supply is based on production costs. The supply of a good or service is defined as the quantity of a good or service that a producer is willing and able to sell at different prices during a given period of time. Market equilibrium occurs when the buying decisions of buyers are equal to the selling decisions of sellers, or when the demand and supply curves intersect. At this point, the quantity that sellers want to sell at a particular price is equal to the quantity the buyers want to buy at that price. This is the market equilibrium price.

SKILL 10.2 Compare and contrast the characteristics and importance of currency.

There are various forms of **currency**. The United States utilizes the dollar, Europe uses the euro, Japan uses the yen, and countries including Chile, Colombia, Cuba, and the Dominican Republic use the peso. A competent authority, usually a central bank, determines and guarantees the value of each currency.

See also Skill 10.5

SKILL 10.3 Identify and analyze the role of markets from production through distribution to consumption.

Free enterprise, individual entrepreneurship, competitive markets, and consumer sovereignty are all parts of a market economy. Individuals have the right to make their own decisions as to what they want to do as a career. The financial incentives are there for individuals who are willing to take the risk. A successful venture earns profit. It is these financial incentives that serve to motivate inventors and small businesses. The same is true for larger businesses. They are free to determine which production technique they want to use and what output they want to produce within the confines of the legal system. They can make investments based on their own decisions.

A **MARKET** is technically whatever mechanism brings buyers and sellers in contact with each other so that they can buy and sell. Buyers and sellers do not have to meet face to face. When a consumer buys a good from a catalog or over the Internet, the buyer never comes face to face with the seller, yet both buyer and seller are part of a bona fide market. Markets exist on both the input and output sides of the economy.

The **INPUT MARKET** is the market in which factors of production, or resources, are bought and sold. Factors of production, or inputs, fall into four broad categories: land, labor, capital and entrepreneurship. Each of these inputs in used in the production of every good and service.

OUTPUT MARKETS are the markets in which goods and services are sold. When the consumer goes to the local shoe store to buy a pair of shoes, the shoes are the output and the consumer is taking part in the output market. However, the shoe store is a participant in both the input and output market. The sales clerk and store workers are hiring out their resource (labor) in return for a wage rate. They are participating in the input market.

MARKET: whatever mechanism brings buyers and sellers in contact with each other so that they can buy and sell

INPUT MARKET: the market in which factors of production, or resources, are bought and sold

OUTPUT MARKET: the market in which goods and services are sold

In a market-oriented economy, all of these markets function on the basis of supply and demand, whether they are input or output markets. The equilibrium price is determined where the buying decisions of buyers coincide with the selling decision of sellers. This is true whether the market is an input market with a market wage rate or an output market with a market output price. This results in the most efficient allocation of resources.

The best place to see supply and demand and markets in action is at a stock exchange or at a commodity futures exchange. Buyers and sellers come face to face in the trading pit and accomplish trades by open outcry. Sellers wanting to sell stocks or futures contracts call out the prices they will sell at. Buyers wanting to buy stocks or futures contracts call out the prices they will buy at. When they agree on price, a trade is made. This process goes on throughout trading hours.

The same kinds of forces are at work at your local shopping mall or grocery store, even though the price is given to you, the consumer. That price was reached through the operation of supply and demand. The equilibrium price is the price that "clears the markets," which means that there are no shortages or surpluses. If the price is too high, consumers won't buy the product and the store will have a surplus of the good. The store will have to lower prices to eliminate the surplus merchandise. If the price is too low, consumers will buy so much that there will be a shortage. The shortage will be alleviated as the price is bid up, rationing the good to those (stores) that are willing and able to pay the higher price for the good and then charge their customers the higher price. In cases where the government imposes legally mandated prices, either above or below the market, the result is shortages (with a price imposed below the market price) or surpluses (with a price imposed above the market price). The existence of price supports in agriculture is the reason for the surplus in agricultural products.

See also Skill 10.4

SKILL 10.4 Identify and analyze factors to consider when making consumer decisions.

Time and money are scarce resources.

Consumers do not have enough time and money to do everything that they want and to buy everything that they want. Time and money are scarce resources. Scarcity is evident in personal financial management. Scarcity here refers to dollars and paying bills. There are only so many dollars available. People's paychecks have to cover the bills or they find themselves in the position of paying one bill and not another.

Scarcity means that consumers can't have all of the goods that they want and do all of the activities that they want to do. Choices have to be made and all of these choices involve opportunity costs.

The scarcity of resources is the basis for the existence of economics. Economics is defined as the study of how scarce resources are allocated to satisfy unlimited wants. Resources refer to the four factors of production: labor, capital, land, and entrepreneurship. Labor refers to anyone who sells his/her ability to produce goods and services. Capital is anything that is manufactured to be used in the production process. Land refers to the land and everything occurring naturally on it, like oil, minerals, lumber, etc. Entrepreneurship is the ability of an individual to combine the three inputs with his/her own talents to produce a viable good or service. The entrepreneur takes the risk and experiences the losses or profits.

The fact that the supply of these resources is finite means that society cannot have as much of everything as it wants. There is a constraint on production and consumption and on the kinds of goods and services that can be produced and consumed. Scarcity means that choices have to be made. If a society decides to produce more of one good, this means there are fewer resources available for the production of other goods.

> If a society decides to produce more of one good, this means there are fewer resources available for the production of other goods

Assume that a society can produce two goods, good X and good Y. The society uses resources in the production of each good. If producing one unit of good X requires the number of resources used to produce three units of good Y, then producing one more unit of good X results in a decrease in three units of good Y. In effect, one unit of good X "costs" three units of good Y. This cost is referred to as **opportunity cost**. Opportunity cost is the value of the sacrificed alternative, the value of what had to be given up in order to have the output of good X. Opportunity cost does not just refer to production. Your opportunity cost of studying with this guide is the value of what you are not doing because you are studying, whether it is reading a novel, watching TV, spending time with family, or working. Every choice has an opportunity cost.

Because resources are scarce, society doesn't want to waste them. The members of society don't want their scarce resources wasted through inefficiency. This means producers of goods must choose an efficient production process, which is the lowest-cost means of production. High costs mean wasted resources. Consumers also don't want society's resources wasted by producing goods that they don't want. How do producers know what goods consumers want? Consumers buy the goods they want, voting with their dollar spending. A desirable good, one that consumers want, earns a profit. A good that incurs losses is a good that society doesn't want its resources wasted on.

Trade

> The nation that can produce a good more cheaply should specialize in the production of that good and trade for the good in which it has the comparative disadvantage.

The theory of comparative advantage says that trade should be based on the comparative opportunity costs between two nations. The nation that can produce a good more cheaply should specialize in the production of that good and trade for the good in which it has the comparative disadvantage. In this way, both nations will experience gains from trade. A basis for trade exists if there are differing comparative costs in each country.

Suppose country A can produce ten units of good x or ten units of good y with its resources. Country B can produce thirty units of x or ten units of y with its resources. What are the relative costs in each country? In country A, one x costs one unit of y, and in country B, one x costs three units of y. Good y is cheaper in country B than it is in country A, $1/3x = 1y$ in country B versus $1y = 1x$ in country A. Country B has the comparative advantage in the production of y and country A has the comparative advantage in the production of good x. According to trade theory, each country should specialize in the production of the good in which it has the comparative advantage. Country B will devote all of its resources to the production of good y, and country A will devote all of its resources to the production of good x. Each country will trade for the good in which it has the comparative disadvantage.

In today's world, markets are international. Nations are all part of a global economy. No nation exists in complete isolation or is totally independent of other nations. An economy that is entirely self-sufficient is said to be an autarky. Membership in a global economy means that what one nation does affects other nations because economies are linked through international trade, commerce, and finance. International transactions affect the levels of income, employment, and prices in each of the trading economies.

> In a country like the United States, trade represents only a small percentage of GDP. In other nations, trade may represent over 50 percent of GDP.

The relative importance of trade is based on what percentage of gross domestic product (GDP) trade constitutes. In a country like the United States, trade represents only a small percentage of GDP. In other nations, trade may represent over 50 percent of GDP. For those countries, changes in international transactions can cause many economic fluctuations and problems.

Trade barriers

Trade barriers are one way economic problems are caused in other countries. Suppose a domestic government is confronted with rising unemployment in a domestic industry due to cheaper foreign imports. Consumers are buying the cheaper foreign import instead of the higher-priced domestic good. In order to protect domestic labor, the government imposes a tariff, thus raising the price of the more efficiently produced foreign good. The result of the tariff is that consumers buy more of the domestic good and less of the foreign good. The problem is that the foreign good is the product of the foreign nation's labor. A decrease in the demand for the foreign good means foreign producers don't need as much labor, so they lay off workers in the foreign country.

The result of the trade barrier is that unemployment has been exported from the domestic country to the foreign country. Treaties like the North American Free Trade Agreement (NAFTA) are a way of lowering or eliminating trade barriers on a regional basis. As trade barriers are lowered or eliminated, labor and output markets change. Some grow; some shrink. These adjustments are taking place now for Canada, the United States, and Mexico.

Capital Markets

The same thing can happen through the exchange rate and other capital markets. Capital goes where it receives the highest rate of return, regardless of national borders. Nations can affect their exchange rate values by buying and selling foreign exchange in the currency markets. Suppose the United States decides that a lower-valued dollar will stimulate its exports, leading to higher employment levels in the United States. The United States, in effect, sells dollars on the open market, thus increasing the supply of dollars on the world market. The effect is a depreciation of the dollar. The lower-valued dollar makes U.S. exports more attractive to foreigners, who buy the relatively cheaper U.S. exports instead of the now relatively higher priced domestic goods. The increased demand for U.S. exports leads to higher employment levels in the export industries in the United States. The lower demand for domestic products in the foreign country leads to unemployment in its domestic industries.

Labor Costs

The existence of multinational corporations means that plants also go where the costs are lowest because it leads to higher levels of profits for them.

**SKILL Identify human, natural, and capital resources and evaluate how
10.6 these resources are used in the production of goods and services.**

RESOURCE: an input into
the production process

A RESOURCE is an input into the production process. When resources are limited in supply, they are scarce. There are not enough of them to produce all of the goods and services that society wants. Resources are called "factors of production" and there are four factors of production: labor, capital, land, and entrepreneurship. Labor refers to all kinds of labor used in the production process. It doesn't matter if the labor is skilled or unskilled, part-time or full-time. All laborers are selling their ability to produce goods and services. Capital refers to anything that is made or manufactured for use in the production process. Included in this definition are plants, equipment, machines, tools, etc. Land includes land and all natural resources—lumber, minerals, oil, etc.

An entrepreneur is an individual who has the ability to combine land, labor, and capital to produce a good or service. The entrepreneur is the one who bears the risks of failure and loss and the one who will gain from the profits if the product is successful. Every good and service that is produced uses some combination of each of the four inputs. The production process refers to the way the four factors are combined to produce the output. If the production technique uses a lot of machinery with very few laborers, then it is a capital-intensive production process. If the process requires many workers with very little machinery, then it is said to be a labor-intensive production process. Whatever the production technique, there are not enough resources to produce all of the goods and services that a society wants.

The scarcity of resources functions as a constraint on the amounts and kinds of goods and services that the economy can produce and consume. The scarcity of resources affects the production, distribution, and consumption decisions of the society. Production is determined by the available resource supply, both quantity and quality. For example, if there are not enough workers for a particular production technique, then smart owners will find machinery that requires fewer workers if they are going to stay in business. Consumers can't consume goods and services that can't be produced or distributed.

DOMAIN III
SCIENCE

PERSONALIZED STUDY PLAN

PAGE	COMPETENCY AND SKILL	
179	**11:** **Knowledge of effective science instruction**	☐
	11.1: Analyze and apply developmentally appropriate researched-based strategies for teaching science practices	☐
	11.2: Select and apply safe and effective instructional strategies to utilize manipulatives, models, scientific equipment, real-world examples, and print and digital representations to support and enhance science instruction	☐
	11.3: Identify and analyze strategies for formal and informal learning experiences to provide science curriculum that promotes students' innate curiosity and active inquiry	☐
	11.4: Select and analyze collaborative strategies to help students explain concepts, to introduce and clarify formal science terms, and to identify misconceptions	☐
	11.5: Identify and apply appropriate reading strategies, mathematical practices, and science-content materials to enhance science instruction for learners at all levels	☐
	11.6: Apply differentiated strategies in science instruction and assessments based on student needs	☐
	11.7: Identify and apply ways to organize and manage a classroom for safe, effective science teaching that reflect state safety procedures and restrictions	☐
	11.8: Select and apply appropriate technology, science tools and measurement units for students' use in data collection and the pursuit of science	☐
	11.9: Select and analyze developmentally appropriate diagnostic, formative and summative assessments to evaluate prior knowledge, guide instruction, and evaluate student achievement	☐
	11.10: Choose scientifically and professionally responsible content and activities that are socially and culturally sensitive	☐
192	**12:** **Knowledge of the nature of science**	☐
	12.1: Analyze the dynamic nature of science models, laws, mechanisms, and theories that explain natural phenomena	☐
	12.2: Identify and apply science and engineering practices through integrated process skills	☐
	12.3: Differentiate between the characteristics of experiments and other types of scientific investigations	☐
	12.4: Identify and analyze attitudes and dispositions underlying scientific thinking	☐
	12.5: Identify and select appropriate tools, including digital technologies, and units of measurement for various science tasks	☐
	12.6: Evaluate and interpret pictorial representations, charts, tables, and graphs of authentic data from scientific investigations to make predictions, construct explanations, and support conclusions	☐
	12.7: Identify and analyze ways in which science is an interdisciplinary process and interconnected to STEM disciplines	☐
	12.8: Analyze the interactions of science and technology with society including cultural, ethical, economic, political, and global factors	☐

PERSONALIZED STUDY PLAN

KNOWN MATERIAL/ SKIP IT

PAGE	COMPETENCY AND SKILL	
202	**13: Knowledge of physical sciences**	☐
	13.1: Identify and differentiate among the physical properties of matter	☐
	13.2: Identify and differentiate between physical and chemical changes	☐
	13.3: Compare the properties of matter during phase changes through the addition and/or removal of energy	☐
	13.4: Differentiate between the properties of homogeneous mixtures and heterogeneous mixtures	☐
	13.5: Identify examples of and relationships among atoms, elements, molecules, and compounds	☐
	13.6: Identify and compare potential and kinetic energy	☐
	13.7: Differentiate among forms of energy, transformations of energy, and their real-world applications	☐
	13.8: Distinguish among temperature, heat, and forms of heat transfer	☐
	13.9: Analyze the functionality of an electrical circuit based on its conductors, insulators, and components	☐
	13.10: Identify and apply the characteristics of contact forces, at-a-distance forces, and their effects on matter	☐
214	**14: Knowledge of Earth and space**	☐
	14.1: Identify characteristics of geologic formations and the mechanisms by which they are changed	☐
	14.2: Identify and distinguish among major groups and properties of rocks and minerals and the processes of their formations	☐
	14.3: Identify and analyze the characteristics of soil, its components and profile, and the process of soil formation	☐
	14.4: Identify and analyze processes by which energy from the Sun is transferred through Earth's systems	☐
	14.5: Identify and analyze the causes and effects of atmospheric processes and conditions	☐
	14.6: Identify and analyze various conservation methods and their effectiveness in relation to renewable and nonrenewable natural resources	☐
	14.7: Analyze the Sun-Earth-Moon system in order to explain repeated patterns such as day and night, phases of the Moon, tides, and seasons	☐
	14.8: Compare and differentiate the composition and various relationships among the objects of our Solar System	☐
	14.9: Identify major events in the history of space exploration and their effects on society	☐

PERSONALIZED STUDY PLAN

KNOWN MATERIAL/ SKIP IT

PAGE	COMPETENCY AND SKILL	
238	**15: Knowledge of life science**	☐
	15.1: Identify and compare the characteristics of living and nonliving things	☐
	15.2: Analyze the cell theory as it relates to the functional and structural hierarchy of all living things	☐
	15.3: Identify and compare the structures and functions of plant and animal cells	☐
	15.4: Classify living things into major groups and compare according to characteristics	☐
	15.5: Compare and contrast the structures, functions, and interactions of human and other animal organ systems	☐
	15.6: Distinguish among infectious agents, their transmission, and their effects on the human body	☐
	15.7: Identify and analyze the processes of heredity and natural selection and the scientific theory of evolution	☐
	15.8: Analyze the interdependence of living things with each other and with their environment	☐
	15.9: Identify and analyze plant structures and the processes of photosynthesis, transpiration, and reproduction	☐
	15.10: Predict the responses of plants to various stimuli	☐
	15.11: Identify and compare the life cycles and predictable ways plants and animals change as they grow, develop, and age	☐

COMPETENCY 11
KNOWLEDGE OF EFFECTIVE SCIENCE INSTRUCTION

**SKILL Analyze and apply developmentally appropriate researched-based
11.1 strategies for teaching science practices.**

Individual teaching should be the method for exceptional students and those
who need more attention than the regular student. A few minutes of explaining
the lesson or the task on hand will be very helpful. In the case of pair share or
collaborative pairs, a small assignment could be given and a time frame set, at the
end of which students will share as a class what they have learned. This is very
good if an exceptional student and a bright student are paired. A small group
is very productive since there are many things involved in that situation, such
as sharing information, waiting for one's turn, listening to other's ideas, views,
and suggestions, and taking responsibility for doing a job in the group (writing/
presenting/drawing etc.) which also teach basic manners. Teaching as a class
involves traditional and modern methods such as lecture, lecture/demonstration,
pause and lecture, etc. The same applies for experimental, field and nonexperi-
mental work.

**SKILL Select and apply safe and effective instructional strategies to utilize
11.2 manipulatives, models, scientific equipment, real-world examples,
and print and digital representations to support and enhance science
instruction.**

Today's learning, especially science, is largely inquiry-based. Sometimes it becomes
part of teaching to encourage the students to ask questions. Sufficient time must
be given to students to ask these questions.

As a teacher, one must be a good manager of not only the classroom but also of
time, resources, and space. The teacher needs to plan how much time should
be given to exceptional students, bright students, regular students, and disruptive students. The exceptional and the disruptive students must get more of the
teacher's time. Next will be the regular and last the bright students, since they
are a few steps ahead of the rest. If they finish work quickly, however, bright
students need to be engaged, so some extra work must be available. In terms of
space the same things apply. Resources must be shared equally as far as possible,

since everybody has the right to have equal opportunity. However, there must be modification of resources suitable for the exceptional students, if required.

One thing is most important—a teacher must use logic and be able to think laterally since all the answers are not in books. The best teaching is part original thinking and part innovation and ingenuity.

Scientific questions are very important because they are the starting point for learning. Students need to be encouraged, provoked and challenged to ask questions. The questions need not necessarily make sense at the beginning, but as time goes by, these questions begin to make more and more sense.

First and foremost, the teacher must encourage students to ask questions and to learn how to frame questions on their own.

There are a few ways in which the students can be encouraged to ask questions:

1. **Brainstorming** the topic under study

2. **Discussing** it in the class and inviting students to ask questions

3. By letting students **discuss in small groups** and come up with questions—this is extremely useful to students who are introverts and shy by nature.

There can be other ways as well besides those mentioned above. The teacher must realize that **questioning** is an important tool in teaching and it can be an effective in learning as well. It must be mentioned here that not all students are curious and inquisitive. Not all parents encourage their children to ask questions. In such cases the teacher needs to show lot of patience in encouraging the students to be inquisitive and curious. This takes time and a classroom environment in which risk-taking is valued.

The next step in this process of teaching students to question is, **refining questions**. By now the students have learned to ask questions. These questions may not be completely relevant to the topic under discussion, but the students have at least formulated a set of questions. At this stage the teacher needs to support students in refining their queries to develop open-ended questions (such as 'how' and 'why') that require investigation. Many times the students may end up asking questions such as: *Who landed on the moon?* These sorts of questions are not really knowledge generating questions. They are not thought provoking questions. The teacher can modify this question to *What did the missions to moon accomplish?* With this type of question, a lot of discussion will be generated. Who landed on the moon first, as well as the weather of the moon, moon rock samples, etc.

The next step is focusing. The questions need to be focused on the topic under discussion or investigation. Focusing is absolutely important because it is very easy to be carried away and to be side tracked. The students need to be made aware of being able to focus on a topic understand and not to deviating from it, however tempting it may be.

The last step in this is testing scientific questions and hypotheses. Not all questions can be tested. Some questions can be answered by research. The previously mentioned question about the moon landing, for example, cannot be tested, but it can be answered through research. A wealth of information could be discovered and most of the questions will be answered.

However, some questions can be tested and answers can be found. For example, *Which fertilizer is best for rose cuttings?* This kind of question can best be answered with the use of experimentation.

<blockquote>
SKILL 11.3 **Identify and analyze strategies for formal and informal learning experiences to provide science curriculum that promotes students' innate curiosity and active inquiry** (e.g., hands-on experiences, active engagement in the natural world, student interaction).
</blockquote>

Learning styles are the ways in which individuals learn best. Physical settings, instructional arrangements, materials available, techniques, and individual preferences are all factors in the teacher's choice of instructional strategies and materials. Information about students' preferences can be obtained through a direct interview or a Likert-style checklist on which the student rates his or her preferences.

Physical Settings

1. **Noise:** The amount of background noise or talking that students can tolerate without getting distracted or frustrated varies.

2. **Temperature and lighting:** Students' preferences for lighter or darker areas of the room, tolerance for coolness or heat, and ability to see the chalkboard, screen, or other areas of the room vary.

3. **Physical factors:** These include a student's need for workspace and preference for type of work area, such as desk, table, or learning center. Depending on the student, proximity factors such as closeness to other students, the teacher, or high-traffic areas such as doorways or pencil sharpeners may help the student feel secure and stay on task or may serve as distractions.

Instructional Arrangements

Some students work well in large groups; others prefer small groups or one-on-one instruction with the teacher, aide, or volunteer. Instructional arrangements also involve peer-tutoring situations with the student as tutor or tutee. The teacher needs to consider how well each student works independently with seatwork.

Instructional Techniques

Considering the following factors will help the teacher choose instructional techniques and select optimal times to schedule certain types of assignments.

- How much time the student needs to complete work

- Time of day the student works best

- How student functions under timed conditions

- How much teacher demonstration and attention is needed for the task

- The student's willingness to approach new tasks

- The student's willingness to give up

- The student's preference for verbal or written instruction

- The student's frustration tolerance when faced with difficulty

- The number of prompts and cues and the level of attention needed for the student to maintain expected behavior

Material and Textbook Preferences

Students vary in their ability to respond to and learn from different techniques of lesson presentation. They likewise vary in their preference for and ability to learn from different types of materials. Depending on the student's preferences and abilities, the teacher can choose from these types of instructional materials:

- Self-correcting materials

- Worksheets with or without visual cues

- Worksheets with a reduced number of items or lots of writing space

- Manipulative materials

- Flash cards, commercial or student-prepared

- Computers

- Commercial materials

- Teacher-made materials

- Games, board or card

- Student-made instructional materials

Learning Styles

Students also display preferences for certain learning styles. The teacher should consider these preferences when selecting presentation methods and materials.

1. **Visual:** Students who are visual may enjoy working with and remember best from books, films, pictures, pictures, modeling, audiovisual presentations, demonstrations, and writing.

2. **Auditory:** Students who are auditory may enjoy working with and remember best from listening to recordings, auditory directions, people, radio, read-aloud stories, and lectures.

3. **Tactile:** Students who are tactile may enjoy drawing, tracing, and manipulating and working with materials such as clay or paints.

4. **Kinesthetic:** Students who are kinesthetic may enjoy writing, experiments, operating machines such as typewriters or calculators, motor activities and games, and taking pictures.

SKILL 11.4 **Select and analyze collaborative strategies to help students explain concepts, to introduce and clarify formal science terms, and to identify misconceptions.**

Using scientific terms and phrases consistently during science activities allows science educators to model scientific thinking and questioning and also to clear up any scientific misconceptions. The more opportunities provided for students to experience scientific endeavors, the more natural their scientific vocabulary and understanding of topics will become. Teachers should maximize these opportunities beginning with very young learners, and include the chance for collaboration on a regular basis.

It is effective to incorporate pictures and labels into science instruction. The use of visual reinforcement supports comprehension and retention. Repeating words as much as possible helps clarify pronunciation and provides opportunities to transfer words from working memory to long-term memory. Expose students to vocabulary words often, and in various contexts. This gives students a model for how words are used appropriately. Conduct collaborative group work. Build on students' prior knowledge. An important part of this is identifying students' misconceptions and addressing them. Engage students in instructional conversations so the topics become relevant and have meaning to them. Provide students with opportunities to brainstorm ideas about science and encourage them to wonder and talk about the natural world. Students are likely to become more confident in science through the use of these strategies and suggestions.

> ### SKILL 11.5 Identify and apply appropriate reading strategies, mathematical practices, and science-content materials to enhance science instruction for learners at all levels.

Applying appropriate reading strategies to science instruction is essential to quality science learning. Confidence with vocabulary, non-fiction text, making predictions, and analysis skills will help learners to fully understand concepts. Mathematics helps us to understand science and to design, conduct, and analyze the results of scientific experiments. Science requires us to collect data, interpret it for significant patterns, and make conclusions that further our knowledge. To collect and analyze data, students must be able to apply mathematical content and practices. This includes selecting appropriate tools, using those tools to model the data by describing it mathematically, and reasoning both quantitatively and abstrctly to both understand the data itself and to draw conclusions from it.

Providing students with a variety of materials to enhance their learning is critical. Tapping into prior knowledge, providing clear-cut explanations and relevant vocabulary, as well as strategies that students will find useful are all important to enhancing science instruction. Help students understand that error is a regular part of scientific experimentation. They need to be able to determine why an error might be occurring and how to account for it (e.g., incorrect measurement, limitations in measuring tools, imperfect models). Give students the opportunity to step back and reflect on how using tools to investigate, identify patterns, and develop theories contributes to the accumulation of scientific knowledge. Ask questions to guide students' thinking about the use and significance of mathematics in a scientific context. Support their efforts to understand by explicitly asking about the connections between data and concepts. Always consider each student's needs and learning style when making decisions regarding instruction.

See also Skill 11.4

SKILL 11.6 Apply differentiated strategies in science instruction and assessments based on student needs.

Science teachers should be aware of the multitude of strategies they can use to assess the scientific knowledge students have and how they can determine areas of strength or weakness. While science is a content area in which students engage in experimentation, teachers should not just look at the result of the experiments the students create. Assessment should take the form of discussing all aspects of the scientific model and determining whether students can adequately explain their experiments, offering reasons for the results obtained.

Other techniques used in the assessment of science may include:

- The use of open-ended questions to prompt students to develop their own inquiries on the topic

- Projects in which pairs or groups of students work together to create an experiment and prepare a report

- Different types of writing, such as journals and logbooks, informative writing, and technical writing, reporting results of experiments over a period of time

- Portfolio assessments, which can show growth in scientific knowledge and higher-order thinking skills over a period of time

SKILL 11.7 Identify and apply ways to organize and manage a classroom for safe, effective science teaching that reflect state safety procedures and restrictions (e.g., procedures, equipment, disposal of chemicals, classroom layout, use of living organisms).

Some of the most common laboratory activities are dissections; preserving, staining, and mounting microscopic specimens; and preparing laboratory solutions.

Laboratory Safety Procedures

Students should wear safety goggles when performing dissections, heating, or while using acids and bases. Hair should always be tied back and objects should never be placed in the mouth. Food should not be consumed while in the laboratory. Hands should always be washed before and after laboratory experiments. In case of an accident, eyewashes and showers should be used for eye contamination or a chemical spill that covers a student's body. Small chemical spills should only be contained and cleaned by the teacher. Kitty litter or a chemical spill kit should be used to clean up a spill. For large spills, the school administration and the local fire department should be notified. Biological spills should also be handled only by the teacher. Contamination with biological waste can be cleaned by using bleach when appropriate.

Accidents and injuries should always be reported to the school administration and local health facilities. The severity of the accident or injury will determine the course of action to pursue.

> It is the responsibility of the teacher to provide a safe environment for all students.

It is the responsibility of the teacher to provide a safe environment for all students. Proper supervision greatly reduces the risk of injury, and a teacher should never leave a class for any reason without providing alternate supervision. After an accident, two factors are considered: foreseeability and negligence. **Foreseeability** is the anticipation that an event may occur under certain circumstances. **Negligence** is the failure to exercise ordinary or reasonable care. Safety procedures should be a part of the science curriculum and a well-managed classroom is important to avoid potential lawsuits.

Procedures and tools

Chemicals should not be stored on bench tops or near heat sources. They should be stored in groups based on their reactivity with one another and in protective storage cabinets. All containers in the lab must be labeled. Suspected and known carcinogens must be labeled as such and segregated in trays to contain potential leaks and spills. Chemical waste should be disposed of in properly labeled containers. Waste should be separated based on its reactivity with other chemicals.

Biological material should never be stored near food or water meant for human consumption. All biological material should be appropriately labeled. All blood and body fluids should be put in a well-secured container with a secure lid to prevent leaking. All biological waste should be disposed of in biological hazardous waste bags.

Safety Equipment

All science labs should contain the following safety equipment, which is required by law:

- Fire blanket that is visible and accessible
- Ground fault circuit interrupters (GFCIs) within two feet of water supplies
- Emergency shower capable of providing a continuous flow of water
- Signs designating room exits
- Emergency eyewash station, which can be activated by the foot or forearm

- Eye protection for every student and a means of sanitizing equipment

- Emergency exhaust fans providing ventilation to the outside of the building

- Master cutoff switches for gas, electric, and compressed air. Switches must have permanently attached handles. Cutoff switches must be clearly labeled.

- An ABC fire extinguisher

- Storage cabinets for inflammable materials

Also recommended, but not required by law:

- Chemical spill control kit

- Fume hood with a spark-proof motor

- Protective laboratory aprons made of flame-retardant material

- Signs that will alert people to potentially hazardous conditions

- Containers for broken glassware, inflammables, corrosives, and waste

- Containers should be labeled

It is the responsibility of teachers to provide a safe environment for their students. Proper supervision greatly reduces the risk of injury, and a teacher should never leave a classroom for any reason without providing alternate supervision. After an accident, two factors are considered: foreseeability and negligence. **Foreseeability** is the anticipation that an event may occur under certain circumstances. **Negligence** is the failure to exercise ordinary or reasonable care.

Hazardous Chemicals

The **Right-to-Know law** covers science teachers who work with potentially hazardous chemicals. Briefly, the law states that employees must be informed of potentially toxic chemicals. An inventory, containing information about the hazards and properties of the chemicals, must be made available if requested. Training must be provided in the safe handling and interpretation of the material safety data sheet (MSDS).

The following chemicals are potential carcinogens and are not allowed in school facilities: acrylonitrile, arsenic compounds, asbestos, benzidine, benzene, cadmium compounds, chloroform, chromium compounds, ethylene oxide, ortho-toluidine, nickel powder, mercury.

All laboratory solutions should be prepared as directed in the lab manual. Care should be taken to avoid contamination. All glassware should be rinsed thoroughly with distilled water before using and cleaned well after use. Safety goggles should be worn while working with glassware in case of an accident. All solutions should be made with distilled water because tap water contains dissolved particles, which may affect the results of an experiment. Chemical storage should be located in a secured, dry area and should be stored in accordance with reactability. Acids must be locked in a separate area. Used solutions should be disposed of according to local disposal procedures. Any questions regarding safe disposal or chemical safety can be directed to the local fire department.

Dissection

Animals that are not obtained from recognized sources should not be used. Decaying animals or those of unknown origin may harbor pathogens and/or parasites. Specimens should always be rinsed before handling. Students should use latex gloves; if gloves are not available, students with sores or scratches should be excused from the activity. Formaldehyde is a carcinogen and should be avoided or disposed of according to district regulations. Students who object to dissection for moral reasons should be given an alternative assignment.

Live Specimens

No dissections may be performed on living mammalian vertebrates or birds. Lower-order life and invertebrates can be used.

Biological experiments can be done with all animals except mammalian vertebrates or birds. No physiological harm can result to the animal. All animals housed and cared for in the school must be handled in a safe and humane manner. Animals are not to remain on school premises during extended vacations unless adequate care is provided. Many state laws stipulate that any instructor who intentionally refuses to comply with the laws may be suspended or dismissed.

Microbiology

Pathogenic organisms must never be used for experimentation. Students should adhere to the following rules at all times when working with microorganisms to avoid accidental contamination:

- Treat all microorganisms as if they were pathogenic
- Maintain sterile conditions at all times

If you are taking a national-level exam, you should check with the Department of Education for your state's safety procedures. You will want to know what your state expects of you not only for the test but also for performance in the classroom and for the welfare of your students.

> ### SKILL 11.8
> **Select and apply appropriate technology, science tools and measurement units for students' use in data collection and the pursuit of science.**

Bunsen Burners

Hot plates should be used whenever possible to avoid the risk of burns or fire. If Bunsen burners are used, the following precautions should be taken:

- Know the location of fire extinguishers and safety blankets and train students in their use. Long hair and long sleeves should be secured and out of the way.

- Turn the gas all the way on and make a spark with the striker. The preferred method to light burners is to use strikers rather than matches.

- Adjust the air valve at the bottom of the Bunsen burner until the flame shows an inner cone.

- Adjust the flow of gas to the desired flame height by using the adjustment valve.

- Do not touch the barrel of the burner (it is hot).

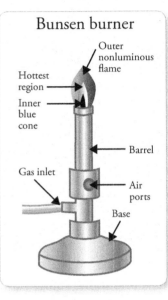

Bunsen burner

Graduated Cylinders

Graduated cylinders are used for precise measurements. They should always be placed on a flat surface. The surface of the liquid will form a meniscus (lens-shaped curve). The measurement is read at the bottom of this curve.

Balances

Electronic balances are easier than triple-beam balances to use, but more expensive. An electronic balance should always be tared (returned to zero) before measuring and used on a flat surface. Substances should always be placed on a piece of paper to avoid spills and/or damage to the instrument. Triple-beam balances must be used on a level surface. There are screws located at the bottom of the balance to make any adjustments.

Start with the largest counterweight first and proceed toward the last notch that does not tip the balance. Do the same with the next largest, etc., until the pointer remains at zero. The total mass is the total of all of the readings on the beams.

Burets

A buret is used to dispense precisely measured volumes of liquid. A stopcock is used to control the volume of liquid being dispensed.

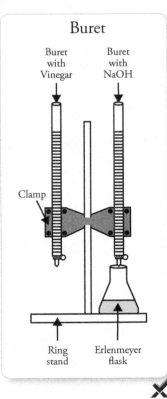

Buret

Light Microscopes

Light microscopes are commonly used in laboratory experiments. Several procedures should be followed to properly care for this equipment:

- Clean all lenses with lens paper only

- Carry microscopes with two hands: one on the arm, and one on the base

- Always begin focusing on low power, then switch to high power

- Store microscopes with the low-power objective down

- Always use a coverslip when viewing wet-mount slides

- Bring the objective down to its lowest position, then focus by moving up to avoid breaking the slide or scratching the lens

Wet-mount slides should be made by placing a drop of water on the specimen and then putting a glass coverslip on top of the drop of water. Dropping the coverslip at a forty-five degree angle will help avoid air bubbles. Total magnification is determined by multiplying the ocular (usually 10X) and the objective (usually 10X on low, 40X on high).

SKILL 11.9 Select and analyze developmentally appropriate diagnostic, formative and summative assessments to evaluate prior knowledge, guide instruction, and evaluate student achievement.

Assessment should be tailored to a specific purpose and should be reliable, valid, and fair for that purpose. Assessment should be age appropriate in both content and the method of data collection. Different types of science assessments can give teachers different kinds of evaluation information. Teachers should utilize a variety of assessment types, both formative and summative. Educators can use classroom discussions, informal observations of children, examination of children's work products, and short interviews to decide what students can do and what they might be ready for next. Project-based learning and formal written tests may be effective as well. Most important for diagnostic assessment is that teachers are clear about what they expect to do in their science teaching and know what qualities they hope to bring out in their students. Using an array of formative and summative assessments can help determine students' strengths and weaknesses, meet the science standards, and shape instruction.

SKILL 11.10 Choose scientifically and professionally responsible content and activities that are socially and culturally sensitive.

Science should be taught in ways that acknowledge gender equity goals and also the diverse groups that exist in the United States, such as urban students, English language learners (ELLs), and students with disabilities. Instruction and curriculum content should reflect cultural, ethnic, and gender diversity, and employ instruction and assessment that builds on students' prior knowledge, culture, and language. Appropriate classroom practices examine biases and assumptions, and encourage students to make meaning. Educators should respect diversity throughout their classrooms during science and across all subject areas. Offering all children access to quality science education experiences will help prepare them fully and allow them to understand the potential for extended learning opportunities while possibly encouraging interest in a career in science.

COMPETENCY 12
KNOWLEDGE OF THE NATURE OF SCIENCE

> **SKILL** **Analyze the dynamic nature of science models, laws, mechanisms,**
> **12.1** **and theories that explain natural phenomena** *(e.g., durability, tentativeness,*
> *replication, reliance on evidence).*

Students will be asked to relate the process of scientific inquiry and understand the variety of natural phenomena that take place in the science world.

Teachers will be expected to teach and model for students the following frameworks:

- Analyzing all processes by which hypotheses and scientific knowledge are generated

- Analyzing ethical issues related to the process of science and scientific experiments

- Evaluating the appropriateness of specified experiment and design a test to relate to the given hypothesis

- Recognize the role of communication between scientists, public, and educational realms.

Science is a way of learning about the natural world. Students must know how science has built a model for increasing knowledge by understanding physical, mathematical, and conceptual models. Students must also understand that these concepts don't answer all of science questions. Students must to understand that investigations are used to depict the events of the natural world. Methods and models are used to build, explain, and attempt to investigate. They help us to draw conclusions that serve as observations and increase our understanding of how the systems of the natural world work.

**SKILL Identify and apply science and engineering practices through
12.2 integrated process skills** *(e.g., observing, classifying, predicting, hypothesizing, designing and carrying out investigations, developing and using models, constructing and communicating explanations).*

Science can be defined as a body of knowledge that is systematically derived from study, observations, and experimentation. Its goal is to identify and establish principles and theories that can be applied to solve problems.

Scientific inquiry starts with observation. After observation, a question is formed, which starts with *why* or *how*. To answer these questions, experimentation is necessary. Between observation and experimentation, there are three more important steps: gathering information (or researching the problem), forming a hypothesis, and designing the experiment.

Designing an experiment involves identifying a control, constants, independent variables, and dependent variables. A control, or standard, is something with which to compare results at the end of the experiment. It is like a reference. Constants are the factors that must remain the same in an experiment to get reliable results. Independent variables are factors that are changed in an experiment. There should always be more constants than variables to obtain reproducible results in an experiment.

The first step in scientific inquiry is posing a question to be answered. Next, a hypothesis is formed to provide a plausible explanation for said question. An experiment is then proposed and performed to test the hypothesis. The next step is a comparison between the predicted and observed results. Conclusions determine whether the hypothesis is correct or incorrect. If incorrect, the next step is to form a new hypothesis and repeat the process.

> *Classifying is grouping items according to their similarities. It is important for students to understand relationships and similarities as well as differences to reach a reasonable conclusion in a lab experience.*

Data Collection

The procedure used to obtain data is important to the outcome of the experiment. Experiments consist of **controls** and **variables**. A control is the experiment run under normal conditions. A variable is a factor that is changed. In biology, the variable may be light, temperature, pH, time, etc. The differences in tested variables can be used to make a prediction or form a hypothesis. Only one variable should be tested at a time.

An **independent variable** is one that is changed or manipulated by the researcher. This could be the amount of light given to a plant or the temperature at which bacteria is grown. The **dependent variable** is influenced by the independent variable.

After the experiment is complete, it is repeated and results are graphically presented. The results are then analyzed and conclusions drawn.

After the conclusion is drawn, the final step is communication. The conclusions must be communicated clearly using accurate data, visual presentations like graphs, tables/charts, diagrams, artwork, and other appropriate media such as a presentation.

The Scientific Method

The scientific method is the basic process behind science. It involves several steps, beginning with hypothesis formulation and working through to the conclusion.

1. **Posing a question:** Although many discoveries happen by chance, the standard thought process of a scientist begins with forming a question to research. The more limited the question, the easier it is to set up an experiment to answer it.

2. **Forming a hypothesis:** Once the question is formulated, researchers should take an educated guess about the answer to the problem or question. This "best guess" is the hypothesis.

3. **Doing the test:** To make a test fair, data from an experiment must have a variable or a condition that can be changed, such as temperature or mass. A good test will try to manipulate as few variables as possible to see which variable is responsible for the result. This requires a control. A control is an extra setup in which all the conditions are the same except for the variable being tested.

4. **Observing and recording the data:** Recording the data should include the specifics of how measurements were calculated. For example, a graduated cylinder needs to be read using proper procedures. For beginning students, technique must be part of the instructional process so as to give validity to the data.

5. **Drawing a conclusion:** After recording data, compare your data with the data of other groups. A conclusion is the judgment derived from results of your data.

Graphs and Lab Reports

Graphs utilize numbers to demonstrate patterns. The patterns offer a visual representation, making it easier to draw conclusions.

Normally, knowledge is integrated in the form of a lab report. A report has many sections. It should include a specific title that tells exactly what is being studied. The abstract is a summary of the report written at the beginning of the paper. The purpose should always be defined to state the problem. The purpose should include the hypothesis (educated guess) of what is expected from the outcome of the experiment. The entire experiment should relate to this problem.

It is important to describe exactly what was done to prove or disprove a hypothesis. A control is necessary to prove that the results occurred from the changed conditions and would not have happened normally. Only one variable should be manipulated at a time. Observations and results of the experiment, including all results from data, should be recorded. Drawings, graphs, and illustrations should be included to support information. Observations are objective, whereas analysis and interpretation are subjective. A conclusion should explain why the results of the experiment either proved or disproved the hypothesis.

A **SCIENTIFIC THEORY** is an explanation of a set of related observations based on a proven hypothesis. A **SCIENTIFIC LAW** usually lasts longer than a scientific theory and has more experimental data to support it.

> **SCIENTIFIC THEORY:** an explanation of a set of related observations based on a proven hypothesis

> **SCIENTIFIC LAW:** usually lasts longer than a scientific theory and has more experimental data to support it.

SKILL 12.3 **Differentiate between the characteristics of experiments** *(e.g., multiple trials, control groups, variables)* **and other types of scientific investigations** *(e.g., observations, surveys).*

Most research in the scientific field is conducted using the scientific method to discover the answer to a scientific problem. The **SCIENTIFIC METHOD** is the process of thinking through possible solutions to a problem and testing each possibility to find the best solution. The scientific method generally involves the following steps: forming a hypothesis, choosing a method and design, conducting experimentation (collecting data), analyzing data, drawing a conclusion, and reporting the findings. Depending on the hypothesis and data to be collected and analyzed, different types of scientific investigation may be used.

> **SCIENTIFIC METHOD:** the process of thinking through possible solutions to a problem and testing each possibility to find the best solution

Descriptive studies are often the first form of investigation used in new areas of scientific inquiry. The most important element in descriptive reporting is a specific, clear, and measurable definition of the disease, condition, or factor in question. Descriptive studies always address the five W's: *who, what, when, where,* and *why.* They also add an additional "so what?" Descriptive studies include case reports, case-series reports, cross-sectional students, surveillance studies with individuals, and correlational studies with populations. Descriptive studies are used primarily for trend analysis, health-care planning, and hypothesis generation.

CONTROLLED EXPERIMENT: a form of scientific investigation in which one variable, the independent or control variable, is manipulated to reveal the effect on another variable, the dependent (experimental) variable, while are other variables in the system remain fixed

A **CONTROLLED EXPERIMENT** is a form of scientific investigation in which one variable, the independent or control variable, is manipulated to reveal the effect on another variable, the dependent (experimental) variable, while all other variables in the system remain fixed. The control group is virtually identical to the dependent variable except for the one aspect whose effect is being tested. Testing the effects of bleach water on a growing plant, the plant receiving bleach water would be the dependent group, while the plant receiving plain water would be the control group. It is best practice to have several replicate samples for the experiment being performed. This allows for results to be averaged or obvious discrepancies to be discarded.

COMPARATIVE DATA ANALYSIS: a statistical form of investigation that allows the researcher to gain new or unexpected insight into data based primarily on graphic representation

COMPARATIVE DATA ANALYSIS is a statistical form of investigation that allows the researcher to gain new or unexpected insight into data based primarily on graphic representation. Comparative data analysis, whether within the research of an individual project or a meta-analysis, allows the researcher to maximize the understanding of the particular data set, uncover underlying structural similarities between research, extract important variables, test underlying assumptions, and detect outliers and anomalies. Most comparative data analysis techniques are graphical in nature with a few quantitative techniques. The use of graphics to compare data allows the researcher to explore the data open-mindedly.

SKILL 12.4 **Identify and analyze attitudes and dispositions underlying scientific thinking** (e.g., curiosity, openness to new ideas, appropriate skepticism, cooperation).

Teachers should expect to encounter curiosity, openness to new ideas, some skepticism, and various dispositions from students. There are many common misconceptions about science. For instance: "The Earth is the center of the solar system" and "Rain comes from the holes in the clouds."

Some useful strategies when teaching science include:

1. **Planning appropriate activities,** so that the students will see for themselves where there are misconceptions.

2. **Web search** is a very useful tool to dispel misconceptions. Students need to be guided in how to look for answers on the Web, and if necessary the teacher should explain scientific literature to help the students understand it.

3. **Science journals** are a great source of information. Recent research is highly beneficial for the senior science students.

4. **Critical thinking** and **reasoning** are two important skills that the students should be encouraged to use to discover facts—for example, that heat is a form of energy. Here, the students have to be challenged to use their critical thinking skills to reason that heat can cause change—for example, causing water to boil—and so it is not a thing but a form of energy, since only energy can cause change.

> **SKILL 12.5** **Identify and select appropriate tools, including digital technologies, and units of measurement for various science tasks.**

While a certain amount of information will always be presented in lecture form or through textbooks, technology, both new and old, can help students understand concepts and become more engaged in discovering new facts using the scientific method.

Hands-on Experiments and Demonstrations

Some of the oldest and simplest technologies can be used to demonstrate concepts for students. These include basic chemical equipment such as Bunsen burners and devices that display physical phenomena such as gyroscopes. Some simple experiments may be appropriate for elementary-age students. Ideas for experiments can be found in many places:

- **Software and simulations:** When hands-on experiments are costly, complicated, dangerous, or otherwise not possible, students may benefit from software programs that simulate them. While these experiences are less "hands-on" than actual experiments, many software programs are highly interactive, allowing students to become involved in what they are learning. Multimedia software packages can be used to expose students to image and sounds of subjects they are studying.

- **Online resources:** There are many science-focused websites designed for elementary-age children. Web resources can be particularly useful when a class is following a current event in science. For instance, the NASA website frequently allows the tracking of space missions in progress, which can be an exciting experience for students.

See also Skill 11.8

SKILL
12.6 **Evaluate and interpret pictorial representations, charts, tables, and graphs of authentic data from scientific investigations to make predictions, construct explanations, and support conclusions.**

The starting point for any scientific investigation is systematic observation. **SYSTEMATIC OBSERVATION** is observing and recording the occurrence of specific (naturally occurring) behaviors.

> **SYSTEMATIC OBSERVATION**: observing and recording the occurrence of specific (naturally occurring) behaviors

There are four descriptive observation methods:

1. **Naturalistic observation:** Recording general occurrences of naturally occurring behavior

2. **Systematic observation:** Recording the occurrences of certain specific naturally occurring behaviors

3. **Case study:** Gathering detailed information about one individual

4. **Archival research:** Using existing behavior to establish occurrence of behavior

Each approach has potential problems and limitations. Systematic observation emphasizes gathering quantitative data on specific behaviors. The researcher is interested in a limited set of behaviors. This allows the researcher to study and test specific hypotheses.

It is imperative that teachers are able to teach students the skills necessary to evaluate scientific principles and ideas and to lead students to their own discoveries. This promotes a better understanding of science and its topics of study. **CRITICAL-THINKING SKILLS** are necessary for a student to understand all processes of science. For example, students must be able to apply the principles of scientific inquiry to the question they are considering. This requires students to use higher-level thinking skills rather than just repeating terms or facts found in a text. The following is a good example of a higher-level thinking or critical-thinking question.

> *If five appliances are all in place in a parallel circuit and all separately connected to the voltage source, and there is a microwave plugged in at the beginning of the circuit, will all the appliances operate? Why or why not?*

Asking such questions force student to think about the answer rather than just define a vocabulary term. Logical reasoning skills are equally important for students' understanding. **LOGICAL REASONING SKILLS** involve comprehending scientific possibilities and how they may occur. For example, when studying earthquakes and natural disasters, students should be able to reason that fault lines that

> **LOGICAL REASONING SKILLS**: comprehending scientific possibilities and how they may occur

normally have some movement but have not moved in the past 10 years would be expected to move within the next few years, possibly resulting in an earthquake.

Finally, scientific problem solving will lead students to a greater understanding of scientific tools and processes. SCIENTIFIC PROBLEM SOLVING involves inquiry, assessment, and solving or drawing conclusions. These are steps of the scientific method. Students should be given the opportunity to use their problem-solving skills to display their scientific knowledge. An excellent opportunity for this would be a science fair or an engineering fair.

Students must communicate their conclusions by clearly describing the information using accurate data, a visual presentation, and other media such as a multimedia slideshow presentation. Examples of visual presentations are graphs (bar/line/pie), tables/charts, diagrams, and artwork. Teachers should incorporate computer technology whenever possible. The method of communication must be suitable to the audience. Written communication is as important as oral communication. The scientist's strongest ally is a solid set of reproducible data.

> **SCIENTIFIC PROBLEM SOLVING**: inquiry, assessment, and solving or drawing conclusions

SKILL 12.7 Identify and analyze ways in which science is an interdisciplinary process and interconnected to STEM disciplines *(i.e., science, technology, engineering, mathematics)*.

Scientific discoveries often lead to technological advances and, conversely, advances in technology often expand the reach of scientific discoveries. In addition, biology and the other scientific disciplines share several concepts and processes that help unify the study of science. Finally, because biology is the science of living systems, biology has a direct impact on society and everyday life.

Science and technology are closely related. Technology often results from the application of scientific discoveries, and advances in technology can increase the impact of scientific discoveries. For example, James D. Watson and Francis Crick discovered the structure of DNA, a discovery that led to many biotechnological advances in the manipulation of DNA. These advances greatly influenced the medical and pharmaceutical fields; however, the success of Watson and Crick's experiments depended on the technology available at the time. Without the technology, their experiments would have failed.

The combination of biology and technology has improved the human standard of living in many ways; however, the impact of increasing human life expectancy and population growth on the environment is problematic. In addition, advances in biotechnology (e.g., genetic engineering, cloning) produce ethical dilemmas that society must consider.

> *The combination of biology and technology has improved the human standard of living in many ways.*

Biologists use a variety of tools and technologies to perform tests, collect and display data, and analyze relationships. Examples of commonly used tools include computer-linked probes, spreadsheets, and graphing calculators.

Computer-linked probes are used to measure various environmental factors including temperature, dissolved oxygen, pH, ionic concentration, and pressure. The advantage of these probes, as compared to more traditional observational tools, is that they automatically gather data and present it in an accessible format, eliminating the need for constant human observation and manipulation.

Biologists use spreadsheets to organize, analyze, and display data. For example, conservation ecologists use spreadsheets to model population growth and development, apply sampling techniques, and create statistical distributions to analyze relationships. Spreadsheet use simplifies data collection and manipulation and facilitates the presentation of data in a logical and understandable format.

Graphing calculators are another technology with many scientific applications. For example, biologists use algebraic functions to analyze growth, development, and other natural processes. Graphing calculators can manipulate algebraic data and create graphs for analysis and observation. In addition, biologists use the matrix function of graphing calculators to model problems in genetics. The use of graphing calculators simplifies the creation of graphical displays including histograms, scatter plots, and line graphs. Biologists can also transfer data and displays to computers for further analysis. Finally, they can connect computer-linked probes, used to collect data, to graphing calculators to ease the collection, transmission, and analysis of data.

SKILL 12.8 Analyze the interactions of science and technology with society including cultural, ethical, economic, political, and global factors.

Scientific and technological breakthroughs greatly influence other fields of study and the job market. All academic disciplines utilize computer and information technology to simplify research and information sharing. In addition, advances in science and technology influence the types of available jobs and the desired work skills. For example, machines and computers continue to replace unskilled laborers and computer and technological literacy is now a requirement for many jobs and careers. Finally, science and technology continue to change the very nature of careers. Because of science and technology's great influence on all areas of the economy, and the continuing scientific and technological breakthroughs, careers are far less stable than in past eras. Workers can thus expect to change jobs and companies much more often than in the past.

Local, state, national, and global governments and organizations must increasingly consider policy issues related to science and technology. For example, local and state governments must analyze the impact of proposed development and growth on the environment. Governments and communities must balance the demands of an expanding human population with the local ecology to ensure sustainable growth.

In addition, advances in science and technology create challenges and ethical dilemmas that national governments and global organizations must attempt to solve. Genetic research and manipulation, antibiotic resistance, stem cell research, and cloning are just a few of the issues facing national governments and global organizations.

In all cases, policymakers must analyze all sides of an issue and attempt to find a solution that protects society while limiting scientific inquiry as little as possible. For example, policy makers must weigh the potential benefits of stem cell research, genetic engineering, and cloning (e.g., medical treatments) against the ethical and scientific concerns surrounding these practices. Also, governments must tackle problems like antibiotic resistance, which can result from the indiscriminate use of medical technology (i.e., antibiotics), to prevent medical treatments from becoming obsolete.

COMPETENCY 13
KNOWLEDGE OF PHYSICAL SCIENCES

> **SKILL 13.1** **Identify and differentiate among the physical properties of matter** *(e.g., mass, volume, texture, hardness, freezing point).*

Everything in our world is made up of **matter**, whether it is a rock, a building, an animal, or a person. Matter is defined by two characteristics: It takes up space and it has mass.

MASS is the amount of matter in an object. Two objects of equal mass will balance each other on a simple balance scale no matter where the scale is located. For instance, two rocks with the same mass that are in balance on Earth will also be in balance on the moon. However, they will feel heavier on Earth than on the moon because of the gravitational pull of Earth. So, although the two rocks have the same mass, they will have different weight.

WEIGHT is the measure of Earth's pull of gravity on an object. It also can be defined as the pull of gravity between other bodies. Common units of weight measurement are the pound (English measure) and the kilogram (metric measure).

In addition to mass, matter has the property of volume. **VOLUME** is the amount of cubic space that an object occupies. Volume and mass together give a more exact description of the object than either property does on its own. Two objects may have the same volume but different mass, or they may have the same mass but different volumes. For instance, consider two cubes that are each one cubic centimeter, one of which is made from plastic and the other from lead. They have the same volume, but the lead cube has more mass. The measure used to describe the cubes, density, takes into consideration both the mass and the volume. **DENSITY** is the mass of a substance contained per unit of volume. If the density of an object is less than the density of a liquid, then the object will float in the liquid. Conversely, if the object is denser than the liquid, then the object will sink.

Density is stated in grams per cubic centimeter (g/cm^3) where the gram is the standard unit of mass. To find an object's density, you must measure its mass and its volume and then divide the mass by the volume ($D = m/V$).

To discover an object's density, first use a balance to find its mass. Then calculate its volume. If the object is a regular shape, you can find the volume by

MASS: a measure of the amount of matter in an object

WEIGHT: the measure of Earth's pull of gravity on an object

VOLUME: the amount of cubic space that an object occupies

DENSITY: the mass of a substance contained per unit of volume

multiplying the length, width, and height. If it is an irregular shape, you can find the volume by seeing how much water it displaces. Measure the water in a container before and after the object is submerged. The difference will be the volume of the object.

SPECIFIC GRAVITY is the ratio of the density of a substance to the density of water. For instance, the specific density of one liter of turpentine is calculated by comparing its mass (0.81 kg) to the mass of one liter of water (1 kg):

$$\frac{\text{mass of 1 L turpentine}}{\text{mass of 1 L water}} = \frac{0.81 \text{ kg}}{1.00 \text{ kg}} = 0.81$$

SPECIFIC GRAVITY: the ratio of the density of a substance to the density of water

SKILL **Identify and differentiate between physical and chemical changes**
13.2 *(e.g., tearing, burning, rusting).*

Physical properties and chemical properties of matter describe the appearance and behavior of a substance. A physical property can be observed without changing the identity of a substance. For instance, you can describe the color, mass, shape, and volume of a book. A chemical property is the ability of a substance to be changed into new substances. Baking powder goes through a chemical change as it changes into carbon dioxide gas during the baking process.

Matter constantly changes. A physical change is a change that does not produce a new substance. The freezing and melting of water is an example of physical change. A chemical change (or chemical reaction) is any change of a substance into one or more new substances. For example, burning materials turn into smoke, and a seltzer tablet fizzes into gas bubbles.

Rusting and burning are examples of chemical changes.

Conductivity

Substances can be categorized as conductors or insulators. A conductor is a material that transfers a substance easily. That substance may be thermal or electrical in nature. Metals generally are good thermal and electrical conductors. Touch your hand to a hot piece of metal and you know it is a good conductor—the heat transfers to your hand, and you may be burnt. Materials through which electric charges easily flow are called electrical conductors. Metals that are good electrical conductors include silicon and boron. In contrast, an insulator is a material through which electric charges move with difficulty, if at all. Examples of electrical insulators are the nonmetal elements of the periodic table.

Solubility is the amount of a substance (referred to as solute) that will dissolve into another substance, called the solvent. The amount that will dissolve can vary according to the conditions, most notably temperature. This process is called solvation.

Melting point is the temperature at which a solid becomes a liquid. **Boiling point** is the temperature at which a liquid becomes a gas. Melting takes place when there is sufficient energy available to break the intermolecular forces that hold molecules together in a solid. Boiling occurs when there is enough energy available to break the intermolecular forces holding molecules together as a liquid. **Freezing point** is the temperature at which a liquid freezes. The freezing point of water is 32°F, or 0°C.

Hardness describes how difficult it is to scratch or indent a substance. The hardest natural substance is diamond.

> SKILL 13.3 **Compare the properties of matter during phase changes through the addition and/or removal of energy** (e.g., boiling, condensation, evaporation).

A phase of matter (solid, liquid, or gas) is identified by the matter's shape and volume. A solid has a definite shape and volume. A liquid has a definite volume but no definite shape. A gas has no definite shape or volume because it will spread to occupy the space in which it is contained.

ENERGY: the ability to cause change in matter

EVAPORATION: the change in phase from liquid to gas

CONDENSATION: the change in phase from gas to liquid

ENERGY is the ability to cause change in matter. Applying heat to a frozen liquid changes it from solid to liquid. Continue heating it, and it will boil and turn to steam, a gas.

EVAPORATION is the change in phase from liquid to gas. **CONDENSATION** is the change in phase from gas to liquid.

According to the **molecular theory of matter**, molecular motion determines the phase of the matter, and the energy in the matter determines the speed of molecular motion. Solids have vibrating molecules that are in fixed relative positions; liquids have faster molecular motion than their solid forms, and the molecules may move more freely but must still be in contact with one another; gases have even more energy and more molecular motion. Other phases, such as plasma, are even more energetic than gasses. At the freezing point or boiling point of a substance, two phases (liquid and solid and liquid and gas, respectively) may be present.

SKILL 13.4 Differentiate between the properties of homogeneous mixtures (i.e., solutions) and heterogeneous mixtures.

Substances can combine without a chemical change. A **MIXTURE** is any combination of two or more substances in which the substances keep their own properties. A fruit salad is a mixture. So is an ice cream sundae, although you might not recognize each part if they are stirred together. Colognes and perfumes are another example. You may not readily recognize the individual elements, but they can be separated.

MIXTURE: any combination of two or more substances in which the substances keep their own properties

Mixtures:

1. Made up of two or more substances.

2. Not formed by a chemical change.

3. Can be separated by physical changes.

4. Properties of the mixture are the same as those of its parts.

5. Does not have a definite amount of each ingredient.

A **HOMOGENOUS MIXTURE** is a mixture in which the components are evenly distributed throughout the mixture. Examples include air, vinegar, sugar water, and steel. You cannot see the individual ingredients or use a mechanical means to separate them.

HOMOGENOUS MIXTURE: a mixture in which the components are evenly distributed throughout the mixture

A **HETEROGENEOUS MIXTURE** is a mixture in which the components are not uniform. Different samples of the mixture are not identical to one another. Examples include salad dressing, gravel, cereal in milk, mixed nuts, and soil.

HETEROGENEOUS MIXTURE: a mixture in which the components are not uniform

SKILL 13.5 Identify examples of and relationships among atoms, elements, molecules, and compounds.

An **ATOM** is a nucleus surrounded by a cloud with moving electrons.

ATOM: a nucleus surrounded by a cloud with moving electrons

The **nucleus** is the center of the atom. The positive particles inside the nucleus are called **protons**. The mass of a proton is about 2,000 times the mass of an electron. The number of protons in the nucleus of an atom is called the **atomic number**. All atoms of the same element have the same atomic number.

Neutrons are another type of particle in the nucleus. Neutrons and protons have about the same mass, but neutrons have no charge. Neutrons were discovered because scientists observed that not all atoms of neon gas have the same mass. This discovery led to the identification of isotopes. **Isotopes** of an element have the same number of protons in the nucleus but different masses. Neutrons explain the difference in mass, because they have mass but no charge.

The mass of matter is measured against a standard mass such as the gram. Scientists measure the mass of an atom by comparing it to that of a standard atom. The result is relative mass. The **relative mass** of an atom is its mass expressed in terms of the mass of the standard atom. The isotope of the element carbon is the standard atom. It has six neutrons and is called carbon-12. It is assigned a mass of 12 atomic mass units (amu). Therefore, the **ATOMIC MASS UNIT (AMU)** is the standard unit for measuring the mass of an atom. It is equal to the mass of a carbon atom.

The **mass number** of an atom is the sum of its protons and neutrons. In any element, there is a mixture of isotopes, some with slightly more or slightly fewer neutrons. The **atomic mass** of an element is an average of the mass numbers of its atoms.

> *The mass of matter is measured against a standard mass such as the gram.*

> **ATOMIC MASS UNIT (AMU):** the standard unit for measuring the mass of an atom; it is equal to the mass of a carbon atom

TERMS USED TO DESCRIBE ATOMIC NUCLEI			
Term	**Example**	**Meaning**	**Characteristic**
Atomic number	Number of protons (p)	Same for all atoms of a given element	Carbon (C) Atomic number = 6 (6p)
Mass number	Number of protons + number of neutrons (p + n)	Changes for different isotopes of an element	C -12 (6p + 6n) C -13 (6p + 7n)
Atomic mass	Average mass of the atoms	Usually not a whole number of the element	Atomic mass of carbon = 12.011

Each atom has an equal number of electrons (negative) and protons (positive). Therefore, atoms are neutral. Electrons orbiting the nucleus occupy energy levels that are arranged in order, and the electrons tend to occupy the lowest energy level available. An atom with a **stable electron arrangement** has all of its electrons in the lowest possible energy levels.

Each energy level holds a maximum number of electrons; however, an atom with more than one level does not hold more than eight electrons in its outermost shell.

LEVEL	FIRST	SECOND	THIRD	FOURTH
Name	K shell	L shell	M shell	N shell
Max. Number of Electronss	2	8	18	32

This can help explain why chemical reactions occur. Atoms react with each other when their outer levels are unfilled. When atoms either exchange or share electrons with each other, these energy levels become filled and the atom becomes more stable.

As an electron gains energy, it moves from one energy level to a higher energy level. The electron cannot leave one level until it has enough energy to reach the next level. **Excited electrons** are electrons that have absorbed energy and have moved farther from the nucleus.

Electrons can also lose energy. When they do, they fall to a lower level. However, they can only fall to the lowest level that has room for them. This explains why atoms do not collapse.

SKILL 13.6 **Identify and compare potential and kinetic energy.**

Energy exists in two forms: potential and kinetic. **KINETIC ENERGY** is the energy of a moving object. **POTENTIAL ENERGY** is the energy stored in matter due to its position relative to other objects.

In any object—solid, liquid, or gas—the atoms and molecules that make up the object are constantly moving (vibrational, translation, and rotational motion) and colliding with one another. They are not stationary.

Due to this motion, the object's particles have varying amounts of kinetic energy. A fast-moving atom can push a slower-moving atom during a collision, so it has energy. All moving objects have energy, and that energy depends on the object's mass and velocity. Kinetic energy is calculated with this equation: K.E. $= \frac{1}{2}mv^2$.

The temperature of an object is proportional to the average kinetic energy of the particles in the substance. Increase the temperature of a substance and its particles move faster, so their average kinetic energies increase as well. However, temperature is not an energy, so it is not conserved.

The energy an object has due to its position or the arrangement of its parts is called potential energy. Potential energy due to position is equal to the mass of the object times the gravitational pull on the object times the height of the object, or:

$$PE = mgh$$

Where PE = potential energy; m = mass of object; g = gravity; and h = height.

> **KINETIC ENERGY:** the energy of a moving object

> **POTENTIAL ENERGY:** the energy stored in matter due to its position relative to other objects

Kinetic motion

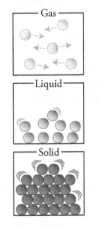

HEAT: energy that is transferred between objects caused by differences in their temperatures

HEAT is energy that is transferred between objects caused by differences in their temperatures. Heat passes spontaneously from an object of higher temperature to one of lower temperature. This transfer continues until both objects reach the same temperature. Both kinetic energy and potential energy can be transformed into heat energy. When you step on the brake in your car, the kinetic energy of the car is changed to heat energy by friction between the brake and the wheels. Energy also can transform from kinetic to potential. Since most of the energy in our world is in a form that is not easily used, both people and nature have developed some clever ways of changing one form of energy into another form that may be more useful.

SKILL 13.7 **Differentiate among forms of energy, transformations of energy, and their real-world applications** *(e.g., chemical, electrical, mechanical, heat, light, sound).*

Many chemical reactions give off **energy**. Like matter, energy can change form, but it can be neither created nor destroyed during a chemical reaction.

Burning fossil fuels causes air pollution as sulfur oxide, unburned hydrocarbons, and carbon monoxide are released into the air. Natural gas burns much cleaner and has the advantage of being able to be pumped through pipes to where it can be used.

SOLAR ENERGY: radiation from the Sun

SOLAR ENERGY is radiation from the Sun. Solar energy must be stored for use when the Sun is not shining. Storage methods include heating water or rocks or converting the Sun's rays into electricity using a photoelectric cell. Photoelectric cells are very expensive to make. Enormous amounts of water or rocks must be heated and insulated in storage to make use of the solar energy.

HYDROELECTRICITY: electricity produced by moving water

HYDROELECTRICITY is produced by moving water. Building a dam and changing the flow of a river to produce hydroelectricity can harm the environment, can kill fish, and frequently destroys plant life. Hydroelectricity is dependent on the cycle of rain and snow; heavy rain and snowfall in the mountains result in greater production while arid conditions lead to shortfalls.

Wind is captured by wind turbines and used to generate electricity. Wind power generation is clean; it doesn't cause air, soil, or water pollution. However, wind farms must be located on large tracts of land or along coastlines to capture the greatest wind movement. Devoting those areas to wind power generation sometimes conflicts with other priorities, such as agriculture, urban development, or waterfront views from homes in prime locations.

Heat within the earth is called GEOTHERMAL ENERGY. Geothermal power plants produce little, if any, pollution or environmental hazards and can operate continuously for many years.

THERMODYNAMICS is the study of energy and energy transfer. The first law of thermodynamics states that the energy of the universe is constant. Thus, interactions involving energy deal with the transfer and transformation of energy, not the creation or destruction of energy.

Electricity is an important source of energy. Ovens and electric heaters convert electrical energy into heat energy. Electrical energy energizes the filament of a light bulb to produce light. The movement of electrical charges creates magnetic fields. Charges moving in a magnetic field experience a force, which is a transfer of energy.

The process of photosynthesis converts light energy from the Sun into chemical energy (sugar). Cellular respiration later converts the sugar into ATP, a major energy source of all living organisms. Plants and certain types of bacteria carry out photosynthesis. The actions of the green pigment chlorophyll convert unusable light energy into usable chemical energy.

> **GEOTHERMAL ENERGY:** heat within the earth

> **THERMODYNAMICS:** the study of energy and energy transfer

---

SKILL 13.8 Distinguish among temperature, heat, and forms of heat transfer (e.g., conduction, convection, radiation).

Heat and Temperature

Heat and temperature are different physical quantities. Heat is a measure of energy. Temperature is the measure of how hot (or cold) a body is with respect to a standard object.

Two concepts are important in the discussion of temperature changes. Objects are in thermal contact if they can affect each other's temperature. Set a hot cup of coffee on a desktop. The two objects are in thermal contact with each other and will begin affecting each other's temperature. The coffee will become cooler and the desktop warmer. Eventually, they will have the same temperature. When this happens, they are in thermal equilibrium.

We cannot rely on our sense of touch to determine temperature because the heat from a hand may be conducted more efficiently by certain objects than others, making them feel colder. Thermometers are used to measure temperature. In thermometers, a small amount of mercury in a capillary tube will expand when heated. The thermometer and the object whose temperature it is measuring are

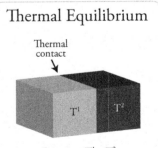

Thermal Equilibrium

Thermal contact

T^1 T^2

Over time $T^1 = T^2$

put in contact long enough for them to reach thermal equilibrium. The temperature can then be read from the thermometer scale.

Three temperature scales are used:

- **Celsius:** The freezing point of water is set at 0 degrees and the steam (boiling) point is 100 degrees. The interval between the two is divided into 100 equal parts called degrees Celsius.

- **Fahrenheit:** The freezing point of water is 32 degrees and the boiling point is 212 degrees. The interval between is divided into 180 equal parts called degrees Fahrenheit.

Temperature readings can be converted from one to the other as follows:

Fahrenheit to Celsius	Celsius to Fahrenheit
$C = \frac{5}{9}(F - 32)$	$C = \left(\frac{9}{5}\right)C + 32$

- **Kelvin:** The Kelvin scale has degrees that are the same size as those of the Celsius scale, but the zero point is moved to the triple point of water. Water inside a closed vessel is in thermal equilibrium in all three states (ice, water, and vapor) at 273.15 degrees Kelvin. This temperature is equivalent to .01 degrees Celsius. Because the degrees are the same in the two scales, temperature changes are the same in Celsius and Kelvin.

Temperature readings can be converted from Celsius to Kelvin:

Celsius to Kelvin	Kelvin to Celsius
$K = C + 273.15$	$C = K - 273.15$

The **heat capacity** of an object is the amount of heat energy it takes to raise the temperature of the object by one degree.

Heat capacity (C) per unit mass (m) is called **specific heat** (c):

$$c = \frac{C}{m} = \frac{Q}{m}$$

There are a number of ways that heat is measured. In each case, the measurement is dependent upon raising the temperature of a specific amount of water by a specific amount. These conversions of heat energy and work are called the **mechanical equivalent of heat**.

CALORIE: the amount of energy it takes to raise one gram of water one degree Celsius

A **CALORIE** is the amount of energy it takes to raise one gram of water one degree Celsius.

A **KILOCALORIE** is the amount of energy it takes to raise one kilogram of water by one degree Celsius. Food calories are kilocalories.

In the International System of Units (SI), the calorie is equal to 4.184 joules.

A British thermal unit (BTU) = 252 calories = 1.054 kilojoules(kJ).

> **KILOCALORIE:** the amount of energy it takes to raise one kilogram of water by one degree Celsius

---

SKILL 13.9 Analyze the functionality of an electrical circuit based on its conductors, insulators, and components.

Electrostatics is the study of stationary electric charges. A plastic rod that is rubbed with fur or a glass rod that is rubbed with silk will become electrically charged and will attract small pieces of paper. The charge on the plastic rod rubbed with fur is negative, and the charge on glass rod rubbed with silk is positive.

Electrically charged objects share these characteristics:

1. Like charges repel one another

2. Opposite charges attract each other

3. Charge is conserved

A neutral object has no net charge. If the plastic rod and fur are initially neutral, when the rod becomes charged by the fur, a negative charge is transferred from the fur to the rod. The net negative charge on the rod is equal to the net positive charge on the fur.

Materials through which electric charges can easily flow are called **CONDUCTORS**. Metals that are good conductors include silicon and boron. On the other hand, an **INSULATOR** is a material through which electric charges do not move easily, if at all. Examples of insulators are the nonmetal elements of the periodic table. A simple device used to indicate the existence of a positive or negative charge is called an electroscope. An electroscope is made up of a conducting knob with very lightweight conducting leaves usually made of foil (gold or aluminum) attached to it. When a charged object touches the knob, the leaves push away from each other because like charges repel. It is not possible to tell whether the charge is positive or negative.

Touch the knob with a finger while a charged rod is nearby. The electrons will be repulsed and flow out of the electroscope through the hand. If you remove your hand while the charged rod remains close, the electroscope will retain the charge.

> **CONDUCTORS:** materials through which electric charges can easily flow

> **INSULATORS:** materials through which electric charges do not move easily, if at all

When an object is rubbed with a charged rod, the object will take on the same charge as the rod; however, charging by induction gives the object the opposite charge as that of the charged rod.

Charge can be removed from an object by connecting it to the earth through a conductor. The removal of static electricity by conduction is called GROUNDING.

GROUNDING: the removal of static electricity by conduction

Electricity can be used to change the chemical composition of a material. For instance, when electricity is passed through water, it breaks the water down into hydrogen gas and oxygen gas.

Circuit breakers in a home monitor the electric current. If there is an overload, the circuit breaker will create an open circuit, stopping the flow of electricity.

Computers can be made small enough to fit inside a plastic credit card by creating what is known as a solid-state device. In this device, electrons flow through solid material such as silicon.

Resistors are used to regulate volume on a television or radio or for a dimmer switch for lights.

A bird can sit on an uninsulated electrical wire without being electrocuted because the bird and the wire have about the same potential; however, if the bird touches two wires at the same time, it would not have to worry about flying south next year.

In an electrical storm, a car is relatively safe from lightning because of the resistance of the rubber tires.

In an electrical storm, a car is relatively safe from lightning because of the resistance of the rubber tires. A metal building would not be a safe place unless it had a lightning rod to attract the lightning and conduct it into the ground.

SKILL 13.10 **Identify and apply the characteristics of contact forces** (e.g., push, pull, friction)**, at-a-distance forces** (e.g., magnetic, gravitational, electrostatic)**, and their effects on matter** (e.g., motion, speed).

DYNAMICS: the study of the relationship between motion and the forces affecting motion

DYNAMICS is the study of the relationship between motion and the forces affecting motion. Force causes motion.

Mass and weight are different quantities. An object's mass gives it a reluctance to change its current state of motion. It also is the measure of an object's resistance to acceleration. The force that Earth's gravity exerts on an object with a specific mass is called the object's weight on Earth. The force of weight is measured in Newtons. Weight (W) = mass times acceleration due to gravity ($W = mg$).

See also Skill 13.1

Newton's Laws of Motion

1. **Newton's first law of motion** is also called the law of inertia. It states that an object at rest will remain at rest and an object in motion will remain in motion at a constant velocity unless acted upon by an external force.

2. **Newton's second law of motion** states that if a net force acts on an object, it will cause the acceleration of the object. The relationship between force and motion is: force equals mass times acceleration ($F = ma$).

3. **Newton's third law** states that for every action there is an equal and opposite reaction. Therefore, if an object exerts a force on another object, that second object exerts an equal and opposite force on the first.

Surfaces that touch each other have a resistance to motion. This resistance is **friction.**

When an object moves in a circular path, a force must be directed toward the center of the circle to keep the motion going. This constraining force is called **centripetal force.** Gravity is the centripetal force that keeps a satellite circling Earth, for instance.

Magnets have a north pole and a south pole. Like poles repel, and opposing poles attract. A **MAGNETIC FIELD** is the space around a magnet where its force will affect objects. The closer you are to a magnet, the stronger the force. As you move away, the force becomes weaker.

> **MAGNETIC FIELD:** the space around a magnet where its force will affect objects

Gravity acts over tremendous distances in space (theoretically, infinite distance, though certainly at least as far as any astronaut has traveled). Gravitational force is inversely proportional to distance from a massive body. This means that when an astronaut is in space, he or she is far enough from the center of mass of any planet that the gravitational force is very small. The result is a feeling of weightlessness.

COMPETENCY 14
KNOWLEDGE OF EARTH AND SPACE

> **SKILL 14.1** Identify characteristics of geologic formations *(e.g., volcanoes, canyons, mountains)* and the mechanisms by which they are changed *(e.g., physical and chemical weathering, erosion, deposition)*.

Mountains

OROGENY: natural mountain building

OROGENY is the term given to natural mountain building. A mountain is terrain that has been raised high above the surrounding landscape by volcanic action or some form of tectonic plate collisions. The plate collisions could either be intercontinental collisions or ocean floor collisions with a continental crust (subduction).

The physical composition of mountains includes igneous, metamorphic, and sedimentary rocks.

The physical composition of mountains includes igneous, metamorphic, and sedimentary rocks; some may have rock layers that are tilted or distorted by plate collision forces.

There are many different types of mountains. The physical attributes of a mountain range depend upon the angle at which plate movement thrusts layers of rock to the surface. Many mountains (the Adirondacks, the Southern Rockies) were formed along high-angle faults.

Folded mountains (the Alps, the Himalayas) are produced by the folding of rock layers during their formation. The Himalayas are the highest mountains in the world; they contain Mount Everest, which rises almost nine kilometers above sea level. The Himalayas were formed when India collided with Asia. The movement that created this collision is still in process at the rate of a few centimeters per year.

Fault-block mountains (in Utah, Arizona, and New Mexico) are created when plate movement produces tension forces instead of compression forces. The area under tension produces normal faults, and rock along these faults is displaced upward.

Dome mountains are formed as magma tries to push up through the crust but fails to break the surface. Dome mountains resemble a huge blister on the Earth's surface.

Upwarped mountains (the Black Hills of South Dakota) are created in association with a broad arching of the crust. They can also be formed by rock thrust upward along high angle faults.

The formation of mountains

Mountains are produced by different types of processes. Most major mountain ranges are formed by the processes of folding and faulting.

In folding, mountains are produced by the folding of rock layers. Crustal movements may press horizontal layers of sedimentary rock together from the sides, squeezing them into wavelike folds. Up-folded sections of rock are called anticlines; down-folded sections of rock are called synclines. The Appalachian Mountains are an example of folded mountains, with long ridges and valleys in a series of anticlines, and synclines formed by folded rock layers.

The Appalachian Mountains are an example of folded mountains.

FAULTS are fractures in the Earth's crust that have been created by either tension or compression forces transmitted through the crust. These forces are produced by the movement of separate blocks of crust. Faultings are categorized on the basis of the relative movement between the blocks on both sides of the fault plane. The movement can be horizontal, vertical, or oblique.

FAULTS: fractures in the Earth's crust that have been created by either tension or compression forces transmitted through the crust

A dip-slip fault occurs when the movement of the plates is vertical and opposite. The displacement is in the direction of the inclination, or dip, of the fault. Dip-slip faults are classified as normal faults when the rock above the fault plane moves down relative to the rock below.

Reverse faults are created when the rock above the fault plane moves up relative to the rock below. Reverse faults with a very low angle to the horizontal are also referred to as thrust faults.

Faults in which the dominant displacement is horizontal movement along the trend or strike (length) of the fault are called strike-slip faults. When a large strike-slip fault is associated with plate boundaries it is called a transform fault. The San Andreas fault in California is a well-known transform fault.

VOLCANISM: the movement of magma through the crust and its emergence as lava onto the Earth's surface

ACTIVE VOLCANO: a volcano that is currently erupting or building to an eruption

Faults that have both vertical and horizontal movement are called oblique-slip faults.

Volcanoes

VOLCANISM is the term given to the movement of magma through the crust and its emergence as lava onto the Earth's surface. Volcanic mountains are built up by successive deposits of volcanic materials.

An ACTIVE VOLCANO is one that is currently erupting or building to an eruption. A DORMANT VOLCANO is one that is between eruptions but still shows signs of internal activity that might lead to an eruption in the future. An EXTINCT VOLCANO is said to be no longer capable of erupting. Most of the world's active volcanoes are found along the rim of the Pacific Ocean, which is also a major earthquake

DORMANT VOLCANO: a volcano that is between eruptions but still shows signs of internal activity that might lead to an eruption in the future

EXTINCT VOLCANO: a volcano no longer capable of erupting

zone. This curving belt of active faults and volcanoes is often called the Ring of Fire. The world's best known volcanic mountains include Mount Etna in Italy and Mount Kilimanjaro in Africa. The Hawaiian Islands are actually the tops of a chain of volcanic mountains that rise from the ocean floor.

There are three types of volcanic mountains:

- **Shield volcanoes** are associated with quiet eruptions. Lava emerges from the vent or opening in the crater and flows freely out over the Earth's surface until it cools and hardens into a layer of igneous rock. A repeated lava flow builds this type of volcano into the largest type of volcanic mountain. Mauna Loa in Hawaii is the largest shield volcano on Earth.

- **Cinder-cone volcanoes** are associated with explosive eruptions as lava is hurled high into the air in a spray of droplets of various sizes. These droplets cool and harden into cinders and particles of ash before falling to the ground. The ash and cinder pile up around the vent to form a steep, cone-shaped hill called the cinder cone. Cinder-cone volcanoes are relatively small but may form quite rapidly.

- **Composite volcanoes** are those built by both lava flows and layers of ash and cinders. Mount Fuji in Japan, Mount St. Helens in the United States (Washington), and Mount Vesuvius in Italy are all famous composite volcanoes.

When lava cools, igneous rock is formed. Igneous rock formation can occur either above or below ground.

INTRUSIVE ROCK: any igneous rock that was formed below the Earth's surface

INTRUSIVE ROCK includes any igneous rock that was formed below the Earth's surface. Batholiths are the largest structures of intrusive rock and are composed of near-granite materials; they are the core of the Sierra Nevada Mountains. **EXTRUSIVE ROCK** includes any igneous rock that was formed at the Earth's surface.

EXTRUSIVE ROCK: any igneous rock that was formed at the Earth's surface

DIKES: old lava tubes formed when magma entered a vertical fracture and hardened

DIKES are old lava tubes formed when magma entered a vertical fracture and hardened. Sometimes magma squeezes between two rock layers and hardens into a thin horizontal sheet called a **sill**. A **laccolith** is formed in much the same way as a sill, but the magma that creates a laccolith is very thick and does not flow easily. It pools and forces the overlying strata outward, creating an obvious surface dome.

CALDERA: normally formed by the collapse of the top of a volcano

A **CALDERA** is normally formed by the collapse of the top of a volcano. This collapse can be caused by a massive explosion that destroys the cone and empties most, if not all, of the magma chamber below the volcano. The cone collapses into the empty magma chamber, forming a caldera.

An inactive volcano may have magma solidified in its pipe. This structure, called a volcanic neck, is resistant to erosion and today may be the only visible evidence of the past presence of an active volcano.

Glaciations

About twelve thousand years ago, a vast sheet of ice covered a large part of the northern United States. This huge, frozen mass had moved southward from the northern regions of Canada as several large bodies of slow-moving ice, or glaciers. A glacier is a large mass of ice that moves or flows over the land in response to gravity. Glaciers form among high mountains and in other cold regions. The term ICE AGE is used to describe a time period in which glaciers advance over a large portion of a continent.

About twelve thousand years ago, a vast sheet of ice covered a large part of the northern United States.

ICE AGE: a time period in which glaciers advance over a large portion of a continent

Evidence of glacial coverage remains as abrasive grooves, large boulders from northern environments dropped in southern locations, glacial troughs created by the rounding out of steep valleys by glacial scouring, and the remains of glacial sources called **cirques** that were created by frost wedging the rock at the bottom of the glacier. Remains of plants and animals found in warm climates that have been discovered in the moraines and outwash plains help support the theory of periods of warmth during past ice ages.

The major ice age began about two to three million years ago. This age saw the advancement and retreat of glacial ice over millions of years. Theories relating to the origin of glacial activity include plate tectonics, through which it can be demonstrated that some continental masses, now in temperate climates, were at one time blanketed by ice and snow. Another theory involves changes in the Earth's orbit around the sun, changes in the angle of the Earth's axis, and the wobbling of the Earth's axis. Support for the validity of this theory has come from deep-ocean research that indicates a correlation between climatic sensitive microorganisms and the changes in the Earth's orbital status.

There are two main types of glaciers: valley glaciers and continental glaciers. Erosion by valley glaciers is characteristic of U-shaped erosion. Valley glaciers produce sharp-peaked mountains such as the Matterhorn in Switzerland. Erosion by continental glaciers is characteristics of glacial movement over mountains, leaving smoothed, rounded mountains and ridges in their paths.

Plate tectonics

Data obtained from many sources led scientists to develop the theory of PLATE TECTONICS. This theory is the most current model that explains not only the movement of the continents but also the changes in the Earth's crust caused by internal forces.

PLATE TECTONICS: the model that explains not only the movement of the continents, but also the changes in the Earth's crust caused by internal forces

Plates are rigid blocks of the Earth's crust and upper mantle. These blocks make up the lithosphere. The Earth's lithosphere is broken into nine large moving sections, or slabs, and several small ones, called **plates**. The major plates are named after the continents they are "transporting."

The plates float on and move with a layer of hot, plastic-like rock in the upper mantle. Geologists believe that the heat currents circulating within the mantle cause this plastic zone of rock to slowly flow, carrying along the overlying crustal plates.

Movement of these crustal plates creates areas where the plates diverge as well as areas where they converge. A major area of divergence is located in the mid-Atlantic. Currents of hot mantle rock rise and separate in this area, creating new oceanic crust at the rate of two to ten centimeters per year.

Convergence is when the oceanic crust collides with either another oceanic plate or a continental plate. The oceanic crust sinks, forming an enormous trench and generating volcanic activity. Convergence also includes continent-to-continent plate collisions. When two plates slide past one another, a transform fault is created.

These movements produce many major features of the Earth's surface, such as mountain ranges, volcanoes, and earthquake zones. Most of these features are located at plate boundaries, where the plates interact by spreading apart, pressing together, or sliding past each other. These movements are very slow, averaging only a few centimeters a year.

Boundaries form between spreading plates where the crust is forced apart in a process called **rifting**. Rifting generally occurs at midocean ridges. Rifting can also take place within a continent, splitting the continent into smaller landmasses that drift away from each other, thereby forming an ocean basin between them. The Red Sea is a product of rifting. As the seafloor spreading takes place, new material is added to the inner edges of the separating plates. In this way the plates grow larger, and the ocean basin widens. This is the process that broke up the supercontinent Pangaea and created the Atlantic Ocean.

Boundaries between plates that are colliding are zones of intense crustal activity. When a plate of ocean crust collides with a plate of continental crust, the more dense oceanic plate slides under the lighter continental plate and plunges into the mantle. This process is called **subduction**. The site where subduction takes place is called a **subduction zone**. A subduction zone is usually seen on the seafloor as a deep depression called a **trench**.

The crustal movement, which is identified by plates sliding sideways past each other, produces a plate boundary characterized by major faults that are capable of unleashing powerful earthquakes. The San Andreas fault forms such a boundary between the Pacific plate and the North American plate.

Identify and distinguish among major groups and properties of rocks and minerals and the processes of their formations.

Rocks are aggregates of minerals. They are classified by the differences in their chemical composition and the way that they are formed. The three major subdivisions of rocks are igneous, sedimentary, and metamorphic; however, it is common for one type of rock to transform into another type, which is known as the rock cycle.

The three major subdivisions of rocks are igneous, sedimentary, and metamorphic; however, it is common for one type of rock to transform into another type, which is known as the rock cycle.

Igneous Rocks

IGNEOUS ROCKS are formed from molten rock called magma. There are two types of igneous rock: volcanic and plutonic. As the name suggests, volcanic rock is formed when magma reaches the Earth's surface as lava. Plutonic rock is also derived from magma, but it is formed when magma cools and crystallizes beneath the surface of the Earth.

IGNEOUS ROCKS: formed from molten rock called magma

Igneous rocks can be classified according to their texture, their composition, and the way that they formed. As magma cools, the elements and compounds begin to form crystals. The more slowly the magma cools, the larger the crystals grow. Rocks with large crystals are said to have a coarse-grained texture. Granite is an example of a coarse-grained rock. Rocks that cool rapidly before any crystals can form have a glassy texture, such as obsidian, also commonly known as volcanic glass.

Sedimentary Rocks

SEDIMENTARY ROCKS are formed by layered deposits of inorganic and/or organic matter. Layers, or strata, of rock are laid down horizontally to form sedimentary rocks. Sedimentary rocks that form as mineral solutions (i.e., seawater) evaporate are called **precipitate**. Those that contain the remains of living organisms are termed **biogenic**. Finally, those that form from the freed fragments of other rocks are called **clastic**. Because the layers of sedimentary rocks reveal chronology and often contain fossils, these types of rock have been key in helping scientists understand the history of the Earth. Chalk, limestone, sandstone, and shale are all examples of sedimentary rock.

SEDIMENTARY ROCKS: formed by layered deposits of inorganic and/or organic matter

Lithification of sedimentary rocks

When fluid sediments are transformed into solid sedimentary rocks, the process is known as **lithification**. A common process affecting sediments is compaction, when the weights of overlying materials compress and compact the deeper sediments. The compaction leads to **cementation**, the process in which sediments are converted to sedimentary rock.

Metamorphic Rocks

> **METAMORPHIC ROCKS:** created when rocks are subjected to high temperatures and pressures

METAMORPHIC ROCKS are created when rocks are subjected to high temperatures and pressures. The original rock, or protolith, may have been igneous, sedimentary, or even an older metamorphic rock. The temperatures and pressures necessary to achieve transformation are higher than those observed on the Earth's surface and are high enough to alter the minerals in the protolith. Because these rocks are formed within the Earth's crust, studying metamorphic rocks gives us clues to conditions in the Earth's mantle. In some metamorphic rocks, different-colored bands are apparent. These bands, called **foliation**, result from strong pressures being applied from specific directions. Examples of metamorphic rock include slate and marble.

Metamorphic rocks are classified into two groups: foliated (leaflike) and unfoliated. Foliated rocks consist of compressed, parallel bands of minerals, which give the rocks a striped appearance. Examples of such rocks include slate, schist, and gneiss. Unfoliated rocks are not banded. Examples include quartzite, marble, and anthracite.

> **SKILL 14.3** Identify and analyze the characteristics of soil, its components and profile, and the process of soil formation.

Soils are composed of particles of sand, clay, various minerals, tiny living organisms, and humus, as well as the decayed remains of plants and animals. Soils are divided into three classes according to their texture:

- **Sandy soils:** Gritty texture with particles that do not bind together firmly. Sandy soils are porous, and water passes through them rapidly. As a result, they have poor **absorption.**

- **Clay soils:** Smooth and greasy texture with particles that bind together firmly. Clay soils are moist and usually do not allow water to easily pass through them. This type of soil has the lowest potential for **runoff.**

- **Loamy soils:** Feel somewhat like velvet, and their particles clump together. Loamy soils are composed of sand, clay, and silt, and they may be able to hold water. Some loamy soils allow for the flow of water. **Percolation**, or the filtering and movement of water through porous materials, is best in this type of soil.

The formation of soil is a process that occurs over millions of years. Various factors come into play that make the soil different in different regions of the world.

There are five important factors involved in the development of soil:

1. **Parent material:** This can be both mineral and organic materials of the Earth. It can be the ash left behind by the eruption of a volcano, material that is carried to and deposited in an area by wind or water, or formed from the decomposition of organisms. It can also be the result of material left behind by glaciers as they melt.

2. **Climate:** Weathering depends on the climate of the area and determines the fineness of the soil that results. Temperature and water are two major forces that affect the amount of weathering that takes place.

3. **Living organisms:** As plants and animals die, they add material to the parent material that has been affected by weathering. These organisms are usually found in the subsoil and the topsoil. As the live animals dig into the soil, they provide more spaces for water to seep through, and in this way more air gets deeper into the soil as well.

4. **Topography:** The flatness or hilliness of an area contributes to the amount of weathering and runoff that takes place.

5. **Time:** Since it takes several centuries to form only one inch of soil, the soils of the Earth are millions of years old.

SKILL 14.4 Identify and analyze processes by which energy from the Sun is transferred *(e.g., radiation, conduction, convection)* through Earth's systems *(e.g., biosphere, hydrosphere, geosphere, atmosphere, cryosphere).*

All heat transfer is the movement of thermal energy from hot to cold matter. This movement down a thermal gradient is a consequence of the second law of thermodynamics. The three methods of heat transfer are:

- **Conduction:** Electron diffusion or photo vibration is responsible for this mode of heat transfer. The bodies of matter themselves do not move; the heat is transferred because adjacent atoms vibrate against each other or electrons flow between atoms. This type of heat transfer is most common when two solids come in direct contact with each other, because molecules in a solid are in close contact with one another. Metals are good conductors of thermal energy because their metallic bonds allow the freest movement of electrons. Similarly, conduction is better in denser solids. Examples of conduction can be seen in the use of copper to quickly convey heat in cookware, the flow of heat from a hot-water bottle to a person's body, or the cooling of a warm drink with ice.

- **Convection:** Convection involves some conduction but involves the movement of warm particles to cooler areas. Convection can be either natural or forced, depending on how the current of warm particles develops. Natural convection occurs when molecules near a heat source absorb thermal energy (typically via conduction), become less dense, and rise. Cooler molecules then take their place and a natural current is formed. Forced convection, as the name suggests, occurs when liquids or gases are moved by pumps, fans, or other means to come into contact with warmer or cooler masses. Because the free motion of particles with different thermal energy is key to this mode of heat transfer, convection is most common in liquid and gases. Convection can, however, transfer heat between a liquid or gas and a solid.

Forced convection is used in "forced hot air" home heating systems and is common in industrial manufacturing processes. Additionally, natural convection is responsible for ocean currents and many atmospheric events. Finally, natural convection often arises in association with conduction, for example, in the air near a radiator or the water in a pot on the stove.

- **Radiation:** This method of heat transfer occurs via electromagnetic radiation. All matter warmer than absolute zero (that is, all known matter) radiates heat. This radiation occurs regardless of the presence of any medium. Thus, it occurs even in a vacuum. Since light and radiant heat are both part of the electromagnetic spectrum, we can easily visualize how heat is transferred via radiation. For instance, like light, radiant heat is reflected by shiny materials and absorbed by dark materials. Common examples of radiant heat include the sunlight traveling from the Sun to warm the Earth, the use of radiators in homes, and the warmth of incandescent lightbulbs.

The Water Cycle

Water that falls to Earth is called precipitation. Precipitation can be in the form of a liquid (rain) or a solid (snow and hail), or it can freeze during the process of precipitating (sleet). Precipitation is part of a continuous process, called the WATER CYCLE, in which water at the Earth's surface evaporates, condenses into clouds, and returns to Earth. Water located below the surface is called groundwater.

> **WATER CYCLE:** a continuous process, in which water at the Earth's surface evaporates, condenses into clouds, and returns to Earth

The Water Cycle

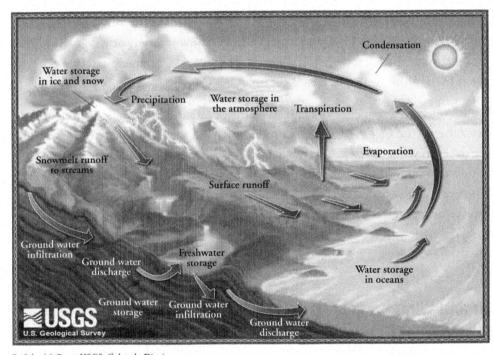

By John M. Evans USGS, Colorado District.

Precipitation can result from a number of atmospheric factors. Air, like any gas, has a limited capacity to hold another dissolved gas (in this case, water vapor). Changes in conditions, such as a decrease in temperature or an increase in water vapor content, can result in condensation of water vapor into liquid water. When this occurs in the atmosphere, clouds begin to form. As the droplets of water, which result from condensation around small particles (condensation nuclei) suspended in the air, grow in size and weight, they eventually reach a point beyond which they can no longer remain suspended in the cloud. The droplets then fall to the ground as precipitation.

Liquid water becomes water vapor through the process of evaporation. This tends to occur more readily in warmer conditions, since more thermal energy is available to allow the water to change from the liquid phase to the gas phase. Evaporation occurs readily when large bodies of water, such as oceans, are present, and it is balanced by the amount of water vapor already contained in the surrounding air. Air can eventually reach saturation, beyond which point no more water vapor can be contained. Addition of further water vapor to saturated air, or reduction of the temperature, results in condensation. In addition to evaporation, water can be transformed directly from the solid phase to the gas phase through sublimation. Sublimation can occur in the presence of snow or ice, especially when the air has low water vapor content.

Water that has evaporated or sublimated into the atmosphere, largely from sizable bodies of water or ice, can later turn into precipitation as atmospheric conditions change. This precipitation, in turn, can either evaporate or sublimate once more, or may return to a larger body of water through above-ground or below-ground transport such as a river. This completes the water cycle, as precipitated water can be returned to the atmosphere as a gas once again.

EL NIÑO: a sequence of changes in the ocean and atmospheric circulation across the Pacific Ocean

EL NIÑO refers to a sequence of changes in the ocean and atmospheric circulation across the Pacific Ocean. The water around the equator is unusually hot every two to seven years. Trade winds normally blow east to west across the equatorial latitudes, piling warm water into the western Pacific. A huge mass of heavy thunderstorms usually forms in the area and produces vast currents of rising air that displace heat poleward. This helps create the strong midlatitude jet streams. The world's climate patterns are disrupted by this change in location of thunderstorm activity.

Air and Wind

Air masses moving toward or away from the Earth's surface are called air currents. Air moving parallel to Earth's surface is called wind. Winds and air currents carrying large amounts of heat and moisture from one part of the atmosphere to another generate weather conditions. Instruments called anemometers are used to measure wind speeds.

Winds and air currents carrying large amounts of heat and moisture from one part of the atmosphere to another generate weather conditions.

The wind belts in each hemisphere consist of convection cells that encircle Earth like belts. There are three major wind belts:

1. Trade winds

2. Prevailing westerlies

3. Polar easterlies

Wind belt formation depends on the differences in air pressure that develop in the doldrums, the horse latitudes, and the polar regions. The doldrums surround the equator. Within this belt, heated air usually rises straight up into Earth's atmosphere. The horse latitudes are regions of high barometric pressure with calm, light winds. The polar regions contain cold, dense air that sinks to the Earth's surface.

Winds caused by local temperature changes include sea breezes and land breezes. A breeze that blows from the land to the ocean or a large lake is called a **land breeze. Sea breezes** are caused by the unequal heating of the land and an adjacent, large body of water. Land heats up faster than water. The movement of cool ocean air toward the land result in a sea breeze. Sea breezes usually begin blowing around midmorning, ending about sunset.

Monsoons are huge wind systems that cover large geographic areas and that reverse direction seasonally. The monsoons of India and Asia are examples of these seasonal winds. They alternate wet and dry seasons. As denser, cooler air over the ocean moves inland, a steady seasonal wind called a summer, or wet, monsoon is produced.

The air temperature at which water vapor begins to condense is called the **DEW POINT.**

RELATIVE HUMIDITY is the actual amount of water vapor in a certain volume of air compared to the maximum amount of water vapor the air could hold at a given temperature.

Storms

A **thunderstorm** is a brief, local storm produced by the rapid upward movement of warm, moist air within a cumulonimbus cloud. Thunderstorms always produce lightning and thunder and are accompanied by strong wind gusts and heavy rain or hail.

A severe storm with swirling winds that may reach speeds of hundreds of kilometers per hour is called a **tornado** or a "twister." Large cumulonimbus clouds and violent thunderstorms cover the sky. A funnel-shaped, swirling cloud may extend downward from a cumulonimbus cloud and reach the ground. Tornadoes are storms that leave a narrow path of destruction on the ground.

A swirling, funnel-shaped cloud that extends downward and touches a body of water is called a **waterspout.**

Hurricanes are storms that develop when warm, moist air carried by trade winds rotates around a low-pressure "eye." In the Pacific region, a hurricane is called a **typhoon.**

DEW POINT: the air temperature at which water vapor begins to condense

RELATIVE HUMIDITY: the actual amount of water vapor in a certain volume of air compared to the maximum amount of water vapor the air could hold at a given temperature

Storms that occur only in the winter are known as blizzards or ice storms. A blizzard is a storm with strong winds, blowing snow, and frigid temperatures. An ice storm consists of falling rain that freezes when it strikes the ground, covering everything with a layer of ice.

Groundwater

Groundwater provides drinking water for fifty-three percent of the population in the United States.

Much groundwater is clean enough to drink without any type of treatment. Although rocks and soil filter impurities from water as it flows over them, many groundwater sources are becoming contaminated. Septic tanks, broken pipes, agricultural fertilizers, garbage dumps, rainwater runoff and leaky underground tanks can all pollute groundwater. Removal of large volumes of groundwater can cause the collapse of soil and rock underground, causing the ground to sink.

Along shorelines, excessive depletion of underground water supplies allows the intrusion of saltwater into the freshwater field, making the groundwater supply undrinkable.

Runoff

Surface runoff is water that flows over land before reaching a river, lake, or ocean. Runoff occurs when precipitation falls at a rate that exceeds the ability of the soil to absorb it or when the soil becomes saturated. Certain human activities have increased runoff by making surfaces increasingly impervious to precipitation. Water is prevented from being absorbed into the ground due to pavement and buildings in urban areas and due to heavily tilled farmland in rural areas. Instead of renewing the groundwater supplies, the precipitation is channeled directly to streams and other bodies of water. Not only does this reduce groundwater supplies, but it can also trigger increased erosion, siltation, and flooding. Increased rates of erosion are particularly damaging to agricultural endeavors, since fertile topsoil is carried away at a higher rate.

Another important environmental effect of human activity on runoff is additional contribution to water pollution. As the runoff flows across land, it picks up and carries particulates and soil contaminants. The pollutants, including agricultural pesticides and fertilizers, can accumulate in lakes and other bodies of water.

Leaching

LEACHING: the liquid extraction of substances contained in a solid

LEACHING is the liquid extraction of substances contained in a solid. Leaching includes the natural processes by which water removes soluble nutrients from soil and minerals from rocks. Agriculturally, the process of leaching is often exploited to lower high salt concentrations in soil. The nutrient loss caused by leaching can be mitigated by special crop planting and fertilizer application techniques.

Leaching may have negative environmental consequences because it can lead to contamination of soil when water liberates contaminants in buried waste (such as nuclear waste or materials in landfills). Water can also dissolve agricultural chemicals and carry them to both above-ground and underground water sources.

Aquifers and reservoirs

An **AQUIFER** is an underground region of porous material that contains water. The material can be porous rock or another substance, such as sand or gravel. Aquifers may or may not be surrounded by nonporous materials and thus may or may not be relatively isolated. The water contained in an aquifer, if it is sufficiently close to the surface, can be tapped by a well to serve residential or other purposes. Since water can flow within an aquifer, contamination and overuse is a danger, thus posing problems in cases of extensive dependence on a particular aquifer for supplying water.

AQUIFER: an underground region of porous material that contains water

Reservoirs are man-made lakes designed for storing water. They may either be the result of a lake bed that is specifically constructed to be filled with water later, or the result of damming a river or other body of water. Reservoirs can serve a number of uses, ranging from water treatment to hydroelectric power generation.

SKILL 14.6 Identify and analyze various conservation methods and their effectiveness in relation to renewable and nonrenewable natural resources.

NATURAL RESOURCES are naturally occurring materials that are critically important or necessary to human life and civilization. A major source of contention in our modern society is the proper use and conservation of our natural resources. Although most people think of coal, oil, iron, and other minerals when they think of natural resources, the definition also includes other often overlooked resources such as forests, soil, water, air, and land.

NATURAL RESOURCES: naturally occurring materials that are critically important or necessary to human life and civilization

Renewable and Nonrenewable Resources

Our natural resources are classified into two broad categories: renewable resources and nonrenewable resources. A **RENEWABLE RESOURCE** is a resource that is capable of replenishment or regeneration on a human timescale. Examples of renewable resources include forests and water.

RENEWABLE RESOURCE: a resource that is capable of replenishment or regeneration on a human timescale

> **NONRENEWABLE RESOURCE:** a resource that, once exhausted, is not capable of replenishment or regeneration on a human timescale

A **NONRENEWABLE RESOURCE** is a resource that, once exhausted, is not capable of replenishment or regeneration on a human timescale. Examples of nonrenewable resources include petroleum and minerals.

As the world's population has increased and civilization has advanced, becoming increasingly dependent on technology, the demand on our natural resources has soared. More important, the per capita consumption of resources has dramatically increased.

The key focus in nonrenewable resources is the ever-increasing demand for energy.

Despite a finite supply of fossil fuels and radioactive fuels such as uranium, the demand for energy continues to increase at a substantial rate. At our present rate of consumption, there are only twenty-eight years of petroleum reserves left, and uranium reserves are estimated to be exhausted in forty years.

To alleviate this predictable energy gap, scientists are exploring new methods of recovering additional fuels from once economically unfeasible sites and researching alternative energy sources.

Alternative Energy Resources

Research efforts into alternative energy sources are directed at producing viable renewable energy sources.

ALTERNATIVE ENERGY SOURCE	
Hydroelectric Power	Power produced from falling water. Waterwheels have been in use for centuries. The drawback to this energy source lies in the availability of suitable locations for dams and the expense of construction.
Wind Power	Windmills are another ancient technology being revisited by engineers. However, wind generators produce very little electricity for the expense involved, and suitable locations with steady, high winds (windfields) are limited.
Tidal Power	The generation of electricity by deflecting and diverting strong tidal currents through offshore turbines that drive electric generators. Again, the presence of proper conditions is necessary (strong tidal power) and suitable locations are limited.

Continued on next page

ALTERNATIVE ENERGY SOURCE	
Geothermal Energy	In some areas of the world, such as New Zealand, Iceland, and Italy, energy is produced from hot igneous rocks within the Earth. Rainwater percolates porous strata near an active magma chamber and turns into steam. Some of the steam returns to the surface through natural fissures or is extracted through drilled vents. The steam is captured and routed to turbine-powered electrical generators to produce geothermal power. The steam can also be used to directly heat buildings. The limitations of this alternative energy source are obvious: Most metropolitan locations are not situated near active magma chambers. However, New Zealand does manage to gather enough power to meet approximately 5 percent of its overall electrical needs.
Solar Energy	Solar power can be utilized directly as a source of heat or to produce electricity. The most common use of solar power is to heat water. An array of dark-colored piping is placed on the roof of a structure. As water circulates through the piping, it is heated. Solar cells produce electricity from the solar radiation. Photons striking the junction between two semiconductors (usually selenium) induce an electrical current that is stored in batteries. Although this source of power is pollution-free, there are two main limitations. First, the production of power is limited by the distribution and periods of insulation. In addition, atmospheric conditions can interfere with collection efforts (e.g., cloud cover, pollution, and storms). Second, the solar cells individually produce very small amounts of electricity (called trickle changes) and must be arrayed in large banks.
Biomass	Plant and animal wastes (decaying or decayed) can be burned to produce heat for steam turbine electrical generators. In most highly developed countries the biomass is first converted to either methane gas (given off by decaying biomass) or alcohol, but in some underdeveloped countries, the biomass is still burned directly as a fuel source. For centuries, peat bogs were used as a traditional source of home-heating and cooking fuel.
Fusion Power	Although the technology does not currently exist, researchers are actively pursuing the means to make fusion power a reality. Unlike fission, the other form of nuclear energy currently in use, fusion does not rely on splitting the atoms of uranium or other potentially deadly radioactive elements. Instead, fusion power mimics the process that produces the energy of the Sun. Fusion energy is produced when small atomic nuclei fuse together to form new atoms. In a fusion reaction, two isotopes of hydrogen, deuterium, and tritium combine to make helium. The most significant advantage offered by fusion power as compared to fission power is that no dangerous radioactive isotopes are produced. The reaction produces only harmless helium that easily diffuses into the atmosphere and escapes into outer space. Additionally, the elements required for a fusion reaction are abundant on Earth (i.e., deuterium and tritium are extracted from seawater) and readily renew themselves through natural processes.

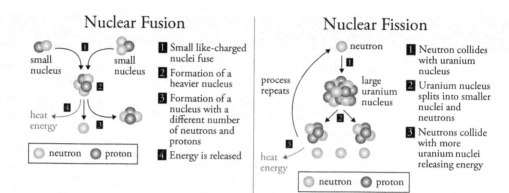

Nuclear Fusion

small nucleus   small nucleus

1 Small like-charged nuclei fuse

2 Formation of a heavier nucleus

3 Formation of a nucleus with a different number of neutrons and protons

4 Energy is released

heat energy

○ neutron ● proton

Nuclear Fission

neutron

large uranium nucleus

process repeats

heat energy

1 Neutron collides with uranium nucleus

2 Uranium nucleus splits into smaller nuclei and neutrons

3 Neutrons collide with more uranium nuclei releasing energy

○ neutron ● proton

Addressing the Issues

Our increasing population, urbanization, and dependence on technology are the key factors that drive the rapid consumption of our resources. How long our natural resources will last depends on future demand and willingness on the part of governments to efficiently manage their energy needs and resources.

As grim as the projected shortfalls may seem, there is some hope. Better agricultural techniques to prevent soil depletion, reclamation of waterways, banning the use of chemicals damaging to the atmosphere, recycling plastics and metals, and seeking alternative energy sources are all examples of ongoing initiatives to ensure resources for future generations.

SKILL 14.7 Analyze the Sun-Earth-Moon system in order to explain repeated patterns such as day and night, phases of the Moon, tides, and seasons.

Phases of the Moon

The Earth's orientation in relation to the solar system is also responsible for our perception of the phases of the moon. While the Earth orbits the Sun within a period of 365 days, the moon orbits the Earth every twenty-seven days. As the moon circles the Earth, its shape in the night sky appears to change. The changes in the appearance of the moon from the Earth are known as **LUNAR PHASES**.

LUNAR PHASES: the changes in the appearance of the moon from the Earth

These phases vary cyclically according to the relative positions of the moon, the Earth, and the Sun. At all times, half of the moon is facing the Sun; thus, it is illuminated by reflecting the Sun's light. As the moon orbits the Earth and the Earth orbits the Sun, the half of the moon that faces the Sun changes. However, the moon is in synchronous rotation around the Earth, meaning that nearly the same side of the moon faces the Earth at all times. This side is referred to as the near side of the moon. Lunar phases occur as the Earth and moon orbit the Sun and the fractional illumination of the moon's near side changes.

When the Sun and Moon are on opposite sides of the Earth, observers on Earth perceive a **full moon**, meaning the Moon appears circular because the entire illuminated half of the Moon is visible. As the Moon orbits the Earth, the Moon "wanes" as the amount of the illuminated half of the Moon that is visible from Earth decreases. A **gibbous moon** is between a full moon and a half moon, or between a half moon and a full moon. When the Sun and the Moon are on the same side of Earth, the illuminated half of the Moon is facing away from Earth, and the Moon appears invisible. This lunar phase is known as the **new moon**. The time between full moons is approximately 29.53 days.

PHASES OF THE MOON		
New Moon		The Moon is invisible or the first signs of a crescent appear
Waxing Crescent		The right crescent of the Moon is visible
First Quarter		The right quarter of the Moon is visible
Waxing Gibbous		Only the left crescent is not illuminated
Full Moon		The entire illuminated half of the Moon is visible
Waning Gibbous		Only the right crescent of the Moon is not illuminated

Continued on next page

Solar System

Montage of planetary images taken by spacecraft managed by the Jet Propulsion Laboratory. Courtesy of NASA Jet Propulsion Laboratory, Pasadena, CA.

PHASES OF THE MOON		
Last Quarter		The left quarter of the Moon is illuminated
Waning Crescent		Only the left crescent of the Moon is illuminated

Viewing the Moon from the Southern Hemisphere causes these phases to occur in the opposite order.

Tides

The orientation of and gravitational interaction between the Earth and the Moon are responsible for the ocean tides that occur on Earth. The term **tide** refers to the cyclic rise and fall of large bodies of water. Gravitational attraction is defined as the force of attraction between all bodies in the universe. At the location on Earth closest to the Moon, the gravitational attraction of the Moon draws seawater toward the Moon in the form of a tidal bulge. On the opposite side of the Earth, another tidal bulge forms in the direction away from the Moon because, at this point, the Moon's gravitational pull is the weakest.

**SPRING TIDES: ** occuring during the full and new moon, the especially strong tides that occur when the Earth, Sun, and Moon are in line, allowing both the Sun and the moon to exert gravitational force on the Earth, thereby increasing tidal bulge height

SPRING TIDES are the especially strong tides that occur when the Earth, Sun, and Moon are in line, allowing both the Sun and the Moon to exert gravitational force on the Earth, thereby increasing tidal bulge height. These tides occur during the full moon and the new moon. **NEAP TIDES** are especially weak tides occurring when the gravitational forces of the Moon and the Sun are perpendicular to one another. These tides occur during quarter moons.

**NEAP TIDES: ** occuring during quarter moons, especially weak tides during which the gravitational forces of the Moon and the Sun are perpendicular to one another

Earth is the third planet away from the Sun in our solar system. Earth's numerous types of motion and states of orientation greatly affect global conditions such as seasons, tides, and lunar phases. The Earth orbits the Sun within a period of 365 days. During this orbit, the average distance between the Earth and the Sun is 93 million miles.

The shape of the Earth's orbit around the Sun deviates from the shape of a circle only slightly. This deviation, known as the Earth's eccentricity, has a very small effect on the Earth's climate. The Earth is closest to the Sun at perihelion, occurring around January 2 of each year, and farthest from the Sun at aphelion, occurring around July 2. Because the Earth is closest to the Sun in January, the northern winter is slightly warmer than the southern winter.

Seasons

The rotation axis of the Earth is not perpendicular to the orbital (ecliptic) plane. The axis of the Earth is tilted 23.45 degrees from the perpendicular. The tilt of this axis is known as the obliquity of the ecliptic, and is mainly responsible for the four seasons of the year by influencing the intensity of solar rays received by the Northern and Southern hemispheres.

The four seasons—spring, summer, fall, and winter—are extended periods of characteristic average temperature, rainfall, storm frequency, and vegetation growth or dormancy. The effect of the Earth's tilt on climate is best demonstrated at the solstices, the two days of the year when the Sun is farthest from the Earth's equatorial plane. At the summer solstice (June), the Earth's tilt on its axis causes the Northern Hemisphere to lean toward the Sun, while the Southern Hemisphere leans away. Consequently, the Northern Hemisphere receives more intense rays from the Sun and experiences summer during this time, while the Southern Hemisphere experiences winter. At the winter solstice (December), it is the Southern Hemisphere that leans toward the Sun and thus experiences summer. Spring and fall are produced by varying degrees of the same tilt toward or away from the Sun.

Rotation Axis of the Earth

23.5° Perpendicular to the Ecliptic

Plane of the Ecliptic

Axis of Rotation

> **SKILL 14.8** Compare and differentiate the composition and various relationships among the objects of our Solar System (e.g., Sun, planets, moons, asteroids, comets).

Planets

There are eight established planets in our solar system: Mercury, Venus, Earth, Mars, Jupiter, Saturn, Uranus, and Neptune. Pluto was an established planet from its discovery in 1930 until 2006, when it was recategorized as a dwarf planet. The planets are divided into two groups based on distance from the sun. The inner planets are Mercury, Venus, Earth, and Mars. The outer planets are Jupiter, Saturn, Uranus, and Neptune.

PLANETS IN THE SOLAR SYSTEM	
Mercury	The closest planet to the Sun. Its surface has craters and rocks. The atmosphere is composed of hydrogen, helium, and sodium. Mercury was named after the Roman messenger god.
Venus	Has a slow rotation when compared to Earth. Venus and Uranus rotate in opposite directions from the other planets. This opposite rotation is called retrograde rotation. The surface of Venus is not visible due to the extensive cloud cover. The atmosphere is composed mostly of carbon dioxide, while sulfuric acid droplets in the dense cloud cover give Venus a yellow appearance. Venus has a greater greenhouse effect than that observed on Earth, and the dense clouds combined with carbon dioxide trap heat. Venus was named after the Roman goddess of love.
Earth	Considered a water planet, with 70 percent of its surface covered by water. Gravity holds the masses of water in place. The different temperatures observed on Earth allow for the different states of water (solid, liquid, gas) to exist. The atmosphere is composed mainly of oxygen and nitrogen. Earth is the only planet known to support life.
Mars	Surface contains numerous craters, active and extinct volcanoes, ridges, and valleys with extremely deep fractures. Iron oxide found in the dusty soil makes the surface seem rust-colored and the skies seem pink in color. The atmosphere is composed of carbon dioxide, nitrogen, argon, oxygen, and water vapor. Mars has polar regions with ice caps composed of water as well as two satellites (moons). Mars was named after the Roman war god.
Jupiter	The largest planet in the solar system. Jupiter has sixteen satellites. The atmosphere is composed of hydrogen, helium, methane, and ammonia. There are white-colored bands of clouds indicating rising gases and dark-colored bands of clouds indicating descending gases. The gas movement is caused by heat resulting from the energy of Jupiter's core. Jupiter has a strong magnetic field and a great red spot that is thought to be a hurricane-like cloud.
Saturn	The second largest planet in the solar system. Saturn has rings of ice, rock, and dust particles circling it. Its atmosphere is composed of hydrogen, helium, methane, and ammonia. It has more than twenty satellites. Saturn was named after the Roman god of agriculture.
Uranus	The third largest planet in the solar system and has retrograde revolution. Uranus is a gaseous planet. It has ten dark rings and fifteen satellites. Its atmosphere is composed of hydrogen, helium, and methane. Uranus was named after the Greek god of the heavens.
Neptune	Another gaseous planet with an atmosphere consisting of hydrogen, helium, and methane. Neptune has three rings and two satellites. It was named after the Roman sea god because its atmosphere is the same color as the seas.

Comets, Asteroids, and Meteors

Astronomers think that most comets originate in a dense comet cloud beyond the dwarf planet Pluto.

Astronomers believe that rocky fragments may be the remains of the birth of the solar system that never formed into a planet. These asteroids are found in the region between Mars and Jupiter.

COMETS are masses of frozen gases, cosmic dust, and small rocky particles. Astronomers think that most comets originate in a dense comet cloud beyond Pluto. A comet consists of a nucleus, a coma, and a tail. A comet's tail always points away from the Sun. The most famous comet, Halley's comet, is named after the person who first discovered it in 240 BCE. It returns to the skies near Earth every seventy-five to seventy-six years.

METEOROIDS are composed of particles of rock and metal of various sizes. When a meteoroid travels through the Earth's atmosphere, friction causes its surface to heat up and it begins to burn. A burning meteoroid falling through the Earth's atmosphere is called a METEOR (also known as a "shooting star").

METEORITES are meteors that strike the Earth's surface. A physical example of a meteorite's impact on the Earth's surface can be seen in Arizona; the Barringer Crater is a huge meteor crater. There are many other meteor craters throughout the world.

Oort Cloud and Kuiper Belt

The OORT CLOUD is a hypothetical spherical cloud surrounding our solar system. It extends approximately three light years or 30 trillion kilometers from the Sun. The cloud is believed to be made up of materials that were ejected from the inner solar system because of interaction with Uranus and Neptune, but are gravitationally bound to the Sun. It is named the Oort cloud after Jan Oort, who suggested its existence in 1950. Comets from the Oort cloud exhibit a wide range of sizes, inclinations, and eccentricities; they are often referred to as long-period comets because they have a period of greater than 200 years.

The KUIPER BELT is the name given to a vast population of small bodies orbiting the Sun beyond Neptune. There are more than 70,000 of these small bodies, some with diameters larger than 100 kilometers extending outwards from the orbit of Neptune to 50AU. They exist mostly within a ring or belt surrounding the Sun. It is believed that the objects in the Kuiper Belt are primitive remnants of the earliest phases of the solar system. It is also believed that the Kuiper Belt is the source of many short-period comets (comets with periods of less than 200 years). It is a reservoir for the comets in the same way that the Oort cloud is a reservoir for long-period comets.

Occasionally, the orbit of a Kuiper Belt object will be disturbed by the interactions of the giant planets in such a way as to cause the object to cross the orbit of Neptune. It will then very likely have a close encounter with Neptune, sending it out of the solar system, into an orbit crossing those of the other giant planets, or even into the inner solar system. Prevailing theory states that scattered disk objects began as Kuiper Belt objects, which were scattered by gravitational interactions with the giant planets.

COMETS: masses of frozen gases, cosmic dust, and small rocky particles

METEOROIDS: composed of particles of rock and metal of various sizes

METEOR: a burning meteoroid falling through the Earth's atmosphere also known as a "shooting star"

METEORITES: meteors that strike the Earth's surface

OORT CLOUD: a hypothetical spherical cloud surrounding our solar system extending approximately three light years or 30 trillion kilometers from the Sun

KUIPER BELT: a vast population of small bodies orbiting the Sun beyond Neptune

Telescopes are one of the oldest technologies used to acquire information about space. Most telescopes are optical, although there are also spectrum telescopes for gathering all types of electromagnetic radiation. Optical telescopes have been used for hundreds of years to observe celestial bodies and phenomena in outer space. As technology has allowed scientists to launch telescopes into outer space, even more detailed information has been obtained. The Hubble telescope, which is in orbit around Earth, is one famous optical telescope that has been utilized in this manner. The Chandra X-ray observatory is another famous telescope, although it collects X-rays.

Some of the earliest forays into space exploration were unmanned missions involving space probes. Space probes are still used for certain applications when risk, cost, or duration make manned missions impractical.

Some of the earliest forays into space exploration were unmanned missions involving space probes. Space probes are controlled remotely from Earth and have been shot into outer space and immediately returned, placed into orbit around our planet, or sent to and past the other planets in our solar system. The USSR's Sputnik I, launched in October 1957, was the first man-made object ever launched into space. This was the beginning of the "space race" between the United States and the USSR. The first successful U.S. launch of a space probe occurred with Vanguard I in December 1957. Space probes are still used for certain applications when risk, cost, or duration make manned missions impractical. The Voyager probes, among the most famous probes, were launched to take advantage of the favorable planetary alignment in the late 1970s. They returned data and fascinating pictures from Jupiter and Saturn as well as information from beyond our solar system. It is hoped that, as technology continues to develop, space probes will allow us to investigate space even farther away from Earth.

The first manned mission occurred in 1961, when the USSR launched Yuri Gagarin aboard Vostok I into space. A year later, the American John Glenn became the first man to orbit the Earth. The United States finally pulled well ahead in the space race in 1969, when Neil Armstrong and Buzz Aldrin became the first men to reach the Moon aboard Apollo 11. Reusable space shuttles were a large step forward in manned missions. The first space shuttle to enter outer space was the Columbia; other famous U.S. shuttles include the Challenger, Atlantis, and Endeavour. Shuttles are now used to conduct experiments and to transport astronauts to and from space stations.

Space stations, which now serve as key tools in space exploration, are artificial structures designed to house, but not transport, humans living in space. The first space station was Salyut 1, launched by the USSR in 1971.

This, like all space stations up to the present, was a low Earth orbital station. Other space stations include Skylab, Salyuts 2–7, Mir, and the International Space Station. Only the International Space Station is currently in use. Space stations offer an excellent environment to run long-term experiments in outer space; however, they are not suitable for human life for more than a few months because of the low gravity, high radiation, and other less understood factors. Much progress needs to be made before human beings will be able to live permanently in space. In fact, the future of manned missions is somewhat uncertain, as there is some debate about how necessary they are. Many speculate that significant cost and risk could be avoided with the use of robots. Currently, humans in space perform many experiments and conduct necessary repairs on equipment.

COMPETENCY 15
KNOWLEDGE OF LIFE SCIENCE

> **SKILL 15.1** Identify and compare the characteristics of living and nonliving things.

Living things are called organisms, a term that describes complex, adaptive systems that function as a whole. Several characteristics have traditionally been used to describe organisms and differentiate them from nonliving things:

- **Living things are made of one or more cells:** The cells grow, reproduce, and die

- **Living things must adapt to environmental changes:** Living things respond to external stimuli

- **Living things carry on metabolic processes:** They use and make energy

Living things also have a similar chemical makeup. First, all organisms are carbon based, that is, they are made primarily of organic molecules with carbon backbones. Even more specifically, they all use the same twenty amino acids as protein building blocks. Finally, they all use nucleic acids to carry genetic information that ultimately codes for proteins and determines the organism's makeup.

While the distinction between living and nonliving things may seem obvious when we compare, for instance, a rock and a dog, there are some gray areas. For example, viruses are not usually considered organisms because they are acellular and must rely on host cells to metabolize and reproduce. However, it can be argued that some obligate parasites and endosymbionts are similarly incapable of "independent" reproduction, but are still considered living things. Additionally, viruses are similar to organisms in that they are carbon based and carry genetic information in the form of nucleic acids.

Some have suggested a broader definition of organisms, such as "any living structure, such as a plant, animal, fungus, or bacterium, capable of growth and reproduction."

Some have suggested a broader definition of organisms, such as "any living structure, such as a plant, animal, fungus, or bacterium, capable of growth and reproduction." Such a definition would encompass both cellular and acellular life and also leave room for synthetic and possibly extraterrestrial life forms. At present, however, it is not likely that viruses will be recharacterized as living things.

Types of Cells

The cell is the basic unit of all living things. The two types of cells are prokaryotic
and eukaryotic. Prokaryotic cells include only bacteria and blue-green algae.
Bacteria were most likely the first cells and date back in the fossil record to 3.5
billion years ago. The important characteristics that differentiate these cells from
eukaryotic cells are:

- They have no defined nucleus or nuclear membrane. The DNA and ribosomes
  float freely within the cell.

- They have a thick cell wall. This is for protection, to give shape, and to keep
  the cell from bursting.

- The cell walls contain amino sugars (glycoproteins). Penicillin works by
  disrupting the cell wall, which is bad for the bacteria but will not harm the
  host.

- Some have a capsule made of polysaccharides, which make the bacteria sticky.

- Some have pili, which is a protein strand. This also allows for attachment of
  the bacteria and may be used for sexual reproduction (conjugation).

- Some have flagella for movement.

Eukaryotic cells are found in protists, fungi, plants, and animals. Features of
eukaryotic cells include:

- They are usually larger than prokaryotic cells.

- They contain many organelles, which are membrane-bound areas for specific
  cell functions.

- They contain a cytoskeleton, which provides a protein framework for the cell.

- They contain cytoplasm to support the organelles and contain the ions and
  molecules necessary for cell function.

Components of Cells

1. Nucleus: The brain of the cell. The nucleus contains:

   - Chromosomes: DNA, RNA, and proteins tightly coiled to conserve
     space while providing a large surface area.

- **Chromatin:** Loose structure of chromosomes. Chromosomes are called chromatin when the cell is not dividing.

- **Nucleoli:** Where ribosomes are made. These are seen as dark spots in the nucleus.

- **Nuclear membrane:** Contains pores that let RNA out of the nucleus. The nuclear membrane is continuous with the endoplasmic reticulum, which allows the membrane to expand or shrink if needed.

2. **Ribosomes:** The site of protein synthesis. Ribosomes may be free-floating in the cytoplasm or attached to the endoplasmic reticulum. There may be up to a half million ribosomes in a cell, depending on how much protein is made by the cell.

3. **Endoplasmic reticulum:** These are folded and provide a large surface area. They are the "roadway" of the cell and allow for the transport of materials. The lumen of the endoplasmic reticulum helps to keep materials out of the cytoplasm and headed in the right direction. The endoplasmic reticulum is capable of building new membrane material.

4. **Golgi complex, or Golgi apparatus:** This structure is stacked to increase surface area. The Golgi complex sorts, modifies, and packages molecules that are made in other parts of the cell. These molecules are either sent out of the cell or to other organelles within the cell.

5. **Lysosomes:** Found mainly in animal cells. Lysosomes contain digestive enzymes that break down food, substances not needed, viruses, damaged cell components, and eventually the cell itself. It is believed that lysosomes are responsible for the aging process.

6. **Mitochondria:** Large organelles that make ATP to supply energy to the cell. Muscle cells have many mitochondria because they use a great deal of energy. The folds inside the mitochondria are called cristae. They provide a large surface where the reactions of cellular respiration occur. Mitochondria have their own DNA and are capable of reproducing themselves if additional energy is required. Mitochondria are found in all cells except bacteria.

7. **Cell wall:** Found in plant cells only, the cell wall is composed of cellulose and fibers. It is thick enough for support and protection, yet porous enough to allow water and dissolved substances to enter. Cell walls are cemented to each other.

8. **Vacuoles:** Hold stored food and pigments. Vacuoles are very large in plants. This allows them to fill with water in order to provide turgor pressure. Lack of turgor pressure causes a plant to wilt.

9. **Cytoskeleton:** Composed of protein filaments attached to the plasma membrane and organelles. The cytoskeleton provides a framework for the cell and aids in cell movement. It constantly changes shape and moves about.

Cell Division

The purpose of cell division is to provide growth and repair in body (somatic) cells and to replenish or create sex cells for reproduction. There are two forms of cell division. MITOSIS is the division of somatic cells and MEIOSIS is the division of sex cells (eggs and sperm).

DIFFERENCES BETWEEN MITOSIS AND MEIOSIS	
Mitosis	**Meiosis**
Division of somatic cell	Division of sex cells
Two cells result from each division	Four cells or polar bodies result from each division
Chromosome number is identical to parent cells	Chromosome number is half the number of parent cells
Division is for cell growth and repair	Recombinations provide genetic diversity

MITOSIS: the division of somatic cells

MEIOSIS: the division of sex cells

The purpose of cell division is to provide growth and repair in body (somatic) cells and to replenish or create sex cells for reproduction.

> **SKILL** Identify and compare the structures and functions of plant and
> **15.3** animal cells.

The structure of a cell is often related to the cell's function. Root hair cells differ from flower stamens or leaf epidermal cells.

The nucleus of an animal cell is a round body inside the cell. It controls the cell's activities. The nuclear membrane contains threadlike structures called chromo-somes. The genes are units that control cell activities found in the nucleus. The cytoplasm has many structures in it. Some vacuoles contain the food for the cell while others contain waste materials. Animal cells differ from plant cells because they have cell membranes.

Plant cells have cell walls. A cell wall differs from a cell membrane. A cell membrane is very thin and is a part of the cell, but a cell wall is thick and is a nonliving part of the cell.

Animal cells differ from plant cells because they have cell membranes.

Differences between Plant and Animal Cells

Because they are both eukaryotic cells, the general structure of plant and animal cells is similar. That is, they both have a nucleus and various membrane-bound organelles. However, plant cells possess two unique features not seen in animal cells: cell walls and chloroplasts. Cell walls are composed of cellulose, hemicellulose, and a variety of other materials, and are found just outside the cell membrane. Chloroplasts are large, double-membrane-bound organelles that contain the light-absorbing substance chlorophyll.

There are a few more subtle differences between plant and animal cells:

- Lysosomes are common in animal cells but rarely seen in plant cells.

- Vacuoles are uncommon in animal cells, and when they appear, are small and often temporary; nearly all plant cells have large vacuoles.

- Centrioles are seen only in the lowest forms of plant life; all animal cells possess centrioles.

- Plastids are seen in the cytoplasm of most plant cells, but never in animal cells.

In both plants and animals, cells combine to make tissues that serve specific functions. Further, as is seen in all types of organisms, the structure of a cell is uniquely related to its function. For example, most plant cells perform two unique functions that are associated with the special features detailed above. The first is photosynthesis, the process by which plants transform sunlight into usable energy. Chlorophyll within the chloroplasts absorbs sunlight and photosynthesis takes place across the membranes. Because animal cells do not photosynthesize, they do not contain chloroplasts.

The second special function of plant cells relates to the manner in which non-woody plants maintain structural integrity. The necessary structure is created using turgor pressure (hydrostatic pressure) and both vacuoles and cell walls are important in this phenomenon. In a plant cell, the large central vacuole fills with water, which exerts pressure on the cell wall. The cell wall prevents the cell from bursting and creates a turgid cell. The pressure of each cell wall against its neighbors creates stiff tissue that allows the plant to stay upright. This also explains why plants that do not have enough water wilt; their vacuoles lose water and can no longer exert pressure, which causes the plant to droop. Such a mechanism is not necessary in animal cells because most animals have specialized tissues (bones, muscles, exoskeletons, etc.) to perform this function. Accordingly, cell walls and large vacuoles are not seen in animal cells.

SKILL **Classify living things into major groups** *(i.e., Linnaean system)* **and**
15.4 **compare according to characteristics** *(e.g., physical features, behaviors, development).*

Carolus Linnaeus is considered the father of taxonomy. **TAXONOMY** is the science of classification. Linnaeus based his system on morphology (study of structure). Later, evolutionary relationships (phylogeny) also were used to sort and group species. The modern classification system uses binomial nomenclature, which is a two-word name for every species. The genus is the first part of the name, and the species is the second part. Notice, in the levels explained below, that Homo sapiens is the scientific name for humans. Starting with the kingdom, the groups get smaller and more alike as one moves down the levels in the classification of humans:

TAXONOMY: the science of classification

> **Kingdom:** Animalia, **Phylum:** Chordata, **Subphylum:** Vertebrata, **Class:** Mammalia, **Order:** Primate, **Family:** Hominidae, **Genus:** Homo, **Species:** sapiens

Species are defined by the ability to successfully reproduce with members of their own kind.

> **Kingdom Monera:** Bacteria and blue-green algae, prokaryotic, having no true nucleus, unicellular.

> **Kingdom Protista:** Eukaryotic, unicellular, some are photosynthetic, some are consumers.

> **Kingdom Fungi:** Eukaryotic, multicellular, absorptive consumers, contain a chitin cell wall.

Bacteria are classified according to their morphology (shape). Bacilli are rod-shaped, cocci are round, and spirillia are spiral-shaped. The gram stain is a staining procedure used to identify bacteria. Gram-positive bacteria pick up the stain and turn purple. Gram-negative bacteria do not pick up the stain and are pink in color. Microbiologists use methods of locomotion, reproduction, and how the organism obtains its food to classify protista.

> **Methods of locomotion:** Flagellates have a flagellum, ciliates have cilia, and ameboids move through use of pseudopodia.

> **Methods of reproduction:** Binary fission is a type of asexual reproduction in which an organism simply divides into two organisms. All new organisms are clones of the parent. Sexual methods of reproduction provide more diversity. Bacteria can reproduce sexually through conjugation, in which genetic material is exchanged.

Methods of obtaining nutrition: Photosynthetic organisms, or producers, convert sunlight to chemical energy. Consumers, or heterotrophs, eat other living things. Saprophytes are consumers that live off dead or decaying material.

> SKILL **Compare and contrast the structures, functions, and interactions**
> 15.5 **of human and other animal organ systems** (e.g., respiration, reproduction, digestion).

Animals

- **Skeletal System:** The skeletal system functions in support. Vertebrates have an endoskeleton, with muscles attached to bones. Skeletal proportions are controlled by area to volume relationships. Body size and shape is limited due to the forces of gravity. Surface area is increased to improve efficiency in all organ systems.

- **Muscular System:** Its function is for movement. There are three types of muscle tissue. Skeletal muscle is voluntary. These muscles are attached to bones. Smooth muscle is involuntary. It is found in organs and enable functions such as digestion and respiration. Cardiac muscle is a specialized type of smooth muscle.

- **Nervous System:** The neuron is the basic unit of the nervous system. It consists of an axon (which carries impulses away from the cell body), the dendrite (which carries impulses towards the cell body), and the cell body itself (which contains the nucleus). Synapses are spaces between neurons. Chemicals called neurotransmitters are found close to the synapse. The myelin sheath, composed of Schwann cells, covers the neurons and provides insulation.

- **Digestive System:** The function of the digestive system is to break down food and absorb it into the blood stream where it can be delivered to all cells of the body for use in cellular respiration. As animals evolved, digestive systems changed from simple absorption to a system with a separate mouth and anus, capable of allowing the animal to become independent of a host.

- **Respiratory System:** This system functions in the gas exchange of oxygen (needed) and carbon dioxide (waste). It delivers oxygen to the bloodstream and picks up carbon dioxide for release out of the body. Simple animals diffuse gases to and from their environment. Gills allow aquatic animals to exchange gases in a fluid medium by removing dissolved oxygen from the water. Lungs maintain a fluid environment for gas exchange in terrestrial animals.

- **Circulatory System:** The function of the circulatory system is to carry oxygenated blood and nutrients to all cells of the body and return carbon dioxide waste to be expelled from the lungs. Animals evolved from an open system to a closed system with vessels leading to and from the heart.

Animal Respiration

Animals take in oxygen and give off waste gases. For instance, a fish uses its gills to extract oxygen from the water. Bubbles are evidence that waste gases are expelled. Respiration without oxygen is called anaerobic respiration. Anaerobic respiration in animal cells is also called lactic acid fermentation. The end product is lactic acid.

Animal Reproduction

Animal reproduction can be asexual or sexual. Geese lay eggs while animals such as bear cubs, deer, and rabbits are born alive. Some animals reproduce frequently while others do not. Some species of animals only produce one baby while others produce many (clutch size).

Animal Digestion

Some animals only eat meat (carnivores) while others only eat plants (herbivores). Many animals eat both (omnivores). The purpose of digestion is to break down carbohydrates, fats, and proteins. Many organs are needed to digest food. The process begins with the mouth. Certain animals, such as birds, have beaks to puncture wood or allow for the consumption of large fish. The tooth structure of a beaver is designed to cut down trees. Tigers are known for their sharp teeth, used to rip through the hides of their prey.

Enzymes are catalysts that help speed up chemical reactions by lowering effective activation energy. Enzyme rate is affected by temperature, pH, and the amount of substrate. Saliva is an enzyme that changes starches into sugars.

Animal Circulation

Mammals are warm-blooded; their blood temperature stays constant regardless of outside temperature. Amphibians are cold-blooded; their blood temperature varies with the outside temperature.

Human Body

Skeletal system

The function of the skeletal system is support. Vertebrates have an endoskeleton, with muscles attached to bones. Skeletal proportions are controlled by area-to-volume relationships. Body size and shape are limited due to the forces of gravity. Surface area is increased to improve efficiency in all organ systems.

The **axial skeleton** consists of the bones of the skull and vertebrae. The **appendicular skeleton** consists of the bones of the legs, arms, tailbone, and shoulder girdle. Bone is a connective tissue. Parts of the bone include compact bone, which gives strength; spongy bone, which contains red marrow to make blood cells; yellow marrow in the center of long bones to store fat cells; and the periostenum, which is the protective covering on the outside of the bone.

A **joint** is defined as a place where two bones meet. Joints enable movement. **Ligaments** attach bone to bone. **Tendons** attach bones to muscles.

Muscular system

The function of the **muscular system** is movement. There are three types of muscle tissue. Skeletal muscle is voluntary. These muscles are attached to bones. Smooth muscle is involuntary. It is found in organs and enables functions such as digestion and respiration. Cardiac muscle is a specialized type of smooth muscle and is found in the heart. Muscles can only contract; therefore they work in antagonistic pairs to allow back-and-forward movement. Muscle fibers are made of groups of myofibrils, which are made of groups of sarcomeres. Actin and myosin are proteins, which make up the sarcomere.

Nervous system

The neuron is the basic unit of the **nervous system**. It consists of an axon, which carries impulses away from the cell body; the dendrite, which carries impulses toward the cell body; and the cell body, which contains the nucleus. Synapses are spaces between neurons. Chemicals called neurotransmitters are found close to the synapse. The myelin sheath, composed of Schwann cells, covers the neurons and provides insulation.

The **reflex arc** is the simplest nerve response. The brain is bypassed. When a stimulus (like touching a hot stove) occurs, sensors in the hand send the message directly to the spinal cord. This stimulates motor neurons that contract the muscles to move the hand. **Voluntary nerve responses** involve the brain. Receptor cells send the message to sensory neurons that lead to association neurons. The message is taken to the brain. Motor neurons are stimulated and the message is transmitted to effector cells that cause the end effect.

Organization of the nervous system

The somatic nervous system is controlled consciously. It consists of the central nervous system (brain and spinal cord) and the peripheral nervous system (nerves that extend from the spinal cord to the muscles). The autonomic nervous system is unconsciously controlled by the hypothalamus in the brain. Smooth muscles, the heart, and digestion are all controlled by the autonomic nervous system. The sympathetic nervous system works in opposition to the parasympathetic nervous system. For example, if the sympathetic nervous system stimulates an action, the parasympathetic nervous system would terminate that action.

The somatic nervous system is controlled consciously. The autonomic nervous system is unconsciously controlled by the hypothalamus in the brain.

Digestive system

The function of the digestive system is to break food down and absorb it into the bloodstream. Once in the blood stream, the broken down food can be delivered to all cells of the body for use in cellular respiration. The teeth and saliva begin digestion by breaking food down into smaller pieces and lubricating it so it can be swallowed. The lips, cheeks, and tongue form a bolus (ball) of food. The food is carried down the pharynx by the process of peristalsis (wave-like contractions) and enters the stomach through the cardiac sphincter, which closes to keep food from going back up.

In the stomach, pepsinogen and hydrochloric acid form pepsin, the enzyme that breaks down proteins. The food is broken down further by this chemical action and turned into chyme. The pyloric sphincter muscle opens to allow the food to enter the small intestine, where most nutrient absorption occurs. Any food left after the trip through the small intestine enters the large intestine. The large intestine functions to reabsorb water and produce vitamin K. The feces, or remaining waste, are passed out through the anus.

Respiratory system

The respiratory system functions in the exchange of oxygen (needed) and carbon dioxide (waste). It delivers oxygen to the bloodstream and picks up carbon dioxide for release out of the body. Air enters the mouth and nose, where it is warmed, moistened, and filtered of dust and particles. Cilia in the trachea trap unwanted material in mucus, which can be expelled. The trachea splits into two bronchial tubes, which divide into smaller and smaller bronchioles in the lungs. The internal surface of the lungs is composed of alveoli, which are thin-walled air sacs. These provide a large surface area for gas exchange. The alveoli are lined with capillaries. Oxygen diffuses into the bloodstream and carbon dioxide diffuses out to be exhaled. The oxygenated blood is carried to the heart and delivered to all parts of the body.

The thoracic cavity holds the lungs. The diaphragm, a muscle below the lungs, makes inhalation possible. As the volume of the thoracic cavity increases, the diaphragm muscle flattens out and inhalation occurs. When the diaphragm relaxes, exhalation occurs.

Circulatory system

The function of the circulatory system is to carry oxygenated blood and nutrients to all cells of the body and return carbon dioxide waste to be expelled from the lungs. Unoxygenated blood enters the heart through the inferior and superior vena cava. The first chamber it encounters is the right atrium. It goes through the tricuspid valve to the right ventricle, on to the pulmonary arteries, and then to the lungs where it is oxygenated. It returns to the heart through the pulmonary vein, into the left atrium. It travels through the bicuspid valve to the left ventricle, where it is pumped to all parts of the body through the aorta.

Heart

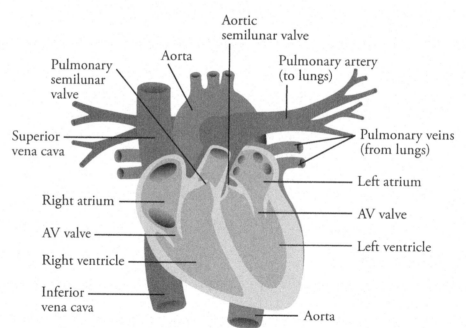

Blood vessels include:

- **Arteries:** Lead away from the heart. All arteries carry oxygenated blood except the pulmonary artery.

- **Arterioles:** Arteries branch off to form these smaller passages.

- **Capillaries:** Arterioles branch off to form tiny capillaries that reach every cell. Blood moves very slowly in capillaries due to their small size.

- **Venules:** Capillaries combine to form larger venules. The vessels are now carrying waste products from the cells.

- **Veins:** Venules combine to form larger veins leading back to the heart. Veins and venules have thinner walls than arteries because they are not under as much pressure. Veins contain valves to prevent the backward flow of blood due to gravity.

Components of the blood include:

- **Plasma:** 60 percent of the blood is plasma, the liquid part of blood. Plasma contains salts called electrolytes, nutrients, and waste.

- **Erythrocytes:** Also called red blood cells; Erthrocytes contain hemoglobin, which carries oxygen molecules.

- **Leukocytes:** Also called white blood cells, which are larger than red blood cells. Leukocytes are phagocytic and can engulf invaders. White blood cells are not confined to the blood vessels and can enter the interstitial fluid between cells.

- **Platelets:** Assist in blood clotting. Platelets are made in the bone marrow.

Lymphatic system (Immune system)

Nonspecific defense mechanisms do not target specific pathogens but instead are a whole-body response. Results of nonspecific mechanisms are seen as symptoms of an infection. These mechanisms include the skin, mucous membranes, and cells of the blood and lymph (i.e., white blood cells, macrophages). Fever is a result of an increase in the member of white blood cells. Pyrogens are released by white blood cells, which set the body's thermostat to a higher temperature. This inhibits the growth of microorganisms. It also increases metabolism to increase phagocytosis and body repair.

Specific defense mechanisms (antibodies) recognize foreign material (antigens) and respond by destroying the invader. These mechanisms are specific in purpose and diverse in type. They are able to recognize individual pathogens. Memory of the invaders provides immunity upon further exposure.

IMMUNITY is the body's ability to recognize and destroy an antigen before it causes harm. Active immunity develops after recovery from an infectious disease such as chicken pox or after a vaccination (e.g., for measles, mumps, and rubella). Passive immunity can be passed from one individual to another; it is not permanent. A good example is the immunities passed from mother to nursing child.

> **IMMUNITY:** the body's ability to recognize and destroy an antigen before it causes harm

Excretory system

The function of the excretory system is to rid the body of nitrogenous wastes in the form of urea. The functional units of excretion are the nephrons, which make up the kidneys. Antidiuretic hormone (ADH), which is made in the hypothalamus and stored in the pituitary, is released when differences in osmotic balance occur. This will cause more water to be reabsorbed. As the blood becomes more dilute, ADH release ceases.

The Bowman's capsule contains the glomerulus, a tightly packed group of capillaries. The glomerulus is under high pressure. Waste and fluids leak out due to pressure. Filtration is not selective in this area. Selective secretion by active and passive transport occur in the proximal convoluted tubule. Unwanted molecules are secreted into the filtrate. Selective secretion also occurs in the loop of Henle. Salt is actively pumped out of the tube and much water is lost due to the hyperosmosity of the inner part (medulla) of the kidney. As the fluid enters the distal convoluted tubule, more water is reabsorbed. Urine forms in the collecting duct, which leads to the ureter, then to the bladder where it is stored. Urine is passed from the bladder through the urethra. The amount of water reabsorbed into the body depends on how much water or fluids an individual has consumed. Urine can be very dilute or very concentrated if dehydration is present.

Endocrine system

The function of the endocrine system is to manufacture proteins called hormones. Hormones are released into the bloodstream and carried to a target tissue where they stimulate an action. Hormones may build up over time to cause their effect, as in puberty or the menstrual cycle.

Hormones are specific and fit receptors on the target tissue cell surface. The receptor activates an enzyme, which converts ATP to cyclic AMP. Cyclic AMP (cAMP) is a second messenger from the cell membrane to the nucleus. The genes found in the nucleus turn on or off to cause a specific response.

There are two classes of hormones. Steroid hormones come from cholesterol and cause sexual characteristics and mating behavior. These hormones include estrogen and progesterone in females and testosterone in males. Peptide hormones are made in the pituitary, adrenal glands (kidneys), and the pancreas. They include:

- Follicle-stimulating hormone (FSH): Production of sperm or egg cells
- Luteinizing hormone (LH): Functions in ovulation
- Luteotropic hormone (LTH): Assists in production of progesterone
- Growth hormone (GH): Stimulates growth

- **Antidiuretic hormone (ADH):** Assists in retention of water
- **Oxytocin:** Stimulates labor contractions at birth and let-down of milk
- **Melatonin:** Regulates circadian rhythms and seasonal changes
- **Epinephrine (adrenaline):** Causes fight-or-flight reaction of the nervous system

Hormones work on a feedback system. The increase or decrease in one hormone may cause the increase or decrease in another. Release of hormones causes a specific response.

Reproductive system

Sexual reproduction greatly increases diversity due to the many combinations possible through meiosis and fertilization. Spermatogenesis begins at puberty in the male. The sperm mature in the seminiferous tubules located in the testes. Oogenesis, the production of egg cells, is usually complete by the birth of a female. Egg cells are not released until menstruation begins at puberty. Meiosis forms one ovum with all the cytoplasm and three polar bodies, which are reabsorbed by the body. The ovum are stored in the ovaries and released each month from puberty to menopause.

Sperm are stored in the seminiferous tubules in the testes, where they mature. Mature sperm are found in the epididymis located on top of the testes. After ejaculation, the sperm travels up the vas deferens, where they mix with semen made in the prostate and seminal vesicles and travel out the urethra.

Eggs are stored in the ovaries. Ovulation releases an egg into the fallopian tube, which is ciliated to move the egg along. Fertilization normally occurs in the fallopian tube. If pregnancy does not occur, the egg passes through the uterus and is expelled through the vagina. Levels of progesterone and estrogen stimulate menstruation. In the event of pregnancy, hormonal levels are affected by the implantation of a fertilized egg, so menstruation does not occur.

Pregnancy

If fertilization occurs, the zygote implants in about two to three days in the uterus. Implantation promotes secretion of human chorionic gonadotropin (HCG). This is what is detected in pregnancy tests. The HCG keeps the level of progesterone elevated to maintain the uterine lining in order to feed the developing embryo until the umbilical cord forms. Labor is initiated by oxytocin, which causes labor contractions and dilation of the cervix. Prolactin and oxytocin cause the production of milk.

> **SKILL 15.6** **Distinguish among infectious agents** *(e.g., viruses, bacteria, fungi, parasites)*, **their transmission, and their effects on the human body.**

Microorganisms include all living things that are too small to be detected by the naked human eye, such as fungi, bacteria, archaea, and protists. Microorganisms may be either prokaryotic or eukaryotic, but are typically single-celled organisms. Viruses and prions are sometimes considered microorganisms, despite the fact that they are acellular. Debate continues regarding whether viruses and prions can truly be classified as living things.

Fungi

FUNGI: heterotrophic, eukaryotic organisms with chitinous cell walls

FUNGI are heterotrophic, eukaryotic organisms with chitinous cell walls. Fungi constitute their own kingdom of organisms and exist as both multicellular and unicellular species. They reproduce both sexually and asexually via spores which are often produced by fruiting bodies. Fungal microorganisms include yeasts and molds. Fungi, especially yeast, have many beneficial uses for humans; bread and alcoholic beverages are made using yeast while other fungi produce antibiotics such as penicillin. However, fungi can also cause diseases in plants and animals, ranging from Dutch elm disease to athlete's foot.

Bacteria

BACTERIA: prokaryotic, unicellular organisms

BACTERIA are prokaryotic, unicellular organisms. This kingdom is extremely diverse because bacteria have adapted to almost every habitat on the Earth. For instance, bacteria have evolved to be chemotrophic, photostophic, and heterotrophic. Bacteria are also diverse in shape and can be spherical, rod-shaped, spiral-shaped, or tightly coiled. Further, some bacteria possess means for locomotion, such as flagella and specially adapted cytoskeletal structures. Though they are typically unicellular, bacteria often associate with one another, and it is particularly common for them to attach to surfaces and form dense aggregations known as biofilms. Bacteria reproduce asexually, although certain mechanisms allow for the transfer of genes between individuals.

When they directly interact with humans, bacteria are both helpful and harmful, although the vast majority have no effect on human health at all. They are important for the proper functioning of the digestive tract (bacteria such as Escherichia coli fulfill this role) and critical to fermentation in wastewater treatment plants and in the production of cheese and yogurt. Additionally, some bacteria have been exploited to produce therapeutic agents.

However, bacteria are the cause of many common diseases, including tuberculosis (caused by several mycobacteria, most notably Mycobacterium tuberculosis), cholera (Vibrio cholerae), staph infections (Staphylococcus), strep infections (Streptococcus), and syphilis (Treponema pallidum).

Archaea

ARCHAEA are also known as archaebacteria because they are single-celled pro-karyotic life forms. In older taxonomical systems, they were classified along with bacteria, but new genetic evidence shows that they are more closely related to eukaryotes. Archaea are noted for their ability to live in harsh conditions that are unsuitable for other organisms; they are often found in environments with extreme temperature, pH, and salinity. At present, there are no known diseases caused by archaeal pathogens.

> **ARCHAEA:** single-celled prokaryotic life forms

Protists

The PROTIST kingdom is composed of eukaryotes that cannot be classified as fungi, animals, or plants. The "catch-all" characteristic of this kingdom is made further apparent by the fact that these organisms do not have a common ancestral species. Rather, they are related by their simple structure; protists are unicellular or, if multicellular, contain no specialized tissue.

> **PROTIST:** eukaryotes that cannot be classified as fungi, animals, or plants

Protists are often described as being animal-like, plant-like, or fungus-like. The animal-like protists are heterotrophic and mobile, and are generally called protozoans. Protozoans are typically classified based on their means of locomotion (flagella, cilia, etc.) and include amoeba, paramecium, and toxoplasma. The plant-like protists are autotrophic, typically photosynthetic organisms. Plant-like protists include red, green, and brown algae. However, in some newer classifications, algae are contained in the plant kingdom. Finally, the fungus-like protists are heterotrophic and produce sporangia. The organisms include the slime and water molds.

While protists serve a critical role in the food chain, their direct interactions with humans tend to be pathogenic. Most notably, malaria is carried by a protozoan.

Viruses

VIRUSES are composed of genetic molecules (DNA or RNA) encased in a protein shell, known as a capsid. Some viruses also contain an outer membrane, similar to a cell membrane. Most viruses have a diameter between 100 and 300 nanometers. A host cell is required for a virus to reproduce, and there are viruses specially suited to almost every type of cell. Viruses are classified by the type of cell they

> **VIRUSES:** genetic molecules (DNA or RNA) encased in a protein shell, known as a capsid

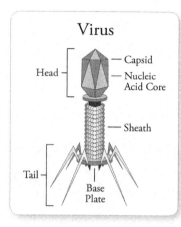

Virus

- Head
  - Capsid
  - Nucleic Acid Core
  - Sheath
- Tail
  - Base Plate

infect, the type and configuration (single- or double-stranded) of genetic material they carry, and their method of infection. Viruses are extremely diverse. For instance, retroviruses are RNA viruses that contain an enzyme that triggers the host cell to copy its RNA into DNA (the reverse of the normal process), while adenoviruses are icosahedral viruses that contain double-stranded DNA and employ a "spike" to attach and infect host cells.

Viruses are typically pathogenic, though in some cases they have little effect on their host. Familiar viruses include human immunodeficiency virus (HIV), the retrovirus that causes AIDS; adenoviruses, which cause diseases of the upper respiratory tract in mammals; and bacteraphages, which infect prokaryotes. However, viruses may ultimately have some clinical value for humans, as they are currently under study for use as vectors in gene therapy treatments.

Bacteriophage

All viruses have a head or protein capsid that contains genetic material. This material is encoded in the nucleic acid and can be DNA, RNA, or even a limited number of enzymes. Some viruses also have a protein tail region. The tail aids in binding to the surface of the host cell and penetrating the surface of the host in order to introduce the virus's genetic material.

Other Examples of Viruses and Their Structures

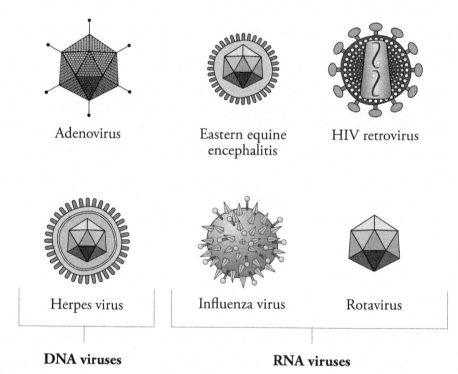

Adenovirus

Eastern equine encephalitis

HIV retrovirus

Herpes virus

Influenza virus

Rotavirus

DNA viruses

RNA viruses

Prions

PRION is an abbreviation for proteinaceous infectious particle that describes infectious agents composed of naked protein. Like viruses, prions are extremely small and require a host to reproduce. Scientists still have much to learn about prions, but current theories are that they alter the folded structure of host proteins. Diseases caused by prions affect neural tissue and include bovine spongiform encephalopathy (BSE), also known as mad cow disease, and Creutzfeldt-Jakob disease (CJD).

> **PRION:** an abbreviation for proteinaceous infectious particle that describes infectious agents composed of naked protein

---

SKILL 15.7 Identify and analyze the processes of heredity and natural selection and the scientific theory of evolution.

Theories of Evolution

Charles Darwin proposed a mechanism for his theory of evolution termed natural selection. NATURAL SELECTION describes the process by which favorable traits accumulate in a population, changing the population's genetic makeup over time. Darwin theorized that all individual organisms, even those of the same species, are different, and those individuals that happen to possess traits favorable for survival would produce more offspring. Thus, in the next generation, the number of individuals with the favorable trait increases, and the process continues.

> **NATURAL SELECTION:** the process by which favorable traits accumulate in a population, changing the population's genetic makeup over time

Darwin, in contrast to other evolutionary scientists, did not believe that traits acquired during an organism's lifetime (e.g., increased musculature), or the desires and needs of the organism, affected the evolution of populations. For example, Darwin argued that the evolution of long trunks in elephants resulted from environmental conditions that favored those elephants that had longer trunks. The individual elephants did not stretch their trunks to reach food or water and pass on the new, longer trunks to their offspring.

Jean Baptiste Lamarck proposed an alternative mechanism of evolution. Lamarck believed that individual organisms develop traits in response to changing environmental conditions and pass on these new traits to their offspring. For example, Lamarck argued that the trunks of individual elephants lengthen as a result of stretching for scarce food and water, and elephants pass on the longer trunks to their offspring.

> *Different molecular and environmental processes and conditions drive the evolution of populations. The various mechanisms of evolution either introduce new genetic variation or alter the frequency of existing variation.*

Mutations—random changes in nucleotide sequence—are a basic mechanism of evolution. Mutations in DNA result from copying errors during cell division, exposure to radiation and chemicals, and interaction with viruses. Simple point mutations, deletions, or insertions can alter the function or expression of existing genes, but do not contribute greatly to evolution. On the other hand, gene duplication—the duplication of an entire gene—often leads to the creation of new genes that may contribute to the evolution of a species. Because gene duplication results in two copies of the same gene, the extra copy is free to mutate and develop without the selective pressure experienced by mutated single-copy genes. Gene duplication and subsequent mutation often leads to the creation of new genes. When new genes resulting from mutations lend the mutated organism a reproductive advantage relative to environmental conditions, natural selection and evolution can occur.

Recombination is the exchange of DNA between a pair of chromosomes during meiosis. Recombination does not introduce new genes into a population, but does affect the expression of genes and the combination of traits expressed by individuals. Thus, recombination increases the genetic diversity of populations and contributes to evolution by creating new combinations of genes.

Isolation is the separation of members of a species by environmental barriers that the organisms cannot cross. Environmental change, either gradual or sudden, often results in isolation. An example of gradual isolation is the formation of a mountain range or desert between members of a species. An example of sudden isolation is the separation of members of a species by a flood or earthquake. Isolation leads to evolution because the separated groups cannot reproduce together and differences arise. In addition, because the environment of each group is different, the groups adapt and evolve differently. Extended isolation can lead to SPECIATION, the development of new species.

SPECIATION: the development of new species

Sexual reproduction and selection contributes to evolution by consolidating genetic mutations and creating new combinations of genes. Genetic recombination during sexual reproduction introduces new combinations of traits and patterns of gene expression. Consolidation of favorable mutations through sexual reproduction speeds the processes of evolution and natural selection. On the other hand, consolidation of deleterious mutations creates individuals with severe defects or abnormalities.

Genetic drift is, along with natural selection, one of the two main mechanisms of evolution. Genetic drift refers to the chance deviation in the frequency of alleles (traits) resulting from the randomness of zygote formation and selection. Because only a small percentage of all possible zygotes become mature adults, parents do not necessarily pass all of their alleles on to their offspring. Genetic drift is particularly important in small populations because chance deviations in allelic frequency can quickly alter the genotypic makeup of the population. In extreme cases, certain alleles may completely disappear from the gene pool. Genetic drift is particularly influential when environmental events and conditions produce small, isolated populations.

**SKILL Analyze the interdependence of living things with each other and
15.8 with their environment** (e.g., food webs, ecosystems, pollution).

Interrelationships among Organisms

Many different types of interactions can occur between different species living together, including predation, parasitism, competition, commensalism, and mutualism.

Predation and parasitism result in a benefit for one species and a detriment for the other. Predation is when a predator eats its prey. The common conception of predation is of a carnivore consuming other animals. Although not always resulting in the death of the plant, herbivory is a form of predation. Some animals eat enough of a plant to cause death. Parasitism involves a predator that lives on or in its host, causing detrimental effects to the host. Insects and viruses that live and reproduce in their hosts are an example of parasitism. Many plants and animals have defenses against predators. Some plants have poisonous chemicals that will harm the predator if ingested, and some animals are camouflaged so they are harder to detect.

Competition occurs when two or more species in a community use the same resources. Competition is usually detrimental to both populations. It is often difficult to find in nature because competition between two populations is not continuous. Either the weaker population will no longer exist, or one population will evolve to utilize other available resources.

Symbiosis is when two species live close together. Parasitism, described above, is one example of symbiosis. Another example is commensalism. Commensalism occurs when one species benefits from the other without causing it harm.

Mutualism is when both species benefit from the other. Species involved in mutualistic relationships must coevolve to survive. As one species evolves, the other must as well if it is to survive. The grouper and a species of shrimp live in a mutualistic relationship. The shrimp feed off parasites living on the grouper; thus the shrimp are fed and the grouper stays healthy. Many microorganisms are in mutualistic relationships.

An ENDANGERED SPECIES is a population of an organism that is at risk of becoming extinct because it is either low in numbers or threatened by changing environmental or predation parameters. The construction of homes all over the world has caused the destruction of habitats for other animals, leading to their extinction. Three major crops feed the world (rice, corn, and wheat); the planting of these crops destroys habitats and pushes animals residing there into other habitats, causing overpopulation or extinction.

ENDANGERED SPECIES: a population of an organism that is at risk of becoming extinct because it is either low in numbers or threatened by changing environmental or predation parameters

Pollution and Climate Change

Although technology gives us many advances, pollution is a side effect of production. Waste disposal and the burning of fossil fuels have polluted our land, water, and air. Global warming and acid rain are two results of burning hydrocarbons and sulfur.

CLIMATE CHANGE: the increase in the average temperature of Earth's near-surface air and oceans

CLIMATE CHANGE is the increase in the average temperature of Earth's near-surface air and oceans. Rainforest depletion and the use of fossil fuels and aerosol sprays have caused an increase in carbon dioxide production. This leads to a decrease in the amount of oxygen, which is directly proportional to the amount of ozone. As the ozone layer is depleted, more heat enters our atmosphere and is trapped. This causes an overall warming effect, which may eventually melt the polar ice caps, causing a rise in water levels and changes in climate that will affect weather systems worldwide.

> **SKILL 15.9** Identify and analyze plant structures and the processes of photosynthesis, transpiration, and reproduction *(i.e., sexual, asexual)*.

PHOTOSYNTHESIS: the process by which plants make carbohydrates from the energy of the Sun, carbon dioxide, and water

PHOTOSYNTHESIS is the process by which plants make carbohydrates from the energy of the Sun, carbon dioxide, and water. Oxygen is simply a waste product of this process. Photosynthesis occurs in the chloroplast where the pigment chlorophyll traps energy from the Sun. It has two major steps:

- **Light reactions:** Sunlight is trapped, water is split, and oxygen is given off. ATP is made and hydrogens reduce NADP to $NADPH_2$. The light reactions occur in light. The products of the light reactions enter into the dark reactions (Calvin cycle).

- **Dark reactions:** Carbon dioxide enters during the dark reactions. This can occur with or without the presence of light. The energy transferred from $NADPH_2$ and ATP allow for the fixation of carbon into glucose.

During times of decreased light, plants break down the products of photosynthesis through cellular respiration. Glucose, with the help of oxygen, breaks down and produces carbon dioxide and water as waste. The plants use approximately fifty percent of the products of photosynthesis for energy.

Water travels up the xylem of the plant through the process of transpiration. Water sticks to itself (cohesion) and to the walls of the xylem (adhesion). As it evaporates through the stomata of the leaves, the water is pulled up the column from the roots. Environmental factors such as heat and wind increase the rate of transpiration. High humidity decreases the rate of transpiration.

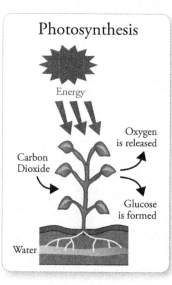

Photosynthesis

Energy

Oxygen is released

Carbon Dioxide

Glucose is formed

Water

Angiosperms are the largest group in the plant kingdom. They are the flowering plants that produce seeds for reproduction. They first appeared about seventy million years ago when the dinosaurs were disappearing. The land was drying up and their ability to produce seeds that could remain dormant until conditions became acceptable allowed for their success. Compared to other plants, they also had more advanced vascular tissue and larger leaves for increased photosynthesis. Angiosperms reproduce through a method of **double fertilization** in which an ovum is fertilized by two sperm. One sperm produces the new plant; the other forms the food supply for the developing plant.

The success of plant reproduction involves the seeds moving away from the parent plant to decrease competition for space, water, and minerals. Seeds can be carried by wind (maple trees), water (palm trees), or animals (burrs), or ingested by animals and released in their feces in another area.

SKILL 15.10 Predict the responses of plants to various stimuli (e.g., heat, light, gravity).

Gravity keeps plants rooted in the ground. Water allows the roots to take nourishment from the soil and extend down into the soil. The fertility of the soil also acts as a stimulus; if the nourishment the plants need does not exist in the ground, they will die.

> Plants do not possess a nervous system, but, like animals, they do respond to stimuli in their environment.

Plants need sunlight to grow and will grow toward the sun. Too much heat causes them to wither and die, but cold weather can have the same result. Plants start to bud in spring as the atmosphere and the ground start to warm up. They die when the weather turns cold and remain dormant in the soil, if they are perennial, until spring.

TROPISM is the term given to the response of plants to grow toward or away from a stimulus in the environment. In phototropism, light sends the hormone auxin to the portion of the plant receiving the most shade so that it starts to grow toward the light. Plants also respond to touch. Some curl up when touched and others tend to flatten, trying to get away from the touch.

> **TROPISM:** the response of plants to grow toward or away from a stimulus in the environment

SKILL 15.11 Identify and compare the life cycles and predictable ways plants and animals change as they grow, develop, and age.

A life cycle consists of the stages through which a living thing goes during its life. In some cases, the process is slow and the changes are gradual. All organisms go through stages of development. Environmental conditions such as water, temperature, and light affect the development of organisms.

A plant's life cycle is how long a plant lives or how long it takes to grow, flower, and set seed. A plant begins as a seed, then its roots form, and then it grows, flowers, possibly provides fruit, and, finally, spreads seeds. At that point, the cycle begins again.

The life cycle of an animal consists of several stages. All animals reproduce. Human babies develop within their mother for nine months before they are born. They grow into children, adolescents, and eventually, adults. In most mammals, the life cycle moves from the fertilized egg, to the fetus, to the juvenile, and then to the adult.

The following are some additional examples of animal life cycles:

- Birds go from the egg, to the chick, to the adult.

- Amphibians go from the egg, to the larva, to the adult.

- Insects go from the egg, to the larva, to the pupa, to the adult.

DOMAIN IV
MATHEMATICS

PERSONALIZED STUDY PLAN

PAGE	COMPETENCY AND SKILL	KNOWN MATERIAL/ SKIP IT
265	**16: Knowledge of student thinking and instructional practices**	☐
	16.1: Analyze and apply appropriate mathematical concepts, procedures, and professional vocabulary to evaluate student solutions	☐
	16.2: Analyze and discriminate among various problem structures with unknowns in all positions in order to develop student understanding of operations	☐
	16.3: Analyze and evaluate the validity of a student's mathematical model or argument used for problem solving	☐
	16.4: Interpret individual student mathematics assessment data to guide instructional decisions and differentiate instruction	☐
	16.5: Select and analyze structured experiences for small and large groups of students according to the cognitive complexity of the task	☐
	16.6: Analyze learning progressions to show how students' mathematical knowledge, skills, and understanding develop over time	☐
	16.7: Distinguish among the components of math fluency	☐
271	**17: Knowledge of operations, algebraic thinking, counting and number in base ten**	☐
	17.1: Interpret and extend multiple representations of patterns and functional relationships by using tables, graphs, equations, expressions, and verbal descriptions	☐
	17.2: Select the representation of an algebraic expression, equation, or inequality that models a real-world situation	☐
	17.3: Analyze and apply the properties of equality and operations in the context of interpreting solutions	☐
	17.4: Determine whether two algebraic expressions are equivalent by applying properties of operations or equality	☐
	17.5: Evaluate expressions with parentheses, brackets, and braces	☐
	17.6: Analyze and apply strategies to solve multistep word problems	☐
	17.7: Apply number theory concepts	☐
	17.8: Identify strategies based on place value to perform multidigit arithmetic	☐

PERSONALIZED STUDY PLAN

KNOWN MATERIAL/ SKIP IT

PAGE	COMPETENCY AND SKILL	
292	**18: Knowledge of fractions, ratios, and integers**	☐
	18.1: Compare fractions, integers, and integers with integer exponents and place them on a number line	☐
	18.2: Convert among standard measurement units within and between measurement systems in the context of multistep, real-world problems	☐
	18.3: Solve problems involving addition, subtraction, multiplication, and division of fractions, including mixing whole numbers and fractions, decimals and percents by using visual models and equations to represent the problems and their solutions	☐
	18.4: Select the representation that best represents the problem and solution, given a word problem or equation involving fractions	☐
	18.5: Solve real-world problems involving ratios and proportions	☐
303	**19: Knowledge of measurement, data, and statistics**	☐
	19.1: Calculate and interpret statistics of variability and central tendency	☐
	19.2: Analyze and interpret data through the use of frequency tables and graphs	☐
	19.3: Select appropriate measurement units to solve problems involving estimates and measurements	☐
	19.4: Evaluate the choice of measures of center and variability, with respect to the shape of the data distribution and the context in which the data were gathered	☐
	19.5: Solve problems involving distance, time, liquid volume, mass, and money, which may include units expressed as fractions or decimals	☐
310	**20: Knowledge of geometric concepts**	☐
	20.1: Apply geometric properties and relationships to solve problems involving perimeter, area, surface area, and volume	☐
	20.2: Identify and locate ordered pairs in all four quadrants of a rectangular coordinate system	☐
	20.3: Identify and analyze properties of three-dimensional shapes using formal mathematical terms such as volume, faces, edges, and vertices	☐
	20.4: Classify two-dimensional figures in a hierarchy based on mathematical properties	☐

COMPETENCY 16
KNOWLEDGE OF STUDENT THINKING AND INSTRUCTIONAL PRACTICES

> **SKILL** **Analyze and apply appropriate mathematical concepts, procedures,**
> **16.1** **and professional vocabulary** *(e.g., subitize, transitivity, iteration, tiling)* **to**
> **evaluate student solutions.**

To understand mathematics and solve problems, one must know the definitions of basic mathematic terms and concepts. For a list of definitions and explanations of basic math terms, visit the following website: *http://home.blarg.net/~math/deflist.html*

Additionally, one must use the language of mathematics correctly and precisely to communicate concepts and ideas.

For example, the statement "minus 10 times minus 5 equals plus 50" is incorrect because "minus" and "plus" are arithmetic operations, not numerical modifiers. The statement should read "negative 10 times negative 5 equals positive 50."

A good teacher presents all information with appropriate vocabulary and provides consistent feedback to students when evaluating their work. Students need to use proper mathematical terms and expressions. For example, when reading decimals, students need to read 0.4 as "four tenths" to promote understanding of the concepts. They should do their work in a neat and organized manner. Students need to be encouraged to verbalize their strategies, both in computation and word problems. Additionally, writing original word problems fosters understanding of math language. Another idea is requiring students to develop their own glossary of mathematical terms. Knowing the answers and being able to communicate them are equally important.

> **SKILL** **Analyze and discriminate among various problem structures with**
> **16.2** **unknowns in all positions in order to develop student understanding**
> **of operations** *(e.g., put-together/take-apart, arrays/area).*

When presenting students with mathematical topics, it is essential to study them from multiple perspectives. For instance, when learning addition and subtraction, fact families ($2 + 4 = 6$, $4 + 2 = 6$, $6 - 2 = 4$, $6 - 4 = 2$) help students relate the two operations and better retain the concepts and the individual math facts. Problem solving techniques can also showcase varied approaches and problem structure. "If Amy spent $20 on 5 boxes of cookies, how much did each box cost?" One student may think division ($20 \div 5 = ?$), while another may use multiplication for their analysis ($5 \times ? = 20$).

Examples and practice problems should be varied as much as possible to incorporate a wide range of numbers, patterns, and nuances within a concept. This will ensure a student's deeper understanding of the material.

> **SKILL 16.3** **Analyze and evaluate the validity of a student's mathematical model or argument** *(e.g., inventive strategies, standard algorithms)* **used for problem solving.**

One of the best-known directives from any good math teacher certainly must be "Show your work." It is usually followed by groans from the student audience. "Why did you take points off if I got the right answer?" is a complaint heard often from disgruntled students. The mathematics teacher must ensure not only that the answer is correct but that the thinking behind the answer is sound and logical as well. Most mathematical skills are taught with fairly structured, standard algorithms that guide the solution process. Student work, then, should mirror these processes. While some variation is possible, the teacher should ensure that the main, most important steps of a certain process are present.

The presentation of mathematical arguments or problem solving steps can also differ in structure. Some explanations can be a series of numbers and calculations, while others can be arguments supported with words and diagrams. Students with different preferences of learning styles may choose one type of solution model over another. While lessons presented by the teacher provide students with a platform of solution models to work from, having students share problem solving techniques with each other exposes them to even more possible mathematical arguments. Additionally students can help each other find weaknesses or errors in their solutions. Ultimately, however, the teacher must be prepared to evaluate a technique for sound, mathematical steps and conclusions. And when an argument is found to have flaws, sharing error analysis with students will further develop their problem solving skills.

SKILL Interpret individual student mathematics assessment data *(e.g.,*
16.4 *diagnostic, formative, progress monitoring)* **to guide instructional decisions and differentiate instruction.**

A good teacher knows that assessment is the tool that guides the learning to come, based on the success of the learning thus far. A student who is forced to "move on" before objectives have been mastered will fail to fully understand future concepts. However, it is impossible to tailor the classroom to perfectly meet the needs of every individual student as children vary in their abilities to process and master new material. Assessment should monitor the successes and failures of students on an individual level, and suggest trends for the learning readiness of the class as a whole.

Initially, a level of readiness for learning can be determined through **diagnostic assessment**: what concepts do children currently understand and what still needs to be learned? Teachers may choose to use a pre-test to assess understanding of prerequisite concepts, or to have students interview each other regarding a list of objectives, to find out what they do or do not know. With these diagnostic results, the teacher will know how to best build an instructional plan.

The lesson-to-lesson progress of students should be monitored with **formative assessments**. These are opportunities for students to informally use their developing skills and check for correctness. Homework, guided in-class practice, and quizzes are some examples of formative assessment. A teacher can analyze the results of these assessments to determine which skills seem to be generally understood in the class and which may need more instruction. Ideally, adjustments in future lessons can be made to address the general learning needs of the class so that by the time the more formal, or **summative assessment**, is given, students will be prepared to successfully demonstrate their learning objectives.

When looking at student growth over multiple learning units, **progress monitoring** should be implemented. On a small scale such as a classroom, a cumulative post-test can be administered to determine how successfully students have retained the bulk of the material to be learned within a quarter or semester. Progress monitoring also takes the form of standardized testing, usually used by schools or districts as a whole, where individual student achievement can be measured within the school year, as well as from one grade to the next. A teacher can use these results to find and address strengths and weaknesses in certain student's performance. Some of these individual needs can be met in the classroom, with extra attention or monitoring, while some may require outside remediation or enrichment.

SKILL 16.5 Select and analyze structured experiences for small and large groups of students according to the cognitive complexity of the task.

Successful teachers select and implement instructional delivery methods that best fit the needs of a particular classroom format. Individual, small-group, and large-group instructional formats require different techniques and methods. **Direct teaching methods**, including lecture and demonstration, are particularly effective in teaching basic mathematical concepts. To stimulate interest, accommodate different learning styles, and enhance understanding, teachers should incorporate manipulatives and technology into their lectures and demonstrations. **Indirect teaching methods**, including cooperative learning, discussion, and projects, promote the development of problem-solving skills. Cooperative learning and discussion allow students to share ideas and strategies with their peers. Projects require students to apply knowledge and develop and implement problem-solving strategies.

Individual instruction allows the teacher to interact closely with the students. Teachers may use a variety of methods in an individual setting that are not practical when working with a large number of students. For example, teachers can use manipulatives to illustrate a mathematical concept.

Teachers can observe and evaluate the student's reasoning and problem-solving skills through verbal questioning and by checking the student's written work. Individual instruction allows the teacher to work problems out with the student, thus familiarizing the student with the problem-solving process.

Small-group formats require the teacher to provide instruction to multiple students at the same time. Because the group is small, instructional methods that encourage student interaction and cooperative learning are particularly effective. For example, group projects, discussion, and question-and-answer sessions promote cooperative learning and maintain student interest. In addition, working problems as a group or in pairs can help students learn problem-solving strategies from one another.

Large-group formats require instructional methods that can effectively deliver information to a large number of students. Lecture is a common instructional method for large groups. In addition, demonstrating methods of problem solving and allowing students to ask questions about homework and test problems are effective strategies for teaching large groups.

SKILL 16.6 Analyze learning progressions to show how students' mathematical knowledge, skills, and understanding develop over time.

Teachers must be aware of the development of a students' knowledge over time. In order to help students become successful and independent, when introducing a new mathematical concept to students, teachers should utilize the concrete-to-representational-to-abstract sequence of instruction. The first step of the instructional progression is the introduction of a concept modeled with concrete materials. The second step is the translation of concrete models into representational diagrams or pictures. The third and final step is the translation of representational models into abstract models using only numbers and symbols.

Teachers should first use concrete models to introduce a mathematical concept because they are easiest to understand. For example, teachers can allow students to use counting blocks to learn basic arithmetic. Teachers should give students ample time and many opportunities to experiment, practice, and demonstrate mastery with the concrete materials.

In addition to building new skills from concrete to abstract levels, teachers should show students how new math concepts relate to previous knowledge. For instance, students may first learn the concept of area with basic rectangles, including use of the formula "base times height." Then, as the study of area progresses to other shapes, formulas can be connected back to the understanding of rectangles. By dividing a rectangle in half with a diagonal, students can make a connection between the area of a rectangle and the formula for the area of a triangle "*one half times base times height.*"

SKILL 16.7 Distinguish among the components of math fluency *(i.e., accuracy, automaticity, rate, flexibility).*

MATH FLUENCY is the ability to accurately, or correctly, and quickly recall basic facts including: addition, subtraction, multiplication, and division. Math fluency is often calculated by determining a student's digits correct per minute for a specific set of facts. Students who possess fluency can recall facts with automaticity, which means they typically think no longer than two seconds before responding with the correct answer. Automaticity is evident when a student solves a problem faster through recall than performing a mental algorithm. Students with math fact fluency have received instruction in the basic math facts and understand the concepts of addition, subtraction, multiplication and division. They possess strategies to determine the answers to math problems and willingly use them when necessary. Additionally, students' confidence and fluency with math skills increase

> **MATH FLUENCY:** the ability to accurately and quickly recall basic facts including: addition, subtraction, multiplication, and division

their level of mathematical flexibility. That is, they can successfully apply skills, as needed, to new problems.

Students with high levels of math fluency have worked with basic facts enough that specific answers have become committed to memory. Instant responses to problems demonstrate automaticity. The response time, or fluency rate, to processing these facts does vary with age. That is, a first grader may be expected to answer 20 addition facts in a minute, while a fourth grader may be able to complete 40 questions in the same amount of time. Students who recall their basic facts accurately and quickly have greater cognitive resources available to learn more complex concepts. For example, if Megan knows her division facts with proficiency, then she has more cognitive resources available to learn and acquire new skills to complete advanced mathematical problems. Students who are fluent with their facts are more likely to complete math problems more quickly and will have more opportunities to respond because it takes less cognitive effort to complete the math tasks.

COMPETENCY 17
KNOWLEDGE OF OPERATIONS, ALGEBRAIC THINKING, COUNTING AND NUMBER IN BASE TEN

SKILL Interpret and extend multiple representations of patterns and
17.1 functional relationships by using tables, graphs, equations,
expressions, and verbal descriptions.

Mathematical concepts can be represented in various ways. Students should gain an understanding of the possibilities.

Examples

Examples, illustrations, and symbolic representations are useful tools in explaining and understanding mathematical concepts. The ability to create examples and alternative methods of expression allows students to solve real-world problems and better communicate their thoughts.

CONCRETE EXAMPLES are real-world applications of mathematical concepts. For example, measuring the shadow produced by a tree or building is a real-world application of trigonometric functions, determining the acceleration or velocity of a car is an application of derivatives, and finding the volume or area of a swimming pool is a real-world application of geometric principles.

> **CONCRETE EXAMPLES:** real world applications of mathematical concepts

Pictorial illustrations of mathematic concepts help clarify difficult ideas and simplify problem solving.

Example: Rectangle R represents the 300 students in School A. Circle represents the 150 students that participated in band. Circle Q represents the 170 students that participated in a sport. 70 students participated in both band and a sport.

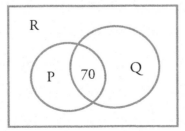

Pictorial representation of above situation.

Example: A ball rolls up an incline and rolls back to its original position. Create a graph of the velocity of the ball.

Velocity starts out at its maximum as the ball begins to roll, decreases to zero at the top of the incline, and returns to the maximum in the opposite direction at the bottom of the incline.

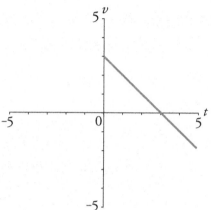

Symbolic representation is the basic language of mathematics. Converting data to symbols allows for easy manipulation and problem solving. Students should have the ability to recognize what the symbolic notation represents and to convert information into symbolic form. For example, from the graph of a line, students should have the ability to determine the slope and intercepts and derive the line's equation from the observed data. Another possible application of symbolic representation is the formulation of algebraic expressions and relations from data presented in word problem form.

Example: Give each group of students 12 tiles and instruct them to build rectangles. Students draw their rectangles on paper.

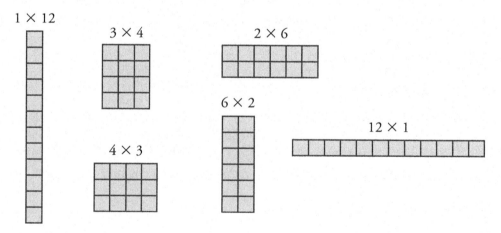

Encourage students to describe their reactions. Extend to 16 tiles. Ask students to form additional problems.

The shaded region represents 47 out of 100 or 0.47 or $\frac{47}{100}$ or 47%.

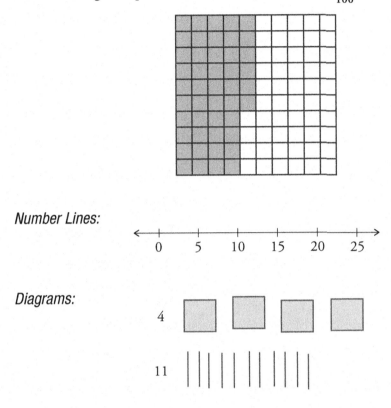

Number Lines:

Diagrams:

To make a **bar graph** or a **pictograph**, determine the scale to be used for the graph. Then determine the length of each bar on the graph or determine the number of pictures needed to represent each item of information. Be sure to include an explanation of the scale in the legend.

Example: A class had the following grades: 4 A's, 9 B's, 8 C's, 1 D, 3 F's. Graph these on a bar graph and a pictograph.

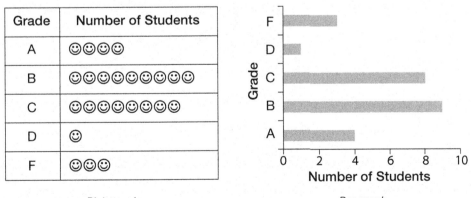

Grade	Number of Students
A	☺☺☺☺
B	☺☺☺☺☺☺☺☺☺
C	☺☺☺☺☺☺☺☺
D	☺
F	☺☺☺

Pictograph

Bar graph

To make a **circle graph**, total all the information that is to be included on the graph. Next, determine the central angle to be used for each sector of the graph using the following formula:

$$\frac{\text{information}}{\text{total information}} \times 360° = \text{degrees in central} \bigcirc$$

Lay out the central angles to these sizes, label each section and include its percent.

Example: Graph this information on a circle graph:

Monthly expenses
Rent, $400
Food, $150
Utilities, $75
Clothes, $75
Church, $100
Misc., $200

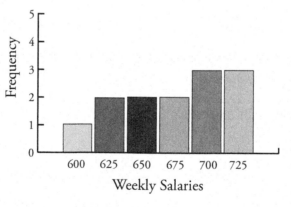

Histograms are used to summarize information from large sets of data that can be naturally grouped into intervals. The vertical axis indicates **frequency** (the number of times any particular data value occurs), and the horizontal axis indicates data values or ranges of data values. The number of data values in any interval is the **frequency of the interval**.

SKILL 17.2 **Select the representation of an algebraic expression, equation, or inequality that models a real-world situation.**

Many algebraic procedures are similar to and rely on number operations and algorithms. Two examples of this similarity are the addition of rational expressions and division of polynomials.

Addition of rational expressions is similar to fraction addition. The basic algorithm of addition for both fractions and rational expressions is the common denominator method. Consider an example of the addition of numerical fractions:

$$\frac{3}{5} + \frac{2}{3} = \frac{3(3)}{3(5)} + \frac{5(2)}{5(3)} = \frac{9}{15} + \frac{10}{15} = \frac{19}{15}$$

To complete the sum, we first find the least common denominator.

Now, consider an example of rational expression addition:

$$\frac{(x+5)}{(x+1)} + \frac{2x}{(x+3)} = \frac{(x+3)(x+5)}{(x+3)(x+1)} + \frac{(x+1)2x}{(x+1)(x+3)}$$

$$\frac{x^2 + 8x + 15}{(x+3)(x+1)} + \frac{2x^2 + 2x}{(x+3)(x+1)} = \frac{3x^2 + 10x + 15}{(x+3)(x+1)}$$

Note the similarity to fraction addition. The basic algorithm, finding a common denominator and adding numerators, is the same.

Division of polynomials follows the same algorithm as numerical long division. Consider an example of numerical long division:

$$\begin{array}{r} 720 \\ 6\overline{)4321} \\ \underline{42} \\ 12 \\ \underline{12} \\ 01 \end{array} \quad \rightarrow 720\frac{1}{6} = \text{final quotient}$$

Compare the process of numerical long division to polynomial division:

$$\begin{array}{r} x - 9 \\ x+1\overline{)x^2 - 8x - 9} \\ \underline{-x^2 - x} \\ -9x - 9 \\ \underline{+19x + 9} \\ 0 + 0 \end{array} \quad \rightarrow x - 9 = \text{final quotient}$$

Note that the step-by-step process is identical in both cases.

Concrete and visual representations can help demonstrate the logic behind operational algorithms. Blocks or other objects modeled on the base-ten system are useful concrete tools. Base-ten blocks represent ones, tens, and hundreds. For example, modeling the partial sums algorithm with base-ten blocks helps clarify the thought process. Consider the sum of 242 and 193. We represent 242 with 2 one-hundred blocks, 4 ten blocks and 2 one blocks. We represent 193 with 1 one-hundred block, 9 ten blocks and 3 one blocks. In the partial sums algorithm, we manipulate each place value separately and total the results. Thus, we group the hundred blocks, ten blocks, and one blocks and derive a total for each place value. We combine the place values to complete the sum.

An example of a visual representation of an operational algorithm is the modeling of a two-term multiplication as the area of a rectangle. For example, consider the product of 24 and 39. We can represent the product in geometric form. Note that the four sections of the rectangle equate to the four products of the partial products method.

	30	9
20	A = 600	A = 180
4	A = 120	A = 36

Thus, the final product is the sum of the areas, or $600 + 180 + 120 + 36 = 936$.

Furthermore, many real world patterns and procedures can convert directly to math expressions and equations.

If the sales tax rate is 7.5%, the final charge can be represented by the expression $1.075T$, where T represents the total amount of goods being purchased.

If a car rental fee, for instance, is based on an initial charge of $20 with the addition of 22 cents per mile, the relationship translates to the expression $20 + 0.22m$, where m is the number of miles driven.

Additionally, if the driver wishes to know how many miles will keep his rental cost under $100, he can solve the equation $100 = 20 + 0.22m$ to determine the maximum number of miles to drive.

> SKILL 17.3 **Analyze and apply the properties of equality and operations in the context of interpreting solutions.**

MATHEMATICAL OPERATIONS: include addition, subtraction, multiplication, and division

MATHEMATICAL OPERATIONS include addition, subtraction, multiplication, and division. **Addition** can be indicated by these expressions: sum, greater than, and, more than, increased by, added to. **Subtraction** can be expressed by difference, fewer than, minus, less than, and decreased by. **Multiplication** is shown by product, times, multiplied by, and twice. **Division** is used for quotient, divided by, and ratio.

Examples:

7 added to a number	$n + 7$
a number decreased by 8	$n - 8$
12 times a number divided by 7	$12n \div 7$
28 less than a number	$n - 28$
the ratio of a number to 55	$\frac{n}{55}$
4 times the sum of a number and 21	$4(n + 21)$

Recognition and understanding of the relationships between concepts and topics is of great value in mathematical problem solving and the explanation of more complex processes.

For instance, multiplication is simply repeated addition. This relationship explains the concept of variable addition. We can show that the expression $4x + 3x = 7x$ is true by rewriting 4 times x and 3 times x as repeated addition, yielding the expression $(x + x + x + x) + (x + x + x)$. Thus, because of the relationship between multiplication and addition, variable addition is accomplished by coefficient addition.

Additionally, the following relationships are stated by the properties of equality:

Reflexive	$x = x$	Every number or variable is equal to itself.
Symmetric	if $x = y$ then $y = x$	Equivalency statements are reversible.
Transitive	if $x = y$ and $y = z$ then $x = z$	Values equal to the same value are equal to each other.
Commutative	You can change the order of the terms or factors as follows. **For addition:** $\quad a + b = b + a$ **For multiplication:** $\quad ab = ba$ Since subtraction is the inverse operation of addition and division is the inverse operation of multiplication, no separate laws are needed for subtraction and division. *Example: $5 + -8 = -8 + 5 = -3$* *Example: $-2 \times 6 = 6 \times (-2) = -12$*	

Continued on next page

Associative	You can regroup the terms as you like.
	For addition: $\quad\quad\quad\quad a + (b + c) = (a + b) + c$
	For multiplication: $\quad\quad a(bc) = (ab)c$
	This rule does not apply for division and subtraction.
	Example: $(-2 + 7) + 5 = -2 + (7 + 5)$ $\quad\quad\quad 5 + 5 = -2 + 12 = 10$
	Example: $(3 \times (-7)) \times 5 = 3 \times (-7 \times 5)$ $\quad\quad\quad -21 \times 5 = 3 \times -35 = -105$
Identity	An identity is a number that when added to a term gives the original term (additive identity) or that when multiplied by a term gives the original term (multiplicative identity).
	For addition: $\quad\quad\quad a + 0 = a \quad$ (0 is additive identity)
	For multiplication: $\quad a \times 1 = a \quad$ (1 is multiplicative identity)
	Example: $17 + 0 = 17$
	Example: $-34 \times 1 = -34$
	The product of any number and 1 is that number.
Inverse	An inverse is a number that when added to another number results in 0, or that when multiplied by another number results in 1.
	For addition: $\quad\quad\quad\quad a + (-a) = 0$
	For multiplication: $\quad\quad a \times \left(\frac{1}{a}\right) = 1$
	$(-a)$ is the additive inverse of a; $\left(\frac{1}{a}\right)$, also called the reciprocal, is the multiplicative inverse of a.
	Example: $25 + -25 = 0$
	Example: $5 \times \frac{1}{5} = 1$
	The product of any number and its reciprocal is 1.
Distributive	The distributive property allows us to operate on terms inside parentheses without first performing operations within the parentheses. This is especially helpful when terms within the parentheses cannot be combined.
	$a(b + c) = ab + ac$
	Example: $6 \times (-4 + 9) = (6 \times (-4)) + (6 \times 9)$ $\quad\quad\quad 6 \times 5 = -24 + 54 = 30$
	To multiply a sum by a number, multiply each addend by the number, then add the products.

Students can experience these properties even when working with basic arithmetic.

Suppose, for instance, that $3 + 2 + 9 + 8 + 7$ is to be calculated. By understanding the use of the associative property, students can regroup the numbers to focus on the sums to 10: $(3 + 7) + (2 + 8) + 9 = 29$.

> **SKILL Determine whether two algebraic expressions are equivalent by**
> **17.4 applying properties of operations or equality.**

Students should be able to identify when two expressions are equivalent (i.e., when the two expressions name the same number regardless of which value is substituted into them).

$$3 + 5 = 4 + 4$$
$$19 - 12 = 37 - 30$$

This holds true with expressions involving variables as well. For example, the expressions $y + y + y$ and $3y$ are equivalent because they name the same number regardless of which number y stands for.

Next, recall the properties of equality that were presented in section 17.3. Understanding and use of these properties become a bit more challenging for students as they are applied to more abstract concepts, such as those found in Algebra.

For instance, suppose two students are solving an equation with variables on both sides. As shown below, they post different looking strategies and results, but should know that they each represent the same solution thanks to the Reflexive Property.

$$2x + 7 = 3x + 4 \qquad 2x + 7 = 3x + 4$$
$$7 = x + 4 \qquad\qquad 2x = 3x + \text{-}3$$
$$3 = x \qquad\qquad\qquad \text{-}x = \text{-}3$$
$$x = 3$$

Additionally, many algebraic procedures require expressions to be rewritten into less complex versions. While the new version is simplified, it is still equivalent to the original expression thanks to properties of operations and equalities.

Example: *Simplify* $5 + 4x + 9 + 2(x - 6)$

    $5 + 4x + 9 + 2x - 12$ is equivalent by the Distributive Property

    $5 + 9 - 12 + 4x + 2x$ is equivalent by the Commutative Property

    $2 + 6x$ is equivalent by the addition operation

The final expression is an equivalent, simpler version of the original.

MATHEMATICS

SKILL Evaluate expressions with parentheses, brackets, and braces.
17.5

See Skill 17.8

SKILL Analyze and apply strategies *(e.g., models, estimation, reasonableness)* to
17.6 solve multistep word problems.

Estimation and approximation can be used to check the reasonableness of answers.

Example: Estimate the answer.

$$\frac{58 \times 810}{1989}$$

58 becomes 60, 810 becomes 800, and 1989 becomes 2000.

$$\frac{60 \times 800}{2000} = 24$$

For word problems, an estimate may sometimes be all that is needed to find the solution.

Example: Janet goes into a store to purchase a CD that is on sale for $13.95. While shopping, she sees two pairs of shoes priced at $19.95 and $14.50. She only has $50. Can she purchase everything?

Solve by rounding:

$19.95 → $20.00
$14.50 → $15.00
$13.95 → $14.00
          $49.00

Yes, she can purchase the CD and the shoes.

SKILL Apply number theory concepts *(e.g., primes, composites, multiples, factors,*
17.7 *parity, rules of divisibility).*

PRIME NUMBERS:
numbers that can only be
factored into 1 and the
number itself

PRIME NUMBERS are numbers that can only be factored into 1 and the number itself. When factoring into prime factors, all the factors must be numbers that cannot be factored again (without using 1). Initially, numbers can be factored into any two factors. Check each resulting factor to see if it can be factored again. Continue factoring until all remaining factors are prime numbers. This produces

FTCE ELEMENTARY EDUCATION K–6

the list of prime factors. Regardless of how the original number was factored, the final list of prime factors will always be the same.

COMPOSITE NUMBERS are whole numbers that have more than two different factors. For example, 9 is a composite number because, besides the factors of 1 and 9, 3 is also a factor. 70 is composite because, besides the factors of 1 and 70, the numbers 2, 5, 7, 10, 14, and 35 are also all factors. The number 1 is neither prime nor composite.

> **COMPOSITE NUMBERS:** whole numbers that have more than two different factors

Example:
Factor 30 into prime factors.
Factor 30 into any two factors.

5×6	Now factor the 6.
$5 \times 2 \times 3$	These are all prime factors.

or

Factor 30 into any two factors.

3×10	Now factor the 10.
$3 \times 2 \times 5$	These are the same prime factors, even though the original factors were different.

Example:
Factor 240 into prime factors.
Factor 240 into any two factors.

24×10	Now factor both 24 and 10.
$4 \times 6 \times 2 \times 5$	Now factor both 4 and 6.
$2 \times 2 \times 2 \times 3 \times 2 \times 5$	These are the prime factors.

This can also be written as $2^4 \times 3 \times 5$.

GCF is the abbreviation for **GREATEST COMMON FACTOR**. The GCF is the largest number that is a factor of all the numbers given in a problem. The GCF can be no larger than the smallest number given in the problem. If no other number is a common factor, then the GCF will be the number 1.

> **GREATEST COMMON FACTOR:** the largest number that is a factor of all the numbers in a problem

To find the GCF, list all possible factors of the smallest number (include the number itself). Starting with the largest factor (which is the number itself), determine if that factor is also a factor of all the other given numbers. If so, that factor is the GCF. If that factor doesn't divide evenly into the other given numbers, try the same method on the next smaller factor. Continue until a common factor is found. That factor is the GCF.

Note: There can be other common factors besides the GCF.

Example: Find the GCF of 12, 20, and 36.

The smallest number in the problem is 12. The factors of 12 are 1, 2, 3, 4, 6, and 12. 12 is the largest of these factors, but it does not divide evenly into 20. Neither does 6. However, 4 will divide into both 20 and 36 evenly.

Therefore, 4 is the GCF.

Example: Find the GCF of 14 and 15.

The factors of 14 are 1, 2, 7 and 14. 14 is the largest factor, but it does not divide evenly into 15. Neither does 7 or 2. Therefore, the only factor common to both 14 and 15 is the number 1, the GCF.

Least Common Multiple

LEAST COMMON MULTIPLE: the smallest number of a group of numbers that all the given numbers will divide into evenly

LCM is the abbreviation for **LEAST COMMON MULTIPLE**. The least common multiple of a group of numbers is the smallest number that all of the given numbers will divide into. The LCM will always be the largest of the given numbers or a multiple of the largest number.

Example: Find the LCM of 20, 30, and 40.

The largest number given is 40, but 30 will not divide evenly into 40. The next multiple of 40 is 80 (2 × 40), but 30 will not divide evenly into 80 either. The next multiple of 40 is 120 (3 × 40). 120 is divisible by both 20 and 30, so 120 is the LCM.

Example: Find the LCM of 96, 16, and 24.

The largest number is 96. 96 is divisible by both 16 and 24, so 96 is the LCM.

Rules of Divisibility

1. A number is divisible by 2 if it is an even number (which means it ends in 0, 2, 4, 6 or 8).

   1,354 ends in 4 so it is divisible by 2. The number 240,685 ends in 5 so it is not divisible by 2.

2. A number is divisible by 3 if the sum of its digits is evenly divisible by 3.

   The sum of the digits of 964 is 9 + 6 + 4 = 19. Since 19 is not divisible by 3, neither is 964. The sum of the digits of 86,514 is 8 + 6 + 5 + 1 + 4 = 24. Since 24 is divisible by 3, then 86,514 is also divisible by 3.

3. A number is divisible by 4 if the number formed by its last two digits is evenly divisible by 4.

The number 113,336 ends with the number 36 in the last two places. Since 36 is divisible by 4, then 113,336 is also divisible by 4. The number 135,627 ends with the number 27 in the last two places. Since 27 is not evenly divisible by 4, then 135,627 is not divisible by 4 either.

4. A number is divisible by 5 if the number ends in either a 5 or a 0.

   The number 225 ends with a 5 so it is divisible by 5. The number 470 is also divisible by 5 because its last digit is 0. The number 2,358 is not divisible by 5 because its last digit is 8, not 5 or 0.

5. A number is divisible by 6 if the number is even and the sum of its digits is evenly divisible by 3.

   The number 4,950 is an even number and its digits add up to 18 ($4 + 9 + 5 + 0 = 18$). Since the number is even, and the sum of its digits is 18 (which is divisible by 3), then 4,950 is divisible by 6. The number 326 is even, but its digits add up to 11. Since 11 is not divisible by 3, then 326 is not divisible by 6. The number 698,135 is not an even number so it cannot possibly be divided evenly by 6.

6. A number is divisible by 8 if the number in its last 3 digits is evenly divisible by 8.

   The number 113,336 ends with the three-digit number 336 in the last three places. Since 336 is divisible by 8, then 113,336 is also divisible by 8. The number 465,627 ends with the number 627 in the last three places. Since 627 is not evenly divisible by 8, then 465,627 is not divisible by 8 either.

7. A number is divisible by 9 if the sum of its digits is evenly divisible by 9.

   The sum of the digits of 874 is $8 + 7 + 4 = 19$. Since 19 is not divisible by 9, neither is 874. The digits of 116,514 are $1 + 1 + 6 + 5 + 1 + 4 = 18$. Since 18 is divisible by 9, the number 116,514 is also divisible by 9.

8. A number is divisible by 10 if the number ends in the digit 0.

   The number 305 ends with 5 so it is not divisible by 10. The number 2,030,270 is divisible by 10 because its last digit is 0. The number 42,978 is not divisible by 10 because its last digit is 8, not 0.

9. Why these rules work:

   By definition, all even numbers are divisible by 2. A two-digit number (with T representing the tens digit and U representing the ones digit) has as its sum of the digits, $T + U$. Suppose this sum of $T + U$ is divisible by 3. Then it equals 3 times some constant, K. So, $T + U = 3K$. Solving for U, $U = 3K - T$. The original two-digit number would be represented by $10T + U$.

Substituting $3K - T$ in place of U, this two-digit number becomes $10T + U = 10T + (3K - T) = 9T + 3K$. This two-digit number is clearly divisible by 3, since each term is divisible by 3. Therefore, if the sum of the digits of a number is divisible by 3, then the number itself is also divisible by 3. Since 4 divides evenly into 100, 200, or 300, it will divide evenly into any number of hundreds. The only part of a number that determines whether 4 will divide into it evenly is the number in the last two places. Numbers divisible by 5 end in 5 or 0. This is clear if you look at the answers to the multiplication table for 5.

Answers to the multiplication table for 6 are all even numbers. Since 6 factors into 2 times 3, the divisibility rules for 2 and 3 must both work. Any number of thousands is divisible by 8. Only the last three places of the number determine whether it is divisible by 8. A two-digit number (with T representing the tens digit and U representing the ones digit) has as its sum of the digits, $T + U$. Suppose this sum of $T + U$ is divisible by 9. Then it equals 9 times some constant, K. So, $T + U = 9K$.

Solving this for U, $U = 9K - T$. The original two-digit number would be represented by $10T + U$. Substituting $9K - T$ in place of U, this two-digit number becomes $10T + U = 10T + (9K - T) = 9T + 9K$. This two-digit number is clearly divisible by 9 since each term is divisible by 9. Therefore, if the sum of the digits of a number is divisible by 9, then the number itself is also divisible by 9. Numbers divisible by 10 must be multiples of 10, which all end in zero.

A pattern of numbers arranged in a particular order is called a **number sequence**. Pre-K children should be able to recognize and extend simple repeating patterns using objects and pictures. By patterns, we mean a sequence of symbols, sounds, movements, or objects that follow a simple rule, such as ABBABBABB. Students should be presented with a simple pattern that they then try to understand. Once they have an understanding of the pattern, they should copy and extend it. Students at this age are capable of assigning letters to their patterns to verbalize how the pattern repeats. These are the very early fundamental stages of algebra.

Many of the traditional ways of talking about this in algebra would certainly not be appropriate. However, many types of patterns and relationships can be addressed. In arithmetic, do the traditional counting with students by 2s, 5s and 10s first. Then have them start at a different number. For example, tell them to count by 5s beginning with 3. As they get better with their addition skills, use larger numbers for the starting number You might also explain how the even and odd counting numbers follow a sequence. Then give them the first few numbers of a sequence and ask them to tell you the pattern. Finally, let them make up some sequences themselves and give them to the other students to guess what the pattern is. The possibilities are endless here. Students in the upper elementary grades should be taught how looking for a pattern or sequence is an important problem-solving tool.

> **SKILL Identify strategies** *(e.g., compensation, combining tens and ones)* **based on**
> **17.8 place value to perform multidigit arithmetic.**

By being knowledgeable with place value concepts, students should be able to perform multidigit arithmetic using various strategies.

Example: A learner should recognize that in a multi-digit whole number, a digit in one place represents ten times what it represents in the place to its right.

Therefore, by applying concepts of place value and division, $700 \div 70 = 10$.

Addition of Whole Numbers

Example: At the end of a day of shopping, a shopper had $24 remaining in his wallet. He spent $45 on various goods. How much money did the shopper have at the beginning of the day?

The total amount of money the shopper started with is the sum of the amount spent and the amount remaining at the end of the day.

$$\begin{array}{r} \$\ 24 \\ +\ 45 \\ \hline \$\ 69 \end{array}$$
The original total was $69.

Example: A race took the winner 1 hr. 58 min. 12 sec. on the first half of the race and 2 hr. 9 min. 57 sec. on the second half. How much time did the entire race take?

1 hr 58 min 12 sec	
+ 2 hr 9 min 57 sec	Add these numbers.
3 hr 67 min 69 sec	
+ 1 min − 60 sec	Change 60 sec to 1 min.
3 hr 68 min 9 sec	
+ 1 hr − 60 min	Change 60 min to 1 hr.
4 hr 8 min 9 sec	Final answer.

Subtraction of Whole Numbers

Example: At the end of his shift, a cashier has $96 in the cash register. At the beginning of his shift, he had $15. How much money did the cashier collect during his shift?

The total collected is the difference between the ending amount and the starting amount.

$$\begin{array}{r} \$\,96 \\ -15 \\ \hline \$\,81 \end{array}$$ The total collected was $81.

Multiplication of Whole Numbers

Multiplication is one of the four basic number operations. In simple terms, multiplication is the addition of a number to itself a certain number of times. For example, 4 multiplied by 3 is equal to $4 + 4 + 4$ or $3 + 3 + 3 + 3$. Another way of conceptualizing multiplication is to think in terms of groups. For example, if we have 4 groups of 3 students, the total number of students is 4 multiplied by 3. We call the solution to a multiplication problem the **PRODUCT**.

The basic algorithm for whole number multiplication begins with aligning the numbers by place value, with the number containing more places on top.

$$\begin{array}{r} 172 \\ \times\,43 \\ \hline \end{array}$$ Note that we placed 172 on top because it has more places than 43 does.

Next, we multiply the ones place of the bottom number by each place value of the top number sequentially.

$$\begin{array}{r} (2) \\ 172 \\ \times\,43 \\ \hline 516 \end{array}$$ {$3 \times 2 = 6$, $3 \times 7 = 21$, $3 \times 1 = 3$}
Note that we had to carry a 2 to the hundreds column because $3 \times 7 = 21$. Note also that we add carried numbers to the product.

Next, we multiply the number in the tens place of the bottom number by each place value of the top number sequentially. Because we are multiplying by a number in the tens place, we place a zero at the end of this product.

$$\begin{array}{r} (2) \\ 172 \\ \times\,43 \\ \hline 516 \\ 6880 \end{array}$$ {$4 \times 2 = 8$, $4 \times 7 = 28$, $4 \times 1 = 4$}

> *Another way of conceptualizing multiplication is to think in terms of groups.*

> **PRODUCT:** the answer to a multiplication problem

Finally, to determine the final product, we add the two partial products.

$$
\begin{array}{r}
172 \\
\times\ 43 \\
\hline
516 \\
+\ 6880 \\
\hline
7396
\end{array}
$$

The product of 172 and 43 is 7,396.

Example: A student buys 4 boxes of crayons. Each box contains 16 crayons. How many total crayons does the student have?

The total number of crayons is 16×4.

$$
\begin{array}{r}
16 \\
\times\ 4 \\
\hline
64
\end{array}
$$

The total number of crayons equals 64.

Division of Whole Numbers

Division, the inverse of multiplication, is another of the four basic number operations. When we divide one number by another, we determine how many times we can multiply the **divisor** (number divided by) before we exceed the number we are dividing (**dividend**). For example, 8 divided by 2 equals 4 because we can multiply 2 four times to reach 8 ($2 \times 4 = 8$ or $2 + 2 + 2 + 2 = 8$). Using the grouping conceptualization we used with multiplication, we can divide 8 into 4 groups of 2 or 2 groups of 4. We call the answer to a division problem the QUOTIENT.

If the **divisor** does not divide evenly into the **dividend**, we express the leftover amount either as a **remainder** or as a fraction with the divisor as the denominator. For example, 9 divided by 2 equals 4 with a remainder of 1, or $4\frac{1}{2}$.

The basic algorithm for division is long division. We start by representing the quotient as follows.

$14\overline{)293}$ → 14 is the divisor and 293 is the dividend. This represents $293 \div 14$.

Next, we divide the divisor into the dividend, starting from the left.

$14\overline{)293}^{\,2}$ → 14 divides into 29 two times with a remainder.

> **QUOTIENT:** the answer to a division problem

Next, we multiply the partial quotient by the divisor, subtract this value from the first digits of the dividend, and bring down the remaining dividend digits to complete the number.

$$14\overline{)293} \rightarrow 2 \times 14 = 28, 29 - 28 = 1, \text{ and bringing down the 3 yields 13.}$$

Finally, we divide again (the divisor into the remaining value) and repeat the preceding process. The number left after the subtraction represents the remainder.

$$14\overline{)293}$$

$13 \rightarrow$ The final quotient is 20 with a remainder of 13. We can also represent this quotient as $20\frac{13}{14}$.

Example: Each box of apples contains 24 apples. How many boxes must a grocer purchase to supply a group of 252 people with one apple each?

The grocer needs 252 apples. Because he must buy apples in groups of 24, we divide 252 by 24 to determine how many boxes he needs to buy.

$$24\overline{)252}$$

$12 \rightarrow$ The quotient is 10 with a remainder of 12.

Thus, the grocer needs 10 boxes plus 12 more apples. Therefore, the minimum number of boxes the grocer can purchase is 11.

Example: At his job, John gets paid $20 for every hour he works. If John made $940 in a week, how many hours did he work?

This is a division problem. To determine the number of hours John worked, we divide the total amount made ($940) by the hourly rate of pay ($20). Thus, the number of hours worked equals 940 divided by 20.

$$20\overline{)940}$$

$0 \rightarrow$ 20 divides into 940 a total of 47 times with no remainder.

John worked 47 hours.

Addition and Subtraction of Decimals

When adding and subtracting decimals, we align the numbers by place value as we do with whole numbers. After adding or subtracting each column, we bring the decimal down, placing it in the same location as in the numbers added or subtracted.

Example: Find the sum of 152.3 and 36.342.

$$\begin{array}{r} 152.300 \\ + \ 36.342 \\ \hline 188.642 \end{array}$$

Note that we placed two zeros after the final place value in 152.3 to clarify the column addition.

Example: Find the difference of 152.3 and 36.342.

$$\begin{array}{cc} \begin{array}{r} 2\ 9\ 10 \\ 152.\cancel{300} \\ -\ 36.342 \\ \hline 58 \end{array} & \begin{array}{r} (4)11(12) \\ 1\cancel{52.300} \\ -\ 36.342 \\ \hline 115.958 \end{array} \end{array}$$

Note how we borrowed to subtract from the zeros in the hundredths and thousandths places of 152.300.

Addition and Subtraction of Fractions

Key points

1. You need a common denominator in order to add and subtract reduced and improper fractions.

   Example:
   $$\frac{1}{3} + \frac{7}{3} = \frac{1+7}{3} = \frac{8}{3} = 2\frac{2}{3}$$

   Example:
   $$\frac{4}{12} + \frac{6}{12} - \frac{3}{12} = \frac{4+6-3}{12} = \frac{7}{12}$$

2. Adding an integer and a fraction of the same sign results directly in a mixed fraction.

   Example:
   $$2 + \frac{2}{3} = 2\frac{2}{3}$$

   Example:
   $$-2 - \frac{2}{3} = -2\frac{2}{3}$$

3. Adding an integer and a fraction with different signs involves the following steps:

   • Get a common denominator

   • Add or subtract as needed

   • Change to a mixed fraction if possible

Example:

$$2 - \frac{1}{3} = \frac{2 \times 3 - 1}{3} = \frac{6 - 1}{3} = \frac{5}{3} = 1\frac{2}{3}$$

Example:

Add $7\frac{3}{8} + 5\frac{2}{7}$

Add the whole numbers, add the fractions, and combine the two results:

$$7\frac{3}{8} + 5\frac{2}{7} = (7 + 5) + \left(\frac{3}{8} + \frac{2}{7}\right)$$
$$= 12 + \frac{(7 \times 3) + (8 \times 2)}{56} \qquad \text{(LCM of 8 and 7)}$$
$$= 12 + \frac{21 + 16}{56} = 12 + \frac{37}{56} = 12\frac{37}{56}$$

Example: Perform the operation.

$$\frac{2}{3} - \frac{5}{6}$$

We first find the LCM of 3 and 6, which is 6.

$$\frac{2 \times 2}{3 \times 2} - \frac{5}{6} \rightarrow \frac{4 - 5}{6} = \frac{-1}{6} \text{(Using method A)}$$

Example:

$$-7\frac{1}{4} + 2\frac{7}{8}$$
$$-7\frac{1}{4} + 2\frac{7}{8} = (-7 + 2) + \left(\frac{-1}{4} + \frac{7}{8}\right)$$
$$= (-5) + \frac{-2 + 7}{8} = (-5) + \left(\frac{5}{8}\right)$$
$$= (-5) + \frac{5}{8} = \frac{-5 \times 8}{1 \times 8} + \frac{5}{8} = \frac{-40 + 5}{8}$$
$$= \frac{-35}{8} = -4\frac{3}{8}$$

Divide 35 by 8 to get 4, remainder 3.

Example:

Caution: A common error would be

$$-7\frac{1}{4} + 2\frac{7}{8} = -7\frac{2}{8} + 2\frac{7}{8} = -5\frac{9}{8} \text{ Wrong.}$$

It is correct to add -7 and 2 to get -5, but adding $\frac{2}{8} + \frac{7}{8} = \frac{9}{8}$ is wrong. It should have been $\frac{-2}{8} + \frac{7}{8} = \frac{5}{8}$. Then, $-5 + \frac{5}{8} = -4\frac{3}{8}$ as before.

This **ORDER OF OPERATIONS** should be followed when evaluating algebraic expressions:

1. Simplify inside grouping characters such as parentheses, brackets, square root, or fraction bars.

2. Multiply out expressions with exponents

3. Do multiplication and/or division, from left to right

4. Do addition and/or subtraction, from left to right

Samples of simplifying expressions with exponents:

Example: $3^3 - 5(b + 2)$
$$= 3^3 - 5b - 10$$
$$= 27 - 5b - 10 = 17 - 5b$$

Example: $2 - 4 \times 2^3 - 2(4 - 2 \times 3)$
$$= 2 - 4 \times 2^3 - 2(4 - 6) = 2 - 4 \times 2^3 = -2(-2)$$
$$= 2 - 4 \times 2^3 + 4 = 2 - 4 \times 8 + 4$$
$$= 2 - 32 + 4 = 6 - 32 = -26$$

COMPETENCY 18
KNOWLEDGE OF FRACTIONS, RATIOS, AND INTEGERS

> **SKILL 18.1** Compare fractions, integers, and integers with integer exponents and place them on a number line.

The **real number system** includes all rational and irrational numbers.

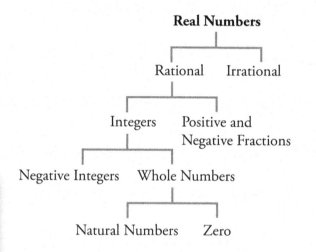

Real Numbers

> **RATIONAL NUMBERS:** can be expressed as the ratio of two integers, $\frac{a}{b}$, where $b > 0$

> **INTEGERS:** the positive and negative whole numbers and zero

> **WHOLE NUMBERS:** the natural numbers and zero

> **NATURAL NUMBERS:** the counting numbers

> **IRRATIONAL NUMBERS:** real numbers that cannot be written as the ratio of two integers

RATIONAL NUMBERS can be expressed as the ratio of two integers, $\frac{a}{b}$, where $b > 0$. For example: $\frac{2}{3}, -\frac{4}{5}, \frac{5}{1} = 5$.

The rational numbers include integers, fractions, mixed numbers, and terminating and repeating decimals. Every rational number can be expressed as a repeating or terminating decimal and can be shown on a number line.

INTEGERS are the positive and negative whole numbers and zero.
...-6, -5, -4, -3, -2, -1, 0, 1, 2, 3, 4, 5, 6,...

WHOLE NUMBERS are the natural numbers and zero.
0, 1, 2, 3, 4, 5, 6...

NATURAL NUMBERS are the counting numbers.
1, 2, 3, 4, 5, 6...

IRRATIONAL NUMBERS are real numbers that cannot be written as the ratio of two integers. They are infinite, nonrepeating decimals.

Examples:

$$\sqrt{5} = 2.2360, \text{pi} = \pi = 3.1415927...$$

PERCENT = per 100 (written with the symbol %). Thus $10\% = \frac{10}{100} = \frac{1}{10}$.

DECIMALS = deci = part of ten. To find the decimal equivalent of a fraction, divide the numerator by the denominator as shown in the following examples.

Example: Find the decimal equivalent of $\frac{7}{10}$.

Since 10 cannot divide into 7 evenly, put a decimal point in the answer row on top; put a 0 behind the 7 to make it 70. Continue the division process. If a remainder occurs, put a 0 by the last digit of the remainder and continue the division.

Thus $\frac{7}{10} = 0.7$

It is a good idea to write a 0 before the decimal point so that the decimal point is emphasized.

Example: Find the decimal equivalent of $\frac{7}{125}$.

$$\begin{array}{r} .056 \\ 125)\overline{7.000} \\ \underline{625} \\ 750 \\ \underline{750} \\ 0 \end{array}$$

Example: Convert 0.056 to a fraction.

Multiplying 0.056 by $\frac{1000}{1000}$ to get rid of the decimal point:

$$0.056 \times \frac{1000}{1000} = \frac{56}{1000} = \frac{7}{125}$$

Example: Find 23% of 1000.

$$= \frac{23}{100} \times \frac{1000}{1} = 23 \times 10 = 230$$

Example: Convert 6.25% to a fraction and to a mixed number.

$$6.25\% = 0.0625 = 0.0625 \times \frac{10000}{10000} = \frac{625}{10000} = \frac{1}{16}$$

PERCENT: a base-ten positional notation system for numbers

DECIMAL: a number written with a whole-number part, a decimal point, and a decimal part

A decimal can be converted to a percent by multiplying by 100, or merely moving the decimal point two places to the right, while a percent can be converted to a decimal by dividing by 100, or moving the decimal point two places to the left.

> A decimal can be converted to a percent by multiplying by 100 or merely moving the decimal point two places to the right. A percent can be converted to a decimal by dividing by 100 or moving the decimal point two places to the left.

Examples:

0.375 = 37.5%	84% = 0.84
0.7 = 70%	3% = 0.03
0.04 = 4%	60% = 0.6
3.15 = 315%	110% = 1.1
	$\frac{1}{2}$% = 0.5% = 0.005

A percent can be converted to a fraction by placing it over 100 and reducing to simplest terms.

Examples:

$$32\% = \frac{32}{100} = \frac{8}{25}$$
$$6\% = \frac{6}{100} = \frac{3}{50}$$
$$111\% = \frac{111}{100} = 1\frac{11}{100}$$

COMMON EQUIVALENTS				
$\frac{1}{2}$	=	0.5	=	50%
$\frac{1}{3}$	=	$0.33\frac{1}{3}$	=	$33\frac{1}{3}$%
$\frac{1}{4}$	=	0.25	=	25%
$\frac{1}{5}$	=	0.2	=	20%
$\frac{1}{6}$	=	$0.16\frac{2}{3}$	=	$16\frac{2}{3}$%
$\frac{1}{8}$	=	$0.12\frac{1}{2}$	=	$12\frac{1}{2}$%
$\frac{1}{10}$	=	0.1	=	10%
$\frac{2}{3}$	=	$0.66\frac{2}{3}$	=	$66\frac{2}{3}$%
$\frac{5}{6}$	=	$0.83\frac{1}{3}$	=	$83\frac{1}{3}$%
$\frac{3}{8}$	=	$0.37\frac{1}{2}$	=	$37\frac{1}{2}$%
$\frac{5}{8}$	=	$0.62\frac{1}{2}$	=	$62\frac{1}{2}$%
$\frac{7}{8}$	=	$0.87\frac{1}{2}$	=	$87\frac{1}{2}$%
1	=	1.0	=	100%

	Word Name	Standard Numeral	Pictorial Model
Decimal	Three-tenths	0.3	
Fraction	One-half	$\frac{1}{2}$	
Integer or Whole Number	Three	3	

The **EXPONENT FORM** is a shortcut method to write repeated multiplication. The basic form is b^n, where b is called the **BASE** and n is the **EXPONENT**. Both b and n are real numbers. The b^n implies that the base b is multiplied by itself n times.

Examples:

$3^4 = 3 \times 3 \times 3 \times 3 = 81$
$2^3 = 2 \times 2 \times 2 = 8$
$(-2)^4 = (-2) \times (-2) \times (-2) \times (-2) = 16$
$-2^4 = -(2 \times 2 \times 2 \times 2) = -16$

When 10 is raised to any power, the exponent tells the numbers of zeros in the product.

Example:

$10^7 = 10,000,000$

Caution: The exponent does not affect the sign unless the negative sign is inside the parentheses and the exponent is outside the parentheses.

$(-2)^4$ implies that -2 is multiplied by itself 4 times.

-2^4 implies that 2 is multiplied by itself 4 times, and then the answer becomes negative.

Scientific Notation

SCIENTIFIC NOTATION is a convenient method for writing very large or very small numbers. It employs two factors. The first factor is a number between 1 and 10. The second factor is a power of 10. This notation is considered "shorthand" for

EXPONENT FORM: a shorthand way of writing repeated multiplication

BASE: the number to be multiplied as many times as indicated by the exponent

EXPONENT: tells how many times the base is multiplied by itself

SCIENTIFIC NOTATION: a convenient method for writing very large and very small numbers

expressing very large numbers (such as the weight of 100 elephants) or very small numbers (such as the weight of an atom in pounds).

Recall that:

10^n	=	Ten multiplied by itself n times
10^n	=	Any nonzero number raised to the zero power is 1
10^1	=	10
10^2	=	$10 \times 10 = 100$
10^3	=	$10 \times 10 \times 10 = 1000$
10^{-1}	=	$\frac{1}{10}$ (deci)
10^{-2}	=	$\frac{1}{100}$ (centi)
10^{-3}	=	$\frac{1}{1000}$ (milli)
10^{-6}	=	$\frac{1}{1,000,000}$ (micro)

KEY EXPONENT RULES: FOR 'a' NONZERO AND 'm' AND 'n' REAL NUMBERS	
Product Rule	$a^m \times a^n = a^{(m+n)}$
Quotient Rule	$\dfrac{a^m}{a^n} = a^{(m-n)}$
Rule of Negative Exponents	$\dfrac{a^{-m}}{a^{-n}} = \dfrac{a^n}{a^m}$

Scientific Notation Format

Convert a number to a form of $b \times 10^n$, where b is a number between −9.9 and 9.9 and n is an integer.

Example: 356.73 can be written in various forms.

$$356.73 = 3567.3 \times 10^{-1}$$
$$= 35673 \times 10^{-2}$$
$$= 35.673 \times 10^1$$
$$= 3.5673 \times 10^2$$
$$= 0.35673 \times 10^3$$

Only (4) is written in proper scientific notation format. The following examples illustrate how to write a number in scientific notation format:

Example: Write 46,368,000 in scientific notation.

1. Introduce a decimal point and decimal places.
   $46,368,000 = 46,368,000.0000$

2. Make a mark between the two digits that give a number between -9.9 and 9.9.
   $4 \wedge 6,368,000.0000$

3. Count the number of digit places between the decimal point and the $\wedge$ mark. This number is the nth power of ten.
   So, $46,368,000 = 4.6368 \times 10^7$.

Example: Write 0.00397 in scientific notation.

1. Decimal point is already in place.

2. Make a mark between the 3 and the 9 to obtain a number between -9.9 and 9.9.

3. Move decimal place to the mark (three hops).
   $0.003 \wedge 97$
   Motion is to the right, so n of 10^n is negative.
   Therefore, $0.00397 = 3.97 \times 10^{-3}$.

Example: Evaluate $\dfrac{3.22 \times 10^{-3} \times 736}{0.00736 \times 32.2 \times 10^{-6}}$.

Since we have a mixture of large and small numbers, convert each number to scientific notation:

$736 = 7.36 \times 10^2$

$0.00736 = 7.36 \times 10^{-3}$

$32.2 \times 10^{-6} = 3.22 \times 10^{-5}$ thus we have,

$\dfrac{3.22 \times 10^{-3} \times 7.36 \times 10^2}{7.36 \times 10^{-3} \times 3.22 \times 10^{-5}}$

$= \dfrac{3.22 \times 7.36 \times 10^{-3} \times 10^2}{7.36 \times 3.22 \times 10^{-3} \times 10^{-5}}$

$= \dfrac{3.22 \times 7.36}{7.36 \times 3.22} \times \dfrac{10^{-1}}{10^{-8}}$

$= \dfrac{3.22 \times 7.36}{7.36 \times 3.22} \times 10^{-1} \times 10^8$

$= \dfrac{23.6992}{23.6992} \times 10^7$

$= 1 \times 10^7 = 10,000,000$

The expanded form of a number can be expressed in words or numbers. In words, the expanded form of 4,213 would be 4 thousands and 2 hundreds and 1 ten and 3 ones. In numeric form, it would be $4 \times 1000 + 2 \times 100 + 1 \times 10 + 3 \times 1$.

$$x^3 = x \times x \times x$$
$$x^{-2} = \frac{1}{x^2}$$
$$x^{\frac{1}{2}} = \sqrt{x}$$

Following are different representations of expressions with exponents and square roots:

If we compare numbers in various forms, we see the following:

The integer $400 = \frac{800}{2}$ (fraction)

$= 400.0$ (decimal) $= 100\%$ (percentage of integer) $= 20^2$ (number with exponent)

$= 4 \times 10^2$ (scientific notation), and

$1 > \frac{7}{8} > 0.65 > 60\% > 2^{-2} > 1 \times 10^{-2}$

SKILL 18.2 **Convert among standard measurement units within and between measurement systems** (e.g., metric, U.S. customary) **in the context of multistep, real-world problems.**

Example: Students are trying to determine the volume of a block.

Direct Measurement: Students pour water into a graduated cylinder and note the volume of the cylinder. They then place the block in the cylinder and note the new volume. By deducting the first reading from the second reading, they can determine the volume of the block by displacement.

Indirect Measurement: Students measure the length, height, and width of the block. They then determine the volume by multiplying the length by the width by the height.

Example: If a packet of sugar weighs 0.5 grams, how many milligrams does it weigh?

Converting from larger units to smaller units (metric): To convert larger units to smaller units, multiply.

1 gram = 1000 milligrams

0.5 grams × 1000 milligrams = 500 milligrams

Example: If an adult Kodiak bear weighs 1,150 pounds, how many tons does it weigh?

Converting from smaller units to larger units (customary):

To convert smaller units to larger units, divide.

$1 \text{ ton} = 2000 \text{ pounds}$

$$\frac{1150 \text{ pounds}}{2000 \text{ pounds}} = 0.575 \text{ tons}$$

> **SKILL 18.3** Solve problems involving addition, subtraction, multiplication, and division of fractions, including mixing whole numbers and fractions, decimals and percents by using visual models and equations to represent the problems and their solutions.

Ratios

Problems involving ratios are solved using multiplication and division.

Example: The ratio of the length of a rectangle to its width is 3:2. If the length of the rectangle is 12 meters, what is the width?

Set up the ratios: $\frac{3}{2} = \frac{\text{length}}{\text{width}}$

Substitute: $\frac{3}{2} = \frac{12}{x}$

Cross-multiply: $3x = 24$

Solve by dividing: $x = 8$

Proportions

Problems involving proportions are solved in the same manner as those involving ratios since proportions are two ratios set equal to each other.

Example: The weight of artificial sweetener in a box of 400 identical sweetener bags is 14 ounces. What is the weight, in ounces, of the sweetener in 12 bags?

Set up two ratios: $\frac{12}{400} = \frac{x}{14}$

Cross-multiply: $400x = 168$

Solve by dividing: $x = 0.42$

Percentages

Percentages are also ratios; for example, $75\% = \frac{75}{100}$. Therefore, problems involving percentages are solved in a manner similar to those involving ratios and proportions.

Example: 15 is what percentage of 75?

Set up two ratios: $\frac{15}{75} = \frac{x}{100}$

Cross-multiply: $75x = 1500$

Solve by dividing: $x = 0.20$ or 20%

Rational Numbers

See also 17.8

Addition and subtraction

If fractions have the same denominators, only addition and subtraction are necessary. However, if a common denominator must be determined, then multiplication is needed to convert the fractions.

Multiplication and division

Multiplication of fractions is the easiest operation involving fractions. You merely multiply the numerators by each other and the denominators by each other.

Division of fractions, on the other hand, calls for multiplication. To divide two fractions, you must multiply the dividend by the reciprocal of the divisor.

Example:

$$\frac{2}{3} \div \frac{3}{4} =$$
$$\frac{2}{3} \times \frac{4}{3} =$$
$$\frac{8}{9}$$

> **SKILL 18.4** **Select the representation** *(e.g., linear, area, set model)* **that best represents the problem and solution, given a word problem or equation involving fractions.**

Operations involving rational numbers represented as fractions require unique algorithms. For example, when adding or subtracting fractions, we use the distributive property of multiplication over division to find common denominators.

When completing operations involving real numbers in decimal form we use similar algorithms to those used with integers. We use the associative, commutative and distributive properties of numbers to generate algorithms.

Certain problem solving methods can give students a better understanding of fractions through visual representation.

A set model can show a student "half of 8" or $\left(\frac{1}{2}\right) \times 8$. Simply show 8 circles and leave one blank for every one that is colored. Then half the circles will be colored and show the answer to be 4.

An area model can identify equivalent fractions. For instance, if a circle is divided into 10 sections, and 5 of those sections are colored in, it will visually match a circle divided into 2 sections with one section colored in. This model would show that $\left(\frac{5}{10}\right) = \left(\frac{1}{2}\right)$.

Linear representation models are useful when comparing fractions with different denominators. With properly partitioned number lines, a student would see that $\left(\frac{5}{8}\right)$, for instance, is greater than $\left(\frac{5}{10}\right)$ as it would be closer to the value of one on the number line.

See also Skill 18.3

SKILL 18.5 Solve real-world problems involving ratios and proportions.

The unit rate for purchasing an item is its price divided by the number of units in the item. The item with the lower unit rate is the lower price.

Example: Find the item with the best unit cost.

$1.79 for 10 ounces
$1.89 for 12 ounces
$5.49 for 32 ounces

$\frac{1.79}{10} = 0.179$ per ounce $\frac{1.89}{12} = 0.1575$ per ounce $\frac{5.49}{32} = 0.172$ per ounce

$1.89 for 12 ounces is the best price.

A second way to find the better buy is to make a proportion, for example, with the price over the number of ounces. Cross-multiply the proportion, writing the products above the numerator that is used. The better price will have the smaller product.

Example: Find the better buy: $8.19 for forty pounds or $4.89 for twenty-two pounds. Find the unit costs.

$$\frac{40}{8.19} = \frac{1}{x}$$ $$\frac{22}{4.89} = \frac{1}{x}$$
$$40x = 8.19$$ $$22x = 4.89$$
$$x = 0.20475$$ $$x = 0.222\overline{27}$$

Because $.20475 < .222\overline{27}$, $8.19 is the lower price and a better buy.

To find the amount of sales tax on an item, change the percentage of sales tax into an equivalent decimal number. Next, multiply the decimal number by the price of the object to find the sales tax. The total cost of the item will be the price of the item plus the sales tax.

Example: A guitar costs $120.00 plus 7% sales tax. How much are the sales tax and the total cost?

7% = .07 as a decimal
(.07)(120) = $8.40 sales tax
$120.00 + $8.40 = $128.40 ← total price

Example: A suit costs $450.00 plus $6\frac{1}{2}$% sales tax. How much are the sales tax and the total cost?

$6\frac{1}{2}$% = .065 as a decimal
(.065)(450) = $29.25 sales tax
$450.00 + $29.25 = $479.25 ← total price

Ratios
Example: The road map Mr. Richards is reading states that 3 inches represent 125 miles. Mr. Richards estimates that the distance to his destination is approximately 5.5 inches on the map. Approximately how many miles would this be?

Solution: Represent the map scale as a ratio: $\frac{3}{125}$
Set the problem up as a proportion: $\frac{3}{125} = \frac{5.5}{x}$
Cross multiply: $3x = 687.5$
Solve: $x \approx 229$ miles

COMPETENCY 19
KNOWLEDGE OF MEASUREMENT, DATA, AND STATISTICS

> **SKILL 19.1** **Calculate and interpret statistics of variability** (e.g., range, mean absolute deviation) **and central tendency** (e.g., mean, median).

Mean, median, and mode are three measures of central tendency. The **MEAN** is the average of the data items. The **MEDIAN** is found by putting the data items in order from smallest to largest and selecting the item in the middle (or the average of the two items in the middle). The **MODE** is the most frequently occurring item. **RANGE** is a measure of variability. It is found by subtracting the smallest value from the largest value.

Example: Find the mean, median, mode, and range of the test scores listed below:

85	77	65
92	90	54
88	85	70
75	80	69
85	88	60
72	74	95

Mean = sum of all scores ÷ number of scores = 78

Median = Put the numbers in order from smallest to largest. Pick the middle number.

54 60 65 69 70 72 74 75 $\boxed{77 \quad 80}$ 85 85 85 88 88 90 92 95

both in middle

Therefore, the median is the average of two numbers in the middle, 78.5.

Mode = most frequent number
   = 85

Range = the largest number minus the smallest number
   = 95 − 54
   = 41

MEAN: the sum of the numbers given, divided by the number of items being averaged

MEDIAN: the middle number of a set

MODE: the number that occurs with the greatest frequency in a set of numbers

RANGE: the difference between the highest and lowest value of data items

Analyze and interpret data through the use of frequency tables and graphs.

To read a bar graph or a pictograph, read the explanation of the scale that was used in the **legend**. Compare the length of each bar with the dimensions on the axes and calculate the value each bar represents.

BAR GRAPHS are used to compare various quantities.

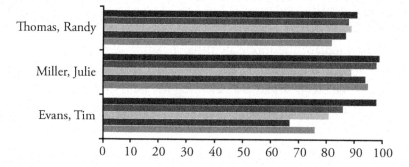

PICTOGRAPHS: show comparison of quantities using symbols; each symbol represents a number of items

A **PICTOGRAPH** shows comparison of quantities using symbols. Each symbol represents a number of items.

¶ ¶ ¶ ¶
¶ ¶ ¶ ¶ ¶ ¶ ¶
¶ ¶ ¶
¶ ¶
¶ ¶ ¶ ¶ ¶

CIRCLE GRAPHS: show the relationship of various parts to each other and the whole as percentages

CIRCLE GRAPHS show the relationship of various parts to each other and the whole. Percentages are used to create circle graphs. To read a circle graph, find the total of the amounts represented on the entire graph. To determine the amount that each sector of the graph represents, multiply the percentage in a sector by the number representing the total amount.

Julie spends eight hours each day in school, two hours doing homework, one hour eating dinner, two hours watching television, ten hours sleeping, and the rest of the time doing other things.

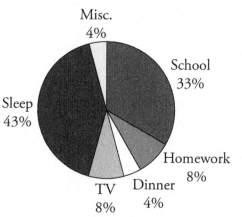

Stem-and-leaf plots are visually similar to line plots. The stems are the digits in the greatest place value of the data values, and the leaves are the digits in the next greatest place value. Stem-and-leaf plots are best suited for small sets of data and are especially useful for comparing two sets of data. The following is an example using test scores:

4	9
5	4 9
6	1 2 3 4 6 7 8 8
7	0 3 4 6 6 6 7 7 7 7 8 8 8 8
8	3 5 5 7 8
9	0 0 3 4 5
10	0 0

To read a chart, read the row and column headings on the table. Use this information to evaluate the information in the chart.

	Test 1	Test 2	Test 3	Test 4	Test 5
Evans, Tim	75	66	80	85	97
Miller, Julie	94	93	88	97	98
Thomas, Randy	81	86	88	87	90

HISTOGRAMS are used to summarize information from large sets of data that can be naturally grouped into intervals. The vertical axis indicates FREQUENCY (the number of times any particular data value occurs), while the horizontal axis indicates data values or ranges of data values. The number of data values in any interval is the FREQUENCY OF THE INTERVAL.

HISTOGRAMS: summarize information from large sets of data that can be naturally grouped into intervals

FREQUENCY: the number of times any particular data value occurs

FREQUENCY OF THE INTERVAL: the number of data values in any interval

Graphical representations of data sets, like **box-and-whisker plots**, help relate the measures of central tendency to data outliers, clusters, and gaps. Consider the hypothetical box-and-whisker plot with one outlier value on each end of the distribution.

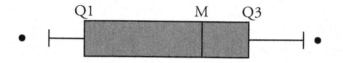

Note the beginning of the box is the value of the first quartile of the data set and the end is the value of the third quartile. We represent the median as a vertical line in the box. The "whiskers" extend to the last point that is not an outlier (i.e., within $\frac{3}{2}$ times the range between Q1 and Q3). The points beyond the figure represent outlier values.

Box-and-whisker graphs are useful when handling large amounts of data. They allow students to explore the data and arrive at an informal conclusion when two or more variables exist. Another name for the visual representation of a box-and-whisker graph is a **five-number summary**. This consists of the median, the quartiles, and the least and greatest numbers in the representation.

In order to create a box-and-whisker graph, first find the median in a list of numbers. Then look at the numbers only to the left of the median and find the median of this set of numbers. This is the lower quartile of the list. Repeat the procedure with the set of numbers to the right of the main median. This is the upper quartile. Use the two medians from the quartile to find the interquartile range by subtracting the lowest from the highest numbers. Then draw the graph on a number line.

Example: Fifteen girls own different numbers of hair elastics.
21 25 30 36 38 42 45 50 51 55 64 66 70 75 80
  The median is the number in the middle: 50.
  The median of the numbers to the left of 50 (the lower quartile) is 36, and the median of the numbers to the right of 50 (the upper quartile) is 66.
  When you subtract (66 − 50), the interquartile range is 16.
  Then you plot these numbers on a number line.

SKILL Select appropriate measurement units to solve problems involving
19.3 estimates and measurements.

Students should be able to determine what unit of measurement is appropriate for a particular problem, as indicated by the following table:

PROBLEM TYPE	UNIT (CUSTOMARY SYSTEM)	UNIT (METRIC SYSTEM)
Length	Inch Foot Yard	Millimeter Centimeter Meter
Distance	Square inches Square feet Square yards Square miles	Square millimeters Square centimeters Square meters Square kilometers
Volume	Cubic inches Cubic feet Cubic yards	Cubic millimeters Cubic centimeters Cubic meters
Liquid Volume	Fluid ounces Cups Pints Quarts Gallons	Milliliters Liters
Mass		Milligrams Centigrams Grams Kilograms
Weight	Ounces Pounds Tons	Milligrams Centigrams Grams Kilograms
Temperature	Degrees Fahrenheit	Degrees Celsius or Kelvin

Here is an example of a real-world problem for which an estimate is more appropriate than an exact measurement:

Ms. Jackson wants to make a 5-by-10-foot braided rug using 1-inch-wide braid.

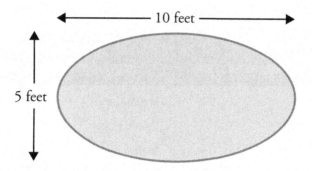

She can estimate how much braid she will need by determining the approximate area of the rug. If the rug were rectangular, the area would be 50 square feet, or 7,200 square inches (50 by 144). Ms. Jackson can use this estimate to make or purchase the amount of braid she needs for the rug.

Here is an example of a real-world problem where an exact measurement is more appropriate than an estimate:

A carpenter is building a staircase to the second floor of a house. If the carpenter estimates instead of using an exact measurement and overestimates the length of the staircase, the staircase will not fit against the second floor. If he underestimates the length, it will not reach to the second floor.

> **SKILL 19.4** **Evaluate the choice of measures of center and variability, with respect to the shape of the data distribution and the context in which the data were gathered.**

See Skill 19.1

Different situations require different information. The mean is the most descriptive value for tightly-clustered data with few outliers. Outlier data, which are values in a data set that are unusually high or low, can greatly distort the mean of a data set. Median, on the other hand, may better describe widely dispersed data and data sets with outliers because outliers and dispersion have little effect on the median value.

If we examine the circumstances under which an ice cream store owner may use statistics collected in the store, we find different uses for different information.

Over a 7-day period, the store owner collected data on the ice cream flavors sold. He found the mean number of scoops sold was 174 per day. The most frequently sold flavor was vanilla. This information was useful in determining how much ice cream to order in all and in what amounts for each flavor. In the case of the ice cream store, the median and range had little business value for the owner.

Retail store owners may be most concerned with the most common dress size so they may order more of that size than any other.

Consider the set of test scores from a math class: 0, 16, 19, 65, 65, 65, 68, 69, 70, 72, 73, 73, 75, 78, 80, 85, 88, and 92. The mean is 64.06 and the median is 71. Since there are only three scores less than the mean out of the eighteen scores, the median (71) would be a more descriptive score.

> SKILL **Solve problems involving distance, time, liquid volume, mass, and**
> 19.5 **money, which may include units expressed as fractions or decimals.**

See Skills 18.3 and 20.1

COMPETENCY 20
KNOWLEDGE OF GEOMETRIC CONCEPTS

SKILL 20.1 **Apply geometric properties and relationships to solve problems involving perimeter, area, surface area, and volume.**

The classifying of angles refers to the angle measure. The naming of angles refers to the letters or numbers used to label the angle.

Example:

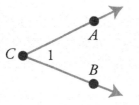

$\overrightarrow{CA}$ (read ray *CA*) and $\overrightarrow{CB}$ are the sides of the angle.
The angle can be called $\angle ACB$, $\angle BCA$, $\angle C$, or $\angle 1$.

Angles are classified according to their size as follows:

- Acute: greater than 0 and less than 90 degrees

- Right: exactly 90 degrees

- Obtuse: greater than 90 and less than 180 degrees

- Straight: exactly 180 degrees

Angles can be classified in a number of ways. Some of those classifications are outlined here.

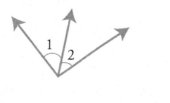

Adjacent angles have a common vertex and one common side but no interior points in common.

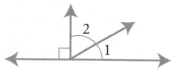

Complementary angles add up to 90 degrees.

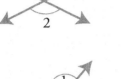

Supplementary angles add up to 180 degrees.

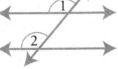

Vertical angles have sides that form two pairs of opposite rays.

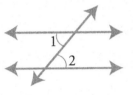

Corresponding angles are in the same corresponding position on two parallel lines cut by a transversal.

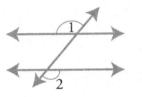

Alternate interior angles are diagonal angles on the inside of two parallel lines cut by a transversal.

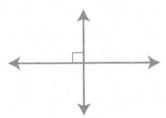

Alternate exterior angles are diagonal on the outside of two parallel lines cut by a transversal.

Parallel lines or planes do not intersect.

Perpendicular lines or planes form a 90 degree angle to each other.

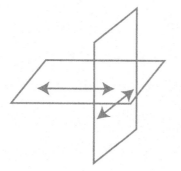

Intersecting lines share a common point, and intersecting planes share a common set of points, or line.

Skew lines do not intersect and do not lie on the same plane.

Finding Perimeter and Area

The **PERIMETER** of a polygon is the sum of the lengths of the sides.

The **AREA** of a polygon is the number of square units covered by the figure.

> **PERIMETER:** the sum of the lengths of the sides

> **AREA:** the number of square units covered by the figure; the space a figure occupies

FIGURE	AREA FORMULA	PERIMETER FORMULA
Rectangle	LW	$2(L + W)$
Triangle	$\frac{1}{2}bh$	$a + b + c$
Parallelogram	bh	sum of lengths of sides
Trapezoid	$\frac{1}{2}h(a + b)$	sum of lengths of sides

Perimeter

Example: A farmer has a piece of land shaped as shown below. He wishes to fence this land at an estimated cost of $25 per linear foot. What is the total cost of fencing this property, to the nearest foot?

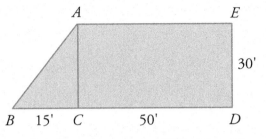

For the right triangle *ABC*, *AC* = 30 and *BC* = 15.
Since $(AB)^2 = (AC)^2 + (BC)^2$, we have
$(AB)^2 = (30)^2 + (15)^2$
So $\sqrt{(AB)^2} = AB = \sqrt{1{,}125} = 33.5410$ feet
To the nearest foot, *AB* = 34 feet.
Perimeter of the piece of land =
= 34 + 15 + 50 + 30 + 50 = 179 feet
Cost of fencing = \$25 × 179 = \$4,475.00

Area

Area is the space that a figure occupies.

Example: What will be the cost of carpeting a rectangular office that measures 12 feet by 15 feet if the carpet costs $12.50 per square yard?

12 ft.

15 ft.

The problem is asking you to determine the area of the office. The area of a rectangle is *length* × *width* = *A*.
Substitute the given values in the equation $A = lw$.

$A = (12\ \text{ft})\,(15\ \text{ft})$
$A = 180\ \text{ft}^2$

The problem asks you to determine the cost of the carpet at \$12.50 per square yard.
First, you need to convert 180 ft² into yd².

1 yd = 3 ft
(1 yd)(1 yd) = (3 ft)(3 ft)
1 yd² = 9 ft²
Hence, $\frac{180\ \text{ft}^2}{1} = \frac{1\ \text{yd}^2}{9\ \text{ft}^2} = \frac{20}{1} = 20\ \text{yd}^2$

The carpet costs \$12.50 per square yard; thus, the cost of carpeting the office is \$12.50 × 20 = \$250.00.

Example: Find the area of a parallelogram whose base is 6.5 cm and the height of the altitude to that base is 3.7 cm.

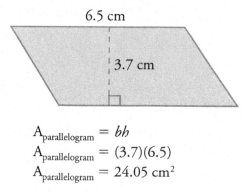

$$A_{parallelogram} = bh$$
$$A_{parallelogram} = (3.7)(6.5)$$
$$A_{parallelogram} = 24.05 \text{ cm}^2$$

Example: Find the area of this triangle.

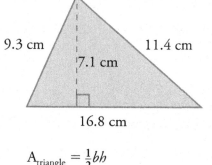

$$A_{triangle} = \frac{1}{2}bh$$
$$= 0.5(16.8)(7.1)$$
$$= 59.64 \text{ cm}^2$$

Example: Find the area of this trapezoid.

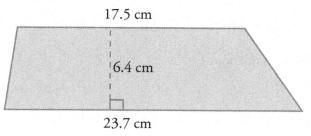

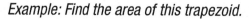

The area of a trapezoid equals one-half the sum of the bases times the altitude.

$$A_{trapezoid} = \frac{1}{2}h(b_1 + b_2)$$
$$= 0.5(6.4)(17.5 + 23.7)$$
$$= 131.84 \text{ cm}^2$$

CIRCUMFERENCE:
distance around a circle

The distance around a circle is called the **CIRCUMFERENCE**. The Greek letter pi represents the ratio of the circumference to the diameter.

$$\pi \approx 3.14 \approx \frac{22}{7}.$$

The circumference of a circle can be found by the formula $C = 2\pi r$ or $C = \pi d$, where r is the radius of the circle and d is the diameter.

The **area of a circle** is found by the formula $A = \pi r^2$.

Example: Find the circumference and area of a circle whose radius is 7 meters.

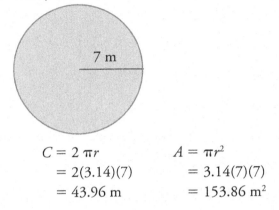

7 m

$$C = 2\,\pi r \qquad\qquad A = \pi r^2$$
$$= 2(3.14)(7) \qquad\quad = 3.14(7)(7)$$
$$= 43.96 \text{ m} \qquad\quad\; = 153.86 \text{ m}^2$$

Volume and Surface Area

We use the following formulas to compute **volume** and **surface area**:

FIGURE	VOLUME TOTAL	SURFACE AREA
Right Cylinder	$\pi r^2 h$	$2\pi rh + \pi r^2$
Right Cone	$\dfrac{\pi r^2 h}{3}$	$\pi r \sqrt{r^2 + h^2} + \pi r^2$
Sphere	$\dfrac{4}{3}\pi r^2 h$	$4\pi r^2$
Rectangular Solid	LWH	$2LW + 2WH + 2LH$

FIGURE	LATERAL AREA	TOTAL AREA	VOLUME
Regular Pyramid	$\frac{1}{2}Pl$	$\frac{1}{2}Pl + B$	$\frac{1}{3}Bh$

P = Perimeter   h = height   B = Area of base   l = slant height

Example: What is the volume of a shoebox with a length of 35 cm, a width of 20 cm, and a height of 15 cm?

Volume of a rectangular solid
$$= \text{Length} \times \text{Width} \times \text{Height}$$
$$= 35 \times 20 \times 15$$
$$= 10{,}500 \text{ cm}^3$$

Example: A water company is trying to decide whether to use traditional cylindrical paper cups or to offer conical paper cups, since both cost the same. The traditional cups are 8 cm wide and 14 cm high. The conical cups are 12 cm wide and 19 cm high. The company will use the cup that holds the most water.

Draw and label a sketch of each.

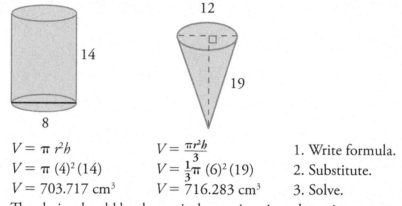

$V = \pi r^2 h$	$V = \frac{\pi r^2 h}{3}$	1. Write formula.
$V = \pi (4)^2 (14)$	$V = \frac{1}{3}\pi (6)^2 (19)$	2. Substitute.
$V = 703.717 \text{ cm}^3$	$V = 716.283 \text{ cm}^3$	3. Solve.

The choice should be the conical cup, since its volume is greater.

Example: How much material do we need to make a basketball that has a diameter of 15 inches? How much air do we need to fill the basketball?

Draw and label a sketch:

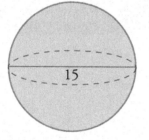

Total surface area	Volume	
$\text{TSA} = 4\pi r^2$	$V = \frac{4}{3}\pi r^3$	1. Write formula.
$= 4\pi (7.5)^2$	$= \frac{4}{3}\pi (7.5)^3$	2. Substitute.
$= 706.858 \text{ in}^2$	$= 1767.1459 \text{ in}^3$	3. Solve.

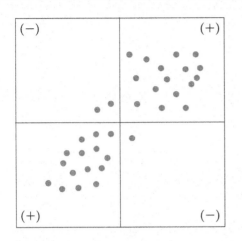

Horizontal and vertical lines are drawn through the **POINT OF AVERAGES**, which is the point on the respective averages of the x and y values. Doing this divides the scatter plot into four quadrants. If a point is in the lower left quadrant, the product of two negatives is positive; in the upper right quadrant, the product of two positives is positive. The positive quadrants are depicted with the positive sign (+). In the two remaining quadrants (upper left and lower right), the product of a negative and a positive is negative. The negative quadrants are depicted with the negative sign (−). If r is positive, then there are more points in the two positive quadrants; if is negative, then there are more points in the two negative quadrants.

POINT OF AVERAGES:
the point on the respective averages of the x and y values

An **ordered pair** is made up of an x-coordinate and a y-coordinate (x, y). The x-coordinate is plotted along the x-axis, and the y-coordinate is plotted along the y-axis.

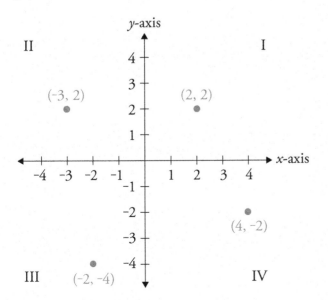

With (0, 0) as the intersection of the two axes, the right side of the *x*-axis is positive, and the left side is negative. The top part of the *y*-axis is positive, and the bottom part is negative. Accordingly, any ordered pair in quadrant I is made up of a positive *x*-coordinate and a positive *y*-coordinate; any ordered pair in quadrant II is made up of a negative *x*-coordinate and a positive *y*-coordinate; any ordered pair in quadrant III is made up of a negative *x*-coordinate and a negative *y*-coordinate; and any ordered pair in quadrant IV is made up of a positive *x*-coordinate and a negative *y*-coordinate.

Example: To locate the point (4, -2), from the origin, (0, 0), you would move to the right 4 units and down 2 units.

> **SKILL 20.3** Identify and analyze properties of three-dimensional shapes using formal mathematical terms such as volume, faces, edges, and vertices.

Three-dimensional figures

CYLINDER: a space figure that has two parallel, congruent circular bases

A **CYLINDER** is a space figure that has two parallel, congruent circular bases.

SPHERE: a space figure having all its points the same distance from the center

A **SPHERE** is a space figure having all its points the same distance from the center.

CONE: a space figure having a circular base and a single vertex

A **CONE** is a space figure having a circular base and a single vertex.

PYRAMID: a space figure with a square base and four triangle-shaped sides

A **PYRAMID** is a space figure with a square base and four triangle-shaped sides.

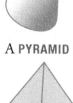

A **TETRAHEDRON** is a four-sided space triangle. Each face is a triangle.

A **PRISM** is a space figure with two congruent, parallel bases that are polygons.

In order to represent three-dimensional figures, we need three coordinate axes (x, y, and z) that are all mutually perpendicular to each other. Since we cannot draw three mutually perpendicular axes on a two-dimensional surface, we use oblique representations.

Example: Represent a cube with sides of 2.
Once again, we draw three sides along the three axes to make things easier.

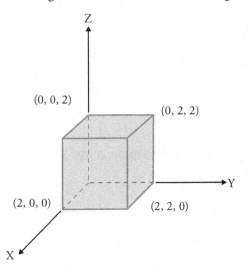

We refer to three-dimensional figures in geometry as solids. A solid is the union of all points on a simple, closed surface and all points in its interior. A poly-hedron is a simple closed surface formed from planar polygonal regions. Each polygonal region is called a face of the polyhedron. The vertices and edges of the polygonal regions are called the vertices and edges of the polyhedron.

We may form a cube from three congruent squares. However, if we tried to put four squares around a single vertex, their interior angle measures would add up to 360° (i.e., four edge-to-edge squares with a common vertex lie in a common plane and therefore cannot form a corner figure of a regular polyhedron).

There are five ways to form corner figures with congruent regular polygons:

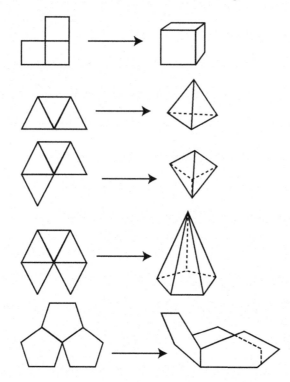

When creating a **three-dimensional figure**, if we know any two values of the vertices, faces, and edges, we can find the remaining value by using **Euler's formula**: $V + F = E + 2$.

Example: We want to create a pentagonal pyramid, and we know it has six vertices and six faces. Using Euler's formula, we compute:

$$V + F = E + 2$$
$$6 + 6 = E + 2$$
$$12 = E + 2$$
$$10 = E$$

Thus, we know that our figure should have 10 edges.

SKILL 20.4 Classify two-dimensional figures in a hierarchy based on mathematical properties.

> **POLYGON:** a simple, closed, two-dimensional figure composed of line segments

Two-Dimensional Figures

We name **POLYGONS**—simple, closed, two-dimensional figures composed of line segments—according to the number of sides they have.

A **QUADRILATERAL** is a polygon with four sides.

The sum of the measures of the angles of a quadrilateral is 360°.

A **TRAPEZOID** is a quadrilateral with exactly one pair of parallel sides.

In an **ISOSCELES TRAPEZOID**, the nonparallel sides are congruent.

A **PARALLELOGRAM** is a quadrilateral with two pairs of parallel sides.

In a parallelogram:

- The diagonals bisect each other
- Each diagonal divides the parallelogram into two congruent triangles
- Both pairs of opposite sides are congruent
- Both pairs of opposite angles are congruent
- Two adjacent angles are supplementary

A **RECTANGLE** is a parallelogram with a right angle.

A **RHOMBUS** is a parallelogram with all sides equal in length.

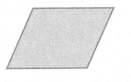

> **QUADRILATERAL:** a polygon with four sides

> **TRAPEZOID:** a quadrilateral with exactly *one* pair of parallel sides

> **ISOSCELES TRAPEZOID:** a quadrilateral in which the nonparallel sides are congruent

> **PARALLELOGRAM:** a quadrilateral with two pairs of parallel sides

> **RECTANGLE:** a parallelogram with a right angle

> **RHOMBUS:** a parallelogram with all sides equal in length

SQUARE: a rectangle with all sides equal in length

A **SQUARE** is a rectangle with all sides equal in length.

Example: True or false?

All squares are rhombuses.	True
All parallelograms are rectangles.	False—<u>some</u> parallelograms are rectangles
All rectangles are parallelograms.	True
Some rhombuses are squares.	True
Some rectangles are trapezoids.	False—trapezoids have only <u>one</u> pair of parallel sides
All quadrilaterals are parallelograms.	False—some quadrilaterals are parallelograms
Some squares are rectangles.	False—all squares are rectangles
Some parallelograms are rhombuses.	True

TRIANGLE: a polygon with three sides

ACUTE TRIANGLE: has exactly three *acute* angles

ACUTE ANGLE: an angle that measures less than 90 degrees

RIGHT TRIANGLE: has one *right* angle

RIGHT ANGLE: an angle that measures 90 degrees

OBTUSE TRIANGLE: has one *obtuse* angle

EQUILATERAL TRIANGLE: all sides are the same length

A **TRIANGLE** is a polygon with three sides. We can classify triangles by the types of angles or the lengths of their sides.

An **ACUTE TRIANGLE** has exactly three *acute* angles. An **ACUTE ANGLE** is an angle that measures less than 90 degrees.

A **RIGHT TRIANGLE** has one *right* angle. A **RIGHT ANGLE** is an angle that measures 90 degrees.

An **OBTUSE TRIANGLE** has one *obtuse* angle. An **OBTUSE ANGLE** measures between 90 degrees and 180 degrees.

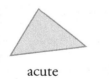

acute   right   obtuse

All three sides of an **EQUILATERAL TRIANGLE** are the same length.

Two sides of an **ISOSCELES TRIANGLE** are the same length.

None of the sides of a **SCALENE TRIANGLE** is the same length.

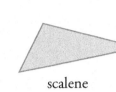

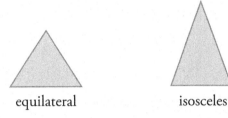

equilateral   isosceles   scalene

> **ISOSCELES TRIANGLE:** two sides are the same length

> **SCALENE TRIANGLE:** no sides are the same length

Example: Can a triangle have two right angles?
No. A right angle measures 90°; therefore, the sum of two right angles would be 180°, and there could not be a third angle.

Example: Can a triangle have two obtuse angles?
No. Since an obtuse angle measures more than 90°, the sum of two obtuse angles would be greater than 180°.

We can represent any two-dimensional geometric figure in the **Cartesian coordinate system** or **rectangular coordinate system**. The Cartesian—or rectangular coordinate system—is formed by two perpendicular axes (coordinate axes): the *X*-axis and the *Y*-axis. If we know the dimensions of a two-dimensional (planar) figure, we can use this coordinate system to visualize the shape of the figure.

Example: Represent an isosceles triangle with two sides of length 4.
Draw the two sides along the *x*- and *y*-axes and connect the points (vertices).

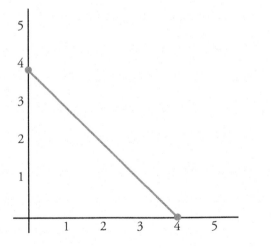

SAMPLE TESTS

Language Arts and Reading

(Rigorous) (Skill 2.1)

1. All of the following are common types of narratives EXCEPT:

    A. Legends

    B. Short stories

    C. Poems

    D. Memoirs

(Easy) (Skill 3.5)

2. All of the following are examples of transitional phrases EXCEPT:

    A. The

    B. However

    C. Furthermore

    D. Although

(Rigorous) (Skill 2.1)

3. Which of the following is NOT a characteristic of a fable?

    A. Animals that feel and talk like humans

    B. Happy solutions to human dilemmas

    C. Teaches a moral or standard for behavior

    D. Illustrates specific peoples or groups without directly naming them

(Rigorous) (Skill 1.8)

4. Effective reading and comprehension requires:

    A. Encoding

    B. Decoding

    C. Both A and B

    D. Neither A nor B

(Rigorous) (Skill 1.11)

5. A sixth-grade science teacher has given her class a paper to read on the relationship between food and weight gain. The writing contains signal words such as "because," "consequently," "this is how," and "due to." This paper has which text structure?

    A. Cause and effect

    B. Compare and contrast

    C. Description

    D. Sequencing

(Rigorous) (Skill 3.5)

6. All of the following are correctly capitalized EXCEPT:

    A. Queen Elizabeth

    B. Congressman McKay

    C. commander Alger

    D. the president of the United States

(Easy) (Skill 3.3)

7. A student has written a paper with the following characteristics: written in first person; characters, setting, and plot; some dialogue; and events organized in chronological sequence with some flashbacks. In what genre has the student written?

    A. Expository writing

    B. Narrative writing

    C. Persuasive writing

    D. Technical writing

(Rigorous) (Skill 5.2)

8. When students present information orally, they should keep the following in mind:

   A. Volume

   B. Pace

   C. Body language

   D. All of the above

(Average) (Skill 3.4)

9. Four athletes are each interested in a different sport. What is the most interesting way to write this information?

   A. Michael liked skating, Henrietta liked hockey, Violet liked archery, and Geoffrey liked football.

   B. Michael and Geoffrey liked skating and football, while Henrietta and Violet liked hockey and archery.

   C. Michael liked skating, but Henrietta liked hockey, and Violet liked archery, but Geoffrey liked football.

   D. Michael preferred skating, Henrietta favored hockey, Violet was wild about archery, and Geoffrey loved football.

(Average) (Skill 3.5)

10. Which of the following sentences shows the correct usage of the hyphen?

    A. Melanie was a real-estate-broker with Hendry and Henderson, so she understood the importance of a well-cared-for home.

    B. Robert dialed Joyce's number since it was easy-to-remember and listened with baited breath.

    C. Although Michael was not an accident-prone person, he knew his older brother did not share this trait.

    D. James and Austin, both twenty-one year old students, had been able to pass the difficult test for medical school.

(Average) (Skill 3.6)

11. Which of the following words best completes the sentence?

    Billy's grandparents had been extremely angry with the experiment on their car that ended badly and his grandfather's red face hung before his eyes like a dark vision: "Before you _____ some other wild plan, talk to me first so nothing else gets damaged."

    A. concoct

    B. invent

    C. make

    D. design

(Average) (Skill 3.6)

12. Which of the following choices best completes the sentence?

When at last Alicia was able to _____ the numerous difficulties associated with the task, she concluded the wisdom of her professor was not only desirable, but absolutely necessary.

A. perceive

B. perception

C. perceptive

D. perceived

(Average) (Skill 3.6)

13. Choose the word that correctly fills the blank the following sentence:

Jessica still needs to finish her home-work: revise her essay, _____ the next chapter, and complete the math problems.

A. reading

B. to read

C. read

D. will read

(Easy) (Skill 3.6)

14. Choose the word that best fills the blank in the following sentence:

Craig is so talented with horses that the skittish colt became _____ once Craig took over his training.

A. frantic

B. docile

C. lucid

D. prudent

(Easy) (Skill 3.6)

15. Choose the word that best fills the blank in the following sentence:

Stanley had never liked Nathan, but he grudgingly _____ Nathan for his idea of holding a car wash for the school fundraiser.

A. exalted

B. praised

C. honored

D. commended

(Easy) (Skill 3.6)

16. Identify the literary device used in the following sentence:

Caroline was rendered speechless to such a degree that she talked of nothing else for the rest of the day.

A. Irony

B. Hyperbole

C. Personification

D. Euphemism

(Rigorous) (Skill 3.6)

17. A magician wants to make all of his tricks a mystery to his audience. What verb should he use to say this?

A. Mysterize

B. Mystify

C. Mysterious

D. Mysteried

(Easy) (Skill 3.6)

18. Identify which spelling of "they're," "there," or "their" is used incorrectly in the following sentence: "They're about to get their boots and go hiking, but there worried about the rain and the mud."

    A. There

    B. They're

    C. Their

    D. None of the above

(Easy) (Skill 3.2)

19. Your best friend asks you how caterpillars turn into butterflies. You know the answer, but it is too complicated to explain in one sentence. How would you best express the explanation for your friend?

    A. Write a paragraph for each step of the process, with each step clearly labeled.

    B. Draw a Venn diagram of the things butterflies and caterpillars have in common.

    C. Look up the facts on how many butterflies fly south to Mexico each year.

    D. Write a paper, beginning with the time when butterflies are the prettiest.

(Easy) (Skill 1.2)

20. At Annie's school, the basketball game on Wednesday precedes the bake sale on Friday. What does the prefix *pre-* mean?

    A. Before

    B. During

    C. After

    D. Until

(Average) (Skill 3.5)

21. You think that longer novels are better than short ones; they give the characters more of a chance to grow and develop. How can you best link these two thoughts together?

    A. Longer novels are better than short ones. They give the characters more of a chance to grow and develop.

    B. Longer novels are better than short ones because they give the characters more of a chance to grow and develop.

    C. Longer novels are better than short ones, therefore they give the characters more of a chance to grow and develop.

    D. Longer novels are better than short ones when they give the characters more of a chance to grow and develop.

(Average) (Skill 1.6)

22. The wound exhibited signs of copious drainage and required medical intervention. Copious means:

    A. Minimal

    B. Clear

    C. Maximal

    D. Foul

(Average) (Skill 1.6)

23. The scientist was able to evoke powerful emotions from her audience. Evoke means:

    A. Sell

    B. Calm

    C. Call forth

    D. Exaggerate

(Average) (Skill 1.6)

24. The official exhibited a heedless attitude when dealing with the dignitaries. Heedless means:

    A. Thoughtless

    B. Pleasant

    C. Friendly

    D. Bitter

(Average) (Skill 1.6)

25. The general tried to instill the hope of victory in his troops. Instill means:

    A. Infuse

    B. Delay

    C. Inscribe

    D. Indict

(Average) (Skill 1.6)

26. The winning team of the World Series often has a jovial attitude. Jovial means:

    A. Merry

    B. Sad

    C. Somber

    D. Laborious

(Average) (Skill 1.6)

27. A lyre was played in ancient Rome. The lyre is a:

    A. Stringed instrument in the harp category

    B. Percussion instrument

    C. Wind instrument in the wind class

    D. Rhythmical percussion device

(Rigorous) (Skill 3.5)

28. Choose the option that best reflects proper comma usage in the sentence below.

    For the Thanksgiving reunion, relatives were sitting in the dining room, on the porch, and in the carport.

    A. Thanksgiving, reunion

    B. were, sitting

    C. porch

    D. No error

(Average) (Skill 3.5)

29. Choose the option that best reflects proper comma usage in the sentence below.

    Lydia seems to be a kind, considerate girl.

    A. seems, to

    B. considerate, girl

    C. kind considerate

    D. No error

(Rigorous) (Skill 3.5)

30. Choose the option that best reflects proper comma usage in the sentence below.

    This fishing pole Nathan, has seen better days.

    A. pole, Nathan,

    B. has, seen

    C. Nathan

    D. No error

(Rigorous) (Skill 1.2)

31. In his first-grade classroom, Mr. DePaul is aware of the importance of his students having a variety of reading readiness experiences. He focuses each week on word patterns to help his students become confident and fluent readers. Building the following type of skills will help his students to understand word patterns:

    A. Syntactic

    B. Morphemic

    C. Phonemic

    D. Semantic

(Rigorous) (Skill 1.6)

32. Types of suffixes that impart new meaning to the base or root word are known as:

    A. Compound words

    B. Prefixes

    C. Inflectional endings

    D. Morphemes

(Rigorous) (Skill 1.7)

33. The underlying message that a writer wants to convey is known as the _____.

    A. setting

    B. main idea

    C. generalization

    D. theme

(Rigorous) (Skill 1.7)

34. Attitude reflected in a statement or passage is:

    A. Author's purpose

    B. Author's tone

    C. Main idea

    D. Inference

(Rigorous) (Skill 1.11)

35. Mrs. Mackey introduces a story that takes place in the city of Atlanta, Georgia. Many students in her classroom have been to Atlanta before. This experience will be helpful to them. When a reader uses prior knowledge, he or she is _____.

    A. making an inference

    B. learning new vocabulary

    C. restating a thesis

    D. providing the main idea

(Rigorous) (Skill 1.10)

36. A _____ skill is a skill target that teachers help students develop to sustain learning in specific subject areas that they can apply in other subject areas.

    A. main idea

    B. thesis

    C. critical thinking

    D. informational text

(Rigorous) (Skill 1.11)

37. This refers to the patterns of textual organization in a piece of writing:

   A. Synthesis

   B. Evaluation

   C. Text structure

   D. Context

(Average) (Skill 1.1)

38. _____ gives readers important clues about what to look for.

   A. A graphic organizer

   B. Text structure

   C. A conclusion

   D. None of the above

(Rigorous) (Skill 1.1)

39. _____ can be accomplished in a number of ways to meet the needs of students with diverse literacy experiences.

   A. Strategic integration

   B. Conspicuous strategies

   C. Language and conventions of print

   D. Mediated scaffolding

(Average) (Skill 1.1)

40. Activities that draw upon _____ include incorporating oral language activities (which discriminate between printed letters and words) into daily read-alouds, as well as frequent opportunities to retell stories, looking at books with predictable patterns, writing messages with invented spelling, and responding to literature through drawing.

   A. background knowledge

   B. conspicuous strategies

   C. language and conventions of print

   D. mediated scaffolding

(Average) (Skill 2.1)

41. A _____ is a traditional narrative or collection of related narratives. It is often popularly regarded as historically factual but is actually a mixture of fact and fiction.

   A. legend

   B. novel

   C. myth

   D. fable

(Average) (Skill 2.1)

42. A play—comedy, modern, or tragedy— typically in five acts, is known as a:

   A. Poem

   B. Romance

   C. Drama

   D. Short story

(Average) (Skill 2.1)

43. These stories about events from the earliest times, such as the origin of the world, are considered true in their own societies.

    A. Myths

    B. Tall tales

    C. Fairy tales

    D. Fables

(Average) (Skill 2.1)

44. Many of the themes found in _____ stories are similar to those in traditional literature. The stories start out based in reality, which makes it easier for the reader to suspend disbelief and enter worlds of unreality.

    A. modern fantasy

    B. science fiction

    C. modern realistic fiction

    D. historical fiction

(Average) (Skill 2.2)

45. In her short story, a sixth grade student included the following line: "The lake was left shivering by the touch of morning wind." This is an example of:

    A. Imagery

    B. Personification

    C. Alliteration

    D. Allegory

(Easy) (Skill 2.2)

46. An _____ is based on the assumption that there is a common body of knowledge shared by the poet and the reader and that a reference to that body of knowledge will be immediately understood.

    A. alliteration

    B. allusion

    C. symbol

    D. imagery

(Easy) (Skill 2.2)

47. Students in Ms. Fernandez's classroom are focusing on figurative language. Mitchell, a student in her classroom, raises his hand to share a winter poem that he has written which contains the phrase 'as cold as ice.' His teacher compliments his use of a _____, or a direct comparison between two things that uses "like" or "as."

    A. simile

    B. metaphor

    C. personification

    D. hyperbole

(Easy) (Skill 2.2)

48. *The New York Times* once stated of crossword puzzles, "The craze evidently is dying out fast." Decades later, *The New York Times* Sunday edition still has the most recognized crossword puzzle. This is an example of:

    A. Irony

    B. Alliteration

    C. Onomatopoeia

    D. Malapropism

(Easy) (Skill 3.1)

49. _____ may include clustering, listing, brainstorming, mapping, free writing, and charting.

    A. Drafting

    B. Prewriting

    C. Revising and editing

    D. Proofreading

(Easy) (Skill 3.2)

50. _____ is discourse that makes an experience available through one of the five senses: seeing, smelling, hearing, feeling, or tasting.

    A. Description

    B. Narration

    C. Exposition

    D. Persuasion

(Average) (Skill 3.2)

51. _____ is a piece of writing—a poem, a play, or a speech—whose purpose is to change the minds of readers or audience members or to get them to do something.

    A. Description

    B. Narration

    C. Exposition

    D. Persuasion

(Rigorous) (Skill 4.2)

52. _____ are notes recorded by the teacher concerning an area of interest in or concern about a particular student.

    A. Anecdotal records

    B. Rating scales

    C. Informal reading inventories

    D. None of the above

(Rigorous) (Skill 4.3)

53. _____ are used to determine individual weaknesses and strengths in specific areas.

    A. Diagnostic assessments

    B. Readiness assessments

    C. Interest assessments

    D. Evaluation assessments

(Rigorous) (Skill 4.3)

54. _____ occurs when you remember things by relating them to each other in some way.

    A. Association

    B. Visualization

    C. Concentration

    D. Repetition

(Average) (Skill 4.3)

55. _____ helps store things in your memory.

    A. Association

    B. Visualization

    C. Concentration

    D. All of the above

(Rigorous) (Skill 1.7)

56. The atmosphere of attitude that an author conveys through descriptive language is known as the _____ of the story.

    A. mood

    B. pragmatics

    C. morphemes

    D. phonemes

(Average) (Skill 1.1)

57. This begins at birth and continues into the preschool years, during which time the child learns how to use and understand language in order to communicate:

    A. Hearing development

    B. Emergent literacy

    C. Alphabetic principle

    D. Context clues

(Rigorous) (Skill 1.1)

58. Around the time a child learns to crawl, the child is often also in the _____ of oral development, which includes baby noises, physical movements, and interactions with others.

    A. transition

    B. language

    C. protolinguistic

    D. cognitive

(Rigorous) (Skill 2.1)

59. _____ are terse tales that offer up a moral.

    A. Legends

    B. Novels

    C. Myths

    D. Fables

(Rigorous) (Skill 2.1)

60. These are purposely exaggerated accounts of individuals with super-human strength:

    A. Myths

    B. Tall tales

    C. Fairy tales

    D. Fables

Language Arts and Reading Answer Key

ANSWER KEY					
1. C	11. A	21. B	31. B	41. A	51. D
2. A	12. A	22. C	32. C	42. C	52. A
3. D	13. C	23. C	33. D	43. A	53. A
4. C	14. B	24. A	34. B	44. A	54. A
5. A	15. D	25. A	35. A	45. A	55. D
6. C	16. A	26. A	36. C	46. B	56. A
7. B	17. B	27. A	37. C	47. A	57. B
8. D	18. A	28. D	38. B	48. A	58. C
9. D	19. A	29. D	39. D	49. B	59. D
10. C	20. A	30. A	40. A	50. A	60. B

Language Arts and Reading Rigor Table

RIGOR TABLE	
Rigor Level	**Questions**
Easy	2, 7, 14, 15, 16, 18, 19, 20, 46, 47, 48, 49, 50
Average	9, 10, 11, 12, 13, 21, 22, 23, 24, 25, 26, 27, 29, 38, 40, 41, 42, 43, 44, 45, 51, 55, 57
Rigorous	1, 3, 4, 5, 6, 8, 17, 28, 30, 31, 32, 33, 34, 35, 36, 37, 39, 52, 53, 54, 56, 58, 59, 60

Language Arts and Reading Answers with Rationales

(Rigorous) (Skill 2.1)

1. **All of the following are common types of narratives EXCEPT:**

    A. Legends

    B. Short stories

    C. Poems

    D. Memoirs

    Answer: C. Poems

    A narrative is a spoken or written story. Legends, short stories, and memoirs all tell different types of stories.

(Easy) (Skill 3.5)

2. **All of the following are examples of transitional phrases EXCEPT:**

    A. The

    B. However

    C. Furthermore

    D. Although

    Answer: A. The

    Transitional phrases create a link between one thought and the next idea. In the given choices, the word "The" is not a word that lends itself to linking ideas together.

(Rigorous) (Skill 2.1)

3. **Which of the following is NOT a characteristic of a fable?**

    A. Animals that feel and talk like humans

    B. Happy solutions to human dilemmas

    C. Teaches a moral or standard for behavior

    D. Illustrates specific peoples or groups without directly naming them

    Answer: D. Illustrates specific peoples or groups without directly naming them

    Fables have distinct characteristics. Some of these are as follows: Animals that feel and talk like humans, positive solutions to human dilemmas, teaching a moral or a standard for behavior.

(Rigorous) (Skill 1.8)

4. **Effective reading and comprehension requires:**

    A. Encoding

    B. Decoding

    C. Both A and B

    D. Neither A nor B

    Answer: C. Both A and B

    Effective reading requires encoding and decoding. Decoding means translating written words into the sounds and meanings of spoken words (often silently). Encoding, or spelling, is the reverse process. Both are necessary skills to have in the process of reading.

(Rigorous) (Skill 1.11)

5.   A sixth-grade science teacher has given her class a paper to read on the relationship between food and weight gain. The writing contains signal words such as "because," "consequently," "this is how," and "due to." This paper has which text structure?

   A.   Cause and effect

   B.   Compare and contrast

   C.   Description

   D.   Sequencing

Answer: A. Cause and effect

Cause and effect is one of several text structures. Information structured as cause and effect explain reasons why something happened or the effects of something.

(Rigorous) (Skill 3.5)

6.   All of the following are correctly capitalized EXCEPT:

   A.   Queen Elizabeth

   B.   Congressman McKay

   C.   commander Alger

   D.   the president of the United States

Answer: C. commander Alger

Commander Alger is a specific title. Therefore, both words need to be capitalized.

(Easy) (Skill 3.3)

7.   A student has written a paper with the following characteristics: written in first person; characters, setting, and plot; some dialogue; and events organized in chronological sequence with some flashbacks. In what genre has the student written?

   A.   Expository writing

   B.   Narrative writing

   C.   Persuasive writing

   D.   Technical writing

Answer: B. Narrative writing

Narrative writing refers to stories. Characteristics include: being written in first person; characters, setting, and plot; some dialogue; and events organized in chronological sequence with some flashbacks.

(Rigorous) (Skill 5.2)

8.   When students present information orally, they should keep the following in mind:

   A.   Volume

   B.   Pace

   C.   Body language

   D.   All of the above

Answer: D. All of the above

When presenting information orally, it is important to focus on volume, pace, and body language to be an effective speaker.

(Average) (Skill 3.4)

9. **Four athletes are each interested in a different sport. What is the most interesting way to write this information?**

   A. Michael liked skating, Henrietta liked hockey, Violet liked archery, and Geoffrey liked football.

   B. Michael and Geoffrey liked skating and football, while Henrietta and Violet liked hockey and archery.

   C. Michael liked skating, but Henrietta liked hockey, and Violet liked archery, but Geoffrey liked football.

   D. Michael preferred skating, Henrietta favored hockey, Violet was wild about archery, and Geoffrey loved football.

   Answer: D. Michael preferred skating, Henrietta favored hockey, Violet was wild about archery, and Geoffrey loved football.

   The different verbs say something about each of the athletes in question, making the sentence more interesting. Repeating the same verb over and over in a sentence can be boring.

(Average) (Skill 3.5)

10. **Which of the following sentences shows the correct usage of the hyphen?**

    A. Melanie was a real-estate-broker with Hendry and Henderson, so she understood the importance of a well-cared-for home.

    B. Robert dialed Joyce's number since it was easy-to-remember and listened with baited breath.

    C. Although Michael was not an accident-prone person, he knew his older brother did not share this trait.

    D. James and Austin, both twenty-one year old students, had been able to pass the difficult test for medical school.

    Answer: C. Although Michael was not an accident-prone person, he knew that his older brother did not share this trait.

    Only choice C correctly uses the hyphen. Hyphens are used for many reasons, such as to make an adjective and a noun a compound word or in numbers (fifty-seven).

(Average) (Skill 3.6)

11. **Which of the following words best completes the sentence?**

    Billy's grandparents had been extremely angry with the experiment on their car that ended badly and his grandfather's red face hung before his eyes like a dark vision: "Before you _____ some other wild plan, talk to me first so nothing else gets damaged."

    A. concoct

    B. invent

    C. make

    D. design

    Answer: A. concoct

    While the words are all very similar in meaning (denotation), only concoct best matches the tone of the passage: Billy is prone to developing wild ideas that result in disaster.

(Average) (Skill 3.6)

12. Which of the following choices best completes the sentence?

    When at last Alicia was able to _____ the numerous difficulties associated with the task, she concluded the wisdom of her professor was not only desirable, but absolutely necessary.

    A. perceive

    B. perception

    C. perceptive

    D. perceived

Answer: A. perceive

This is the correct form of the word for the sentence. The present tense of the verb is needed to complete the sentence.

(Average) (Skill 3.6)

13. Choose the word that correctly fills the blank the following sentence:

    Jessica still needs to finish her homework: revise her essay, _____ the next chapter, and complete the math problems.

    A. reading

    B. to read

    C. read

    D. will read

Answer: C. read

"Read" (the present tense form of the verb) maintains the parallel structure of the sentence and matches the verb tense for "revise" and "complete."

(Easy) (Skill 3.6)

14. Choose the word that best fills the blank in the following sentence:

    Craig is so talented with horses that the skittish colt became _____ once Craig took over his training.

    A. frantic

    B. docile

    C. lucid

    D. prudent

Answer: B. docile

The word "docile" means easily taught or ready to be taught. The sentence should read: Craig is so talented with horses that the skittish colt became docile once Craig took over his training.

(Easy) (Skill 3.6)

15. Choose the word that best fills the blank in the following sentence:

    Stanley had never liked Nathan, but he grudgingly _____ Nathan for his idea of holding a car wash for the school fundraiser.

    A. exalted

    B. praised

    C. honored

    D. commended

Answer: D. commended

Although the word choices all have similar denotations, the context of the sentence, and especially the use of the word "grudgingly," indicate that Stanley gave only a perfunctory congratulations to Nathan for his good idea. The sentence should read: Stanley had never liked

Nathan, but he grudgingly commended Nathan for his idea of holding a car wash for the school fund raiser.

(Easy) (Skill 3.6)

16. Identify the literary device used in the following sentence:

    Caroline was rendered speechless to such a degree that she talked of nothing else for the rest of the day.

    A. Irony

    B. Hyperbole

    C. Personification

    D. Euphemism

    Answer: A. Irony

    Irony is an expression where words are attributed with the opposite of their usual meaning. The fact that Caroline was not rendered speechless, but quite the opposite, is indicated by the fact that she did not stop talking the rest of the day.

(Rigorous) (Skill 3.6)

17. A magician wants to make all of his tricks a mystery to his audience. What verb should he use to say this?

    A. Mysterize

    B. Mystify

    C. Mysterious

    D. Mysteried

    Answer: B. Mystify

    The Latin suffix *-ify* means "to make something become." To *mystify* is to make something become a mystery.

(Easy) (Skill 3.6)

18. Identify which spelling of "they're," "there," or "their" is used incorrectly in the following sentence: "They're about to get their boots and go hiking, but there worried about the rain and the mud."

    A. There

    B. They're

    C. Their

    D. None of the above

    Answer: A. There

    This sentence should end, "but they're worried about the rain and the mud." The word "they're" is a contraction of the words "they" and "are." The word "there" points to a place, as in, "The boot is over there," making its usage in the sentence incorrect.

(Easy) (Skill 3.2)

19. Your best friend asks you how caterpillars turn into butterflies. You know the answer, but it is too complicated to explain in one sentence. How would you best express the explanation for your friend?

    A. Write a paragraph for each step of the process, with each step clearly labeled.

    B. Draw a Venn diagram of the things butterflies and caterpillars have in common.

    C. Look up the facts on how many butterflies fly south to Mexico each year.

    D. Write a paper, beginning with the time when butterflies are the prettiest.

Answer: A. Write a paragraph for each step of the process, with each step clearly labeled.

The best way to answer a complex question is to go through each step of the answer from beginning to end.

(Easy) (Skill 1.2)

20. At Annie's school, the basketball game on Wednesday precedes the bake sale on Friday. What does the prefix *pre-* mean?

    A. Before

    B. During

    C. After

    D. Until

    Answer: A. Before

    "Pre-" is part of a word that means "before." The basketball game on Wednesday comes before, or *precedes,* the bake sale on Friday.

(Average) (Skill 3.5)

21. You think that longer novels are better than short ones; they give the characters more of a chance to grow and develop. How can you best link these two thoughts together?

    A. Longer novels are better than short ones. They give the characters more of a chance to grow and develop.

    B. Longer novels are better than short ones because they give the characters more of a chance to grow and develop.

    C. Longer novels are better than short ones, therefore they give the characters more of a chance to grow and develop.

    D. Longer novels are better than short ones when they give the characters more of a chance to grow and develop.

Answer: B. Longer novels are better than short ones because they give the characters more of a chance to grow and develop.

"Because" is the best word to use when the second part of a sentence supports the first part.

(Average) (Skill 1.6)

22. The wound exhibited signs of copious drainage and required medical intervention. Copious means:

    A. Minimal

    B. Clear

    C. Maximal

    D. Foul

    Answer: C. Maximal

    Copious means profuse or abundant

(Average) (Skill 1.6)

23. The scientist was able to evoke powerful emotions from her audience. Evoke means:

    A. Sell

    B. Calm

    C. Call forth

    D. Exaggerate

    Answer: C. Call forth

    To evoke means to call forth, elicit, or draw out, as emotions.

(Average) (Skill 1.6)

24. The official exhibited a heedless attitude when dealing with the dignitaries. Heedless means:

    A. Thoughtless

    B. Pleasant

    C. Friendly

    D. Bitter

Answer: A. Thoughtless

Heedless means thoughtless: to heed is to pay attention to, mind, or observe something, and heedless is not paying attention/ignoring.

(Average) (Skill 1.6)

25. The general tried to instill the hope of victory in his troops. Instill means:

    A. Infuse

    B. Delay

    C. Inscribe

    D. Indict

Answer: A. Infuse

Infuse is the best synonym here for instill, meaning to impart, inject, introduce or put something into someone or something.

(Average) (Skill 1.6)

26. The winning team of the World Series often has a jovial attitude. Jovial means:

    A. Merry

    B. Sad

    C. Somber

    D. Laborious

Answer: A. Merry

Jovial means happy or merry.

(Average) (Skill 1.6)

27. A lyre was played in ancient Rome. The lyre is a:

    A. Stringed instrument in the harp category

    B. Percussion instrument

    C. Wind instrument in the wind class

    D. Rhythmical percussion device

Answer: A. Stringed instrument in the harp category

A lyre was a stringed instrument played in ancient Greece and Rome, similar to/a precursor of the modern harp.

(Rigorous) (Skill 3.5)

28. Choose the option that best reflects proper comma usage in the sentence below.

    For the Thanksgiving reunion, relatives were sitting in the dining room, on the porch, and in the carport.

    A. Thanksgiving, reunion

    B. were, sitting

    C. porch

    D. No error

Answer: D. No error

There is a comma after the initial modifying prepositional phrase and after the first and second modifying prepositional phrases in the series of three.

(Average) (Skill 3.5)

29. Choose the option that best reflects proper comma usage in the sentence below.

Lydia seems to be a kind, considerate girl.

A. seems, to

B. considerate, girl

C. kind considerate

D. No error

Answer: D. No error

A comma belongs between two consecutive adjectives modifying the same noun.

(Rigorous) (Skill 3.5)

30. Choose the option that best reflects proper comma usage in the sentence below.

This fishing pole Nathan, has seen better days.

A. pole, Nathan,

B. has, seen

C. Nathan

D. No error

Answer: A. pole, Nathan,

The comma after "Nathan" is correct, but there should also be another comma before it. When an address to someone by name is inserted mid-sentence-here between subject and object-it should be set off by commas on both sides.

(Rigorous) (Skill 1.2)

31. In his first-grade classroom, Mr. DePaul is aware of the importance of his students having a variety of reading readiness experiences. He focuses each week on word patterns to help his students become confident and fluent readers. Building the following type of skills will help his students to understand word patterns:

A. Syntactic

B. Morphemic

C. Phonemic

D. Semantic

Answer: B. Morphemic

When readers develop morphemic skills, they are developing an understanding of patterns they see in words. This helps readers recognize and understand words more quickly.

(Rigorous) (Skill 1.6)

32. Types of suffixes that impart new meaning to the base or root word are known as:

A. Compound words

B. Prefixes

C. Inflectional endings

D. Morphemes

Answer: C. Inflectional endings

Inflectional endings change the gender, number, tense, or form of a base or root word.

(Rigorous) (Skill 1.7)

33. The underlying message that a writer wants to convey is known as the _____.

    A. setting

    B. main idea

    C. generalization

    D. theme

Answer: D. theme

Common themes in literature include jealousy, money, love, man/woman vs. nature, friendship, etc.…, and are never explicitly stated in the text.

(Rigorous) (Skill 1.7)

34. Attitude reflected in a statement or passage is:

    A. Author's purpose

    B. Author's tone

    C. Main idea

    D. Inference

Answer: B. Author's tone

A reader can determine the overall tone of a statement or passage through author's word choice.

(Rigorous) (Skill 1.11)

35. Mrs. Mackey introduces a story that takes place in the city of Atlanta, Georgia. Many students in her classroom have been to Atlanta before. This experience will be helpful to them. When a reader uses prior knowledge, he or she is _____.

    A. making an inference

    B. learning new vocabulary

    C. restating a thesis

    D. providing the main idea

Answer: A. making an inference

A reader must use prior knowledge and apply it to what he is she is reading in order to draw an inference and make a conclusion about the text.

(Rigorous) (Skill 1.10)

36. A _____ skill is a skill target that teachers help students develop to sustain learning in specific subject areas that they can apply in other subject areas.

    A. main idea

    B. thesis

    C. critical thinking

    D. informational text

Answer: C. critical thinking

Critical thinking skills are higher-order thinking skills. Developing critical thinking skills in students is not as simple as developing other, simpler, skills. Critical thinking skills must be taught within the context of specific subject matter.

(Rigorous) (Skill 1.11)

37. This refers to the patterns of textual organization in a piece of writing:

    A. Synthesis

    B. Evaluation

    C. Text structure

    D. Context

Answer: C. Text structure

Authors arrange their writing in various structures to make their content more comprehensible. Particularly in informational texts, text structure helps readers make sense of the content.

(Average) (Skill 1.1)

38. _____ gives readers important clues about what to look for.

    A. A graphic organizer

    B. Text structure

    C. A conclusion

    D. None of the above

Answer: B. Text structure

In nonfiction, particularly in textbooks, and sometimes in fiction, text structure gives readers important clues about what to look for.

(Rigorous) (Skill 1.1)

39. _____ can be accomplished in a number of ways to meet the needs of students with diverse literacy experiences.

    A. Strategic integration

    B. Conspicuous strategies

    C. Language and conventions of print

    D. Mediated scaffolding

Answer: D. Mediated scaffolding

Mediated scaffolding can be accomplished in a number of ways to meet the needs of students with diverse literacy experiences. To link oral and written language, for example, teachers may use texts that simulate speech by incorporating oral language patterns or children's writing.

(Average) (Skill 1.1)

40. Activities that draw upon _____ include incorporating oral language activities (which discriminate between printed letters and words) into daily read-alouds, as well as frequent opportunities to retell stories, looking at books with predictable patterns, writing messages with invented spelling, and responding to literature through drawing.

    A. background knowledge

    B. conspicuous strategies

    C. language and conventions of print

    D. mediated scaffolding

Answer: A. background knowledge

All children bring some level of background knowledge (e.g., how to hold a book, awareness of directionality of print) to beginning reading. Teachers can utilize children's background knowledge to help them link their personal literacy experiences to beginning reading instruction, while also closing the gap between students with rich literacy experiences and those with impoverished literacy experiences.

(Average) (Skill 2.1)

41. A _____ is a traditional narrative or collection of related narratives. It is often popularly regarded as historically factual but is actually a mixture of fact and fiction.

    A. legend

    B. novel

    C. myth

    D. fable

Answer: A. legend

A legend is a traditional narrative or collection of related narratives, popularly regarded as historically factual but actually a mixture of fact and fiction.

(Average) (Skill 2.1)

42. A play—comedy, modern, or tragedy—typically in five acts, is known as a:

    A. Poem

    B. Romance

    C. Drama

    D. Short story

Answer: C. Drama

Plays—comedy, modern, or tragedy—typically in five acts are known as dramas. Traditionalists and neoclassicists adhere to Aristotle's unities of time, place, and action. Plot development is advanced via dialogue. Literary devices include asides, soliloquies, and the chorus representing public opinion.

(Average) (Skill 2.1)

43. These stories about events from the earliest times, such as the origin of the world, are considered true in their own societies.

    A. Myths

    B. Tall tales

    C. Fairy tales

    D. Fables

Answer: A. Myths

Myths are stories about events from the earliest times, such as the origin of the world, are considered true in their own societies.

(Average) (Skill 2.1)

44. Many of the themes found in _____ stories are similar to those in traditional literature. The stories start out based in reality, which makes it easier for the reader to suspend disbelief and then enter worlds of unreality.

    A. modern fantasy

    B. science fiction

    C. modern realistic fiction

    D. historical fiction

Answer: A. modern fantasy

Many of the themes found in modern fantasy stories are similar to those in traditional literature. The stories start out based in reality, which makes it easier for the reader to suspend disbelief and enter worlds of unreality. These often appeal to ideals of justice and issues having to do with good and evil; and because children tend to identify with the characters, the message is more likely to be retained.

45. In her short story, a sixth grade student included the following line: "The lake was left shivering by the touch of morning wind." This is an example of:

A. Imagery

B. Personification

C. Alliteration

D. Allegory

Answer: A. Imagery

Imagery describes a word or sequence of words that refers to any sensory experience; anything that can be seen, tasted, smelled, heard, or felt on the skin or with the fingers.

46. An _____ is based on the assumption that there is a common body of knowledge shared by the poet and the reader and that a reference to that body of knowledge will be immediately understood.

A. alliteration

B. allusion

C. symbol

D. imagery

Answer: B. allusion

An allusion is based on the assumption that there is a common body of knowledge shared by the poet and the reader and that a reference to that body of knowledge will be immediately understood. It is very much like a symbol.

47. Students in Ms. Fernandez's classroom are focusing on figurative language. Mitchell, a student in her classroom, raises his hand to share a winter poem that he has written which contains the phrase 'as cold as ice.' His teacher compliments his use of a _____, or a direct comparison between two things that uses "like" or "as."

A. simile

B. metaphor

C. personification

D. hyperbole

Answer: A. simile

A simile is a direct comparison between two things that uses "like" or "as" to compare.

48. *The New York Times* once stated of crossword puzzles, "The craze evidently is dying out fast." Decades later, *The New York Times* Sunday edition still has the most recognized crossword puzzle. This is an example of:

A. Irony

B. Alliteration

C. Onomatopoeia

D. Malapropism

Answer: A. Irony

Expressing something other than and particularly opposite the true meaning, such as words of praise when the author or speaker intends blame is irony. The information above shows an ironic example. In poetry, irony is often used as a sophisticated or resigned awareness of contrast between what is and what ought to be and expresses a controlled pathos without sentimentality.

(Easy) (Skill 3.1)

49. _____ may include clustering, listing, brainstorming, mapping, free writing, and charting.

A. Drafting

B. Prewriting

C. Revising and editing

D. Proofreading

Answer: B. Prewriting

During the prewriting stage of the writing process, students gather ideas before writing. Prewriting may include clustering, listing, brainstorming, mapping, free writing, and charting.

(Easy) (Skill 3.2)

50. _____ is discourse that makes an experience available through one of the five senses: seeing, smelling, hearing, feeling, or tasting.

A. Description

B. Narration

C. Exposition

D. Persuasion

Answer: A. Description

Description is discourse that makes an experience available through one of the five senses: seeing, smelling, hearing, feeling, or tasting. Only by experiencing an

event can the emotions become involved. Poets are experts in using descriptive language.

(Average) (Skill 3.2)

51. _____ is a piece of writing—a poem, a play, or a speech—whose purpose is to change the minds of readers or audience members or to get them to do something.

A. Description

B. Narration

C. Exposition

D. Persuasion

Answer: D. Persuasion

Persuasion is a piece of writing—a poem, a play, or a speech—whose purpose is to change the minds of readers or audience members or to get them to do something. Persuasive writing often uses all forms of discourse. The introduction may be a history or background of the idea being presented (exposition). Details supporting some of the points may be stories (narrations). Descriptive writing will be used to make sure the point is established emotionally.

(Rigorous) (Skill 4.2)

52. _____ are notes recorded by the teacher concerning an area of interest in or concern about a particular student.

A. Anecdotal records

B. Rating scales

C. Informal reading inventories

D. None of the above

Answer: A. Anecdotal Records

Anecdotal records are notes recorded by the teacher concerning an area of interest in or concern about a particular student. These records should focus on observable behaviors and should be descriptive in nature.

(Rigorous) (Skill 4.3)

53. _____ are used to determine individual weaknesses and strengths in specific areas.

    A. Diagnostic assessments

    B. Readiness assessments

    C. Interest assessments

    D. Evaluation assessments

Answer: A. Diagnostic assessments

Diagnostic assessments are used to determine individual weaknesses and strengths in specific areas.

(Rigorous) (Skill 4.3)

54. _____ occurs when you remember things by relating them to each other in some way.

    A. Association

    B. Visualization

    C. Concentration

    D. Repetition

Answer: A. Association

When you associate, you remember things by relating them to each other in some way.

(Average) (Skill 4.3)

55. _____ helps store things in your memory.

    A. Association

    B. Visualization

    C. Concentration

    D. All of the above

Answer: D. All of the above

When you have difficulty remembering textbook information, you should repeat the procedures for association, visualization, and concentration. The repetition helps store the information in your memory more effectively.

(Rigorous) (Skill 1.7)

56. The atmosphere of attitude that an author conveys through descriptive language is known as the _____ of the story.

    A. mood

    B. pragmatics

    C. morphemes

    D. phonemes

Answer: A. mood

Mood helps the reader to better understand the writer's intentions, and usually fits in well with the theme and setting.

(Average) (Skill 1.1)

57. This begins at birth and continues into the preschool years, during which time the child learns how to use and understand language in order to communicate:

    A. Hearing development

    B. Emergent literacy

    C. Alphabetic principle

    D. Context clues

Answer: B. Emergent literacy

Emergent literacy refers to a child's speech and language development. It begins at birth and continues into the preschool years, during which time the child learns how to use and understand language in order to communicate.

(Rigorous) (Skill 1.1)

58. Around the time a child learns to crawl, the child is often also in the _____ of oral development, which includes baby noises, physical movements, and interactions with others.

    A. transition

    B. language

    C. protolinguistic

    D. cognitive

Answer: C. protolinguistic

The protolinguistic phase of oral development includes baby noises, physical movements, and interactions with others.

(Rigorous) (Skill 2.1)

59. _____ are terse tales that offer up a moral.

    A. Legends

    B. Novels

    C. Myths

    D. Fables

Answer: D. Fables

Fables are terse tales that offer up a moral. They often have animals that act uncharacteristically human in them.

(Rigorous) (Skill 2.1)

60. These are purposely exaggerated accounts of individuals with superhuman strength:

    A. Myths

    B. Tall tales

    C. Fairy tales

    D. Fables

Answer: B. Tall tales

Tall tales are purposely exaggerated accounts of individuals with superhuman strength. Examples include Paul Bunyan, John Henry, and Pecos Bill.

Social Sciences

(Easy) (Skill 8.1)

1. **All of the following are oceans EXCEPT:**

    A. Pacific

    B. Atlantic

    C. Mediterranean

    D. Indian

(Rigorous) (Skill 7.4)

2. **Which civilization invented the wheel?**

    A. Egyptians

    B. Romans

    C. Assyrians

    D. Sumerians

(Rigorous) (Skill 8.7)

3. **What was the long-term importance of the Mayflower Compact?**

    A. It established the foundation of all later agreements with the Native peoples

    B. It established freedom of religion in the original English colonies

    C. It ended the war in Europe between Spain, France, and England

    D. It established a model of small, town-based government that was adopted throughout the New England colonies

(Easy) (Skill 9.6)

4. **The belief that the United States should control all of North America was called:**

    A. Westward expansion

    B. Pan Americanism

    C. Manifest Destiny

    D. Nationalism

(Average) (Skill 10.1)

5. **The Westward expansion occurred for a number of reasons; however, the most important reason was:**

    A. Colonization

    B. Slavery

    C. Independence

    D. Economics

(Easy) (Skill 10.1)

6. **The economic collapse of the United States in 1929 is known as the:**

    A. Cold War

    B. New Deal

    C. Unhappy times

    D. Great Depression

(Easy) (Skill 6.3)

7. **Activities that enhance team socialization include all of the following EXCEPT:**

    A. Basketball

    B. Soccer

    C. Golf

    D. Volleyball

(Rigorous) (Skill 7.1)

8. **Cultural diffusion is:**

    A. The process that individuals and societies go through in changing their behavior and organization to cope with social, economic, and environmental pressures

    B. The complete disappearance of a culture

    C. The exchange or adoption of cultural features when two cultures come into regular direct contact

    D. The movement of cultural ideas or materials between populations independent of the movement of those populations

(Average) (Skill 7.4)

9. **Where was the first great human civilization located?**

    A. Egypt

    B. Greece

    C. Mesopotamia

    D. Samaria

(Average) (Skill 9.3)

10. **Which U.S. Founding Father is credited with founding the Federalist Party?**

    A. John Adams

    B. Thomas Jefferson

    C. Alexander Hamilton

    D. George Washington

(Average) (Skill 10.5)

11. **What does the acronym NAFTA stand for?**

    A. North American Federal Tariff Association

    B. North African Free Trade Agreement

    C. Non-American Final Territory Agreement

    D. North American Free Trade Agreement

(Average) (Skill 7.1)

12. **Women, such as Susan Anthony, fought for suffrage and were finally successful in 1920. What does suffrage mean?**

    A. Right to free speech

    B. Right to get an education

    C. Right to vote

    D. Right to work

(Average) (Skill 10.6)

13. **A new dog toy is introduced in pet stores in April for $19.99, but by December, the toy is being sold for $4.99. According to the law of supply and demand, which is most likely to be true about the dog toy?**

    A. Supply for the toy was low but demand was high

    B. Supply for the toy was high but the demand was low

    C. Both the supply and the demand for the toy were low

    D. Both the supply and the demand for the toy were high

(Average) (Skill 10.6)

14. If a drought severely reduces the amount of corn available to consumers, what would you expect to happen?

    A. The supply of corn would go up

    B. The demand for corn would go down

    C. The price of corn would go down

    D. The price of corn would go up

(Average) (Skill 9.1)

15. What type of government does the United States have?

    A. Monarchy

    B. Democracy

    C. Dictatorship

    D. Theocracy

(Average) (Skill 7.7)

16. Franklin Delano Roosevelt's New Deal helped America recover from the Great Depression by providing federal money for construction projects, including schools and roads. How did this help the country recover?

    A. It gave money back to the taxpayers

    B. It created desperately needed jobs at fair wages

    C. It encouraged wealthy people to do the same thing

    D. It made trade easier with Mexico

(Average) (Skill 7.1)

17. The catastrophic 1972 Summer Olympics in which terrorists killed eleven Israeli athletes was held in:

    A. Mexico City

    B. Moscow

    C. Munich

    D. Montreal

(Average) (Skill 7.5)

18. Which of the following nations was NOT once part of the British colonial empire?

    A. Australia

    B. India

    C. Nigeria

    D. Haiti

(Average) (Skill 10.6)

19. In American cities after the Industrial Revolution began, it was not unusual to see children huddled together without shoes, warm clothing, shelter, or decent food. These children illustrated what unhappy effect of industrialization in the United States?

    A. Because the focus was on manufacturing, not enough shoes were made

    B. Because of low wages, many people lived in poverty

    C. Because of protective employment laws, child laborers could no longer be employed

    D. Because of the freedom women experienced in the workplace, many abandoned their children

(Average) (Skill 8.1)

20. Which of these countries does NOT share a border with Israel?

    A. Jordan

    B. Saudi Arabia

    C. Lebanon

    D. Egypt

(Average) (Skill 7.1)

21. Put the following events in order from oldest to most recent.

    1. Martin Luther King led the March on Washington.

    2. *Brown v. Board of Education* overturned the policy of "separate but equal" education.

    3. The Student Non-Violent Coordinating Committee began staging sit-ins at segregated lunch counters in the South.

    4. The arrest of Rosa Parks sparked the Montgomery Bus Boycott.

    A. 2, 4, 3, 1

    B. 1, 3, 2, 4

    C. 3, 4, 1, 2

    D. 2, 1, 4, 3

(Average) (Skill 10.6)

22. An economist who advocated government intervention to prevent and remedy recessions and depressions was:

    A. Adam Smith

    B. John Maynard Keynes

    C. Friedrich Hayek

    D. Milton Friedman

(Easy) (Skill 10.6)

23. Which combination of factors is most likely to cause inflation?

    A. High unemployment and reduced production

    B. Credit restrictions and reduced production

    C. An oversupply of currency and a relatively low number of available goods

    D. An undersupply of currency and a relatively low number of available goods

(Average) (Skill 8.9)

24. The current definition of the term "Latin America" is most correctly described as:

    A. Everywhere in the Americas that Spanish or Portuguese predominantly is spoken

    B. Everywhere in the Americas south of the United States, including the Caribbean

    C. Everywhere in the Americas where a Latinate (i.e. Romance) language is spoken

    D. All of the previous choices can correctly describe a current definition of the term "Latin America"

(Average) (Skill 9.1)

25. Which Supreme Court ruling was the first to strike down a state law as unconstitutional?

    A. *Fletcher v. Peck*

    B. *Marbury v. Madison*

    C. *Martin v. Hunter's Lessee*

    D. *McCullough v. Maryland*

(Average) (Skill 9.2)

26. Which of the following initial principles of Jacksonian Democracy changed most over time?

    A. Expanded suffrage

    B. Manifest Destiny

    C. Political patronage

    D. Strict constructionism

(Rigorous) (Skill 9.3)

27. Which of the following is incorrect concerning the Articles of Confederation?

    A. They established the confederation's name as The United States of America

    B. They gave one vote apiece to each state in the Congress of the Confederation

    C. They established the freedom, sovereignty, and equality of individual states

    D. They did all these things, among many others; therefore, all these are correct

(Rigorous) (Skill 7.7)

28. Which of the following was a country considered to be behind the "Iron Curtain" in post-WWII Europe?

    A. Belgium

    B. Poland

    C. Austria

    D. Greece

(Rigorous) (Skill 6.4)

29. The ancient _____ were warlike and aggressive due to a highly organized military that used horse-drawn chariots.

    A. Sumerians

    B. Assyrians

    C. Egyptians

    D. Phoenicians

(Rigorous) (Skill 6.4)

30. In _____, the caste system was developed, the principle of zero in mathematics was discovered, and the major religion of Hinduism was begun.

    A. China

    B. France

    C. Egypt

    D. India

(Rigorous) (Skill 6.4)

31. Learning about many aspects of a culture is a critical part of understanding it. In his Social Studies class, Mr. Lyons sets up stations with task cards that explain the contributions of the _____ culture. These include drama, epic and lyric poetry, fables, myths, science, astronomy, medicine, mathematics, philosophy, art, architecture, and recording historical events.

    A. Chinese

    B. French

    C. Greek

    D. Indian

(Easy) (Skill 6.3)

32. Documents that reflect the immediate, everyday concerns of people: memoranda, bills, deeds, charters, newspaper reports, pamphlets, graffiti, popular writings, journals or diaries, records of decision-making bodies, letters, receipts, and snapshots are known as:

    A. Secondary sources

    B. Tertiary sources

    C. Primary sources

    D. Historical sources

(Rigorous) (Skill 6.4)

33. _____ were sea traders, well known for their manufacturing skills in glass and metals and the development of their famous purple dye.

    A. Phoenicians

    B. Mycenaeans

    C. Minoans

    D. Israelites

(Easy) (Skill 7.2)

34. The process of putting the features of the Earth onto a flat surface is called _____.

    A. distortion

    B. cartography

    C. projection

    D. illustrating

(Easy) (Skill 7.2)

35. A _____ tells the reader about the various symbols that are used on that particular map and what the symbols represent.

    A. legend

    B. grid

    C. scale

    D. title

(Rigorous) (Skill 7.2)

36. In this type of map, the meridians and parallels are drawn so that the areas shown have the same proportions as they do on the Earth:

    A. Consistent scales

    B. Conformal

    C. Equal areas

    D. Relief

(Easy) (Skill 7.2)

37. A series of lines that are used to find exact places and locations on the map:

    A. Legend

    B. Grid

    C. Scale

    D. Title

(Rigorous) (Skill 6.4)

38. _____ was a long period of peace, which enabled free travel and trade and spread people, cultures, goods, and ideas over a vast area of the known world.

   A. Pax Romana

   B. Daimyon Era

   C. Confucianism

   D. Joseon Dynasty

(Easy) (Skill 7.2)

39. _____ is the distance above or below the sea level.

   A. Contour

   B. Elevation

   C. Relief

   D. Scale

(Easy) (Skill 7.2)

40. This type of map shows the shape of the land surface:

   A. Contour

   B. Elevation

   C. Relief

   D. Scale

(Rigorous) (Skill 7.4)

41. The branch of the science of statistics most concerned with the social well-being of people:

   A. Psychology

   B. Archaeology

   C. Cartography

   D. Demography

(Easy) (Skill 7.2)

42. An important map property is _____, or correct shapes.

   A. consistent scales

   B. conformal

   C. equal areas

   D. relief

(Average) (Skill 7.8)

43. Populations can grow naturally when the rate of birth is higher than the rate of death or by adding new people from other populations through:

   A. Immigration

   B. Migration

   C. Climate change

   D. Economics

(Average) (Skill 7.8)

44. Elevated landforms usually level on top are known as:

   A. Deltas

   B. Mesas

   C. Mountains

   D. Plateaus

(Average) (Skill 7.8)

45. Areas of lowlands formed by soil and sediment deposited at the mouths of rivers:

   A. Deltas

   B. Mesas

   C. Mountains

   D. Plateaus

(Average) (Skill 7.8)

46. The flat tops of hills or mountains usually with steep sides:

    A. Deltas

    B. Mesas

    C. Mountains

    D. Plateaus

(Rigorous) (Skill 8.2)

47. The first ten amendments to the U.S. Constitution:

    A. Declaration of Independence

    B. Articles of Confederation

    C. Federalist Papers

    D. Bill of Rights

(Rigorous) (Skill 8.3)

48. This was adopted on November 15, 1777, creating a league of free and independent states:

    A. Declaration of Independence

    B. Articles of Confederation

    C. Federalist Papers

    D. Bill of Rights

(Average) (Skill 8.4)

49. This branch of the government, headed by the president, who leads the country, recommends new laws, and can veto bills passed by the legislative branch:

    A. Executive

    B. Judicial

    C. Legislative

    D. Presidential

(Average) (Skill 8.4)

50. This branch of the government is made up of the House of Representatives and the Senate:

    A. Executive

    B. Judicial

    C. Legislative

    D. Presidential

(Rigorous) (Skill 8.6)

51. This is considered to be the first modern document that sought to limit the powers of the state authority:

    A. Declaration of Independence

    B. Magna Carta

    C. Petition of Right

    D. Declaration of Rights

(Rigorous) (Skill 8.6)

52. This is the petition addressed to King Charles I by the British parliament in 1628:

    A. Declaration of Independence

    B. Magna Carta

    C. Petition of Right

    D. Declaration of Rights

(Rigorous) (Skill 8.7)

53. This allowed for the organizing the Supreme Court of the United States and establishing a system of federal courts of inferior jurisdiction:

    A. Judiciary Act

    B. Magna Carta

    C. Petition of Right

    D. Federal Act

(Rigorous) (Skill 9.4)

54. The Bill of Rights consists of which amendments?

    A. Amendments 1–5

    B. Amendments 1–10

    C. Amendments 1 and 2

    D. Amendments 1–22

(Skill 7.1) (Rigorous)

55. The area of the United States was effectively doubled through purchase of the Louisiana Territory under which president?

    A. John Adams

    B. Thomas Jefferson

    C. James Madison

    D. James Monroe

(Skill 7.6) (Rigorous)

56. A major quarrel between colonial Americans and the British concerned a series of British Acts of Parliament dealing with:

    A. Taxes

    B. Slavery

    C. Native Americans

    D. Shipbuilding

(Skill 7.9) (Rigorous)

57. The international organization established to work for world peace at the end of the Second World War is the:

    A. League of Nations

    B. United Federation of Nations

    C. United Nations

    D. United World League

(Skill 7.3) (Rigorous)

58. Why is the system of government in the United States referred to as a federal system?

    A. There are different levels of government

    B. There is one central authority in which all governmental power is vested

    C. The national government cannot operate except with the consent of the governed

    D. Elections are held at stated periodic times, rather than as called by the head of the government

(Skill 7.1) (Rigorous)

59. The U.S. Constitution, adopted in 1789, provided for:

    A. Direct election of the president by all citizens

    B. Direct election of the president by citizens meeting a standard of wealth

    C. Indirect election of the president by electors

    D. Indirect election of the president by the U.S. Senate

(Skill 7.8) (Rigorous)

60. From about 1870 to 1900, the settlement of America's "last frontier," the West, was completed. One attraction for settlers was free land, but it would have been to no avail without:

    A. Better farming methods and technology

    B. Surveying to set boundaries

    C. Immigrants and others to seek new land

    D. The railroad to get them there

Social Sciences Answer Key

ANSWER KEY					
1. C	11. D	21. A	31. C	41. D	51. B
2. D	12. C	22. B	32. C	42. A	52. C
3. D	13. B	23. C	33. A	43. A	53. A
4. C	14. D	24. D	34. C	44. D	54. B
5. D	15. B	25. A	35. A	45. A	55. B
6. D	16. B	26. D	36. C	46. B	56. A
7. C	17. C	27. D	37. B	47. D	57. C
8. D	18. D	28. A	38. A	48. B	58. A
9. C	19. B	29. B	39. B	49. A	59. C
10. C	20. B	30. D	40. C	50. C	60. D

Social Sciences Rigor Table

RIGOR TABLE	
Rigor Level	Questions
Easy	1, 4, 6, 7, 23, 32, 34, 35, 37, 39, 40, 42
Average	5, 9, 10, 11, 12, 13, 14, 15, 16, 17, 18, 19, 20, 21, 22, 24, 25, 26, 43, 44, 45, 46, 49, 50
Rigorous	2, 3, 8, 27, 28, 29, 30, 31, 33, 36, 38, 41, 47, 48, 51, 52, 53, 54, 55, 56, 57, 58, 59, 60

Social Sciences Answers with Rationales

(Easy) (Skill 8.1)

1. **All of the following are oceans EXCEPT:**

    A. Pacific

    B. Atlantic

    C. Mediterranean

    D. Indian

Answer: C. Mediterranean

The Pacific, Atlantic, and Indian Oceans are three of the four oceans in the world. The Mediterranean Sea is not an ocean, but was an important route for merchants and travelers during ancient times as it allowed for trade and cultural exchange between emergent peoples of the region.

(Rigorous) (Skill 7.4)

2. **Which civilization invented the wheel?**

    A. Egyptians

    B. Romans

    C. Assyrians

    D. Sumerians

Answer: D. Sumerians

The wheel was invented by the ancient Sumerians. The concept of the wheel actually grew out of a mechanical device that the Sumerians had invented shortly after 3500 B.C.—the potter's wheel. No other civilization of their time had one.

(Rigorous) (Skill 8.7)

3. **What was the long-term importance of the Mayflower Compact?**

    A. It established the foundation of all later agreements with the Native peoples

    B. It established freedom of religion in the original English colonies

    C. It ended the war in Europe between Spain, France, and England

    D. It established a model of small, town-based government that was adopted throughout the New England colonies

Answer: D. It established a model of small, town-based government that was adopted throughout the New England colonies

The Mayflower Compact was a signed agreement to ensure peace between the two groups carried by the Mayflower ship to America. It established a model of small, town-based government that was adopted throughout the New England colonies.

(Easy) (Skill 9.6)

4. **The belief that the United States should control all of North America was called:**

    A. Westward expansion

    B. Pan Americanism

    C. Manifest Destiny

    D. Nationalism

Answer: C. Manifest Destiny

In 1845, John L. O'Sullivan coined the term "Manifest Destiny," which was the belief that the United States should control all of North America.

(Average) (Skill 10.1)

5. The Westward expansion occurred for a number of reasons; however, the most important reason was:

    A. Colonization

    B. Slavery

    C. Independence

    D. Economics

    Answer: D. Economics

    Economics was the most important reason that the Westward Expansion occurred. The opportunities and growth led to a better economy through the development of various new industries.

(Easy) (Skill 10.1)

6. The economic collapse of the United States in 1929 is known as the:

    A. Cold War

    B. New Deal

    C. Unhappy times

    D. Great Depression

    Answer: D. Great Depression

    The Great Depression was a severe worldwide economic depression in the 1930s. The timing of the Great Depression varied across nations; however, in most countries it started in 1929 and lasted until the late 1930s.

(Easy) (Skill 6.3)

7. Activities that enhance team socialization include all of the following EXCEPT:

    A. Basketball

    B. Soccer

    C. Golf

    D. Volleyball

    Answer: C. Golf

    Team socialization is important in all cultures, both on and off the field. Golf is an individual activity, and does not promote this quality.

(Rigorous) (Skill 7.1)

8. Cultural diffusion is:

    A. The process that individuals and societies go through in changing their behavior and organization to cope with social, economic, and environmental pressures

    B. The complete disappearance of a culture

    C. The exchange or adoption of cultural features when two cultures come into regular direct contact

    D. The movement of cultural ideas or materials between populations independent of the movement of those populations

    Answer: D. The movement of cultural ideas or materials between populations independent of the movement of those populations

    Cultural diffusion is the movement of cultural ideas or materials between populations independent of the movement of those populations. The English language is a good example of diffusion, as it contains many words from other languages.

(Average) (Skill 7.4)

9. **Where was the first great human civilization located?**

   A. Egypt

   B. Greece

   C. Mesopotamia

   D. Samaria

Answer: C. Mesopotamia

The first great human civilization was the Sumerian civilization, which was located in Mesopotamia. Mesopotamia encompasses the area between the Tigris and Euphrates Rivers in modern-day Iraq and is also referred to as "the Cradle of Civilization," and includes part of the Fertile Crescent. The Sumerian civilization is credited with being the first to practice serious, year round agriculture.

(Average) (Skill 9.3)

10. **Which U.S. Founding Father is credited with founding the Federalist Party?**

    A. John Adams

    B. Thomas Jefferson

    C. Alexander Hamilton

    D. George Washington

Answer: C. Alexander Hamilton

Alexander Hamilton was the Founding Father who is credited with founding the Federalist Party. Hamilton was a proponent of the idea that the young country required the support of the rich

and powerful in order to survive. This party grew out of Hamilton's political connections in Washington and was particularly popular in the northeastern United States.

(Average) (Skill 10.5)

11. **What does the acronym NAFTA stand for?**

    A. North American Federal Tariff Association

    B. North African Free Trade Agreement

    C. Non-American Final Territory Agreement

    D. North American Free Trade Agreement

Answer: D. North American Free Trade Agreement

NAFTA stands for: North American Free Trade Agreement. Started in 1994, the North American Free Trade Agreement (NAFTA), created one of the world's largest free trade zones and set the foundations for strong economic growth and rising prosperity for Canada, the United States, and Mexico.

(Average) (Skill 7.1)

12. **Women, such as Susan Anthony, fought for suffrage and were finally successful in 1920. What does suffrage mean?**

    A. Right to free speech

    B. Right to get an education

    C. Right to vote

    D. Right to work

Answer: C. Right to vote

Suffrage means the right to vote.

(Average) (Skill 10.6)

13. **A new dog toy is introduced in pet stores in April for $19.99, but by December, the toy is being sold for $4.99. According to the law of supply and demand, which is most likely to be true about the dog toy?**

    A. Supply for the toy was low but demand was high

    B. Supply for the toy was high but the demand was low

    C. Both the supply and the demand for the toy were low

    D. Both the supply and the demand for the toy were high

    Answer: B. Supply for the toy was high but the demand was low

    The supply (availability) of the product was high, but demand (interest) was low. Therefore, the item is being sold at a reduced price.

(Average) (Skill 10.6)

14. **If a drought severely reduces the amount of corn available to consumers, what would you expect to happen?**

    A. The supply of corn would go up

    B. The demand for corn would go down

    C. The price of corn would go down

    D. The price of corn would go up

    Answer: D. The price of corn would go up

    The price of corn would go up because there is not a large quantity available. A consumer will pay more due to a lack of supply.

(Average) (Skill 9.1)

15. **What type of government does the United States have?**

    A. Monarchy

    B. Democracy

    C. Dictatorship

    D. Theocracy

    Answer: B. Democracy

    The United States operates under a Democracy, or a system of government by the whole population or all the eligible members of a state, typically through elected representatives.

(Average) (Skill 7.7)

16. **Franklin Delano Roosevelt's New Deal helped America recover from the Great Depression by providing federal money for construction projects, including schools and roads. How did this help the country recover?**

    A. It gave money back to the taxpayers

    B. It created desperately needed jobs at fair wages

    C. It encouraged wealthy people to do the same thing

    D. It made trade easier with Mexico

    Answer: B. It created desperately needed jobs at fair wages

    The country needed good paying jobs to boost the economy.

(Average) (Skill 7.1)

17. The catastrophic 1972 Summer Olympics in which terrorists killed eleven Israeli athletes was held in:

A. Mexico City

B. Moscow

C. Munich

D. Montreal

Answer: C. Munich

Palestinian terrorists kidnapped and killed eleven Israeli athletes and a police officer. Since this tragedy, security at these games has been of the highest level.

(Average) (Skill 7.5)

18. Which of the following nations was NOT once part of the British colonial empire?

A. Australia

B. India

C. Nigeria

D. Haiti

Answer: D. Haiti

Although an independent nation for many years, Haiti does have a history as a colonial possession of France.

(Average) (Skill 10.6)

19. In American cities after the Industrial Revolution began, it was not unusual to see children huddled together without shoes, warm clothing, shelter, or decent food. These children illustrated what unhappy effect of industrialization in the United States?

A. Because the focus was on manufacturing, not enough shoes were made

B. Because of low wages, many people lived in poverty

C. Because of protective employment laws, child laborers could no longer be employed

D. Because of the freedom women experienced in the workplace, many abandoned their children

Answer: B. Because of low wages, many people lived in poverty

During this era, poverty was common. Low wages cause this detrimental effect.

(Average) (Skill 8.1)

20. Which of these countries does NOT share a border with Israel?

A. Jordan

B. Saudi Arabia

C. Lebanon

D. Egypt

Answer: B. Saudi Arabia

Although both Israel and Saudi Arabia border on the Gulf of Aqaba, Jordan stands between Israel and its giant neighbor to the southeast.

(Average) (Skill 7.1)

21. Put the following events in order from oldest to most recent.

    1. Martin Luther King led the March on Washington.

    2. *Brown v. Board of Education* overturned the policy of "separate but equal" education.

    3. The Student Non-Violent Coordinating Committee began staging sit-ins at segregated lunch counters in the South.

    4. The arrest of Rosa Parks sparked the Montgomery Bus Boycott.

    A. 2, 4, 3, 1

    B. 1, 3, 2, 4

    C. 3, 4, 1, 2

    D. 2, 1, 4, 3

    Answer: A. 2, 4, 3, 1

    Brown v. Board of Education was decided in 1954. Rosa Parks was arrested in 1955. The lunch counter sit-ins were staged in 1960. The March on Washington took place in 1963.

(Average) (Skill 10.6)

22. An economist who advocated government intervention to prevent and remedy recessions and depressions was:

    A. Adam Smith

    B. John Maynard Keynes

    C. Friedrich Hayek

    D. Milton Friedman

    Answer: B. John Maynard Keynes

    Keynesian economics is based on the notion that governments can effectively stimulate economic growth through taxation, adjustment of interest rates, and the funding of public projects. His economic philosophy contrasts sharply with the free-market philosophies of Smith, Hayek, and Friedman.

(Easy) (Skill 10.6)

23. Which combination of factors is most likely to cause inflation?

    A. High unemployment and reduced production

    B. Credit restrictions and reduced production

    C. An oversupply of currency and a relatively low number of available goods

    D. An undersupply of currency and a relatively low number of available goods

    Answer: C. An oversupply of currency and a relatively low number of available goods

    Inflation is an overall increase in prices. Inflation commonly occurs when there is a large amount of printed currency circulating in an economy at a time when there are few available goods relative to that amount.

(Average) (Skill 8.9)

24. The current definition of the term "Latin America" is most correctly described as:

A. Everywhere in the Americas that Spanish or Portuguese predominantly is spoken

B. Everywhere in the Americas south of the United States, including the Caribbean

C. Everywhere in the Americas where a Latinate (i.e. Romance) language is spoken

D. All of the previous choices can correctly describe a current definition of the term "Latin America"

Answer: D. All of the previous choices can correctly describe a current definition of the term "Latin America"

All of these can correctly describe a current definition of the term Latin America because more than one definition of this name can be used.

(Average) (Skill 9.1)

25. Which Supreme Court ruling was the first to strike down a state law as unconstitutional?

A. *Fletcher v. Peck*

B. *Marbury v. Madison*

C. *Martin v. Hunter's Lessee*

D. *McCullough v. Maryland*

Answer: A. *Fletcher v. Peck*

The first American Supreme Court decision ever to strike down a state law as unconstitutional was *Fletcher v. Peck* (1810). The ruling mandated that the State of Georgia could repeal a corrupt land grant previously made.

(Average) (Skill 9.2)

26. Which of the following initial principles of Jacksonian Democracy changed most over time?

A. Expanded suffrage

B. Manifest Destiny

C. Political patronage

D. Strict constructionism

Answer: D. Strict constructionism

Strict constructionism of the Constitution was initially a principle that Jacksonian Democracy shared in common with earlier Jeffersonian Democracy. At first, Andrew Jackson agreed with Thomas Jefferson that the Federal government should be decentralized in order to limit its power.

(Rigorous) (Skill 9.3)

27. Which of the following is incorrect concerning the Articles of Confederation?

A. They established the confederation's name as The United States of America

B. They gave one vote apiece to each state in the Congress of the Confederation

C. They established the freedom, sovereignty, and equality of individual states

D. They did all these things, among many others; therefore, all these are correct

Answer: D. They did all these things, among many others; therefore, all these are correct

The Articles of Confederation did formally establish the name of the United States of America (a) for the new confederation. They did allocate just one vote to each state in the Congress of the Confederation (b), to which each state could send two to seven delegates. They did state that the individual states would keep their sovereignty, freedom, and equality (c) with the government of the confederation, and would maintain "…every power, jurisdiction, and right, which is not by this Confederation expressly delegated."

(Rigorous) (Skill 7.7)

28. **Which of the following was a country considered to be behind the "Iron Curtain" in post-WWII Europe?**

    A. Belgium

    B. Poland

    C. Austria

    D. Greece

    Answer: A. Belgium

    The "Iron Curtain" was a reference to the political and symbolic division of Europe after WWII, separating countries under Soviet influence or control from the rest of Europe.

(Rigorous) (Skill 6.4)

29. **The ancient _____ were warlike and aggressive due to a highly organized military that used horse-drawn chariots.**

    A. Sumerians

    B. Assyrians

    C. Egyptians

    D. Phoenicians

    Answer: B. Assyrians

The ancient Assyrians were warlike and aggressive due to a highly organized military that used horse-drawn chariots.

(Rigorous) (Skill 6.4)

30. **In _____, the caste system was developed, the principle of zero in mathematics was discovered, and the major religion of Hinduism was begun.**

    A. China

    B. France

    C. Egypt

    D. India

    Answer: D. India

    In India, the caste system was developed, the principle of zero in mathematics was discovered, and the major religion of Hinduism was begun. Hinduism was a continuing influence along with the rise of Buddhism. Industry and commerce developed along with extensive trading with the Near East.

(Rigorous) (Skill 6.4)

31. **Learning about many aspects of a culture is a critical part of understanding it. In his Social Studies class, Mr. Lyons sets up stations with task cards that explain the contributions of the _____ culture. These include drama, epic and lyric poetry, fables, myths, science, astronomy, medicine, mathematics, philosophy, art, architecture, and recording historical events.**

    A. Chinese

    B. French

    C. Greek

    D. Indian

Answer: C. Greek

Greece was responsible for the rise of independent, strong city-states. Other important contributions of classical Greece include drama, epic and lyric poetry, fables, myths, science, astronomy, medicine, mathematics, philosophy, art, architecture, and recording historical events.

(Easy) (Skill 6.3)

32. **Documents that reflect the immediate, everyday concerns of people: memoranda, bills, deeds, charters, newspaper reports, pamphlets, graffiti, popular writings, journals or diaries, records of decision-making bodies, letters, receipts, and snapshots are known as:**

    A. Secondary sources

    B. Tertiary sources

    C. Primary sources

    D. Historical sources

Answer: C. Primary sources

Primary sources are works, records, etc., that were created during the period being studied or immediately after it.

(Rigorous) (Skill 6.4)

33. **_____ were sea traders well known for their manufacturing skills in glass and metals and the development of their famous purple dye.**

    A. Phoenicians

    B. Mycenaeans

    C. Minoans

    D. Israelites

Answer: A. Phoenicians

The Phoenicians were sea traders well known for their manufacturing skills in glass and metals and the development of their famous purple dye.

(Easy) (Skill 7.2)

34. **The process of putting the features of the Earth onto a flat surface is called _____.**

    A. distortion

    B. cartography

    C. projection

    D. illustrating

Answer: C. projection

All maps are really map projections. There are many different types. Each one deals in a different way with the problem of distortion. Map projections are made in a number of ways. Some are done using complicated mathematics.

(Easy) (Skill 7.2)

35. **A _____ tells the reader about the various symbols that are used on that particular map and what the symbols represent.**

    A. legend

    B. grid

    C. scale

    D. title

Answer: A. legend

Most maps have a legend. A legend tells the reader about the various symbols that are used on that particular map and what the symbols represent. It is also called a map key.

(Rigorous) (Skill 7.2)

36. In this type of map, the meridians and parallels are drawn so that the areas shown have the same proportions as they do on the Earth:

   A. Consistent scales

   B. Conformal

   C. Equal areas

   D. Relief

Answer: C. Equal areas

One property that maps can have is that of equal areas. In an equal area map, the meridians and parallels are drawn so that the areas shown have the same proportions as they do on the Earth.

(Easy) (Skill 7.2)

37. A series of lines that are used to find exact places and locations on the map:

   A. Legend

   B. Grid

   C. Scale

   D. Title

Answer: B. Grid

A grid is a series of lines that are used to find exact places and locations on the map. There are several different kinds of grid systems in use; however, most maps use the longitude and latitude system, known as the Geographic Grid System.

(Rigorous) (Skill 6.4)

38. _____ was a long period of peace, which enabled free travel and trade and spread people, cultures, goods, and ideas over a vast area of the known world.

   A. Pax Romana

   B. Daimyon Era

   C. Confucianism

   D. Joseon Dynasty

Answer: A. Pax Romana

The contributions and accomplishments of the Romans are numerous, but the greatest included language, engineering, building, law, government, roads, trade, and the Pax Romana.

(Easy) (Skill 7.2)

39. _____ is the distance above or below the sea level.

   A. Contour

   B. Elevation

   C. Relief

   D. Scale

Answer: B. Elevation

Elevation is the distance above or below the sea level. The elevation is usually shown with colors, for instance, all areas on a map which are at a certain level will be shown in the same color.

(Easy) (Skill 7.2)

40. This type of map shows the shape of the land surface:

    A. Contour

    B. Elevation

    C. Relief

    D. Scale

Answer: C. Relief

Relief maps show the shape of the land surface: flat, rugged, or steep. They usually give more detail than simply showing the overall elevation of the land's surface.

(Rigorous) (Skill 7.4)

41. The branch of the science of statistics most concerned with the social well-being of people:

    A. Psychology

    B. Archaeology

    C. Cartography

    D. Demography

Answer: D. Demography

Demography includes the analysis of a population on the basis of such ideals as age, parentage, physical condition, race, occupation, or civil position, giving the actual size and density of each separate area, and changes in a population as a result of birth, marriage, and death.

(Easy) (Skill 7.2)

42. An important map property is _____, or correct shapes.

    A. consistent scales

    B. conformal

    C. equal areas

    D. relief

Answer: A. consistent scales

Many maps attempt to use the same scale on all parts of the map. Generally, this is easier when a map shows a relatively small part of the Earth's surface.

(Average) (Skill 7.8)

43. Populations can grow naturally when the rate of birth is higher than the rate of death or by adding new people from other populations through:

    A. Immigration

    B. Migration

    C. Climate change

    D. Economics

Answer: A. Immigration

Populations can grow naturally when the rate of birth is higher than the rate of death or by adding new people from other populations through immigration. Immigration is often a source of societal change as people from other cultures bring their institutions and language to a new area. Immigration has an impact on a population's educational and economic institutions as immigrants enter the workforce and enroll their children in schools.

(Average) (Skill 7.8)

44. **Elevated landforms usually level on top are known as:**

   A. Deltas

   B. Mesas

   C. Mountains

   D. Plateaus

   Answer: D. Plateaus

   Plateaus are elevated landforms usually level on top. Depending on location, they range from being an area that is very cold to one that is cool and healthful. Some plateaus are dry because they are surrounded by mountains that keep out any moisture.

(Average) (Skill 7.8)

45. **Areas of lowlands formed by soil and sediment deposited at the mouths of rivers:**

   A. Deltas

   B. Mesas

   C. Mountains

   D. Plateaus

   Answer: A. Deltas

   Deltas are areas of lowlands formed by soil and sediment deposited at the mouths of rivers. The soil is generally very fertile and most fertile river deltas are important crop-growing areas. One well known example is the delta of Egypt's Nile River, known for its production of cotton.

(Average) (Skill 7.8)

46. **The flat tops of hills or mountains usually with steep sides:**

   A. Deltas

   B. Mesas

   C. Mountains

   D. Plateaus

   Answer: B. Mesas

   Mesas are the flat tops of hills or mountains usually with steep sides. Mesas are similar to plateaus, but smaller.

(Rigorous) (Skill 8.2)

47. **The first ten amendments to the U.S. Constitution:**

   A. Declaration of Independence

   B. Articles of Confederation

   C. Federalist Papers

   D. Bill of Rights

   Answer: D. Bill of Rights

   The Bill of Rights is the first ten amendments to the U.S. Constitution, which deal with civil liberties and civil rights, written mostly by James Madison.

(Rigorous) (Skill 8.3)

48. **This was adopted on November 15, 1777, creating a league of free and independent states:**

   A. Declaration of Independence

   B. Articles of Confederation

   C. Federalist Papers

   D. Bill of Rights

   Answer: B. Articles of Confederation

During the war, and after independence was declared, the former colonies found themselves independent states. The Second Continental Congress was conducting a war with representation by delegates from thirteen separate states. The Congress had no power to act for the states or to require them to accept and follow its wishes. A permanent united government was desperately needed. On November 15, 1777, the Articles of Confederation were adopted, creating a league of free and independent states.

(Average) (Skill 8.4)

49. **This branch of the government, headed by the president, who leads the country, recommends new laws, and can veto bills passed by the legislative branch:**

   A. Executive

   B. Judicial

   C. Legislative

   D. Presidential

Answer: A. Executive

The executive branch of the government is headed by the president, who leads the country, recommends new laws, and can veto bills passed by the legislative branch. As the chief of state, the president is responsible for carrying out the laws of the country and the treaties and declarations of war passed by the legislative branch. The president appoints federal judges and is commander-in-chief of the military. Other members of the executive branch include the vice-president, various cabinet members, ambassadors, presidential advisers, members of the armed forces, and other appointed officers and

civil servants of government agencies, departments, and bureaus.

(Average) (Skill 8.4)

50. **This branch of the government is made up of the House of Representatives and the Senate:**

   A. Executive

   B. Judicial

   C. Legislative

   D. Presidential

Answer: C. Legislative

The Legislative branch of the government is made up of the House of Representatives and the Senate. Voters in all states elect the members who serve in each respective house of Congress. The legislative branch is responsible for making laws, raising and printing money, regulating trade, establishing the postal service and federal courts, approving the president's appointments, and declaring war and supporting the armed forces.

(Rigorous) (Skill 8.6)

51. **This is considered to be the first modern document that sought to limit the powers of the state authority:**

   A. Declaration of Independence

   B. Magna Carta

   C. Petition of Right

   D. Declaration of Rights

Answer: B. Magna Carta

The Magna Carta is considered to be the first modern document that sought to limit the powers of the state authority.

It guaranteed feudal rights, regulated the justice system, and abolished many abuses of the king's power to tax and regulate trade.

(Rigorous) (Skill 8.6)

52. **This is the petition addressed to King Charles I by the British parliament in 1628:**

    A. Declaration of Independence

    B. Magna Carta

    C. Petition of Right

    D. Declaration of Rights

    Answer: C. Petition of Right

    The Petition of Right was a petition addressed to the King Charles I by the British parliament in 1628. Parliament demanded that the king stop imposing new taxes without its consent. Parliament demanded the cessation of housing soldiers and sailors in the homes of private citizens, the proclamation of martial law in times of peace, and that no subject should be imprisoned without good cause.

(Rigorous) (Skill 8.7)

53. **This allowed for the organizing the Supreme Court of the United States and establishing a system of federal courts of inferior jurisdiction:**

    A. Judiciary Act

    B. Magna Carta

    C. Petition of Right

    D. Federal Act

    Answer: A. Judiciary Act

Congress passed the Judiciary Act in 1789, organizing the Supreme Court of the United States and establishing a system of federal courts of inferior jurisdiction. The states were left to establish their own judicial systems subject to the exclusive overall jurisdiction of the federal courts and to Article VI of the Constitution, declaring the judges of the state courts to be bound to the Constitution and to the laws and treaties of the United States. This created a dual system of judicial power and authority.

(Rigorous) (Skill 9.4)

54. **The Bill of Rights consists of which amendments?**

    A. Amendments 1–5

    B. Amendments 1–10

    C. Amendments 1 and 2

    D. Amendments 1–22

    Answer: B. Amendments 1–10

    The Bill of Rights consists of Amendments 1–10.

(Rigorous) (Skill 7.1)

55. **The area of the United States was effectively doubled through purchase of the Louisiana Territory under which president?**

    A. John Adams

    B. Thomas Jefferson

    C. James Madison

    D. James Monroe

    Answer: B. Thomas Jefferson

The Louisiana Purchase, an acquisition of territory from France in 1803, occurred during the presidency of Thomas Jefferson. (A) John Adams (1735–1826) was president from 1797–1801, before the purchase. (C) James Madison (1751–1836) after the purchase (1809–1817). (D) James Monroe (1758–1831) was actually a signatory on the Purchase, but did not become president until 1817.

(Rigorous) (Skill 7.6)

56. **A major quarrel between colonial Americans and the British concerned a series of British Acts of Parliament dealing with:**

    A. Taxes

    B. Slavery

    C. Native Americans

    D. Shipbuilding

Answer: A. Taxes

Acts of Parliament imposing taxes on the colonists always provoked resentment. Because the colonies had no direct representation in Parliament, they felt it unjust that that body should impose taxes on them, with so little knowledge of their very different situation in America and no real concern for the consequences of such taxes. (B) While slavery continued to exist in the colonies long after it had been completely abolished in Britain, it never was a source of serious debate between Britain and the colonies. By the time Britain outlawed slavery in its colonies in 1833, the American Revolution had already occurred and the United States was free of British control. (C) There was no series of British Acts of Parliament passed concerning Native Americans. (D) Colonial shipbuilding was an industry, which received little interference from the British.

(Rigorous) (Skill 7.9)

57. **The international organization established to work for world peace at the end of the Second World War is the:**

    A. League of Nations

    B. United Federation of Nations

    C. United Nations

    D. United World League

Answer: C. United Nations

The international organization established to work for world peace at the end of the Second World War was the United Nations. From the ashes of the failed League of Nations, established following World War I, the United Nations continues to be a major player in world affairs today.

(Rigorous) (Skill 7.3)

58. **Why is the system of government in the United States referred to as a federal system?**

    A. There are different levels of government

    B. There is one central authority in which all governmental power is vested

    C. The national government cannot operate except with the consent of the governed

    D. Elections are held at stated periodic times, rather than as called by the head of the government

Answer: A. There are different levels of government

(A) The United States is composed of fifty states, each responsible for its own affairs, but united under a federal government. (B) A centralized system is the opposite of a federal system. (C) That national government cannot operate except with the consent of the governed is a founding principle of American politics. It is not a political system like federalism. A centralized democracy could still be consensual, but would not be federal. (D) This is a description of electoral procedure, not a political system like federalism.

(Rigorous) (Skill 7.1)

59. The U.S. Constitution, adopted in 1789, provided for:

   A. Direct election of the president by all citizens

   B. Direct election of the president by citizens meeting a standard of wealth

   C. Indirect election of the president by electors

   D. Indirect election of the president by the U.S. Senate

Answer: C. Indirect election of the president by electors

The United States Constitution has always arranged for the indirect election of the president by electors. The question, by mentioning the original date of adoption, might mislead someone to choose B, but while standards of citizenship have been changed by amendment, the president has never been directly elected. Nor does the Senate have anything to do with presidential elections. The House of

Representatives, not the Senate, settles cases where neither candidate wins in the Electoral College.

(Rigorous) (Skill 7.8)

60. From about 1870 to 1900, the settlement of America's "last frontier," the West, was completed. One attraction for settlers was free land, but it would have been to no avail without:

   A. Better farming methods and technology

   B. Surveying to set boundaries

   C. Immigrants and others to seek new land

   D. The railroad to get them there

Answer: D. The railroad to get them there

From about 1870 to 1900, the settlement of America's "last frontier" in the West was made possible by the building of the railroad. Without the railroad, the settlers never could have traveled such distances in an efficient manner.

Science

(Rigorous) (Skill 14.8)

1. Which of the following is the best definition for meteorite?

   A. A meteorite is a mineral composed of mica and feldspar

   B. A meteorite is material from outer space that has struck the Earth's surface

   C. A meteorite is an element that has properties of both metals and nonmetals

   D. A meteorite is a very small unit of length measurement

(Rigorous) (Skill 15.3)

2. Identify the correct sequence of organization of living things from lower to higher order:

   A. Cell, Organelle, Organ, Tissue, System, Organism

   B. Cell, Tissue, Organ, Organelle, System, Organism

   C. Organelle, Cell, Tissue, Organ, System, Organism

   D. Organelle, Tissue, Cell, Organ, System, Organism

(Average) (Skill 13.3)

3. The following are examples of chemical reactions EXCEPT:

   A. Melting ice into water

   B. Dissolving a seltzer tablet in water

   C. Using a fire-cracker

   D. Burning a piece of plastic

(Average) (Skill 14.9)

4. All of the following professions are classified under "Earth Sciences" EXCEPT:

   A. Geologist

   B. Meteorologist

   C. Seismologist

   D. Biochemist

(Average) (Skill 11.2)

5. When teaching Science rules pertaining to safety, Mrs. Miller explains to her students that chemicals should be stored

   A. in the principal's office.

   B. in a dark room.

   C. in an off-site research facility.

   D. according to their reactivity with other substances.

(Average) (Skill 10.4)

6. Social skills and values developed by activity include all of the following EXCEPT:

   A. Winning at all costs

   B. Making judgments in groups

   C. Communicating and cooperating

   D. Respecting rules and property

(Average) (Skill 14.8)

7. Which of the following statements about galaxies is true?

    A. Galaxies are the only structures in the universe that do not contain dark matter.

    B. Galaxies are gravitationally bound, meaning structures within the galaxy orbit around its center.

    C. Galaxies typically contain over one trillion stars.

    D. Galaxies are comprised of clusters and superclusters.

(Rigorous) (Skill 15.11)

8. Which of the following correctly lists the periods that comprise the Mesozoic era, from earliest to most recent?

    A. Jurassic, Triassic, Cretaceous

    B. Permian, Triassic, Jurassic

    C. Triassic, Jurassic, Cretaceous

    D. Triassic, Jurassic, Permian

(Average) (Skill 13.7)

9. A glass rod becomes positively charged when it is rubbed with silk. This net positive charge accumulates because the glass rod:

    A. Gains electrons

    B. Gains protons

    C. Loses electrons

    D. Loses protons

(Average) (Skill 13.8)

10. Which property determines the direction of the exchange of internal energy between two objects?

    A. Temperature

    B. Specific heat

    C. Mass

    D. Density

(Average) (Skill 13.3)

11. Which statement is consistent with the kinetic theory of ideal gases?

    A. Molecules transfer energy through collisions.

    B. Molecules are always stationary.

    C. The force of attraction between molecules is constant.

    D. The size of the molecules is large compared to the distance that separates them.

(Average) (Skill 13.8)

12. What is the boiling point of water at standard pressure on the Kelvin Scale?

    A. 272 K

    B. 273 K

    C. 372 K

    D. 373 K

(Average) (Skill 13.1)

13. Sunglasses that reduce glare are:

    A. Transparent

    B. Translucent

    C. Cloudy

    D. Polarized

(Average) (Skill 13.1)

14. **Which of the following is translucent?**

    A. A car windshield

    B. A convex mirror

    C. A frosted light bulb

    D. A concrete block

(Easy) (Skill 13.8)

15. **Light is a form of:**

    A. Heat

    B. Electricity

    C. Energy

    D. Sound

(Average) (Skill 13.8)

16. **Which is NOT found in the electromagnetic spectrum?**

    A. X-rays

    B. Infrared light

    C. FM radio waves

    D. Sound waves

(Average) (Skill 13.10)

17. **An object's ability to float depends on its:**

    A. Size

    B. Temperature

    C. Insulation

    D. Density

(Rigorous) (Skill 13.8)

18. **The molecules of a _____ tend to be packed tightly in an organized way.**

    A. gas

    B. solid

    C. liquid

    D. neutron

(Average) (Skill 13.3)

19. **Water can turn from liquid to gas by evaporating or _____.**

    A. condensing

    B. pouring

    C. boiling

    D. freezing

(Average) (Skill 14.4)

20. **Earth gets its heat from:**

    A. Trees

    B. Convection

    C. Greenhouses

    D. The Sun

(Average) (Skill 14.5)

21. **When a cool air mass and a warm air mass meet and stay over an area for days without moving, this is referred to as a(n):**

    A. Warm front

    B. Occluded front

    C. Stationary front

    D. Cool front

(Average) (Skill 13.7)

22. **A balance between energy lost and energy gained is called:**

    A. The greenhouse effect

    B. Climate

    C. Solar energy

    D. Radiative balance

(Rigorous) (Skill 14.2)

23. **The main ingredient in soil is:**

    A. Bacteria

    B. Weathered rock

    C. Decayed animal material

    D. Decayed plant material

(Rigorous) (Skill 14.2)

24. **Fossils are most often found in:**

    A. Sedimentary rock

    B. Lava

    C. Sand

    D. Igneous rock

(Rigorous) (Skill 14.4)

25. **The moon is unlivable compared to the Earth because:**

    A. There is no air to breathe

    B. There is no water to drink

    C. The surface temperature can be hotter than boiling water

    D. All of the above

(Rigorous) (Skill 14.4)

26. **Earth's thickest layer is called the:**

    A. Mantle

    B. Crust

    C. Inner core

    D. Outer core

(Rigorous) (Skill 15.1)

27. **Insects, spiders, lobsters, and crabs are all:**

    A. Mammals

    B. Amphibians

    C. Arthropods

    D. Syrphids

(Rigorous) (Skill 14.4)

28. **Which statement explains why the Sun appears to rise and set each day?**

    A. Earth rotates

    B. The Sun rotates

    C. The Sun revolves around Earth

    D. Earth revolves around the Sun

(Average) (Skill 15.1)

29. **The skeletons of sharks are made up of:**

    A. Scales

    B. Bones

    C. Fins

    D. Cartilage

(Average) (Skill 15.1)

30. Adult frogs breathe with their:

    A. Gills

    B. Lungs

    C. Cartilage

    D. Mollusks

(Average) (Skill 13.10)

31. A baseball and a sheet of paper are dropped at the same time from the same height. If there is no air resistance, then:

    A. The baseball will land first

    B. The paper will float slowly through the air

    C. The baseball will float slowly through the air

    D. The baseball and the paper will land at the same time

(Average) (Skill 13.10)

32. An object is accelerated when it is acted on by:

    A. An unbalanced force

    B. A balanced force

    C. Inertia

    D. Velocity

(Easy) (Skill 13.1)

33. Everything in our world is made up of _____.

    A. matter

    B. cells

    C. grams

    D. molecules

(Average) (Skill 14.8)

34. The closest planet to the Sun, its surface has craters and rocks, and its atmosphere is composed of hydrogen, helium, and sodium:

    A. Mercury

    B. Mars

    C. Jupiter

    D. Venus

(Easy) (Skill 13.1)

35. During his lesson, Mr. McGovern's pen rolled off his desk. He used this example to demonstrate that _____ is the measure of the Earth's pull of gravity on an object.

    A. matter

    B. weight

    C. mass

    D. molecules

(Average) (Skill 13.2)

36. This does not produce a new substance:

    A. Physical property

    B. Chemical property

    C. Physical change

    D. Chemical change

(Rigorous) (Skill 13.2)

37. During class, Ms. Barnes asked her students to help her follow a recipe for baking a cake. She noted to them that the substances she was using were being turned into another substance. This example demonstrates a:

    A. Physical property

    B. Chemical property

    C. Physical change

    D. Chemical change

(Rigorous) (Skill 13.2)

38. The ability of a substance to be changed into new substances:

    A. Physical property

    B. Chemical property

    C. Physical change

    D. Chemical change

(Rigorous) (Skill 13.4)

39. The smallest particle of an element that retains the properties of that element.

    A. Molecule

    B. Substance

    C. Compound

    D. Atom

(Easy) (Skill 13.8)

40. A measure of energy:

    A. Temperature

    B. Heat

    C. Mass

    D. Conduction

(Rigorous) (Skill 13.8)

41. The amount of heat energy it takes to raise the temperature of the object by one degree Celsius:

    A. Temperature

    B. Heat capacity

    C. Heat energy

    D. Conduction

(Rigorous) (Skill 13.2)

42. These are made up of one kind of particle, formed during a chemical change, and broken down only by chemical changes:

    A. Elements

    B. Solutions

    C. Mixtures

    D. Compounds

(Rigorous) (Skill 13.2)

43. All _____ contain the elements oxygen and hydrogen.

    A. bases

    B. solutions

    C. mixtures

    D. compounds

(Rigorous) (Skill 13.2)

44. _____ are compounds that are formed when oxygen combines with another element.

    A. Bases

    B. Oxides

    C. Mixtures

    D. Solutions

(Rigorous) (Skill 13.3)

45. _____ is the ability to cause change in matter.

    A. Movement

    B. Motion

    C. Conduction

    D. Energy

(Rigorous) (Skill 13.2)

46. Plasma is a gas that has been _____, meaning that at least one electron has been removed from some of its atoms.

    A. depleted

    B. compressed

    C. ionized

    D. condensed

(Rigorous) (Skill 13.2)

47. A nucleus surrounded by a cloud with moving electrons:

    A. Atom

    B. Proton

    C. Neutron

    D. Molecule

(Easy) (Skill 13.8)

48. The amount of energy it takes to raise one gram of water one degree Celsius:

    A. Thermal equilibrium

    B. Thermal unit

    C. Kilocalorie

    D. Calorie

(Rigorous) (Skill 13.8)

49. An object's _____ gives it a reluctance to change its state of motion. It is also the measure of an object's resistance to _____.

    A. weight; gravity

    B. mass; gravity

    C. weight; acceleration

    D. mass; acceleration

(Easy) (Skill 13.8)

50. A resistance to motion is known as:

    A. Friction

    B. Force

    C. Gravity

    D. Acceleration

(Rigorous) (Skill 14.8)

51. The second largest planet in the solar system, this planet has rings of ice, rock, and dust particles circling it, and its atmosphere is composed of hydrogen, helium, methane, and ammonia.

    A. Jupiter

    B. Mars

    C. Saturn

    D. Uranus

(Easy) (Skill 13.8)

52. The centripetal force that keeps a satellite circling the Earth:

    A. Friction

    B. Force

    C. Gravity

    D. Acceleration

(Easy) (Skill 13.8)

53. Materials through which electric charges can easily flow are called:

    A. Conductors

    B. Insulators

    C. Neutrons

    D. Ions

(Easy) (Skill 14.1)

54. _____ are those built by both lava flows and layers of ash and cinders.

    A. Shield volcanoes

    B. Ash volcanoes

    C. Cinder-cone volcanoes

    D. Composite volcanoes

(Easy) (Skill 14.1)

55. When lava cools, this type of rock is formed:

    A. Metamorphic

    B. Sedimentary

    C. Igneous

    D. Composite

(Rigorous) (Skill 14.1)

56. Huge wind systems that cover large geographic areas and that reverse direction seasonally are known as:

    A. El Niño

    B. Hurricanes

    C. Monsoons

    D. Sea breezes

(Rigorous) (Skill 14.8)

57. The largest planet in the solar system containing sixteen satellites and an atmosphere composed of hydrogen, helium, methane, and ammonia:

    A. Jupiter

    B. Mars

    C. Venus

    D. Uranus

(Easy) (Skill 11.8)

58. Mr. Michalak's lab groups are measuring a liquid using graduated cylinders. Before expecting the students to accurately measure, he must teach them to read each measurement in the following way:

    A. At the highest point of the liquid

    B. At the bottom of the meniscus curve

    C. At the closest mark to the top of the liquid

    D. At the top of the plastic safety ring

(Easy) (Skill 12.1)

59. When is a hypothesis formed?

    A. Before the data is taken

    B. After the data is taken

    C. After the data is analyzed

    D. Concurrent with graphing the data

(Average) (Skill 14.6)

60. Which of the following is the most accurate definition of a nonrenewable resource?

A. A nonrenewable resource is never replaced once used.

B. A nonrenewable resource is replaced on a time scale that is very long relative to human life-spans.

C. A nonrenewable resource is a resource that can only be manufactured by humans.

D. A nonrenewable resource is a species that has already become extinct.

Science Answer Key

ANSWER KEY					
1. B	11. A	21. C	31. A	41. B	51. C
2. C	12. D	22. D	32. A	42. D	52. C
3. A	13. D	23. B	33. A	43. A	53. A
4. D	14. C	24. A	34. A	44. B	54. D
5. D	15. C	25. D	35. B	45. D	55. C
6. A	16. D	26. A	36. C	46. C	56. C
7. B	17. D	27. C	37. D	47. A	57. A
8. C	18. B	28. A	38. B	48. D	58. B
9. C	19. C	29. D	39. D	49. D	59. A
10. A	20. D	30. B	40. B	50. A	60. B

Science Rigor Table

RIGOR TABLE	
Rigor Level	Questions
Easy	15, 33, 35, 40, 48, 50, 52, 53, 54, 55, 58, 59
Average	3, 4, 5, 6, 7, 9, 10, 11, 12, 13, 14, 16, 17, 19, 20, 21, 22, 29, 30, 31, 32, 34, 36, 60
Rigorous	1, 2, 8, 18, 23, 24, 25, 26, 27, 28, 37, 38, 39, 41, 42, 43, 44, 45, 46, 47, 49, 51, 56, 57

Science Answers with Rationales

(Rigorous) (Skill 14.8)

1. Which of the following is the best definition for meteorite?

   A. A meteorite is a mineral composed of mica and feldspar

   B. A meteorite is material from outer space that has struck the Earth's surface

   C. A meteorite is an element that has properties of both metals and nonmetals

   D. A meteorite is a very small unit of length measurement

   Answer: B. A meteorite is material from outer space that has struck the Earth's surface

   More than 90 percent of meteorites are of rock, while the remainder consist mostly or partly of iron and nickel.

(Rigorous) (Skill 15.3)

2. Identify the correct sequence of organization of living things from lower to higher order:

   A. Cell, Organelle, Organ, Tissue, System, Organism

   B. Cell, Tissue, Organ, Organelle, System, Organism

   C. Organelle, Cell, Tissue, Organ, System, Organism

   D. Organelle, Tissue, Cell, Organ, System, Organism

Answer: C. Organelle, Cell, Tissue, Organ, System, Organism

This sequence correctly organizes from lower to higher order: Organelle, Cell, Tissue, Organ, System, Organism.

(Average) (Skill 13.3)

3. The following are examples of chemical reactions EXCEPT:

   A. Melting ice into water

   B. Dissolving a seltzer tablet in water

   C. Using a fire-cracker

   D. Burning a piece of plastic

   Answer: A. Melting ice into water

   Melting ice into water is not considered a chemical reaction. A chemical reaction is the change of a substance into a new one that has a different chemical identity.

(Average) (Skill 14.9)

4. All of the following professions are classified under "Earth Sciences" EXCEPT:

   A. Geologist

   B. Meteorologist

   C. Seismologist

   D. Biochemist

   Answer: D. Biochemist

   A career in biochemistry falls under the Life Sciences category.

(Average) (Skill 11.2)

5. **When teaching Science rules pertaining to safety, Mrs. Miller explains to her students that chemicals should be stored**

   A. in the principal's office.

   B. in a dark room.

   C. in an off-site research facility.

   D. according to their reactivity with other substances.

   Answer: D. according to their reactivity with other substances.

   Chemicals should be stored with other chemicals of similar properties (e.g. acids with other acids), to reduce the potential for either hazardous reactions in the store-room, or mistakes in reagent use. Certainly, chemicals should not be stored in anyone's office, and the light intensity of the room is not very important because light-sensitive chemicals are usually stored in dark containers. In fact, good lighting is desirable in a store-room, so that labels can be read easily. Chemicals may be stored off-site, but that makes their use inconvenient. Therefore, the best answer is (D).

(Average) (Skill 10.4)

6. **Social skills and values developed by activity include all of the following EXCEPT:**

   A. Winning at all costs

   B. Making judgments in groups

   C. Communicating and cooperating

   D. Respecting rules and property

   Answer: A. Winning at all costs

"Winning at all costs" does not emphasize social skills and values.

(Average) (Skill 14.8)

7. **Which of the following statements about galaxies is true?**

   A. Galaxies are the only structures in the universe that do not contain dark matter.

   B. Galaxies are gravitationally bound, meaning structures within the galaxy orbit around its center.

   C. Galaxies typically contain over one trillion stars.

   D. Galaxies are comprised of clusters and superclusters.

   Answer: B. Galaxies are gravitationally bound, meaning structures within the galaxy orbit around its center.

   It is true that galaxies are gravitationally bound so that structures within them orbit around the center. Galaxies do contain dark matter, and only the largest "giant" galaxies contain over one trillion stars. The smallest "dwarf" galaxies contain as few as 10 million stars. Clusters and superclusters are comprised of many galaxies.

(Rigorous) (Skill 15.11)

8. **Which of the following correctly lists the periods that comprise the Mesozoic era, from earliest to most recent?**

   A. Jurassic, Triassic, Cretaceous

   B. Permian, Triassic, Jurassic

   C. Triassic, Jurassic, Cretaceous

   D. Triassic, Jurassic, Permian

   Answer: C. Triassic, Jurassic, Cretaceous

The Mesozoic era is comprised of the Triassic, Jurassic, and Cretaceous periods. It was preceded by the Paleozoic era, of which the Permian is the last period. The Triassic period ended about 200 million years ago, and was followed by the Jurassic period. The Jurassic period gave way to the Cretaceous period just under 150 million years ago.

(Average) (Skill 13.7)

9. **A glass rod becomes positively charged when it is rubbed with silk. This net positive charge accumulates because the glass rod:**

    A. Gains electrons

    B. Gains protons

    C. Loses electrons

    D. Loses protons

    Answer: C. Loses electrons

    A glass rod becomes positively charged when it is rubbed with silk. This net positive charge accumulates because the glass rod loses electrons.

(Average) (Skill 13.8)

10. **Which property determines the direction of the exchange of internal energy between two objects?**

    A. Temperature

    B. Specific heat

    C. Mass

    D. Density

    Answer: A. Temperature

Temperature determines the direction of the exchange of internal energy between two objects.

(Average) (Skill 13.3)

11. **Which statement is consistent with the kinetic theory of ideal gases?**

    A. Molecules transfer energy through collisions.

    B. Molecules are always stationary.

    C. The force of attraction between molecules is constant.

    D. The size of the molecules is large compared to the distance that separates them.

    Answer: A. Molecules transfer energy through collisions.

    Molecules transfer energy through collisions. This is a consistent statement true to the kinetic theory of all ideal gases.

(Average) (Skill 13.8)

12. **What is the boiling point of water at standard pressure on the Kelvin Scale?**

    A. 272 K

    B. 273 K

    C. 372 K

    D. 373 K

    Answer: D. 373 K

    The boiling point of water is 373 K.

(Average) (Skill 13.1)

13. **Sunglasses that reduce glare are:**

   A. Transparent

   B. Translucent

   C. Cloudy

   D. Polarized

Answer: D. Polarized

Sunglasses that reduce glare are polarized.

(Average) (Skill 13.1)

14. **Which of the following is translucent?**

   A. A car windshield

   B. A convex mirror

   C. A frosted light bulb

   D. A concrete block

Answer: C. A frosted light bulb

A frosted light bulb is translucent, meaning that it allows light to pass through it in a diffused manner.

(Easy) (Skill 13.8)

15. **Light is a form of:**

   A. Heat

   B. Electricity

   C. Energy

   D. Sound

Answer: C. Energy

Light is a form of energy.

(Average) (Skill 13.8)

16. **Which is NOT found in the electromagnetic spectrum?**

   A. X-rays

   B. Infrared light

   C. FM radio waves

   D. Sound waves

Answer: D. Sound waves

Sound waves are not found in the electromagnetic spectrum.

(Average) (Skill 13.10)

17. **An object's ability to float depends on its:**

   A. Size

   B. Temperature

   C. Insulation

   D. Density

Answer: D. Density

An object's ability to float depends on its density.

(Rigorous) (Skill 13.8)

18. **The molecules of a _____ tend to be packed tightly in an organized way.**

   A. gas

   B. solid

   C. liquid

   D. neutron

Answer: B. solid

A characteristic of a solid is its tightly-packed molecules.

(Average) (Skill 13.3)

19. **Water can turn from liquid to gas by evaporating or _____.**

    A. condensing

    B. pouring

    C. boiling

    D. freezing

Answer: C. boiling

Water can turn from liquid to gas by evaporating or boiling.

(Average) (Skill 14.4)

20. **Earth gets its heat from:**

    A. Trees

    B. Convection

    C. Greenhouses

    D. The Sun

Answer: D. The Sun

Earth gets its heat from the Sun.

(Average) (Skill 14.5)

21. **When a cool air mass and a warm air mass meet and stay over an area for days without moving, this is referred to as a(n):**

    A. Warm front

    B. Occluded front

    C. Stationary front

    D. Cool front

Answer: C. Stationary front

A stationary front is a collection of air masses, neither of which is strong enough to replace the other. On a weather map, this is shown by an inter-playing series of blue spikes pointing one direction and red domes pointing the other.

(Average) (Skill 13.7)

22. **A balance between energy lost and energy gained is called:**

    A. The greenhouse effect

    B. Climate

    C. Solar energy

    D. Radiative balance

Answer: D. Radiative balance

Radiative balance is the balance between energy lost and energy gained.

(Rigorous) (Skill 14.2)

23. **The main ingredient in soil is:**

    A. Bacteria

    B. Weathered rock

    C. Decayed animal material

    D. Decayed plant material

Answer: B. Weathered rock

The main ingredient in soil is weathered rock.

(Rigorous) (Skill 14.2)

24. **Fossils are most often found in:**

    A. Sedimentary rock

    B. Lava

    C. Sand

    D. Igneous rock

    Answer: A. Sedimentary rock

    Fossils are found in sedimentary rock.

(Rigorous) (Skill 14.4)

25. **The moon is unlivable compared to the Earth because:**

    A. There is no air to breathe

    B. There is no water to drink

    C. The surface temperature can be hotter than boiling water

    D. All of the above

    Answer: D. All of the above

    Humans cannot live on the moon because there is no air to breathe, no water to drink, and the surface temperature can be hotter than boiling water.

(Rigorous) (Skill 14.4)

26. **Earth's thickest layer is called the:**

    A. Mantle

    B. Crust

    C. Inner core

    D. Outer core

    Answer: A. Mantle

    Earth's thickest layer is known as the mantle.

(Rigorous) (Skill 15.1)

27. **Insects, spiders, lobsters, and crabs are all:**

    A. Mammals

    B. Amphibians

    C. Arthropods

    D. Syrphids

    Answer: C. Arthropods

    Insects, spiders, lobsters, and crabs are all arthropods. An arthropod is an invertebrate animal having an exoskeleton, a segmented body, and jointed appendages.

(Rigorous) (Skill 14.4)

28. **Which statement explains why the Sun appears to rise and set each day?**

    A. Earth rotates

    B. The Sun rotates

    C. The Sun revolves around Earth

    D. Earth revolves around the Sun

    Answer: A. Earth rotates

    The Earth rotates, therefore the Sun appears to rise and set each day.

(Average) (Skill 15.1)

29. **The skeletons of sharks are made up of:**

    A. Scales

    B. Bones

    C. Fins

    D. Cartilage

    Answer: D. Cartilage

    Shark skeletons are made purely of cartilage and connective tissue, or muscle.

(Average) (Skill 15.1)

30. **Adult frogs breathe with their:**

    A. Gills

    B. Lungs

    C. Cartilage

    D. Mollusks

    Answer: B. Lungs

    As a frog matures from tadpole to adult, it loses its gills and develops functioning lungs.

(Average) (Skill 13.10)

31. **A baseball and a sheet of paper are dropped at the same time from the same height. If there is no air resistance, then:**

    A. The baseball will land first

    B. The paper will float slowly through the air

    C. The baseball will float slowly through the air

    D. The baseball and the paper will land at the same time

    Answer: A. The baseball will land first.

    If a baseball and sheet of paper are dropped at the same time from the same height, the baseball will land first.

(Average) (Skill 13.10)

32. **An object is accelerated when it is acted on by:**

    A. An unbalanced force

    B. A balanced force

    C. Inertia

    D. Velocity

Answer: A. An unbalanced force

An object is accelerated when it is acted on by an unbalanced force.

(Easy) (Skill 13.1)

33. **Everything in our world is made up of _____.**

    A. matter

    B. cells

    C. grams

    D. molecules

Answer: A. matter

Everything in our world is made up of matter. Matter is defined by two characteristics: It takes up space and it has mass.

(Average) (Skill 14.8)

34. **The closest planet to the Sun, its surface has craters and rocks, and its atmosphere is composed of hydrogen, helium, and sodium:**

    A. Mercury

    B. Mars

    C. Jupiter

    D. Venus

Answer: A. Mercury

The closest planet to the Sun, Mercury's surface has craters and rocks. The atmosphere is composed of hydrogen, helium, and sodium. Mercury was named after the Roman messenger god.

(Easy) (Skill 13.1)

35. During his lesson, Mr. McGovern's pen rolled off his desk. He used this example to demonstrate that _____ is the measure of the Earth's pull of gravity on an object.

    A. matter

    B. weight

    C. mass

    D. molecules

Answer: B. weight

Weight is the measure of the Earth's pull of gravity on an object. It can also be defined as the pull of gravity between other bodies. The units of weight measurement commonly used are the pound (English measure) and the kilogram (metric measure).

(Average) (Skill 13.2)

36. This does not produce a new substance:

    A. Physical property

    B. Chemical property

    C. Physical change

    D. Chemical change

Answer: C. Physical change

A physical change is a change that does not produce a new substance. The freezing and melting of water is an example of a physical change.

(Rigorous) (Skill 13.2)

37. During class, Ms. Barnes asked her students to help her follow a recipe for baking a cake. She noted to them that the substances she was using were being turned into another substance. This example demonstrates a:

    A. Physical property

    B. Chemical property

    C. Physical change

    D. Chemical change

Answer: D. Chemical change

A chemical change (or chemical reaction) is any change of a substance into one or more other substances. Burning materials turn into smoke; a seltzer tablet fizzes into gas bubbles. When steel rusts, the composition of the material has undergone a change. Rusting and burning are examples of chemical changes.

(Rigorous) (Skill 13.2)

38. The ability of a substance to be changed into new substances:

    A. Physical property

    B. Chemical property

    C. Physical change

    D. Chemical change

Answer: B. Chemical property

A chemical property describes the ability of a substance to be changed into new substances. Baking powder goes through a chemical change as it changes into carbon dioxide gas during the baking process.

(Rigorous) (Skill 13.4)

39. **The smallest particle of an element that retains the properties of that element.**

    A. Molecule

    B. Substance

    C. Compound

    D. Atom

Answer: D. Atom

An atom is the smallest particle of an element that retains the properties of that element. All of the atoms of a particular element are the same. The atoms of each element are different from the atoms of other elements.

(Easy) (Skill 13.8)

40. **A measure of energy:**

    A. Temperature

    B. Heat

    C. Mass

    D. Conduction

Answer: B. Heat

Heat is a measure of energy. It is known as thermal energy.

(Rigorous) (Skill 13.8)

41. **The amount of heat energy it takes to raise the temperature of the object by one degree Celsius:**

    A. Temperature

    B. Heat capacity

    C. Heat energy

    D. Conduction

Answer: B. Heat capacity

The heat capacity of an object is the amount of heat energy it takes to raise the temperature of the object by one degree. Heat capacity (C) per unit mass (m) is called specific heat.

(Rigorous) (Skill 13.2)

42. **These are made up of one kind of particle, formed during a chemical change, and broken down only by chemical changes:**

    A. Elements

    B. Solutions

    C. Mixtures

    D. Compounds

Answer: D. Compounds

Compounds are made up of one kind of particle, formed during a chemical change, broken down only by chemical changes, their properties are different from their parts, and they have a specific amount of each of their ingredients.

(Rigorous) (Skill 13.2)

43. **All _____ contain the elements oxygen and hydrogen.**

    A. bases

    B. solutions

    C. mixtures

    D. compounds

Answer: A. bases

All bases contain the elements oxygen and hydrogen (OH). Many household cleaning products contain bases.

(Rigorous) (Skill 13.2)

44. _____ are compounds that are formed when oxygen combines with another element.

    A. Bases

    B. Oxides

    C. Mixtures

    D. Solutions

Answer: B. Oxides

Oxides are compounds that are formed when oxygen combines with another element. Rust is an oxide formed when oxygen combines with iron.

(Rigorous) (Skill 13.3)

45. _____ is the ability to cause change in matter.

    A. Movement

    B. Motion

    C. Conduction

    D. Energy

Answer: D. Energy

Energy is the ability to cause change in matter. Applying heat to a frozen liquid changes it from solid back to liquid. Continue heating it and it will boil and give off steam, a gas.

(Rigorous) (Skill 13.2)

46. Plasma is a gas that has been _____, meaning that at least one electron has been removed from some of its atoms.

    A. depleted

    B. compressed

    C. ionized

    D. condensed

Answer: C. ionized

While plasma is a type of gas, its properties are so distinct that it is considered a unique phase of matter. Plasma is a gas that has been ionized, meaning that at least one electron has been removed from some of its atoms.

(Rigorous) (Skill 13.2)

47. A nucleus surrounded by a cloud with moving electrons:

    A. Atom

    B. Proton

    C. Neutron

    D. Molecule

Answer: A. Atom

An atom is a nucleus surrounded by a cloud with moving electrons.

(Easy) (Skill 13.8)

48. The amount of energy it takes to raise one gram of water one degree Celsius:

    A. Thermal equilibrium

    B. Thermal unit

    C. Kilocalorie

    D. Calorie

FTCE ELEMENTARY EDUCATION K–6

Answer: D. Calorie

A calorie is the amount of energy it takes to raise one gram of water one degree Celsius.

(Rigorous) (Skill 13.8)

49. An object's _____ gives it a reluctance to change its state of motion. It is also the measure of an object's resistance to _____.

    A. weight; gravity

    B. mass; gravity

    C. weight; acceleration

    D. mass; acceleration

Answer: D. mass; acceleration

An object's mass gives it a reluctance to change its state of motion. It is also the measure of an object's resistance to acceleration. The force that the Earth's gravity exerts on an object with a specific mass is called the object's weight on Earth.

(Easy) (Skill 13.8)

50. A resistance to motion is known as:

    A. Friction

    B. Force

    C. Gravity

    D. Acceleration

Answer: A. Friction

Surfaces that touch each other have a certain resistance to motion. This resistance is friction.

(Rigorous) (Skill 14.8)

51. The second largest planet in the solar system, this planet has rings of ice, rock, and dust particles circling it, and its atmosphere is composed of hydrogen, helium, methane, and ammonia.

    A. Jupiter

    B. Mars

    C. Saturn

    D. Uranus

Answer: C. Saturn

The second largest planet in the solar system, Saturn has rings of ice, rock, and dust particles circling it. Its atmosphere is composed of hydrogen, helium, methane, and ammonia. It has more than twenty satellites. Saturn was named after the Roman god of agriculture.

(Easy) (Skill 13.8)

52. The centripetal force that keeps a satellite circling the Earth:

    A. Friction

    B. Force

    C. Gravity

    D. Acceleration

Answer: C. Gravity

When an object moves in a circular path, a force must be directed toward the center of the circle in order to keep the motion going. This constraining force is called centripetal force. Gravity is the centripetal force that keeps a satellite circling the Earth.

(Easy) (Skill 13.8)

53. **Materials through which electric charges can easily flow are called:**

   A. Conductors

   B. Insulators

   C. Neutrons

   D. Ions

   Answer: A. Conductors

   Materials through which electric charges can easily flow are called conductors. Metals that are good conductors include silicon and boron.

(Easy) (Skill 14.1)

54. **_____ are those built by both lava flows and layers of ash and cinders.**

   A. Shield volcanoes

   B. Ash volcanoes

   C. Cinder-cone volcanoes

   D. Composite volcanoes

   Answer: D. Composite volcanoes

   Composite volcanoes are those built by both lava flows and layers of ash and cinders. Mount Fuji in Japan, Mount St. Helens in the United States, and Mount Vesuvius in Italy are all famous composite volcanoes.

(Easy) (Skill 14.1)

55. **When lava cools, this type of rock is formed:**

   A. Metamorphic

   B. Sedimentary

   C. Igneous

   D. Composite

   Answer: C. Igneous

   When lava cools, igneous rock is formed. This formation can occur either above or below ground.

(Rigorous) (Skill 14.1)

56. **Huge wind systems that cover large geographic areas and that reverse direction seasonally are known as:**

   A. El Niño

   B. Hurricanes

   C. Monsoons

   D. Sea breezes

   Answer: C. Monsoons

   Monsoons are huge wind systems that cover large geographic areas and that reverse direction seasonally. The monsoons of India and Asia are examples of these seasonal winds. They alternate wet and dry seasons. As denser, cooler air over the ocean moves inland, a steady seasonal wind called a summer, or wet, monsoon is produced.

(Rigorous) (Skill 14.8)

57. The largest planet in the solar system containing sixteen satellites and an atmosphere composed of hydrogen, helium, methane, and ammonia:

    A. Jupiter

    B. Mars

    C. Venus

    D. Uranus

Answer: A. Jupiter

The largest planet in the solar system, Jupiter has sixteen satellites. The atmosphere is composed of hydrogen, helium, methane, and ammonia. There are white-colored bands of clouds indicating rising gases and dark-colored bands of clouds indicating descending gases. The gas movement is caused by heat resulting from the energy of Jupiter's core. Jupiter has a strong magnetic field and a great red spot that is thought to be a hurricane-like cloud.

(Easy) (Skill 11.8)

58. Mr. Michalak's lab groups are measuring a liquid using graduated cylinders. Before expecting the students to accurately measure, he must teach them to read each measurement in the following way:

    A. At the highest point of the liquid

    B. At the bottom of the meniscus curve

    C. At the closest mark to the top of the liquid

    D. At the top of the plastic safety ring

Answer: B. At the bottom of the meniscus curve

To measure water in glass, you must look at the top surface at eye-level, and ascertain the location of the bottom of the meniscus (the curved surface at the top of the water). The meniscus forms because water molecules adhere to the sides of the glass, which is a slightly stronger force than their cohesion to each other. This leads to a U-shaped top of the liquid column, the bottom of which gives the most accurate volume measurement. (Other liquids have different forces, e.g. mercury in glass, which has a convex meniscus.) This is consistent only with answer (B).

(Easy) (Skill 12.1)

59. **When is a hypothesis formed?**

    A. Before the data is taken

    B. After the data is taken

    C. After the data is analyzed

    D. Concurrent with graphing the data

Answer: A. Before the data is taken

A hypothesis is an educated guess, made before undertaking an experiment. The hypothesis is then evaluated based on the observed data. Therefore, the hypothesis must be formed before the data is taken, not during or after the experiment. This is consistent only with answer (A).

(Average) (Skill 14.6)

60. **Which of the following is the most accurate definition of a nonrenewable resource?**

    A. A nonrenewable resource is never replaced once used.

    B. A nonrenewable resource is replaced on a time scale that is very long relative to human life-spans.

    C. A nonrenewable resource is a resource that can only be manufactured by humans.

    D. A nonrenewable resource is a species that has already become extinct.

    Answer: B. A nonrenewable resource is replaced on a time scale that is very long relative to human life-spans.

    Renewable resources are those that are renewed, or replaced, in time for humans to use more of them. Examples include fast-growing plants, animals, or oxygen gas. (Note that while sunlight is often considered a renewable resource, it is actually a nonrenewable but extremely abundant resource.) Nonrenewable resources are those that renew themselves only on very long time scales, usually geologic time scales. Examples include minerals, metals, or fossil fuels. Therefore, the correct answer is (B).

Mathematics

(Rigorous) (Skill 16.3)

1. Which of the following is an irrational number?

    A. 0.36262626262...

    B. 4

    C. 8.2

    D. -5

(Easy) (Skill 16.3)

2. 4,087,361

    What number represents the ten-thousands place?

    A. 4

    B. 6

    C. 0

    D. 8

(Rigorous) (Skill 16.6)

3. Two kids are selling lemonade on the side of the road and want to raise at least $320. If the materials needed (lemons, pitcher, table, etc.) to run a lemonade stand cost $15, how many glasses of lemonade will they need to sell if each glass costs $6?

    A. 210 glasses

    B. 61 glasses

    C. 74 glasses

    D. 53 glasses

(Average) (Skill 19.1)

4. If a right triangle has a hypotenuse of 10 cm and one leg of 6 cm, what is the measure of the other leg?

    A. 7 cm

    B. 5 cm

    C. 8 cm

    D. 9 cm

(Easy) (Skill 18.3)

5. 3 km is equivalent to:

    A. 300 cm

    B. 300 m

    C. 3000 cm

    D. 3000 m

(Average) (Skill 19.3)

6. All of the following are examples of obtuse angles EXCEPT:

    A. 110 degrees

    B. 90 degrees

    C. 135 degrees

    D. 91 degrees

(Average) (Skill 19.1)

7. Given the formula $d = rt$ (where d = distance, r = rate, and t = time), calculate the time required for a vehicle to travel 585 miles at a rate of 65 miles per hour.

    A. 8.5 hours

    B. 6.5 hours

    C. 9.5 hours

    D. 9 hours

(Rigorous) (Skill 16.7)

8. Permutation is:

A. The number of possible arrangements, without repetition, where order of selection is not important

B. The number of possible arrangements, with repetition, where order of selection is not important

C. The number of possible arrangements of items, without repetition, where order of selection is important

D. The number of possible arrangements of items, with repetition, where order of selection is important

(Average) (Skill 17.1)

9. If 300 peppermints cost you x dollars, how many peppermints can you purchase for 50 cents at the same rate?

A. $\frac{150}{x}$

B. $150x$

C. $6x$

D. $\frac{1500}{x}$

(Average) (Skill 17.2)

10. Megan is able to sell a painting for $670, a 35% profit over her cost. How much did the painting originally cost her?

A. $496.30

B. $512.40

C. $555.40

D. $574.90

(Average) (Skill 17.2)

11. If Melinda can paint a house in 4 hours, and David can paint the same house in 6 hour, how long will it take for both of them to paint the house together?

A. 2 hours and 24 minutes

B. 3 hours and 12 minutes

C. 3 hours and 44 minutes

D. 4 hours and 10 minutes

(Rigorous) (Skill 17.2)

12. Sam arrived at work at 8:15 A.M. and left work at 10:30 P.M. If Sam gets paid by the hour at a rate of $10 and time and $\frac{1}{2}$ for any hours worked over 8 in a day. How much did Sam get paid?

A. $120.25

B. $160.75

C. $173.75

D. $180

(Rigorous) (Skill 17.1)

13. Angelo wants to invest $4,000 at 6% simple interest rate for 5 years. How much interest will he receive?

A. $240

B. $480

C. $720

D. $1,200

(Average) (Skill 17.3)

14. The sales price of a motorcycle is $12,590, which is 20% off the original price. What is the original price?

    A. $14,310.40

    B. $14,990.90

    C. $15,290.70

    D. $15,737.50

(Average) (Skill 17.2)

15. You need to add 240 pencils and 6 staplers to your supply list for next school year. Pencils are purchased in sets of 6 for $2.35 per pack. Staplers are sold in sets of 2 for 12.95. How much will purchasing these products cost?

    A. $132.85

    B. $145.75

    C. $162.90

    D. $225.25

(Easy) (Skill 17.8)

16. Round 917.457 to the nearest tens place.

    A. 918.0

    B. 920

    C. 917.5

    D. 900

(Average) (Skill 17.2)

17. Over the course of a week, Landon spent $28.49 on lunch. What was the average cost per day?

    A. $4.07

    B. $3.57

    C. $6.51

    D. $2.93

(Easy) (Skill 17.8)

18. In the number 913.85, which digit represents the tenths space?

    A. 8

    B. 3

    C. 1

    D. 5

(Easy) (Skill 19.1)

19. What is the median of the following list of numbers?

    4, 5, 7, 9, 10, 12

    A. 6

    B. 7.5

    C. 7.8

    D. 8

(Average) (Skill 17.1)

20. What is the absolute value of -9?

    A. -9

    B. 9

    C. 0

    D. -1

(Rigorous) (Skill 19.5)

21. A scale on a map states that every $\frac{1}{4}$ of an inch represents 20 miles. If two cities are $3\frac{1}{2}$ inches apart, how many miles are actually between the two cities?

    A. 20 miles

    B. 125 miles

    C. 230 miles

    D. 280 miles

(Average) (Skill 18.5)

22. A women's basketball team won 24 games and lost 32. What is the ratio of games lost to the number of games played?

    A. 32:24

    B. 4:3

    C. 3:4

    D. 4:7

(Average) (Skill 19.5)

23. Maddox has a 20 dollar bill and a 5 dollar bill. If he purchases two items, one for $11.23 and the other for $8.32, then how much money does he have left over?

    A. $3.75

    B. $5.45

    C. $6.34

    D. $7.77

(Average) (Skill 20.1)

24. In triangle *ABC*, *AB* = *BC* and (*C*'s measure is 65°). What is the measure of angle *B*?

    A. 40°

    B. 50°

    C. 60°

    D. 65°

(Average) (Skill 17.2)

25. If $8x + 5 = 21$, then $3x + 4 =$

    A. 2

    B. 5

    C. 10

    D. 16

(Rigorous) (Skill 19.5)

26. A salesman sold 20 cars in the month of April and 40 cars in the month of May. What is the percent increase in the number of cars the salesman sold?

    A. 50%

    B. 100%

    C. 150%

    D. 200%

(Average) (Skill 18.3)

27. Change $4\frac{3}{5}$ to an improper fraction.

    A. $\frac{23}{5}$

    B. $\frac{7}{5}$

    C. $\frac{12}{20}$

    D. $\frac{20}{12}$

(Average) (Skill 17.2)

28. If $8x + 5 = 21$, then $3x + 4 =$

    A. 2

    B. 5

    C. 10

    D. 16

(Average) (Skill 20.1)

29. If one side of a square is 5 units, what is the area of the square?

    A. 10

    B. 15

    C. 20

    D. 25

(Average) (Skill 17.1)

30. Which of the following is a **true** statement?

    A. The product of two negative numbers is negative.

    B. The product of one negative and one positive number is positive.

    C. When dividing a positive number by a negative number, the results are negative.

    D. When dividing a negative number by a positive number, the results are positive.

(Easy) (Skill 17.1)

31. Jordan wants to get $200,000 for his house. An agent charges 20% of the selling price for selling the house for Jordan. What should the selling price be?

    A. $250,000

    B. $225,000

    C. $270,000

    D. $240,000

(Rigorous) (Skill 17.2)

32. It took Miguel 3.5 hours to drive from city A to city B. On his way back to city A, he increased his speed by 20 km per hour and it took him 3 hours. Find the average speed for the whole journey.

    A. 180.2 km per hour

    B. 180 km per hour

    C. 120 km per hour

    D. 129.2 km per hour

(Average) (Skill 20.1)

33. The length of a rectangular field is $\frac{7}{5}$ its width. If the perimeter of the field is 240 meters, what are the length and width of the field?

    A. Width = 50 m, Length = 70 m

    B. Width = 70 m, Length = 50 m

    C. Width = 60 m, Length = 80 m

    D. Width = 40 m, Length = 120 m

(Rigorous) (Skill 17.3)

34. Which of these relations does NOT represent a function?

    A. {(2, 3), (–4, 3), (7, 3)}

    B. {(0, 0), (–1, –1), (2, 2)}

    C. {(–1, 3), (–5, 3), (–9, 0)}

    D. {(2, 3), (–5, 3), (2, 7)}

(Rigorous) (Skill 16.7)

35. Examples of _____ are 2, 3, 5, 7, 11, 13, 17, and 19.

    A. prime numbers

    B. composite numbers

    C. greatest common factors

    D. least common multiples

(Rigorous) (Skill 16.7)

36. The number 1 is _____.

    A. composite, but not prime

    B. prime, but not composite

    C. neither prime nor composite

    D. both prime and composite

(Rigorous) (Skill 16.5)

37. Ms. Jesop is teaching her students the correct order of operations when solving algebraic problems. She pauses during her lesson to check their understanding and asks them to answer the following: When following the order of operation, which step should come first?

    A. Do addition and/or subtraction, from left to right

    B. Do multiplication and/or division, from left to right

    C. Multiply out expressions with exponents

    D. Simplify inside grouping characters such as parentheses, brackets, square root, and fraction bars

(Easy) (Skill 20.1)

38. An acute angle is:

    A. Greater than 90° and less than 180°

    B. Greater than 0° and less than 90°

    C. Exactly 90°

    D. Exactly 180°

(Easy) (Skill 17.1)

39. In a cafeteria, 3 coffees and 4 donuts cost $10.05. In the same cafeteria, 5 coffees and 7 donuts cost $17.15. How much do you have to pay for 4 coffees and 6 donuts?

    A. $13.25

    B. $14.80

    C. $14.20

    D. $15.60

(Rigorous) (Skill 20.1)

40. These angles have a common vertex and one common side but no interior points in common:

    A. Adjacent

    B. Complementary

    C. Supplementary

    D. Straight

(Rigorous) (Skill 17.1)

41. Evaluate: $-18 + 4(6 \div 2)^2$

    A. 6

    B. -18

    C. 54

    D. 18

(Rigorous) (Skill 20.1)

42. Angles A and B are complementary and the measure of angle A is twice the measure of angle B. Find the measures of angles A and B.

    A. 60°

    B. 120°

    C. 45°

    D. 90°

(Rigorous) (Skill 20.1)

43. The size of angle *AOB* is equal to 132° and the size of angle *COD* is equal to 141°. Find the size of angle *DOB*.

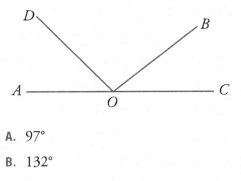

A. 97°

B. 132°

C. 141°

D. 93°

(Average) (Skill 17.1)

44. Going for a long trip, Thomas drove for 2 hours and had lunch. After lunch, he drove for 3 more hours at a speed that is 20 km/hour more than before lunch. The total trip was 460 km. What was his speed after lunch?

A. 130 km/hr

B. 140 km/hr

C. 120 km/hr

D. 100 km/hour

(Average) (Skill 20.1)

45. The rectangle below is made up of 12 congruent (same size) squares. Find the perimeter of the rectangle if the area of the rectangle is equal to 432 square cm.

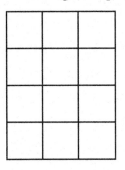

A. 36 cm

B. 72 cm

C. 84 cm

D. 66 cm

(Average) (Skill 20.1)

46. The sum of all of the faces of a prism or sphere:

A. Surface area

B. Circumference

C. Volume

D. Perimeter

(Average) (Skill 20.1)

47. Which is a three-dimensional measurement?

A. Surface area

B. Circumference

C. Volume

D. Perimeter

(Easy) (Skill 20.2)

48. This is made up of an *x*-coordinate and a *y*-coordinate (*x, y*):

   A. Point of average

   B. Coordinate plane

   C. Ordered pair

   D. Quadrant

(Easy) (Skill 20.1)

49. A circular garden with a diameter of 10 meters is surrounded by a walkway of width 1 meter. Find the area of the walkway (shaded part).

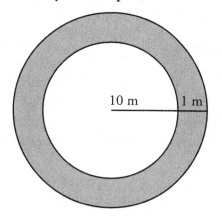

10 m   1 m

   A. 11π square meters

   B. 21π square meters

   C. 32π square meters

   D. 24π square meters

(Easy) (Skill 19.1)

50. This measure of variability is found by subtracting the smallest value from the largest value:

   A. Mean

   B. Median

   C. Mode

   D. Range

(Easy) (Skill 17.2)

51. Mrs. Kline's classroom store is having a sale. An item that sells for $3.75 is put on sale for $1.20. What is the percent of decrease?

   A. 25%

   B. 28%

   C. 68%

   D. 34%

(Rigorous) (Skill 17.1)

52. What is the greatest common factor of 16, 28, and 36?

   A. 2

   B. 4

   C. 8

   D. 16

(Average) (Skill 20.1)

53. What is the area of a square whose side is 13 feet?

   A. 169 ft

   B. 169 ft^2

   C. 52 ft

   D. 52 ft^2

(Rigorous) (Skill 20.1)

54. Find the surface area of a box which is 3 feet wide, 5 feet tall, and 4 feet deep.

   A. 47 ft^2

   B. 60 ft^2

   C. 94 ft^2

   D. 188 ft^2

(Average) (Skill 20.1)

55. Which term most accurately describes two coplanar lines without any common points?

    A. Perpendicular

    B. Parallel

    C. Intersecting

    D. Skew

(Rigorous) (Skill 20.1)

56. Given similar polygons with corresponding sides 6 and 8, what is the area of the smaller if the area of the larger is 64?

    A. 48

    B. 36

    C. 144

    D. 78

(Rigorous) (Skill 20.1)

57. Find the midpoint of (2, 5) and (7, –4).

    A. (9, –1)

    B. (5, 9)

    C. $\left(\frac{9}{2}, -\frac{1}{2}\right)$

    D. $\left(\frac{9}{2}, \frac{1}{2}\right)$

(Rigorous) (Skill 17.2)

58. Mary did comparison shopping on her favorite brand of coffee. Over half of the stores priced the coffee at $1.70. Most of the remaining stores priced the coffee at $1.80, except for a few who charged $1.90. Which of the following statements is true about the distribution of prices?

    A. The mean and the mode are the same.

    B. The mean is greater than the mode.

    C. The mean is less than the mode.

    D. The mean is less than the median.

(Easy) (Skill 17.2)

59. What is the mode of the data in the following sample?

    9, 10, 11, 9, 10, 11, 9, 13

    A. 9

    B. 9.5

    C. 10

    D. 11

(Average) (Skill 17.1)

60. What is the 40th term in this sequence?

    {1, 4, 7, 10, …}

    A. 118

    B. 121

    C. 43

    D. 120

Mathematics Answer Key

ANSWER KEY					
1. A	11. A	21. D	31. A	41. D	51. C
2. D	12. C	22. D	32. D	42. A	52. B
3. B	13. D	23. B	33. A	43. D	53. B
4. C	14. A	24. B	34. D	44. D	54. C
5. D	15. A	25. C	35. A	45. C	55. B
6. B	16. B	26. B	36. C	46. A	56. B
7. D	17. A	27. A	37. D	47. C	57. D
8. C	18. A	28. C	38. B	48. C	58. B
9. A	19. D	29. D	39. C	49. B	59. A
10. A	20. B	30. C	40. A	50. D	60. A

Mathematics Rigor Table

RIGOR TABLE	
Rigor Level	Questions
Easy	2, 5, 16, 18, 19, 31, 38, 39, 48, 49, 50, 51, 59
Average	4, 6, 7, 9, 10, 11, 14, 15, 17, 20, 22, 23, 24, 25, 27, 28, 29, 30, 33, 44, 45, 46, 47, 53, 55, 60
Rigorous	1, 3, 8, 12, 13, 21, 26, 32, 34, 35, 36, 37, 40, 41, 42, 43, 52, 54, 56, 57, 58

Mathematics Answers with Rationales

(Rigorous) (Skill 16.3)

1. Which of the following is an irrational number?

   A. 0.36262626262…

   B. 4

   C. 8.2

   D. -5

   Answer: A. 0.36262626262…

   0.36262626262… is an irrational number.

(Easy) (Skill 16.3)

2. 4,087,361

   What number represents the ten-thousands place?

   A. 4

   B. 6

   C. 0

   D. 8

   Answer: D. 8

   The 8 in the number 4,087,361 represents the ten-thousands place.

(Rigorous) (Skill 16.6)

3. Two kids are selling lemonade on the side of the road and want to raise at least $320. If the materials needed (lemons, pitcher, table, etc.) to run a lemonade stand cost $15, how many glasses of lemonade will they need to sell if each glass costs $6?

   A. 210 glasses

   B. 61 glasses

   C. 74 glasses

   D. 53 glasses

   Answer: B. 61 glasses

   At $6 each, they kids would need to sell 61 glasses.

   61 glasses $\times$ $6 each = $366

   The kids would make a profit of $366 − $15 operating costs = $351 in overall profit.

(Average) (Skill 19.1)

4. If a right triangle has a hypotenuse of 10 cm and one leg of 6 cm, what is the measure of the other leg?

   A. 7 cm

   B. 5 cm

   C. 8 cm

   D. 9 cm

   Answer: C. 8 cm

   Use the following formula to calculate:

   $a^2 + b^2 = c^2$
   $a^2 + 36 = 100$
   $100 - 36 = 64$

   The square root of 64 is 8, so the missing length is 8 cm.

(Easy) (Skill 18.3)

5. **3 km is equivalent to:**

   A. 300 cm

   B. 300 m

   C. 3000 cm

   D. 3000 m

   Answer: D. 3000 m

   3 km = 3,000 m

(Average) (Skill 19.3)

6. **All of the following are examples of obtuse angles EXCEPT:**

   A. 110 degrees

   B. 90 degrees

   C. 135 degrees

   D. 91 degrees

   Answer: B. 90 degrees

   Obtuse angles are those that are greater than 90 degrees.

(Average) (Skill 19.1)

7. **Given the formula $d = rt$ (where d = distance, r = rate, and t = time), calculate the time required for a vehicle to travel 585 miles at a rate of 65 miles per hour.**

   A. 8.5 hours

   B. 6.5 hours

   C. 9.5 hours

   D. 9 hours

Answer: D. 9 hours

$d = rt$

585 miles = 65 mph $\times t$

585 ÷ 65 = 9

$t = 9$ hours

(Rigorous) (Skill 16.7)

8. **Permutation is:**

   A. The number of possible arrangements, without repetition, where order of selection is not important

   B. The number of possible arrangements, with repetition, where order of selection is not important

   C. The number of possible arrangements of items, without repetition, where order of selection is important

   D. The number of possible arrangements of items, with repetition, where order of selection is important

Answer: C. The number of possible arrangements of items, without repetition, where order of selection is important

Permutation is the number of possible arrangements of items, without repetition, where order of selection is important.

(Average) (Skill 17.1)

9. **If 300 peppermints cost you x dollars, how many peppermints can you purchase for 50 cents at the same rate?**

   A. $\frac{150}{x}$

   B. $150x$

   C. $6x$

   D. $\frac{1500}{x}$

Answer: A. $\frac{150}{x}$

50 cents is half of one dollar, thus the ratio is written as half of 300, or 150, to x. The equation representing this situation is $\frac{300}{x} \times \frac{1}{2} = \frac{150}{x}$.

10. Megan is able to sell a painting for $670, a 35% profit over her cost. How much did the painting originally cost her?

   A. $496.30

   B. $512.40

   C. $555.40

   D. $574.90

Answer: A. $496.30

$670 = \text{Cost} + 0.35(\text{Cost}) = 1.35(\text{Cost})$
$\text{Cost} = \$670 \div 1.35 = \$496.30$

11. If Melinda can paint a house in 4 hours, and David can paint the same house in 6 hour, how long will it take for both of them to paint the house together?

   A. 2 hours and 24 minutes

   B. 3 hours and 12 minutes

   C. 3 hours and 44 minutes

   D. 4 hours and 10 minutes

Answer: A. 2 hours and 24 minutes

Melinda can paint $\frac{1}{4}$ of the house in 1 hour. David can paint $\frac{1}{6}$ of the same house in 1 hour. In order to determine how long it will take them to paint the house, when working together, the following equation may be written:

$\frac{1}{4}x + \frac{1}{6}x = 1$. Solving for x gives $\frac{5}{12}x = 1$, where $x = 2.4$ hours, or 2 hours, 24 minutes.

12. Sam arrived at work at 8:15 A.M. and left work at 10:30 P.M. If Sam gets paid by the hour at a rate of $10 and time and $\frac{1}{2}$ for any hours worked over 8 in a day. How much did Sam get paid?

   A. $120.25

   B. $160.75

   C. $173.75

   D. $180

Answer: C. $173.75

From 8:15 A.M. to 4:15 P.M., he gets paid $10 per hour, with the total amount paid represented by the equation, $10 \times 8 = \$80$. From 4:15 P.M. to 10:30 P.M., he gets paid $15 per hour, with the total amount paid represented by the equation, $15 \times 6.25 = \$93.75$. The sum of $80 and $93.75 is $173.75, so he was paid $173.75 for 14.25 hours of work.

13. Angelo wants to invest $4,000 at 6% simple interest rate for 5 years. How much interest will he receive?

   A. $240

   B. $480

   C. $720

   D. $1,200

Answer: D. $1,200

Simple interest is represented by the formula, $I = Prt$, where P represents the principal amount, r represents the interest rate, and t represents the time. Substituting $4,000 for P, 0.06 for r, and 5 for t gives $I = (4000)(0.06)(5)$, or $I = 1,200$. So, he will receive $1,200 in interest.

(Average) (Skill 17.3)

14. The sales price of a motorcycle is $12,590, which is 20% off the original price. What is the original price?

   A. $14,310.40

   B. $14,990.90

   C. $15,290.70

   D. $15,737.50

   Answer: A. $14,310.40

In order to solve for A, both sides of the equation may first be multiplied by 3. This is written as $3\left(\frac{2A}{3}\right) = 3(8 + 4A)$ or $2A = 24 + 12A$. Subtraction of $12A$ from both sides of the equation gives $-10A = 24$. Division by -10 gives $A = -2.4$.

(Average) (Skill 17.2)

15. You need to add 240 pencils and 6 staplers to your supply list for next school year. Pencils are purchased in sets of 6 for $2.35 per pack. Staplers are sold in sets of 2 for 12.95. How much will purchasing these products cost?

   A. $132.85

   B. $145.75

   C. $162.90

   D. $225.25

   Answer: A. $132.85

You will need 40 packs of pencils and 3 sets of staplers. Thus, the total cost may be represented by the expression, $40(2.35) + 3(12.95)$. The total cost is $132.85.

(Easy) (Skill 17.8)

16. Round 917.457 to the nearest tens place.

   A. 918.0

   B. 920

   C. 917.5

   D. 900

   Answer: B. 920

When rounding the decimal to the nearest tens place, look to the digit that is one place to the right, or the ones place. Since the digit in the ones place is greater than 5, the number will be rounded up to the next 10, giving a rounded number of 920.

(Average) (Skill 17.2)

17. Over the course of a week, Landon spent $28.49 on lunch. What was the average cost per day?

   A. $4.07

   B. $3.57

   C. $6.51

   D. $2.93

   Answer: A. $4.07

The average is equal to the ratio of the amount spent to the number of days in a week. Thus, the average may be written as 28.49 divided by 7. Landon spent an average of $4.07 per day.

(Easy) (Skill 17.8)

18. In the number 913.85, which digit represents the tenths space?

    A. 8

    B. 3

    C. 1

    D. 5

Answer: A. 8

The tenths place is one place to the right of the decimal. Thus, 8 represents the digit in the tenths place.

(Easy) (Skill 19.1)

19. What is the median of the following list of numbers?

    4, 5, 7, 9, 10, 12

    A. 6

    B. 7.5

    C. 7.8

    D. 8

Answer: D. 8

Since this list (already written in ascending order) has an even number of values, the median is the average of the two middle values. The average of 7 and 9 is 8, thus the median is 8.

(Average) (Skill 17.1)

20. What is the absolute value of -9?

    A. -9

    B. 9

    C. 0

    D. -1

Answer: B. 9

The absolute value of a number is the distance the number is from 0. The integer, -9, is 9 units from the whole number, 0. Thus, it has an absolute value of 9.

(Rigorous) (Skill 19.5)

21. A scale on a map states that every $\frac{1}{4}$ of an inch represents 20 miles. If two cities are $3\frac{1}{2}$ inches apart, how many miles are actually between the two cities?

    A. 20 miles

    B. 125 miles

    C. 230 miles

    D. 280 miles

Answer: D. 280 miles

The following proportion may be written: $\frac{\left(\frac{1}{4}\right)}{20} = \frac{\left(3\frac{1}{2}\right)}{x}$, which simplifies to $\frac{1}{4}x = 70$, where $x = 280$. Thus, there are actually 280 miles between the two cities.

(Average) (Skill 18.5)

22. A women's basketball team won 24 games and lost 32. What is the ratio of games lost to the number of games played?

    A. 32:24

    B. 4:3

    C. 3:4

    D. 4:7

Answer: D. 4:7

The ratio may be written as $\frac{32}{56}$, which reduces to $\frac{4}{7}$. Thus, the ratio of games lost to games played is 4:7.

(Average) (Skill 19.5)

23. Maddox has a 20 dollar bill and a 5 dollar bill. If he purchases two items, one for $11.23 and the other for $8.32, then how much money does he have left over?

    A. $3.75

    B. $5.45

    C. $6.34

    D. $7.77

    Answer: B. $5.45

    The solution may be represented by the expression, $25 - (11.23 + 8.32)$, which equals 5.45. Thus, she has $5.45 left over.

(Average) (Skill 20.1)

24. In triangle ABC, $AB = BC$ and (C's measure is 65°). What is the measure of angle B?

    A. 40°

    B. 50°

    C. 60°

    D. 65°

    Answer: B. 50°

    Each of the base angles measures 65°, since the triangle is isosceles. Thus, the same of the base angles is 130°. The measure of angle B is equal to the difference of 180° and 130°, or 50°.

(Average) (Skill 17.2)

25. If $8x + 5 = 21$, then $3x + 4 =$

    A. 2

    B. 5

    C. 10

    D. 16

Answer: C. 10

The first equation may be solved for x. Doing so gives $x = 2$. Substituting 2 for x, into the second equation, gives $3(2) + 4$, or 10.

(Rigorous) (Skill 19.5)

26. A salesman sold 20 cars in the month of April and 40 cars in the month of May. What is the percent increase in the number of cars the salesman sold?

    A. 50%

    B. 100%

    C. 150%

    D. 200%

Answer: B. 100%

The percent increase may be represented as $\frac{(40 - 20)}{20}$, which equals 1. $1 = 100\%$. So, the percent increase was 100%.

(Average) (Skill 18.3)

27. Change $4\frac{3}{5}$ to an improper fraction.

    A. $\frac{23}{5}$

    B. $\frac{7}{5}$

    C. $\frac{12}{20}$

    D. $\frac{20}{12}$

Answer: A. $\frac{23}{5}$

In order to change the mixed number to an improper fraction, the denominator should first be multiplied by the whole number. Next, the numerator should be added to this product. The resulting value should be placed over the original denominator of the fractional portion of the mixed number. $4\frac{3}{5} = \frac{23}{5}$ because

$(5 \times 4) + 3 = 23$ and 23 divided by 5 is written as $\frac{23}{5}$.

(Average) (Skill 17.2)
28. If $8x + 5 = 21$, then $3x + 4 =$

A. 2

B. 5

C. 10

D. 16

Answer: C. 10

The first equation may be solved for x. Doing so gives $x = 2$. Substituting 2 for x, into the second equation, gives $3(2) + 4$, or 10.

(Average) (Skill 20.1)
29. If one side of a square is 5 units, what is the area of the square?

A. 10

B. 15

C. 20

D. 25

Answer: D. 25

$A = s^2$, so the area may be written as $A = 5^2$; $A = 25$. The area of the square is 25 square units.

(Average) (Skill 17.1)
30. Which of the following is a true statement?

A. The product of two negative numbers is negative.

B. The product of one negative and one positive number is positive.

C. When dividing a positive number by a negative number, the results are negative.

D. When dividing a negative number by a positive number, the results are positive.

Answer: C. When dividing a positive number by a negative number, the results are negative.

Dividing a positive number by a negative number gives a negative quotient. For example, $\frac{4}{(-2)} = -2$.

(Easy) (Skill 17.1)
31. Jordan wants to get $200,000 for his house. An agent charges 20% of the selling price for selling the house for Jordan. What should the selling price be?

A. $250,000

B. $225,000

C. $270,000

D. $240,000

Answer: A. $250,000

Let x be the selling price:
$x - 20\%x = 200,000$

Solve for x to find $x = \$250,000$.

The selling price should be $250,000.

(Rigorous) (Skill 17.2)

32. It took Miguel 3.5 hours to drive from city A to city B. On his way back to city A, he increased his speed by 20 km per hour and it took him 3 hours. Find the average speed for the whole journey.

    A. 180.2 km per hour

    B. 180 km per hour

    C. 120 km per hour

    D. 129.2 km per hour

Answer: D. 129.2 km per hour

Let x and $x + 20$ be the speeds of the car from A to B and then from B to A. Therefore, the distance from A to B may expressed as $3.5x$ and the distance from B to A as $3(x + 20)$.

The average speed = total distance ÷ total time = $(3.5x + 3(x + 20)) ÷ (3.5 + 3)$

The distance from A to B is equal to the distance from B to A, so: $3.5x = 3(x + 20)$. Solve for x to obtain $x = 120$ km/hr.

We now substitute x by 120 in the formula for the average speed to obtain.

Average Speed = 129.2 km per hour

(Average) (Skill 20.1)

33. The length of a rectangular field is $\frac{7}{5}$ its width. If the perimeter of the field is 240 meters, what are the length and width of the field?

    A. Width = 50 m, Length = 70 m

    B. Width = 70 m, Length = 50 m

    C. Width = 60 m, Length = 80 m

    D. Width = 40 m, Length = 120 m

Answer: A. Width = 50 m, Length = 70 m

Let L be the length and W be the width.
$L = \left(\frac{7}{5}\right)W$

Perimeter: $2L + 2W = 240$,
$2\left(\frac{7}{5}\right)W + 2W = 240$

Solve the above equation to find:
$W = 50$ m and $L = 70$ m.

(Rigorous) (Skill 17.3)

34. Which of these relations does NOT represent a function?

    A. {(2, 3), (-4, 3), (7, 3)}

    B. {(0, 0), (-1, -1), (2, 2)}

    C. {(-1, 3), (-5, 3), (-9, 0)}

    D. {(2, 3), (-5, 3), (2, 7)}

Answer: D. {(2, 3), (-5, 3), (2, 7)}

For the relation in D, when $x = 2$, there are two possible values of y: 3 or 7 and therefore the relation in D is not a function.

(Rigorous) (Skill 16.7)

35. Examples of _____ are 2, 3, 5, 7, 11, 13, 17, and 19.

    A. prime numbers

    B. composite numbers

    C. greatest common factors

    D. least common multiples

Answer: A. prime numbers

Prime numbers are whole numbers greater than 1 that have only two factors: 1 and the number itself. Examples of prime numbers are 2, 3, 5, 7, 11, 13, 17, and 19. Note that 2 is the only even prime number. When factoring into prime factors, all the factors must be numbers that cannot be factored again (without using 1). Initially, numbers can be factored into any two factors.

(Rigorous) (Skill 16.7)

36. The number 1 is _____.

    A. composite, but not prime

    B. prime, but not composite

    C. neither prime nor composite

    D. both prime and composite

    Answer: C. neither prime nor composite

    Prime numbers are whole numbers greater than 1 that have only two factors: 1 and the number itself. Composite numbers are whole numbers that have more than two different factors. The number 1 is neither prime nor composite.

(Rigorous) (Skill 16.5)

37. Ms. Jesop is teaching her students the correct order of operations when solving algebraic problems. She pauses during her lesson to check their understanding and asks them to answer the following: When following the order of operation, which step should come first?

    A. Do addition and/or subtraction, from left to right

    B. Do multiplication and/or division, from left to right

    C. Multiply out expressions with exponents

    D. Simplify inside grouping characters such as parentheses, brackets, square root, and fraction bars

Answer: D. Simplify inside grouping characters such as parentheses, brackets, square root, and fraction bars

This order of operations should be followed when evaluating algebraic expressions:

1. Simplify inside grouping characters such as parentheses, brackets, square root, and fraction bars.

2. Multiply out expressions with exponents.

3. Do multiplication and/or division, from left to right.

4. Do addition and/or subtraction, from left to right.

(Easy) (Skill 20.1)

38. An acute angle is:

    A. Greater than 90° and less than 180°

    B. Greater than 0° and less than 90°

    C. Exactly 90°

    D. Exactly 180°

    Answer: B. Greater than 0° and less than 90°

    Angles are classified according to their size. Acute angles are greater than 0° and less than 90°.

(Easy) (Skill 17.1)

39. In a cafeteria, 3 coffees and 4 donuts cost \$10.05. In the same cafeteria, 5 coffees and 7 donuts cost \$17.15. How much do you have to pay for 4 coffees and 6 donuts?

   A. \$13.25

   B. \$14.80

   C. \$14.20

   D. \$15.60

Answer: C. \$14.20

Let x be the price of 1 coffee and y be the price of 1 donut.

We now use "3 coffees and 4 donuts cost \$10.05" to write the equation

$$3x + 4y = 10.05$$

and use "5 coffees and 7 donuts costs \$17.15" to write the equation

$$5x + 7y = 17.15$$

Subtract the terms of the first equation from the terms of the second equation to obtain

$$2x + 3y = 7.10$$

Multiply all terms of the last equation to obtain

$$4x + 6y = 14.2$$

4 coffees and 6 donuts cost \$14.20.

(Rigorous) (Skill 20.1)

40. These angles have a common vertex and one common side but no interior points in common:

   A. Adjacent

   B. Complementary

   C. Supplementary

   D. Straight

Answer: A. Adjacent

Angles can be classified in a number of ways. Adjacent angles have a common vertex and one common side but no interior points in common.

(Rigorous) (Skill 17.1)

41. Evaluate: $-18 + 4(6 \div 2)^2$

   A. 6

   B. -18

   C. 54

   D. 18

Answer: D. 18

According to order of operations, inner brackets first:

$$-18 + 4(6 \div 2)^2 = -18 + 4(3)^2$$

According to order of operations, power next:

$$= -18 + 4*9$$

According to order of operations, multiplication next:

$$= -18 + 36$$
$$= 18$$

(Rigorous) (Skill 20.1)

42. Angles A and B are complementary and the measure of angle A is twice the measure of angle B. Find the measures of angles A and B.

    A. 60°

    B. 120°

    C. 45°

    D. 90°

Answer: A. 60°

Let A be the measure of angle A and B be the measure of angle B.

$A = 2B$

Angles A and B are complementary; hence

$A + B = 90°$

But $A = 2B$; hence

$2B + B = 90$
$\quad 3B = 90$
$\quad\quad B = 90 \div 3 = 30°$
$A = 2B = 60°$

The measure of Angle $A = 60°$.

(Rigorous) (Skill 20.1)

43. The size of angle AOB is equal to 132° and the size of angle COD is equal to 141°. Find the size of angle DOB.

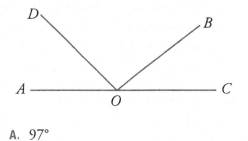

    A. 97°

    B. 132°

    C. 141°

    D. 93°

Answer: D. 93°

Angle $AOB = 132°$ and is also the sum of angles AOD and DOB.

angle AOD + angle $DOB = 132°$ (I)

Angle $COD = 141°$ and is also the sum of angles COB and BOD.

angle COB + angle $DOB = 141°$ (II)

We now add the left sides together and the right sides together to obtain a new equation.

angle AOD + angle DOB + angle COB + angle $DOB = 132° + 141°$ (III)

Note that angle AOD + angle DOB + angle $COB = 180°$.

Substitute angle AOD + angle DOB + angle COB in (III) by 180° and solve for angle DOB.

$180°$ + angle $DOB = 132° + 141°$
angle $DOB = 273° - 180° = 93°$

(Average) (Skill 17.1)

44. Going for a long trip, Thomas drove for 2 hours and had lunch. After lunch, he drove for 3 more hours at a speed that is 20 km/hour more than before lunch. The total trip was 460 km. What was his speed after lunch?

    A. 130 km/hr

    B. 140 km/hr

    C. 120 km/hr

    D. 100 km/hour

Answer: D. 100 km/hr

Let x be the speed before lunch, hence the distance driven before lunch is equal to $2x$. After lunch his speed is 20 km/hr more than before lunch and is therefore $x + 20$. The distance after lunch is $3(x + 20)$.

The total distance is 460, hence the equation: $2x + 3(x + 20) = 460$

Solve the above equation to find speed before lunch $x = 80$ km/hr

The speed after lunch is 20 km/hr more than before lunch and is therefore equal to 80 km/hr + 20 km/hr = 100 km/hr.

(Average) (Skill 20.1)

45. The rectangle below is made up of 12 congruent (same size) squares. Find the perimeter of the rectangle if the area of the rectangle is equal to 432 square cm.

    A. 36 cm

    B. 72 cm

    C. 84 cm

    D. 66 cm

Answer: C. 84 cm

If the total area of the rectangle is 432 square cm, the area of one square is equal to

$432 \div 12 = 36$ square cm

Let x be the side of one small square. The area of one small circle equal to 36 is

$x^2 = 36$

Solve for x.

$x = 6$ cm

The length L of the perimeter is equal to $4x$ and the width W is equal to $3x$. Therefore:

$L = 4 \times 6 = 24$ cm and $W = 3 \times 6 = 18$ cm

The perimeter P of the rectangle is given by:

$P = 2\,(L + W) = 2(24 + 18) = 84$ cm

(Average) (Skill 20.1)

46. **The sum of all of the faces of a prism or sphere:**

    A. Surface area

    B. Circumference

    C. Volume

    D. Perimeter

Answer: A. Surface area

Surface area is the sum of all of the faces of a prism or sphere. In the case of a rectangular prism, this is $2lw + 2lh + 2w$.

(Average) (Skill 20.1)

47. **Which is a three-dimensional measurement?**

    A. Surface area

    B. Circumference

    C. Volume

    D. Perimeter

Answer: C. Volume

Volume is a three-dimensional measurement. For example, the volume of a rectangular prism is equal to *lwh*.

(Easy) (Skill 20.2)

48. **This is made up of an *x*-coordinate and a *y*-coordinate (*x, y*):**

    A. Point of average

    B. Coordinate plane

    C. Ordered pair

    D. Quadrant

Answer: C. Ordered pair

An ordered pair is made up of an *x*-coordinate and a *y*-coordinate (*x, y*). The *x*-coordinate is plotted along the *x*-axis, and the *y*-coordinate is plotted along the *y*-axis.

(Easy) (Skill 20.1)

49. **A circular garden with a diameter of 10 meters is surrounded by a walkway of width 1 meter. Find the area of the walkway (shaded part).**

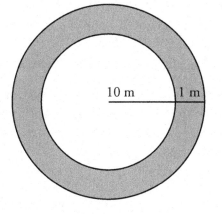

    A. 11π square meters

    B. 21π square meters

    C. 32π square meters

    D. 24π square meters

Answer: B. 21π square meters

The walkway is enclosed between a smaller circle of radius 10 meters and a larger circle of radius 11 meters and therefore the area of the walkway is equal to the area enclosed by the larger circle minus the area enclosed by the smaller circle and is equal to:

$\pi \times 112 - \pi \times 102 = 121\pi - 100\pi$
$= 21\pi$ square meters

(Easy) (Skill 19.1)

50. This measure of variability is found by subtracting the smallest value from the largest value:

    A. Mean

    B. Median

    C. Mode

    D. Range

    Answer: D. Range

    The range is the difference between the highest and lowest value of data items.

(Easy) (Skill 17.2)

51. Mrs. Kline's classroom store is having a sale. An item that sells for $3.75 is put on sale for $1.20. What is the percent of decrease?

    A. 25%

    B. 28%

    C. 68%

    D. 34%

    Answer: C. 68%

    This problem can be solved without using the decimals. Use $(1 - x)$ as the discount: $375x = 120$.

    $$375(1 - x) = 120$$
    $$375 - 375x = 120$$
    $$-375x = -255$$
    $$x = 0.68 = 68\%$$

(Rigorous) (Skill 17.1)

52. What is the greatest common factor of 16, 28, and 36?

    A. 2

    B. 4

    C. 8

    D. 16

    Answer: B. 4

    The smallest number in this set is 16; its factors are 1, 2, 4, 8 and 16. 16 is the largest factor, but it does not divide into 28 or 36. Neither does 8. 4 does factor into both 28 and 36.

(Average) (Skill 20.1)

53. What is the area of a square whose side is 13 feet?

    A. 169 ft

    B. 169 ft^2

    C. 52 ft

    D. 52 ft^2

    Answer: B. 169 ft^2

    Area = length times width (lw).

    Length = 13 ft

    Width = 13 ft (square, so length and width are the same).

    Area = 13 ft × 13 ft
          = 169 ft^2

    Area is measured in square feet.

(Rigorous) (Skill 20.1)

54. Find the surface area of a box which is 3 feet wide, 5 feet tall, and 4 feet deep.

    A. 47 ft^2

    B. 60 ft^2

    C. 94 ft^2

    D. 188 ft^2

Answer: C. 94 ft^2

Let's assume the base of the rectangular solid (box) is 3 by 4, and the height is 5. Then the surface area of the top and bottom together is $2(12) = 24$. The sum of the areas of the front and back are $2(15) = 30$, while the sum of the areas of the sides are $2(20) = 40$. The total surface area is therefore 94 square feet.

(Average) (Skill 20.1)

55. Which term most accurately describes two coplanar lines without any common points?

    A. Perpendicular

    B. Parallel

    C. Intersecting

    D. Skew

Answer: B. Parallel

By definition, parallel lines are coplanar lines without any common points.

(Rigorous) (Skill 20.1)

56. Given similar polygons with corresponding sides 6 and 8, what is the area of the smaller if the area of the larger is 64?

    A. 48

    B. 36

    C. 144

    D. 78

Answer: B. 36

In similar polygons, the areas are proportional to the squares of the sides.

$$\frac{36}{64} = \frac{x}{64}$$

(Rigorous) (Skill 20.1)

57. Find the midpoint of (2, 5) and (7, –4).

    A. (9, –1)

    B. (5, 9)

    C. $\left(\frac{9}{2}, -\frac{1}{2}\right)$

    D. $\left(\frac{9}{2}, \frac{1}{2}\right)$

Answer: D. $\left(\frac{9}{2}, \frac{1}{2}\right)$

Using the midpoint formula:

$$x = \frac{(2 + 7)}{2}$$
$$y = \frac{(5 + \text{–}4)}{2}$$

(Rigorous) (Skill 17.2)

58. Mary did comparison shopping on her favorite brand of coffee. Over half of the stores priced the coffee at $1.70. Most of the remaining stores priced the coffee at $1.80, except for a few who charged $1.90. Which of the following statements is true about the distribution of prices?

A. The mean and the mode are the same.

B. The mean is greater than the mode.

C. The mean is less than the mode.

D. The mean is less than the median.

Answer: B. The mean is greater than the mode.

Over half the stores priced the coffee at $1.70, so this means that this is the mode. The mean would be slightly over $1.70 because other stores priced the coffee at over $1.70.

(Easy) (Skill 17.2)

59. What is the mode of the data in the following sample?

9, 10, 11, 9, 10, 11, 9, 13

A. 9

B. 9.5

C. 10

D. 11

Answer: A. 9

The mode is the number that appears most frequently. 9 appears 3 times, which is more than the other numbers.

(Average) (Skill 17.1)

60. What is the 40th term in this sequence?

{1, 4, 7, 10, ...}

A. 118

B. 121

C. 43

D. 120

Answer: A. 118

The repeating pattern adds 3 to each number.

The nth term is $a + (n - 1)d$.

$1 + (3 \times 39) = 118$

Interested in dual certification?

XAMonline offers over 20+ FTCE study guides which are aligned to current standards and provide a comprehensive review of the core test content. Want certification success on your first exam? Trust XAMonline's study guides to help you succeed!

FTCE Series:

- **Educational Media Specialist PK-12**
  978-1-58197-578-9
- **Middle Grades General Science 5-9**
  978-1-60787-008-1
- **Middle Grades Social Science 5-9**
  978-1-60787-010-4
- **Exceptional Education Ed. K-12**
  978-1-60787-473-7
- **Guidance and Counseling PK-12**
  978-1-58197-586-4
- **Prekindergarten/Primary PK-3**
  978-1-60787-386-0
- **FELE Florida Education Leadership**
  978-1-60787-001-2
- **Elementary Education K–6**
  978-1-60787-506-2
- **Middle Grades English 5-9**
  978-1-58197-597-0
- **Middle Grades Math 5-9**
  978-1-60787-464-5
- **Physical Education K-12**
  978-1-58197-616-8

- **General Knowledge Test**
  978-1-60787-533-8
- **Mathematics 6–12**
  978-1-60787-383-9
- **Professional Education**
  978-1-60787-474-4
- **Social Science 6–12**
  978-1-60787-381-5
- **English 6-12**
  978-1-60787-463-8
- **ESOL K–12**
  978-1-60787-530-7
- **Biology 6-12**
  978-1-58197-689-2
- **Chemistry 6-12**
  978-1-58197-046-3
- **Physics 6-12**
  978-1-58197-044-9
- **Reading K-12**
  978-1-58197-659-5
- **FTCE Spanish K-12**
  978-1-60787-093-7

Don't see your test? Visit our website: www.xamonline.com

XAMonline.com

CPSIA information can be obtained
at www.ICGtesting.com
Printed in the USA
BVOW04s1631271217
503784BV00024B/1162/P